DK Children's Illustrated Dictionary

John McIlwain

DK

DORLING KINDERSLEY

Contents

DK

LONDON, NEW YORK,
MELBOURNE, MUNICH, AND DELHI

Senior Editors Nicola Tuxworth,
Susan Peach
Senior Art Editor Rowena Alsey
Project Editor Lee Simmons
Art Editor Marcus James
Editor Claire Watts
Designers Cheryl Telfer, Diane Clouting

Managing Editor Jane Yorke
Managing Art Editor Chris Scollen
Production Jayne Wood

Photography by Andy Crawford,
Steve Gorton, Susanna Price,
and Tim Ridley

Illustrated by Grahame Corbett,
Peter Dennis, Bill Le Fever,
Nicholas Hewetson, Louis Mackay,
Roger Stewart, and Jolyon Webb
Language Consultants The Centre for Literacy
in Primary Education, London
Pronunciation Consultant Sheila Dignen

2009 Edition:
Project Editor Niki Foreman
Senior Art Editor Sheila Collins
Managing Editor Linda Esposito
Managing Art Editor Diane Thistlethwaite
Publishing Manager Andrew Macintyre
Category Publisher Laura Buller
Production Editors Maria Elia,
Vivianne Ridgeway
Jacket Editor Mariza O'Keeffe
Jacket Designer Akiko Kato
Geography Consultant Simon Mumford

DK India
Head of Publishing Aparna Sharma
Design Manager Arunesh Talapatra
Editorial Manager Glenda Fernandes
Assistant Editor Samira Sood
Designers Malavika Talukder,
Govind Mittal
DTP Co-ordinator Sunil Sharma
DTP Designers Dheeraj Arora,
Preetam Singh

First published in Great Britain in 1994.
This revised edition published in 2009 by
Dorling Kindersley Limited,
80 Strand, London, WC2 ORL

Copyright © 1994, 2009
Dorling Kindersley Limited
A Penguin Company

2 4 6 8 10 9 7 5 3 1
CD207 – 05/09

A CIP catalogue record for this book is available
from the British Library.

ISBN 978-1-4053-5252-9

Colour reproduction by Colourscan, Singapore
Printed and bound by Toppan Printing Co Ltd, China

Introduction

The Dorling Kindersley Children's Illustrated Dictionary is specifically aimed at children of seven years and up, an age when children are becoming increasingly independent readers and writers, and when a dictionary can be a valuable companion.

In addition, this book will help children develop their awareness of words and the relationships between them. An introductory section explains the concept of parts of speech, such as nouns and verbs, which are also listed under each entry in the dictionary, while the end section looks at word beginnings and endings, spelling patterns, and common abbreviations.

Words and pictures

Unlike many other dictionaries, *The Children's Illustrated Dictionary* is not just about words – it also contains pictures. Children today are used to information being presented in a visual form through television, film, and computers, and are skilled readers of images. As a result, they require books to be increasingly visually sophisticated.

The colourful photographs and illustrations in this dictionary are fresh, exciting, and highly relevant to children's interests and concerns. These images will help to draw young readers into the book, and also work with the text to give clear and concise definitions.

A dictionary with a difference

A unique feature of this dictionary is the 26 full-page entries, where words and pictures are grouped by theme.

Browsing through these word collections, on subjects as diverse as costume and time, children will enjoy recognizing known words and concepts, and discovering new vocabulary and information. These pages offer many opportunities for discussion and provide the basis for further exploration of a wide range of topics and themes.

Vital skills for readers and writers

Using a dictionary can teach children many useful skills. One of the most important is the ability to locate information that is organized in alphabetical order. Once acquired, this skill will enable them to use many other reference books, from telephone directories to encyclopedias, which are organized along the same principle. The clear design and layout of this dictionary make it easy for children to learn how to look things up.

The Children's Illustrated Dictionary can also help to widen vocabulary and improve spelling. Young readers and writers can find out for themselves what an unfamiliar word means, or check any spellings about which they are unsure.

A lasting work of reference

The Children's Illustrated Dictionary combines a core of common vocabulary with words that have a high interest level for children of this age group. It provides them with both a rich source of information about the world and an important resource for developing their reading and writing skills.

The Centre for Literacy in Primary Education, London

All about words

In every sentence that we speak or write, there are several types of word. They are called "parts of speech". Each of them has its own name and its own job to do in the sentence. In this dictionary, each word entry has its part of speech printed below it in *italic* type. The parts of speech that are labelled in the dictionary (verbs, adverbs, adjectives, interjections, prepositions, and nouns) are explained on these two pages.

Verbs

Verbs are sometimes called "action words" because they are words that describe what a person or a thing is doing. **Sit**, **think**, **sleep**, **sing**, and **climb** are all verbs. A sentence must contain a verb to make sense. There are a few special kinds of verb, such as "being" and "helping" verbs, that do slightly different jobs in a sentence.

*She **runs** to school every morning.*

*The dog often **lies** on the floor.*

*They **were** both very angry.*

Being verbs

Being words, such as **am**, **is**, **are**, **was**, and **were** all come from the verb **to be**. They link someone or something with the words that describe them.

Helping verbs

Verbs such as **have**, **be**, **will**, **must**, **may**, and **do**, are sometimes used with other verbs in a sentence. They show how possible or necessary it is that an action takes place. Helping verbs can also show a verb's tense.

*It **may rain** tomorrow.*

*I **do like** sandwiches!*

Verb tenses

The form of a verb shows whether the action it describes takes place in the present, the past, or the future. This is called the verb's tense. When a verb, such as **hang**, appears in this dictionary, the entry looks like this:

hang
hangs hanging hung
verb

The second line of the entry shows how the verb is written in three different tenses – the present, the continuous present, and the past tense. These tenses are used like this:

Present tense:
*She **hangs** up her T-shirt.*

Continuous present tense:
*She **is hanging** up her T-shirt.*

Past tense:
*She **hung** up her T-shirt.*

Adverbs

An adverb is a word that gives more information about a verb, an adjective, or another adverb. Adverbs can tell us how, when, where, how often, or how much. **Slowly**, **yesterday**, **upwards**, and **very** are all adverbs. Many adverbs end with the letters "ly".

*These newspapers are all published **daily**.*

*They played **happily** with the balloon.*

Nouns

A noun is a word that names a thing, a person, or a place. **Cat**, **teacher**, **spoon**, and **city** are all nouns. Nouns do not have to be things that you can see – words like **truth** and **geography** are also nouns.

*They often went to the **café** for a **snack**.*

*The **present** came in a round **box**, tied with **ribbon**.*

Adjectives

An adjective is a word that is used to describe a noun. **Fat**, **yellow**, **sticky**, **dark**, and **hairy** are all adjectives.

*The car was **big**, **red**, and **shiny**.*

*A **tall**, **green**, **prickly** cactus.*

Interjections

Interjections are words such as **hello** and **goodbye** which can be used on their own, without being part of a full sentence. Exclamations, such as **Oh**! and **Ouch**!, are also interjections.

Conjunctions

Conjunctions are words such as **and**, **but**, and **of**, which are used to join parts of sentences together.

Prepositions

Prepositions, such as **in**, **with**, **behind**, and **on**, show how one person or thing relates to another.

*She held the ball **above** her head.*

Comparatives and superlatives

If you want to compare a person or thing with another, you often use an adjective in the comparative or superlative form. **Taller**, **easier**, **better**, and **quicker** are comparatives. **Tallest**, **easiest**, **best**, and **quickest** are superlatives. Comparatives either end with the letters "-er", or include the word "more". Superlatives either end with the letters "-est" or include the word "most".

Adjective:
*This ball is **big**.*

Comparative:
*This ball is **bigger**.*

Superlative:
*This ball is the **biggest**.*

a b c d e f g h i j k l m n o p q r s t u v w x y z

5

How to use this dictionary

Read the information on these two pages to find out how to get the most from your dictionary. Most pages in the book look like the double page from the letter **R** section shown below. There are also 26 full-page entries in the dictionary, which provide a whole page of pictures and vocabulary on a theme. The page shown here is about cars.

What's on a page

Guide word

Use the guide word at the top of the page to help you find the page a word is on. The left-hand guide word, **rabbi**, tells you that this is the first word on the page.

Headword

This is the word you are looking up. The headword is printed in heavy, black letters at the start of the entry. The definition underneath explains what the headword means.

Guide word

The right-hand guide word, **rate**, tells you that this is the last word on this page.

New letter section

Each new letter section starts with a big letter, like this **R**.

Pictures

The photos and illustrations show you exactly what things look like and help to define the headwords.

Alphabet

Use the alphabet running down the side of the page to help you find your place in the dictionary. The highlighted letter tells you that you are in the **R** section.

Word box

Families of linked words are enclosed in a box. All the words in this box start with the same word, **rain**.

Alphabetical order

The headwords in this dictionary are listed in alphabetical order – the same order as the letters of the alphabet. Words that begin with **A** are grouped at the start of the dictionary, followed by **B** words, and so on up to **Z**. Where several words start with the same letter, the second letters of the words are used to decide which comes first. So **cat** comes before **cot**, because **A** comes before **O** in the alphabet. If words start with the same two letters, then the third letter decides the order. So **radius** comes before **raft**, because **D** comes before **F**.

Full-page entries

All the pictures and labels on a full-page entry are linked to the main headword. This page shows types of car, with their various parts labelled.

How the entries work

Headword
The headword is printed at the start of the entry. This shows you how to spell the word.

Plural
This tells you how to write a noun when there is more than one of the thing it is referring to. Here, **rams** is the plural of the headword **ram**.

Definition
This part of the entry explains what the headword means. If a word has more than one meaning, the first meaning given is normally the one that is most common. Other meanings are listed below.

ram
rams *noun*
1 a male sheep.

2 a device for pushing against something with force.

*They used the log as a **ram** to break down the door.*
ram *verb*

Part of speech
This shows whether the word is a noun, verb, adjective, interjection, adverb, or preposition. Find out more about parts of speech on pages 4–5.

Tenses of verbs
These three forms of the verb **share** show how it is written in the present, continuous present, and past tenses. These tenses are explained on page 4.

share
shares sharing shared
verb
1 to have or use together.
2 to divide something into parts to give to others.

*They **shared** the melon.*

Sample sentence
The sentence that follows the definition gives you an example of how the headword is used. In the sample sentence the headword is always written in heavy, black type like this: ***shared***.

Comparisons
The two forms of an adjective that are shown here are called the comparative and superlative. They are explained on page 5. **Rarer** means "more rare" and **rarest** means "the most rare".

rare
adjective
unusual or not common.

*A **rare** blue morpho butterfly.*
■ comparisons **rarer rarest**
■ opposite **common**

Opposite
This tells you the word that is the opposite of the headword. For example, **common** is the opposite of the headword **rare**.

Pronunciation guide
This guide helps you to pronounce difficult words. It respells the word so that you can sound out the letters. Part of the guide is in heavy, black type. This shows you which part of the word to stress, or say more loudly.

radioactivity
noun
the energy released by the centre of atoms breaking up in some substances. High amounts of radioactivity can be harmful to living things.

*They tested for **radioactivity** outside the nuclear power station.*
■ say **ray**-dee-oh-**ak**-tiv-i-tee
radioactive *adjective*

Related words
Other words that are related to the headword are listed here. This related word, **radioactive**, is the adjective that comes from the headword **radioactivity**.

a
b
c
d
e
f
g
h
i
j
k
l
m
n
o
p
q
r
s
t
u
v
w
x
y
z

Dictionary games

See if you can solve these word puzzles, using your dictionary to help you. The games will help you learn how to use the dictionary quickly and easily. You can play all of the games on your own, but you could also play with a friend. Try giving a point for each correct answer and then see which of you gets the highest score. The answers to all the puzzles are somewhere in this dictionary. Have fun!

Alphabetical birds

How quickly can you arrange these 12 bird names in alphabetical order? You could use the alphabet at the side of the page to help you to sort them out. For more help, turn to page 6, where alphabetical order is explained in detail.

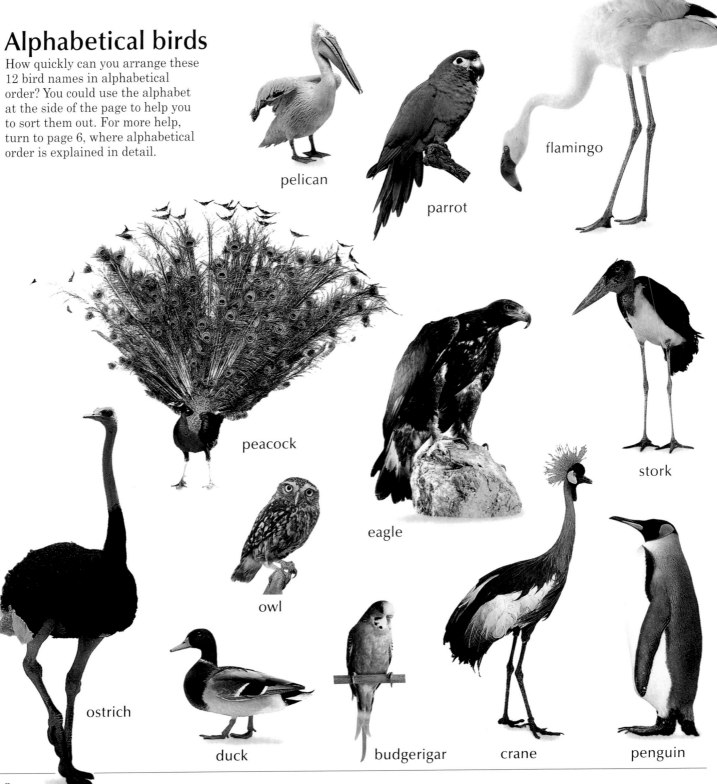

pelican

parrot

flamingo

peacock

stork

eagle

owl

ostrich

duck

budgerigar

crane

penguin

True or false?

Here are some word definitions for you to read. Can you tell which are true and which are false? Remember to check every part of the definition before you decide whether it is true. You can find out whether you were right by looking up the words in the dictionary.

An **elephant** is a huge mammal that lives in Europe and North America.

A **microscope** is an instrument that magnifies very tiny things so that they can be seen in detail.

A **harp** is a musical instrument that you hit with sticks or your hands to make a noise.

A **stethoscope** is an instrument that is used by doctors for looking in your ears.

An **iguana** is a large lizard found mainly in Central and South America.

A **mosaic** is a picture or pattern made of small squares of coloured stone.

A **plumber** is a person who repairs the glass in broken windows.

An **amphibian** is an animal that can live in water and on land.

Sound alikes

Below are some pairs of pictures. The two words that go with each pair sound the same but are spelt differently. Can you work out what they are? The first letter of each answer is shown as a clue.

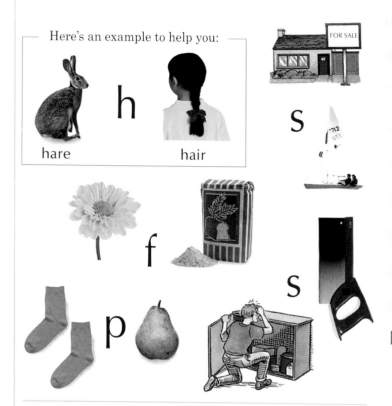

Here's an example to help you:

hare   h   hair

f

p

s

s

Sound unlikes

This is the opposite of the game above. The two words that go with these pairs of pictures are spelt the same, but sound different. Can you work out what the words are? The first letter of each answer is given as a clue.

b

t

w

Odd word out

If you look carefully at these pictures of animals and objects, you will see that in each group there is an "odd word out". Which is it and why? If you get stuck, the special full-page entries in the dictionary will help you.

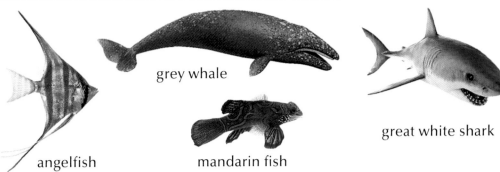

angelfish

grey whale

mandarin fish

great white shark

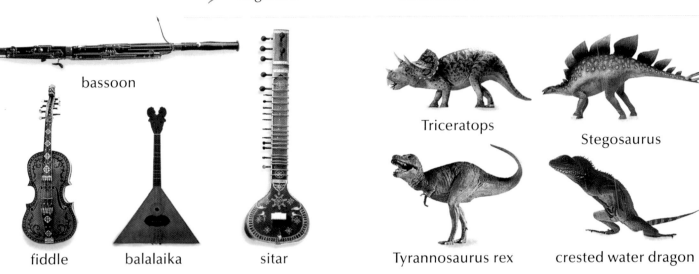

bassoon

fiddle

balalaika

sitar

Triceratops

Stegosaurus

Tyrannosaurus rex

crested water dragon

Action words

The people in these pictures are all doing something. The words in the list are all "action words", or verbs. Can you match the right verb to each of the pictures? There are more verbs than pictures, so choose carefully. Check your answers by looking up the words in the dictionary.

juggle
kneel
climb
throw
hit
crouch
bend
stretch
drum
explore

A B C D E F G H I J K L M N O P Q R S T U V W X Y Z

Word detective

Be a detective and follow the clues to answer these questions. The answers are all in the dictionary.

- Which mammal gnaws down trees to build dams in rivers?
Look for a word beginning with b.

- What are emeralds, sapphires, and rubies?
Look for a page of sparkly things.

- Which word connects an egg, a nut, and a crab?
Look on page 183.

- What is the opposite of few?
Check on page 125.

- What is the name of a planet and also the name of the silver-coloured metal used in thermometers?
Look for a word beginning with m on page 229.

- Which animal has withers, hocks, and a forelock?
Look for a page of large, plant-eating mammals.

- Where would you find a sprit, a main sheet, and a daggerboard?
Look for a page of vessels that travel on water.

Guess the word

Some words have more than one meaning. Each of these groups of pictures illustrates three different meanings of the same word. Can you work out what it is? Check in the dictionary to see if you are right.

Here's an example to help you:

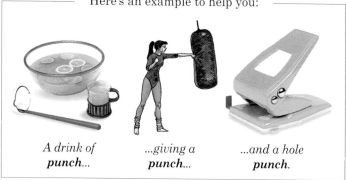

A drink of **punch**... ...*giving a* **punch**... ...*and a hole* **punch**.

Rhyming words

This is a game where you have to spot the "odd word out". The words that go with each of these groups of pictures all rhyme except one. Which one is it?

The first letter of each word is there to give you a clue. Remember that there can be lots of different ways of spelling the same sound.

o
b
t
s
k

f
f
t
p
c

a b c d e f g h i j k l m n o p q r s t u v w x y z

A a

abacus
abacuses *noun*
a frame with sliding beads, used for counting.

abbreviation
abbreviations *noun*
a short way of writing a word or a group of words.
*Ave is an **abbreviation** of avenue.*
■ say a-bree-vee-**ay**-shun.

abdomen
abdomens *noun*
the part of an animal's or a person's body that contains the intestines and stomach (see **insect** on page 108 and **sea life** on page 178).
■ say **ab**-do-men

ability
abilities *noun*
a talent for doing something.

*He had the **ability** to play many instruments at once.*

about
preposition
1 on the subject of.
*We talked **about** the play.*
2 around.
*The baby crawled **about** the room.*

about
adverb
more or less.
*There were **about** 300 people at the circus.*

above
preposition
over, or higher than something.

Above her head.
■ opposite **below**

abroad
adverb
in or to another country.
*She went **abroad** for her holiday.*

absent
adjective
not there, or away.
*He was **absent** from school because he had a cold.*
■ opposite **present**

absorb
absorbs absorbing absorbed
verb
to soak up.

*A sponge **absorbs** liquid.*
absorbent *adjective*

absurd
adjective
silly or ridiculous.

*She looked **absurd** leaving for school in her pyjamas.*

accent
accents *noun*
1 the way people say words.
*She had a foreign **accent**.*
2 a mark on a letter showing you how to pronounce it.
Café is pronounced kafay.

accept
accepts accepting accepted *verb*
to take something that is offered to you.

accident
accidents *noun*
something that goes wrong by chance.

*He spilt the juice, but it was an **accident**.*

accordion
accordions *noun*
a musical instrument that you squeeze to make a sound.

accurate
adjective
exactly right.
*A stopwatch gives **accurate** time.*
■ say ak-yoo-rut

accuse
accuses accusing accused *verb*
to say someone has done something wrong.
*She **accused** him of lying.*
■ say a-**kyooz**

ace
aces *noun*
a playing card that has one main symbol in the centre.

ache
aches aching ached *verb*
to feel a steady pain.

*Her tooth **ached**.*
■ rhymes with **cake**

acid
acids *noun*
a sharp-tasting, sour liquid.
*Some **acids** can burn you.*

acorn
acorns *noun*
the seed of
an oak tree.

acrobat
acrobats *noun*
a person who performs
gymnastics on a stage or
in a circus.

across
preposition
from one side to the other.

Across the bridge.

act
acts acting acted *verb*
1 to behave in a certain way.
*He was acting
very strangely.*
2 to take part in a play,
a film, or a television
programme.

action
actions *noun*
anything that
somebody does.
*His quick action put out
the fire.*

activity
noun
1 energetic movement.
active *adjective*
2 something that has been
planned for you to do.

adapt
adapts adapting adapted *verb*
to change something to
suit a special purpose.

*This mug has been adapted so
that a baby can drink from it.*

add
adds adding added *verb*
1 to put one thing
with another.

Add cherries to the mixture.
2 to find the sum of two or
more numbers.

21+54=75

*Twenty-one added to fifty-four
equals seventy-five.*
addition *noun*

addict
addicts *noun*
someone who cannot give up
a habit that they have.

address
addresses *noun*
the building and area where
someone lives or works.

Jane Horne
1 Highrise flats
Bristol
BS43 1PQ

adjective
adjectives *noun*
a word that is used to
describe a noun.

adjust
adjusts adjusting adjusted *verb*
to make a small
change to something.

She adjusted her belt.

admire
admires admiring admired *verb*
to think that something is
nice or good.

*She admired herself in
the mirror.*

admit
admits admitting admitted *verb*
1 to say reluctantly that
something is true.
2 to allow someone to enter.
*A ticket admits you to
the cinema.*

adopt
adopts adopting adopted *verb*
to take a child into your
home as part of your family.

adult
adults *noun*
a grown-up person.
■ opposite **child**

advantage
advantages *noun*
something
that is
useful
to have.
*Her long legs
gave her an
advantage.*
■ opposite **disadvantage**

adventure
adventures *noun*
something you do that
is exciting and new.
*Exploring the river was
a real adventure.*
adventurous *adjective*

adverb
adverbs *noun*
a word that describes a verb,
adjective, or another adverb.
The tortoise moved slowly.

advertisement
advertisements *noun*
words or pictures that try to
persuade you to buy or to do
something. Advertisement
can be shortened
to advert
or ad.

■ say ad-**ver**-tiss-ment

advice
noun
suggestions to help you
decide what you should do.
*Follow your dentist's advice
on brushing your teeth.*
advise *verb*

a
b
c
d
e
f
g
h
i
j
k
l
m
n
o
p
q
r
s
t
u
v
w
x
y
z

aerial
aerials noun
a device for receiving radio and television signals (see **car** on page 39).

aerial
adjective
in the air.
*An **aerial** photograph.*
■ say **air**-ee-al

aerobics
noun
energetic physical exercises that are done in time to music.

■ say air-**roh**-biks

aerosol
aerosols noun
a can that forces out liquid in a fine spray.
■ say air-**roh**-sol

affect
affects affecting affected verb
to make something or someone different.
*The drought badly **affected** the harvest.*

affection
noun
the feeling that you like someone very much.
affectionate adjective

afford
affords affording afforded verb
to have enough money to buy something.
*We can **afford** to go away on holiday this year.*

afraid
adjective
scared.

*He was **afraid** of mice.*

after
preposition
1 later than.

*It is **after** 8 o'clock.*
2 behind.
*He was **after** me in the queue.*
3 following.
*The cat ran **after** the mouse.*

afternoon
afternoons noun
the period of time between midday and evening.

again
adverb
once more.
*The fans cheered when their team scored **again**.*

against
preposition
1 next to something, touching it.

***Against** the fence.*
2 opposed to, or not on the same side.
*She was **against** the decision.*

age
noun
1 how old someone or something is.

*The number of rings in a tree's trunk show its **age**.*
2 a period in history.
*The Iron **Age**.*

aggressive
adjective
ready to attack.

*Cats can be **aggressive** if they are frightened.*
aggressively adverb

agony
agonies noun
extreme pain.
*The footballer was in **agony** when he broke his leg.*

agree
agrees agreeing agreed verb
to think the same as someone else.
■ opposite **disagree**

agriculture
noun
farming.

*One kind of **agriculture** in Thailand is rice growing.*
agricultural adjective

aground
adverb
stranded on rocks or sand, or in shallow water.
*The ship ran **aground** in the storm.*

ahead
adverb
in front.

*He walked on **ahead** of the others.*

aid
noun
1 help.
*The helicopter came to the **aid** of the stranded walkers.*
2 a machine or a device that helps you do something.

hearing aid

aim
aims aiming aimed verb
1 to point an object at someone or something.

***Aiming** at the target.*
2 to try to do something.
*We **aim** to please.*
aim noun

air
noun
the mixture of gases that plants and animals breathe. *A layer of **air** surrounds Earth.*

aircraft
noun
any vehicle that can fly.

aeroplane

aircraft-carrier
aircraft-carriers *noun*
a ship for aircraft to take off from and land on.

airline
airlines *noun*
a company that owns and flies aircraft.

airmail
noun
post that is carried by aeroplane.

airport
airports *noun*
a place where people go to travel by aeroplane.

ajar
adjective
slightly open.

*The door is **ajar**.*

alarm
noun
1 a loud noise that warns you of something.

2 a feeling of fear.

*burglar **alarm***

album
albums *noun*
a blank book for displaying pictures and other items. *A photograph **album**.*

alcohol
noun
a strong drink, such as wine or beer.
■ say al-ka-hol

alert
adjective
watching and listening very carefully.

*The dog looked very **alert**.*

alien
aliens *noun*
something that seems strange or foreign.
■ say ay-lee-en
alien *adjective*

alike
adjective
very similar.

*These brothers look **alike**.*

alive
adjective
living.

*Flowers need water to stay **alive**.*
■ opposite **dead**

all
adjective
every part of, or everyone. *He ate **all** the cake himself.*

allergy
allergies *noun*
an unpleasant reaction to something that doesn't affect most people.

*He has an **allergy** to cats.*
allergic *adjective*

alligator
alligators *noun*
a large reptile that lives in swamps and rivers. Alligators eat fish and other animals that come close to the water's edge.

allow
allows allowing allowed *verb*
to let someone do something.

*Her parents **allowed** her to stay up and watch the programme.*
■ opposite **forbid**

almost
adverb
nearly.

*The bottle is **almost** empty.*

alone
adjective
by yourself, without anyone else.

*He was **alone** on the island.*

along
preposition
from one end to another. *We walked **along** the beach.*

aloud
adverb
so that it can be heard. *He read the letter **aloud**.*

a
b
c
d
e
f
g
h
i
j
k
l
m
n
o
p
q
r
s
t
u
v
w
x
y
z

alphabet

alphabets *noun*

a series of letters or symbols, written in a particular order, which people use to write words.

alphabetical *adjective*

ABCDEFGHIJKLMNOPQRSTUVWXYZ
abcdefghijklmnopqrstuvwxyz

Roman **alphabet**

aeiou — *letters* — **bcdfghjklmnpqrstvwxyz**
vowels   *consonants*

ΑΒΓΔΕΖΗΘΙΚΛΜΝΞΟΠΡΣΤΥΦΧΨΩ
αβγδεζηθικλμνξοπρστυφχψω

Greek **alphabet**

АБВГДЕЁЖЗИЙКЛМНОПРСТУФХЦЧШЩЪЫЬЭЮЯ
абвгдеёжзийклмнопрстуфхцчшщъыьэюя

Cyrillic **alphabet**

א ב ג ד ה ו ז ח ט י כ ל מ נ ס ע פ צ ק ר ש ת

Hebrew **alphabet**

أ ب ت ث ج ح خ د ذ ر ز س ش ص ض ط ظ ع غ ف ق ك ل م ن هـ و

Arabic **alphabet**

Gujarati **alphabet**

あいうえおかきくけこさしすせそたちつてとなにぬ
ねのはひふへほまみむめもやゆよらりるれろわをん

Japanese **alphabet**

All of these messages say "Happy Birthday" in different alphabets.

Happy Birthday
Roman

Χρονια Πολλά
Greek

с днем рождения
Cyrillic

Hebrew

Arabic

Gujarati

Japanese

already
adverb
by this time.
*She was **already** eating breakfast when he woke up.*

also
adverb
as well.
*Sue is **also** coming with us.*

alter
alters altering altered *verb*
to change something.
*I have **altered** my story to give it a happy ending.*

altogether
adverb
including everyone or everything.

*There are eight apples **altogether**.*

aluminium
noun
a silvery-white metal that is light but strong.

aluminium container
■ say al-yoo-**min**-ee-um

always
adverb
1 very often.
*He is **always** playing loud music.*
2 forever.
*I will **always** remember our holiday.*
■ opposite **never**

amazing
adjective
very surprising or out of the ordinary.

*An **amazing** hat.*
amaze *verb*

ambition
ambitions *noun*
what you want to be or do.
*Her **ambition** is to travel to the Moon.*

ambulance
ambulances *noun*
a vehicle for taking sick or injured people to and from hospital.

ambush
ambushes ambushing ambushed *verb*
to hide and wait for someone, then attack them by surprise when they come along.

among
preposition
in the middle of.

*There are poppies growing **among** the corn.*

amount
amounts *noun*
how much there is of something.

*Twice the **amount** of flour as brown sugar.*

amphibian
amphibians *noun*
an animal that can live in water and on land.

tree frog

■ say am-**fib**-ee-an
amphibious *adjective*

amplifier
amplifiers *noun*
a piece of equipment to make music sound louder.

amuse
amuses amusing amused *verb*
to make someone smile or laugh.
*The cartoon **amused** them.*

anaesthetic
anaesthetics *noun*
a medicine given to patients so that they don't feel pain during an operation.
■ say an-us-**thet**-ik

ancestor
ancestors *noun*
a relative from a previous generation.

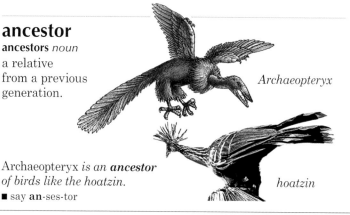

Archaeopteryx

hoatzin

*Archaeopteryx is an **ancestor** of birds like the hoatzin.*
■ say **an**-ses-tor

anchor
anchors *noun*
a large, heavy, metal hook that digs into the seabed to stop a ship from drifting away.

■ say **an**-ker

ancient
adjective
very old.

ancient Roman statue

angel
angels *noun*
a messenger from a god or God.

anger
noun
a strong feeling of annoyance.
angry *adjective*

a
b
c
d
e
f
g
h
i
j
k
l
m
n
o
p
q
r
s
t
u
v
w
x
y
z

A
B
C
D
E
F
G
H
I
J
K
L
M
N
O
P
Q
R
S
T
U
V
W
X
Y
Z

angle
angles *noun*

a corner where two lines or surfaces meet.

right **angle** *(90°)*

animal
animals *noun*

any living thing that breathes and moves about. Insects, fish, birds, mammals, and reptiles are all types of animal.

bird

fish

insect

mammal

reptile

animation
animation *noun*

still pictures, often in cartoon form, which appear to move.

ankle
ankles *noun*

the joint between your leg and your foot.

anniversary
anniversaries *noun*

a special event that is remembered every year on the same date. *Wedding* **anniversary**.

announce
announces announcing announced *verb*

to say something for everyone to hear. *"I'm going", he* **announced**.

annoy
annoys annoying annoyed *verb*
to make someone cross.

The flies **annoyed** *her.*
annoyance *noun*

annual
adjective

happening every year. *Wimbledon is an* **annual** *tennis competition.*
annually *adverb*

anonymous
adjective

without a name. *An* **anonymous** *letter.*
■ say a-**non**-ee-mus

another
adjective

1 different. *Have you got* **another** *pen? I think this one is broken.*
2 one more. *Do you want* **another** *biscuit?*

answer
answers answering answered *verb*

to reply to a question.
answer *noun*

ant
ants *noun*

an insect that lives in large, organized groups. The males and egg-laying females have wings.

wood **ant**

antelope
antelopes *noun*

a mammal that is found on dry plains in Africa and Asia. Antelopes eat grass and other plants.

nyala

antenna
antennae or **antennas** *noun*

1 a long, thin part on certain animals' heads that is used for feeling (see **insect** on page 108 and **sea life** on page 178).
2 an aerial (see **universe** on page 229).

antibiotic
antibiotics *noun*

a medicine that kills bacteria.

antiseptic
antiseptics *noun*

a substance put on cuts and grazes to prevent infection.

anxious
adjective

worried or nervous.
■ say **ank**-shus

any
adjective

some or every.
♦ **Anybody** *can do that, it's easy!*
♦ *She didn't tell* **any**one *what she had seen.*
♦ *I'm going out, and you can't do* **anything** *to stop me!*
♦ *It might be cloudy, but we could go for a picnic* **anyway**.
♦ *Have you seen my pet mouse* **anywhere**?

apart
adverb

away from each other, or separate.

Standing with feet **apart**.

apartment
apartments *noun*

a home that is made up of a set of rooms inside a larger building.

ape
apes *noun*

a mammal that lives in forests in warm regions, and feeds on insects and fruit. Apes have no tails and can walk on two legs.

gibbon

apologize
apologizes apologizing apologized *verb*

to say you are sorry.

apparatus
noun

the equipment you need for a particular task.

*scientific **apparatus***

appear
appears appearing appeared verb

to come into view.
*The sun **appeared** from behind the clouds.*
■ opposite **disappear**

appendix
appendices or **appendixes** noun

a very small part of your lower intestine.

stomach

appendix   *intestine*

appetite
appetites noun

a desire for food.

*He has a huge **appetite**.*

applause
noun

clapping and cheering.
*The **applause** rang out as the team ran onto the pitch.*

apple
apples noun

an edible fruit with a smooth skin and crisp flesh.

appointment
appointments noun

a meeting at a certain time.
*A dental **appointment**.*

appreciate
appreciates appreciating appreciated verb

to be grateful for something.
*She **appreciated** the flowers that her daughter sent her.*
■ say a-**pree**-shee-ate

approach
approaches approaching approached verb

to come near to something.
*The train slowed down as it **approached** the station.*

approve
approves approving approved verb

to think that something is right or good.
*Does your Mum **approve** of your new shoes?*

approximate
adjective

almost accurate, or not exact.

*The **approximate** number of marbles in the jar is 50.*
approximately adverb

apricot
apricots noun

an edible fruit with soft flesh and a stone in its centre.

aquarium
aquariums or **aquaria** noun

a glass tank to keep fish and other water animals and plants in.

arch
arches noun

a curved part of a building or bridge.

architect
architects noun

a person who designs buildings.
■ say **ar**-kee-tekt

area
areas noun

1 a certain piece of ground or space, or part of a surface.
*This is a play **area**.*
2 the amount of space something covers.
*The wood covers a large **area**.*

argue
argues arguing argued verb

to talk angrily with someone because you disagree with them.
argument noun

arithmetic
noun

the adding, subtracting, multiplying, and dividing of numbers.

$$25+17=42$$
adding

$$36-25=11$$
subtracting

$$14\times7=98$$
multiplying

$$28\div2=14$$
dividing

arm
arms noun
the part of your body between your shoulder and your hand.

armpit

arm

armadillo
armadillos noun

a nocturnal mammal that lives in North and South America, and eats insects, snakes, and frogs. The armadillo's body is protected by hard, bony plates.

a
b
c
d
e
f
g
h
i
j
k
l
m
n
o
p
q
r
s
t
u
v
w
x
y
z

A
B
C
D
E
F
G
H
I
J
K
L
M
N
O
P
Q
R
S
T
U
V
W
X
Y
Z

armchair
armchairs *noun*
a soft, padded chair with arms.

armour
noun
a suit of thick, metal plates worn long ago to protect knights in battle.

army
armies *noun*
a group of people and machines that fight on land.

around
adverb
1 nearby.
*I left my bag **around** here.*
2 in every direction.
*For miles **around**.*

around
preposition
1 from place to place.
*We walked **around** the city.*
2 on all sides.
*We sat **around** the table.*

arrange
arranges arranging arranged *verb*
1 to plan something.
*She **arranged** to meet me at 10 o'clock.*
2 to place something in a special order.

arrest
arrests arresting arrested *verb*
to catch hold of someone and officially accuse them of breaking the law.

arrive
arrives arriving arrived *verb*
to come to a place.
*The plane **arrived** at the airport.*
arrival *noun*

arrow
arrows *noun*
1 a pointed piece of metal that is shot from a bow.

2 a pointed shape that shows you which way to go or look.

art
noun
the creation of something, often through drawing, painting, sculpture, or design.

artery
arteries *noun*
one of the tubes that carries blood from the heart to the rest of the body.

artery

heart

artificial
adjective
something false that is made to look like the real thing.

*an **artificial** flower*
■ ar-tee-**fish**-al

artist
artists *noun*
someone who creates pictures, sculptures, music, or other beautiful things.

artistic *adjective*

ash
ashes *noun*
1 the grey powder that is left behind after something has been burnt.

*wood **ash***

2 a deciduous, broad-leaved tree, with spreading branches that grow in pairs. The female ash produces winged seeds. The wood is hard and strong.

***ash** leaves*

ashamed
adjective
feeling guilty about something you have done.
*She felt **ashamed** about teasing her little brother.*

ask
asks asking asked *verb*
to try to find something out from someone.
***Ask** your dad if you can come with us.*

asleep
adjective
resting the whole body and mind with the eyes closed.

sleep *verb*

aspirin
aspirins *noun*
a type of medicine taken as a pill, used for relieving pain and fever.

assemble
assembles assembling assembled *verb*
1 to put something together.
*I **assembled** a model boat.*
2 to meet together.
*They **assembled** in the hall.*
assembly *noun*

assist
assists assisting assisted *verb*
to help somebody.

*He **assisted** the customer with his coat.*
assistance *noun*   shop **assistant**

assortment
assortments *noun*
a collection of different types of the same thing.

*An **assortment** of buttons.*

asthma
noun
an illness or allergy that can make breathing difficult.
■ say **as**-ma
asthmatic *adjective*

astonish
astonishes astonishing astonished *verb*
to amaze someone very much.
*She **astonished** the crowd by winning the race.*

astronaut
astronauts *noun*
a person who is trained to travel into space.

astronomy
noun
the scientific study of stars and planets.

ate
from the verb **to eat**
*I **ate** a whole loaf of bread yesterday.*

athlete
athletes *noun*
a person who takes part in races or sports competitions.

athletics *noun*

atlas
atlases *noun*
a book of maps.

atmosphere
noun
1 the layer of air that surrounds Earth.
2 the feeling in a room or a place.
*The dark room had a gloomy **atmosphere**.*

atom
atoms *noun*
a very tiny part of any substance.

*magnified **atom***

attach
attaches attaching attached *verb*
to fasten.

Attached with a paper-clip.

attack
attacks attacking attacked *verb*
to try to hurt a person or an animal.
*The wild dog **attacked** the flock of geese.*

attempt
attempts attempting attempted *verb*
to try to do something.
*They **attempted** to climb the wall, but had to give up.*

attend
attends attending attended *verb*
to go to an event, or to go somewhere regularly.
*I **attended** school for 11 years.*

attention
noun
1 listening carefully.
*Pay **attention**!*
2 standing stiff and straight.
*Stand to **attention**.*

attic
attics *noun*
a room at the top of a house, usually in the space under the roof.

attract
attracts attracting attracted *verb*
1 to interest.
*The museum **attracts** many visitors.*
2 to make something come closer.

Magnets attract iron filings.

attractive
adjective
pleasing to the eye, mind, and senses.

audience
audiences *noun*
the people who come to watch a show or concert.

aunt
aunts *noun*
the sister of someone's parent, or their uncle's wife.

author
authors *noun*
a person who writes books, poems, or plays.

autograph
autographs *noun*
a signature, usually of a famous person.
■ say **or**-toe-grarf

automatic
adjective
1 without thinking.
*Blinking is **automatic**.*
2 working by itself, without any assistance.
Automatic doors.

automobile
automobiles *noun*
another name for a car. Cars are often called automobiles in America.

*vintage **automobile***

autumn
autumns *noun*
one of the four seasons. Autumn follows summer and comes before winter. It is the time when the leaves on some trees change colour and fall to the ground.

a
b
c
d
e
f
g
h
i
j
k
l
m
n
o
p
q
r
s
t
u
v
w
x
y
z

A
B
C
D
E
F
G
H
I
J
K
L
M
N
O
P
Q
R
S
T
U
V
W
X
Y
Z

avalanche
avalanches noun
a large amount of snow, rocks, and ice that suddenly slides down a mountain.

avenue
avenues noun
a type of street. It is often wide and sometimes has a line of trees down each side.

average
adjective
ordinary.
*He was of **average** height for his age.*

average
averages noun
1 a usual amount.
*My marks were above **average**.*
2 a number of things spread out equally.
*He eats 14 apples a week, an **average** of 2 a day.*

avocado
avocados noun
a green, pear-shaped tree fruit with a leathery skin and smooth, creamy flesh.

avoid
avoids avoiding avoided verb
to keep away from something.

*The car swerved to **avoid** the dog.*

awake
adjective
not asleep.
*I stayed **awake** all night.*

award
awards noun
a prize.
*A rosette is an **award**.*
award verb

aware
adjective
knowing something.
*He became **aware** that someone was watching him.*

away
adverb
1 not here.
*The teacher was **away** today.*
2 to another place.
*I put all my games **away**.*

awful
adjective
very bad.

awkward
adjective
1 difficult to use or inconvenient.
2 clumsy.

*A new-born foal looks **awkward** on its feet.*
awkwardly adverb

axe
axes noun
a tool that is used to chop wood.

baboon
baboons noun
a large monkey that is found all over Africa. Baboons live on the ground and eat plants and small animals.

baby
babies noun
a very young child (see **growth** on page 94).

back
adverb
returning.
*I am going to the shops. I'll be **back** later.*

back
backs noun
1 the part of your body that is opposite your chest, and between your neck and your bottom.

back

backpack
backpacks noun
a large bag with shoulder straps, often worn by walkers to hold clothes and equipment.

backwards
adverb
moving towards the back.
*I fell **backwards** into a prickly bush.*

bacon
noun
salted meat from the back or side of a pig.

2 the part opposite the front.
back adjective

***back** of a clock*

---

bacteria
noun

very small organisms. Some cause disease, while others help your body.
*Some **bacteria** help break down food in your stomach.*

■ say bak-**tee**-ree-a

bad
adjective

1 wrong.
*Stealing is very **bad**.*
2 serious.
*I've got a **bad** earache.*
3 rotten, or faulty.
*The food had gone **bad**.*

■ comparisons **worse worst**

badge
badges *noun*

a decoration that can be pinned or sewn onto clothes.

*sheriff's **badge***

badminton
noun

an indoor game played by two or four people on a court. Each player uses a racket to hit a shuttlecock over a net (see **sport** on page 197).

baffle
baffles baffling baffled *verb*

to confuse someone or make a person puzzled.
*The quiz completely **baffled** him.*

bag
bags *noun*

a container that you can carry things in, usually made of material, plastic, or paper.

baggy
adjective

fitting loosely.

***baggy** trousers*

bake
bakes baking baked *verb*

to cook in an oven or fire. Pies, cakes, and bread are baked.

*A baker **bakes** bread.*

balance
balances balancing balanced *verb*

to keep steady so you do not fall over.
*The tightrope walker **balanced** on the high wire.*

balcony
balconies *noun*

a platform for standing on that is attached to the wall of a building above the ground.

bald
adjective

without any hair.
*A **bald** head.*

ball
balls *noun*

1 a rounded object used to play many games and sports.

*beach **ball***

2 a big, grand party where there is dancing.
*A summer **ball**.*

ballet
ballets *noun*

a performance on stage that tells a story in music and dance.

■ say **bal**-lay

***ballet** dancers*

balloon
balloons *noun*

a bag of rubber or other material filled with air or another gas.

*hot-air **balloon***

bamboo
noun

a tall, tropical grass with hard, hollow stems. Bamboo can be used to make garden poles and furniture.

***bamboo** poles*

ban
bans banning banned *verb*

to forbid people to do something.
*Smoking is **banned** on public transport.*

banana
bananas *noun*

a tree fruit with a smooth, thick, outer skin and a soft, edible centre. Bananas grow in hot, damp regions.

band
bands *noun*

1 a group of people who play music together.

2 a strip of material such as fabric, elastic, or metal that holds things together.

*elastic **band***

bandage
bandages *noun*

a strip of material that is used to wrap around a wound to keep it clean.

23

A
B
C
D
E
F
G
H
I
J
K
L
M
N
O
P
Q
R
S
T
U
V
W
X
Y
Z

bang
bangs *noun*
a sudden, loud noise.
The firework went off with a loud bang.

bank
banks *noun*
1 a steep, sloping piece of ground, often on the side of a river.

2 a company that looks after people's money and also lends money.

banner
banners *noun*
a large flag or piece of cloth that has a picture or a message on it.

bar
bars *noun*
1 a long, narrow piece of metal.

weight-lifting bar

2 a counter or a room where drinks or snacks are sold.

barbecue
barbecues *noun*
1 a grill over an open fire that is lit outdoors and used for cooking meat, fish, or vegetables.

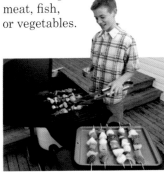

2 a party or special meal where food is cooked on a barbecue.
■ say **bar**-bi-kew

bare
adjective
without any covering.

bare feet

bargain
bargains *noun*
something bought cheaply.
My shoes were a real bargain in the sale.

bark
noun
the rough wood on the outside of a tree trunk.

bark
barks barking barked *verb*
to make a rough, loud noise like a dog.
bark *noun*

barley
noun
a type of cereal grown on farms to make food and beer.

barn
barns *noun*
a large farm building used as a store or for keeping animals in.

barrel
barrels *noun*
a large, rounded, wooden or metal container for storing beer and other liquids.

barrier
barriers *noun*
a structure built to stop someone or something from passing through.
The police placed a barrier across the road.

base
bases *noun*
the bottom of something.

lamp base

baseball
noun
a game for two teams of nine players, which started in the USA. The winning team is the one that runs the biggest number of runs around the pitch (see **sport** on page 197).

basement
basements *noun*
a floor in a building that is partly or completely below ground level.

basin
basins *noun*
a bowl-shaped container. A wash-basin is used for washing in, and a pudding-basin is used for cooking in.

basket
baskets *noun*
a container for carrying things in, usually made of cane, twigs, or straw.

basketball
noun
a team game with five players on each side. Points are scored by throwing a ball through a raised hoop called the basket (see **sport** on page 197).

bat
bats *noun*
1 a stick, often made of wood or metal that is used to hit a ball (see **sport** on page 197).

softball **bat**

2 a nocturnal mammal with wings. Bats live in caves and dark places, and eat insects, fruit, or small animals. They rest hanging upside-down (see **mammal** on page 124).

long-eared **bat**

bath
baths *noun*
a large tub for washing the whole of your body.

baton
batons *noun*
a thin piece of wood or metal. Conductors of orchestras and band leaders use different types of batons to keep time.

band leader's **baton**

battery
batteries *noun*
a closed container of chemicals that makes and stores small amounts of electricity.

watch **battery**

battle
battles *noun*
a fight between two armies that are at war.

bawl
bawls bawling bawled *verb*
to shout or cry very loudly.

bay
bays *noun*
a deep, inward curve in a coastline or the edge of a lake.

beach
beaches *noun*
land at the edge of a sea or lake, usually covered in pebbles or sand.

bead
beads *noun*
a small piece of wood, stone, or glass that can be threaded onto string.

beak
beaks *noun*
the hard, bony mouth of a bird or dinosaur (see **dinosaur** on page 61).

beam
beams *noun*

1 a long, narrow ray of light.

2 a long, strong piece of wood or metal, often used in buildings to hold up the roof.

bean
beans *noun*
a seed or pod that is eaten as a vegetable.

broad **bean**

bear
bears *noun*
a large mammal with thick fur that usually lives in forests. All bears eat meat, but some also eat honey, roots, plant buds, berries, and fruit.

Canadian black **bear**

toucan's **beak**

bear
bears bearing bore born or borne *verb*
1 to produce or give birth to.
This plant **bears** *red berries.*
2 to carry or support.
Can that branch **bear** *your weight?*
3 to put up with.
I can't **bear** *to think about it.*

beard
beards *noun*
the hair that grows on the lower part of a man's face if he does not shave.

beat
beats beating beat beaten *verb*
1 to defeat someone.
My friend **beat** *me at chess.*
2 to hit or stir repeatedly.
She **beat** *the eggs.*
3 to make a repeated movement, or noise.
My heart is **beating** *loudly.*

beat
beats *noun*
a steady stroke or sound.
A metronome ticks with a steady **beat.**

beautiful
adjective
very pleasant to look at.
What a **beautiful** *view!*
■ say **byoo**-te-ful

beaver
beavers *noun*
a large rodent that gnaws down trees to build dams and island homes, called lodges, in rivers. Beavers eat bark, roots, and twigs.

a b c d e f g h i j k l m n o p q r s t u v w x y z

A
B
C
D
E
F
G
H
I
J
K
L
M
N
O
P
Q
R
S
T
U
V
W
X
Y
Z

beckon
beckons beckoning beckoned
verb
to make a sign that tells someone to come to you.

become
becomes becoming became
verb
to change or grow into.
*A tadpole **becomes** a frog.*

bed
beds *noun*
1 a piece of furniture that you sleep on.
2 the bottom of a river, lake, or the sea.

bee
bees *noun*
a flying insect that usually lives in large, well-organized groups. Bees feed on pollen, nectar, and the honey they make from nectar.

beech
beeches *noun*
a deciduous forest tree with smooth, grey bark and spreading branches (see **tree** on page 223).

beech leaf

beef
noun
the meat from a cow or bull.

beehive
beehives *noun*
a type of box that people keep bees in. They collect the honey that the bees make.

beer
beers *noun*
an alcoholic drink made from cereal grains.

beetle
beetles *noun*
an insect with hard, often brightly coloured wing cases. Some beetles eat small insects, others eat wood and plants.

*jewel **beetle***

beetroot
beetroots *noun*
the hard, red root of the beet plant, which is eaten as a vegetable (see **vegetable** on page 233).

before
preposition
earlier than.

Before four o'clock.

before
adverb
in the past.
*I've heard that story **before**.*

beg
begs begging begged *verb*
to ask for something very strongly.

*The dog **begged** for a piece of meat.*

begin
begins beginning began begun
verb
to start something.
*The story **begins** in a castle.*
beginning *noun*

behave
behaves behaving behaved *verb*
to act in a particular way in front of other people.
*Our class **behaved** well at the zoo.*
behaviour *noun*

behind
preposition
at the back of.

*She stood **behind** her friend.*
behind *adverb*

being
beings *noun*
someone or something that exists.

believe
believes believing believed *verb*
to feel strongly that something is true.

bell
bells *noun*
a cup-shaped piece of metal that makes a ringing sound when it is struck.

belong
belongs belonging belonged
verb
to be someone's possession or property.
*That book **belongs** to me.*

below
preposition
lower than.

Below her waist.
■ opposite **above**

belt
belts *noun*
a narrow strip of fabric or leather that you wear around your waist.

bench
benches *noun*
1 a long, wooden seat.

*park **bench***

2 a work table.

bend

bends bending bent *verb*
to change something straight
into a curved shape.

She **bent**
over to touch
her toes.

bend

bends *noun*
a curve.

Bends in the road.

benefit

benefits benefiting benefited
verb
to receive help from someone
or something.
*The school would **benefit** from
having new computers.*
benefit *noun*

beret

berets *noun*
a soft, flat hat.

■ say **ber**-ray

berry

berries *noun*
a small, round
juicy fruit with
seeds inside.

*blue**berries***

beside

preposition
at the side of.

*The ball is **beside** her.*

best

*from the adjective **good***
better than any other.

bet

bets betting bet *verb*
to believe that something
is going to happen.
*I **bet** it's going to rain later.*

better

*from the adjective **good***
1 more able.
*You are good at science but he
is **better**.*
2 well again.
*I'm feeling **better**, thanks.*

between

preposition
in the
middle of.

Between her knees.

beware

verb
to be careful of something.
Beware of the dog.

beyond

preposition
further away than.
*The hills lay **beyond** the river.*

bicycle

bicycles *noun*
a vehicle with two wheels
that you ride by turning
the pedals with your feet.
Bicycle can be shortened
to bike.

big

adjective
large in
width
or size.

*The jacket is too **big** for him.*
■ comparisons **bigger biggest**

bikini

bikinis *noun*
a swimming
costume with
two pieces,
worn by girls
and women.

bill

bills *noun*
1 the hard, bony mouth of
a bird.

bill

2 a piece of paper that shows
you how much you have to
pay for something.
*The waiter brought us the **bill**
at the end of our meal.*
3 a plan for a new law that
must be voted on by
a country's government.
*The new education **bill**
will be discussed in
Parliament today.*

billow

billows billowing billowed *verb*
to spread out and be blown
about in the wind.
*Smoke **billowed** out from
the chimneys.*

bin

bins *noun*
a container for things you
want to throw away.

binoculars

noun
two small telescopes joined
together that make things
that are far away look closer.

biodegradable

adjective
able to be broken down
by bacteria.
*Most paper is **biodegradable**.*
■ say by-oh-dee-**gray**-da-bul

a
b
c
d
e
f
g
h
i
j
k
l
m
n
o
p
q
r
s
t
u
v
w
x
y
z

bird

birds *noun*

an animal that has warm blood, feathers on its body, and wings (see **skeleton** on page 188).

shaft

vane

quill

macaw's feather

kestrel

hooked beak

talon

song thrush's nest

osprey's egg

nostril   *beak*

nape

mantle

breast

plumage

finch

tail feathers

budgerigar

crest

belly

claw

flight feathers

roller   *toe*

lorikeet

cockatoo

knee

train of feathers

webbed foot

flamingo

peacock

kiwi

flipper

penguin

birthday
birthdays *noun*
the anniversary of the day you were born.

birthday cake
birthday cakes *noun*
a special cake with candles on top that is baked for your birthday.

birthday card
birthday cards *noun*
a card that people send to you on your birthday, to congratulate you on being a year older.

birthday party
birthday parties *noun*
a party to celebrate someone's birthday.

birthday present
birthday presents *noun*
a gift that you give to someone on their birthday.

biscuit
biscuits *noun*
a small, flat, crisp type of cake made from dough.
■ say **bis**-kit

bit
bits *noun*
a small piece of something. *The mouse nibbled a **bit** of cheese.*

bite
bites biting bit bitten *verb*
to use your teeth in a cutting action, usually with food.

bite *noun*

bitter
adjective
having a sour, sharp taste. *Strong coffee can taste **bitter**.*

black
noun
1 a colour.

2 very dark. *A **black** night.*

blackberry
blackberries *noun*
a black or dark purple fruit that grows on prickly stems called brambles.

blackbird
blackbirds *noun*
a bird that lives in gardens and fields, and eats insects and seeds. The male has black feathers and the female has brown feathers.

blackboard
blackboards *noun*
a board that has been painted black. Blackboards can be written on with chalk.

blade
blades *noun*
1 the flat, sharp, metal part of a knife or a sword.

*knife **blade***

2 a stem of grass.

blade

blame
blames blaming blamed *verb*
to think or say that someone has done something wrong. *She always **blames** me for letting the toast burn.*

blank
blanks *noun*
An empty space.

A hen lays ___.

*The last word has been left **blank**.*
blank *adjective*

blanket
blankets *noun*
a soft covering, usually made of wool that is used to keep people or animals warm.

blast
blasts *noun*
a powerful explosion or gust of wind. *A **blast** of cold air came in through the window.*

blaze
blazes blazing blazed *verb*
to burn very brightly.

*The fire **blazed** through the old building.*
blaze *noun*

blazer
blazers *noun*
a jacket that is often worn as part of a uniform.

bleach
noun
a very powerful chemical that removes colour. Bleach can burn your skin.

a b c d e f g h i j k l m n o p q r s t u v w x y z

29

A
B
C
D
E
F
G
H
I
J
K
L
M
N
O
P
Q
R
S
T
U
V
W
X
Y
Z

bleed
bleeds bleeding bled *verb*
to lose blood.
*My nose started to bleed
when I fell over.*

blind
adjective
unable to see.

*Some blind people have
guide dogs.*

blink
blinks blinking blinked *verb*
to open and shut your
eyes quickly.
*The bright light made
me blink.*

blister
blisters *noun*
a bubble of watery liquid that
forms under your skin when
it has been burnt or rubbed.
Tight shoes give me blisters.

blizzard
blizzards *noun*
a very heavy snowstorm.

blob
blobs *noun*
a small lump of something
with no shape.

*a blob of
face cream*

block
blocks *noun*
1 a solid
shape, such
as a block
of wood.
2 a very big building or
a group of buildings.

block
blocks blocking blocked *verb*
to be in the way.
*The road was blocked
by the fallen tree.*

blond / blonde
adjective
having light-coloured hair.
Blond is used for boys and
men, and blonde is used for
girls and women.

blond boy

blonde girl

blood
noun
the red liquid that flows
around our body through
veins and arteries. Blood
carries nutrients and oxygen
to our skin and muscles.

bloom
blooms blooming bloomed *verb*
to produce flowers.
*Fruit trees bloom in
the spring.*

blossom
blossoms *noun*
the flowers on a tree
that appear
before
the fruit.

hawthorn blossom

blot
blots *noun*
a stain on paper, usually
made by ink or paint that
has been spilt.

blouse
blouses *noun*
a type of shirt, usually worn
by girls or women.

blow
blows blowing blew blown *verb*
1 to move in air, or be moved
in air.
2 to force air out of your nose
or mouth.

He blew up the balloon.

blue
noun
a colour.

bluff
bluffs bluffing bluffed *verb*
to trick someone into
believing something.
*She pretended to be brave,
but she was bluffing.*

blunt
adjective
having a rounded end or edge.

■ opposite **sharp**

blur
blurs blurring blurred *verb*
to make something unclear
and difficult to see.
*The view through the window
was blurred by rain.*

blush
blushes blushing blushed *verb*
to turn red because you are
embarrassed or shy.

board
boards *noun*
a flat piece of wood, or very
stiff paper.

boast
boasts boasting boasted *verb*
to tell people about
something in a proud and
annoying way.
He boasted about his money.

boat

boats *noun*
a small open vessel that carries goods and people across water.

sprit

sail

boom

tiller

mast

stern

main sheet

rudder

bow

daggerboard

dinghy

anchor

hull

junk

blade

lifebuoy

propeller

prow

fishing **boat**

cockpit

reed **boat**

paddle

cabin

thwart

keel

coble (fishing **boat**)

rudder

yard

stay

powerboat

propeller

narrowboat

deck

sailing **boat**

A
B
C
D
E
F
G
H
I
J
K
L
M
N
O
P
Q
R
S
T
U
V
W
X
Y
Z

body
bodies *noun*
all the physical parts that make up an animal or person.

boil
boils boiling boiled *verb*
to heat a liquid until it starts to bubble and steam rises from it.

bold
adjective
brave and fearless.
*The **bold** knight marched up to the dragon's cave.*

bolt
bolts *noun*
1 a metal rod that is used to fasten things together.

2 a sliding metal bar that is used for fastening a door.

bomb
bombs *noun*
an exploding weapon that can cause damage to anything around it.
■ say **bom**

bone
bones *noun*
the hard parts of an animal's or person's body that make up the skeleton.

*femur (upper leg **bone**)*
bony *adjective*

bonfire
bonfires *noun*
a large outdoor fire.

book
books *noun*
printed pieces of paper, joined together inside a cover.

boom
booms booming boomed *verb*
to make a deep, loud sound.
*His voice **boomed** out through the loudspeaker.*

boomerang
boomerangs *noun*
a curved piece of wood that comes back to you when you throw it. Boomerangs were used in the past as a weapon by Australian Aboriginals.

boot
boots *noun*
a type of shoe that covers your foot and part of your leg.

*wellington **boot***

border
borders *noun*
1 the boundary between two countries.

*country **border***

2 a strip around the edge of something.

*blue **border***

bore
bores boring bored *verb*
1 to be very uninteresting.
*She **bored** us for weeks by telling the same joke.*
2 to make a round hole in something.
*They **bored** a hole in the ground in search of oil.*

bore
from the verb **to bear**
1 *She **bore** 10 children.*
2 *Luckily, the bridge **bore** the truck's weight.*

born
from the verb **to bear**
*I was **born** 10 years ago, so I am 10 years old.*

borrow
borrows borrowing borrowed *verb*
to take something for a while and then return it.
*I **borrowed** my friend's pen.*
■ opposite **lend**

boss
bosses *noun*
the person who is in charge at work.

both
adjective
not just one thing, but two.

Both bowls contain rice.

bother
bothers bothering bothered *verb*
to worry or annoy someone.

bottle
bottles *noun*
a container for liquids, usually made of glass or plastic.

bottom
bottoms *noun*
1 the lowest part of something.

*The **bottom** of the sea.*
■ opposite **top**

2 the part of your body that you sit on.

bought

from the verb **to buy**

I bought a present for my friend yesterday.

■ say **bort**

bounce

bounces bouncing bounced *verb*

to spring up and down.

bounce *noun*

boundary

boundaries *noun*

the edge of a piece of land.

bouquet

bouquets *noun*

a bunch of flowers that has been specially arranged and wrapped.

■ say bo-**kay**

bow

bows bowing bowed *verb*

to bend from the waist as a greeting or a sign of respect.

■ rhymes with **now**

bow

bows *noun*

the front of a ship.

■ rhymes with **now**

bow

bows *noun*

1 a knot with two loops.

2 a curved piece of wood with a string attached to each end, used for shooting arrows.

3 a wooden stick with horse hair attached at each end, used for playing musical instruments.

violin **bow**

■ rhymes with **go**

bowl

bowls *noun*

a curved, open container, usually used for food.

bowl

bowls bowling bowled *verb*

1 to throw a ball for someone to hit.
2 to roll a ball in the game of lawn bowls.
3 to roll a ball in tenpin bowling.

bowling in cricket

box

boxes *noun*

a container to store things in.

cardboard **box**

boy

boys *noun*

a young male person.

brace

braces *noun*

a piece of wire that is fitted over your teeth to help straighten them.

bracelet

bracelets *noun*

a decorative band or chain that is worn around your wrist. Bracelets are usually made of metal or beads.

braille

noun

a type of writing, where letters are represented by raised dots. People who are blind read the dots by feeling them with their fingertips.

■ say **brayl**

brain

brains *noun*

the part of your body inside your head that controls how you think and move.

brake

brakes *noun*

a part of a vehicle that slows it down or stops it.

brake

brakes braking braked *verb*

to slow down or stop a vehicle by using the brakes.

branch

branches *noun*

the part of a tree that grows out of the trunk.

trunk / **branch**

brass

noun

a hard, yellow-coloured metal made from a mixture of copper and zinc.

brass *door knocker*

brave

adjective

willing to do something even though you are afraid.

*The **brave** girl dived into the lake to rescue her brother.*

■ comparisons **braver bravest bravery** *noun*

A
B
C
D
E
F
G
H
I
J
K
L
M
N
O
P
Q
R
S
T
U
V
W
X
Y
Z

bread

noun

a food made from flour and baked in an oven.

break

breaks breaking broke broken *verb*

to damage something so that it cannot be used.

*The cat is always **breaking** things.*

break

breaks *noun*

a period of rest.

breakfast

breakfasts *noun*

the first meal of the day, eaten in the morning.

breathe

breathes breathing breathed *verb*

to take air in and out of your lungs, through your nose or mouth.
breath *noun*

breathless

adjective

having difficulty in breathing.
*Running for the bus made the old man **breathless**.*

breed

breeds breeding bred *verb*

to keep animals so that they produce young.
*She **breeds** racehorses.*

breed

breeds *noun*

a particular type of animal.

*A dalmatian is a **breed** of dog.*

breeze

breezes *noun*

a gentle wind.

bribe

bribes bribing bribed *verb*

to pay someone secretly to do something that they shouldn't do.
*The prisoner **bribed** the guard to set him free.*

brick

bricks *noun*

a block for building with, made out of baked clay.

bride

brides *noun*

a woman on the day she gets married.

bride

bridge

bridges *noun*

a structure that is built over an obstacle such as a railway line or a river.

brief

adjective

short in time.
*He made a **brief** speech, lasting only five minutes.*

bright

adjective

1 giving off a lot of light.
*A car has **bright** headlights.*
2 clever.
*The **bright** pupil knew all the answers.*
■ comparisons **brighter brightest**
brightly *adverb*

brilliant

adjective

1 very clever indeed.
*The inventor had a **brilliant** idea.*
2 very bright.
*Diamonds are **brilliant**.*

brim

brims *noun*

1 the edge of a hat.

brim

2 the top of a container, such as a glass or a cup.

*Full to the **brim**.*

bring

brings bringing brought *verb*

to take something or someone with you when you go somewhere.
*Can I **bring** my friend along?*

bristle

bristles *noun*

stiff hairs, usually on an animal or a brush.

nail-brush

brittle

adjective

easily broken.
*Icicles are very **brittle**.*

broad

adjective

very wide.

*The river was **broad** at its mouth.*
■ comparisons **broader broadest**

broadcast

broadcasts broadcasting broadcast *verb*

to send sound or pictures by radio or television.
*The Olympic games are **broadcast** all over the world.*

broccoli

noun

a vegetable with edible green or purple buds. Broccoli is related to the cauliflower.

brochure

brochures *noun*

a small book that contains information.
■ say **broh**-sher

broke

from the verb **to break**
I broke my pencil in half.

bronze

noun

a brown-coloured metal made from a mixture of copper and tin.

An ornament made of bronze.

brooch

brooches *noun*

a piece of jewellery that is usually pinned onto clothes.
■ say **broach**

broom

brooms *noun*

a stiff, long-handled brush that is used for sweeping.

brother

brothers *noun*

a male person who has the same mother and father as someone else.

brought

from the verb **to bring**
I brought my dog with me.
■ say **brort**

brown

noun
a colour.

brush

brushes brushing brushed *verb*
1 to sweep.
2 to touch something lightly as you pass by it.
The woman brushed past me in the street.

brush

brushes *noun*
a tool with a handle and bristles.

animal brush

bubble

bubbles *noun*
a light ball of liquid with air inside.

bubble verb

bucket

buckets *noun*
a large container with a handle, usually used for carrying liquids.

buckle

buckles *noun*
an object for fastening two ends of a belt or strap.

bud

buds *noun*
a small swelling on a plant, containing young leaves or flowers (see **tree** on page 223).

tree bud

Buddhist

Buddhists *noun*
a person who follows the teachings of Buddha, a religious teacher who lived about 2,500 years ago.
■ say **buh**-dist

buffalo

buffaloes *noun*
a large mammal that lives on open plains and eats grass.

bugle

bugles *noun*
a brass musical instrument that you blow through to produce sound.

build

builds building built *verb*
to join things together to make a structure.
The bird built a nest out of twigs.

building

buildings *noun*
a structure, usually with walls and a roof, for sheltering people or objects.

bulb

bulbs *noun*
1 the rounded glass part of an electric light.

light bulb

2 the rounded part of some plants that grows underground.

daffodil bulb

bulge

bulges bulging bulged *verb*
to swell or be lumpy.
Her pockets bulged with food.

bull

bulls *noun*
1 a male mammal of the cattle family.
2 the male of some large animals, such as elephants, whales, and seals.

bulldozer

bulldozers *noun*
a machine with a large, metal blade at the front for moving earth and rocks.

bullet

bullets *noun*
a pointed metal object fired from a gun.

bully

bullies *noun*
an unpleasant person who frightens others.
bully *verb*

A
B
C
D
E
F
G
H
I
J
K
L
M
N
O
P
Q
R
S
T
U
V
W
X
Y
Z

bump
bumps bumping bumped *verb*
to knock into something.

bump
bumps *noun*
a rounded shape on
a smooth surface.
*It was difficult to ride
my bike over the **bumps**.*
bumpy *adjective*

bunch
bunches *noun*
a group
of things
together.

bunch of carrots

bundle
bundles *noun*
a group of things that are
loosely joined together.

bundle of twigs

bungalow
bungalows *noun*
a house with all its rooms
on one level.

bunk bed
bunk beds *noun*
one of a pair of beds that are
placed one on top of the other.

buoy
buoys *noun*
an object that is tied
to an anchor and floats on
water. Buoys are used as
a warning or guide for ships
and boats.

■ say **boy**

burglar
burglars *noun*
a person who steals things
from people's houses.

burn
burns burning burnt or **burned**
verb
to damage or destroy by fire.

burrow
burrows *noun*
an animal's underground
home.

*rabbit **burrow***

burst
bursts bursting burst *verb*
to split open.
*The water-pipe **burst** and
flooded the kitchen.*

bury
buries burying buried *verb*
to put something in
the ground and cover it over.
*The dog **buried** its bone.*

■ say **ber**-ree

bus
buses *noun*
a road vehicle for carrying a
large number of passengers.

bush
noun
1 a large plant with a rounded
shape. Bushes are smaller
than trees, and have many
branches low to the ground.

2 the wild countryside in
Australia, New Zealand,
and Africa.

business
businesses *noun*
1 an organization that sells
products or services.
2 the things that only you
should know about and
look after.
*Mind your own **business**.*

■ say **biz**-nis

busy
adjective
doing lots of things.

■ say **bizzy**

butcher
butchers *noun*
a person who prepares and
sells meat.

butter
noun
a soft, yellow food made
from cream.

buttercup
buttercups *noun*
a small,
wild flower.

butterfly
butterflies *noun*
an insect with wings covered
in very fine, coloured scales.
Butterflies begin life as
caterpillars. Most butterflies
eat plants (see **growth** on
page 94).

birdwing
butterfly

button
buttons *noun*
1 a small object used
to fasten two
parts of a piece
of clothing
together.

2 a switch to activate
an electronic device.

buy
buys buying bought *verb*
to pay for something.
*I'm going to **buy** a CD
with my pocket money.*

buzz
buzzes buzzing buzzed *verb*
to make a low,
humming noise.
*The bees **buzzed** in the hive.*

byte
bytes *noun*
a piece of information that a
computer stores in its memory.

Cc

cabbage
cabbages *noun*
a vegetable with a short stem and tightly wrapped layers of broad leaves.

cabin
cabins *noun*
1 a hut, often made of logs.

2 a room for passengers or crew on an aeroplane or ship.

cable
cables *noun*
1 a very strong rope or chain.

2 a bundle of wires for carrying electrical power or signals, often laid underground.

electric cable

cactus
cacti or cactuses *noun*
a plant that grows in hot deserts. Cacti store water in their stems, and have prickly spines that protect them from animals.

café
cafés *noun*
a place where people buy and eat meals, snacks, and drinks.
■ say **kaf**-ay

cage
cages *noun*
a container with metal bars for keeping animals or birds in.

cake
cakes *noun*
a sweet food that is made from flour, sugar, eggs, and butter and baked in an oven.

calculator
calculators *noun*
a small electronic machine for doing maths quickly.

■ say **kal**-kew-late-or

calendar
calendars *noun*
a chart of all the days, weeks, and months of the year.

calf
calves *noun*
1 a young cow or bull.
2 some young mammals, such as elephants or whales.

3 the back of your leg below the knee.

calf

call
calls calling called *verb*
1 to shout out.
They called for help.
2 to give something a name.
I called my dog Spot.
3 to phone or visit somebody.
My cousin called to see me.

calligraphy
noun
beautiful handwriting, using ink or paint.

■ say kal-**ig**-ra-fee

calm
adjective
1 still and quiet.
The sea was calm after the storm had passed.
2 peaceful.
Yoga makes her feel calm.
■ say **karm**
■ comparisons calmer calmest

came
from the verb to come
He came with us yesterday.

37

A
B
C
D
E
F
G
H
I
J
K
L
M
N
O
P
Q
R
S
T
U
V
W
X
Y
Z

camel
camels *noun*
a mammal with one or two humps on its back that lives in hot deserts. Camels store fat in their humps to help them go without water or food for long periods of time.

dromedary camel with one hump

camera
cameras *noun*
a piece of equipment used for taking photographs, or for making videos or films.

digital camera

camouflage
camouflages *noun*
a disguise that helps to hide an animal or person.

■ say **kam**-o-flarj
camouflage *verb*

leaf insect

camp
camps camping camped *verb*
to stay in a tent outdoors.

camping *noun*

campaign
campaigns *noun*
a series of events organized for the same aim. *She led a **campaign** to stop the new motorway.*
■ say kam-**pain**

can
can could *verb*
to be able to or to know how to do something. *She **can** touch her toes.*
■ opposite **cannot** or **can't**
■ always used with another verb

can
cans *noun*
a metal container used for preserving food or drink.

canal
canals *noun*
a water channel that has been built across land for boats and ships to travel on.

canary
canaries *noun*
a yellow bird that is often kept as a pet because it sings. Wild canaries are green.

cancel
cancels cancelling cancelled *verb*
to stop something that has been planned. *We **cancelled** our trip.*
■ say **kan**-sel
cancellation *noun*

cancer
cancers *noun*
a serious disease in which harmful cells spread through the body.
■ say **kan**-ser

candidate
candidates *noun*
someone who enters an exam, or someone who tries to be elected or to get a job. *Presidential **candidate**.*

candle
candles *noun*
a stick of wax with a string called a wick running through it. Candles are burnt to give light.

candy
candies *noun*
a type of sweet food.

cane
canes *noun*
1 a walking stick.
2 the thick, hollow stem of some plants.

*sugar **cane***

canoe
canoes *noun*
a light, narrow boat. A paddle is used to move the canoe along.

canyon
canyons *noun*
a steep-sided, rocky valley.

capable
adjective
having ability or skill at something. *They are both **capable** cooks.*

capacity
capacities *noun*
the amount that something will hold.

*These jars have different **capacities**.*

capital
capitals *noun*
1 a city where a country has its government offices and parliament. *Moscow is the **capital** of Russia.*
2 a large letter of the alphabet used to start a sentence or a special name.

capture
captures capturing captured *verb*
to catch and hold on to someone or something.

car

cars *noun*

a vehicle with wheels
that is moved by
an engine, and used
to carry people from
place to place.

New York taxicab

London taxi

number plate

spare wheel

fuel can

jeep

tow hook

aerial

rear view mirror

roof rack

tailgate

family **car**

wheel trim

bumper

silencer

exhaust pipe

wheel hub

tyre

spoke

wheel

windscreen wiper

hatchback

wing mirror

headlamp

mascot

mudguard

XR 366

starting handle

vintage **car**

tyre tread

radiator grille

piston

fan

engine

windscreen

steering wheel

bonnet

hood

boot

exhaust pipe

sports **car**

indicator lamp

a b **c** d e f g h i j k l m n o p q r s t u v w x y z

caravan
caravans *noun*
1 a home on wheels in which people live or have holidays.
2 a group of people travelling together for safety, usually across deserts.

cardboard
noun
a very strong, stiff type of paper used to make boxes.

care
cares caring cared *verb*
1 to be interested.
*I **care** about what you do.*
2 to look after someone.
*I **care** for my sick mother.*
3 to feel affection for someone.
*He **cares** for his girlfriend.*

career
careers *noun*
the jobs someone has during their working life, usually in the same occupation.
*She taught in three schools during her **career**.*

careful
adjective
being aware of dangers or problems.

*Be **careful** when you cross the river.*
■ opposite **careless**

cargo
cargoes *noun*
all the different goods that a ship or aircraft carries.
*A **cargo** of bananas.*

carnival
carnivals *noun*
a special event with a street procession, music, and dancing.

carrot
carrots *noun*
a hard, sweet-tasting root vegetable.

carry
carries carrying carried *verb*
to hold something while you move it somewhere.

carton
cartons *noun*
a small cardboard container for holding liquid or food.

cartoon
cartoons *noun*
1 a funny drawing that makes people laugh.
2 a moving film made by photographing thousands of drawings one by one.

cartridge
cartridges *noun*
a container of ink for use in a pen or computer printer.

carve
carves carving carved *verb*
to cut something into a shape.

case
cases *noun*
1 a container.
2 a particular event or example.
*There have been several **cases** of flu at school.*

cast
casts casting cast *verb*
1 to choose someone for a part in a play or film.
*He was **cast** as the king.*
2 to shape something in a mould.
*A statue **cast** in bronze.*

castle
castles *noun*
a large house with high stone walls and strong defences against attacking armies.

cat
cats *noun*
a mammal that is often kept as a pet. Cats eat small animals and are fierce hunters (see **pet** on page 148).

catalogue
catalogues *noun*
a book that shows you the things you can buy from a shop or a company.
■ say **kat**-a-log

catch
catches catching caught *verb*
1 to get hold of something that is thrown to you.

2 to get on a vehicle.
*I **catch** the bus to work.*
3 to get an infection.
*I **caught** measles from my sister.*

caterpillar
caterpillars *noun*
the larva of a butterfly or moth.

cattle
noun
cows, bulls, or oxen.

cauliflower
cauliflowers *noun*
a vegetable with a short stem and a hard centre, made of small flowers.

caution
noun
attention to possible danger.
Drive with **caution**.
- say **kor**-shun
cautious *adjective*

ceiling
ceilings *noun*
the surface of a room that is above your head.
- say **see**-ling

celebrate
celebrates celebrating celebrated *verb*
to do something enjoyable for a special reason.
We had a party to **celebrate** *my birthday.*
- say **sell**-ee-brate
celebration *noun*

cell
cells *noun*
1 a small room in a prison.

2 the smallest living part of an animal or plant.

animal **cell**

cellar
cellars *noun*
an underground room.

cellphone
noun
a hand-held mobile telephone that connects to other telephones by radio waves.

She is speaking on her **cellphone**.

cement
noun
a clay powder that becomes hard when mixed with water.

centipede
centipedes *noun*
a tiny, blind animal with many pairs of legs, which lives in dark places. They paralyse their prey with a poisonous bite.
- say **sen**-tee-peed

centre
centres *noun*
1 the middle.

The tomato is in the **centre** *of the plate.*
2 a building where particular events take place.
A sports **centre**.

century
centuries *noun*
a period of a hundred years.
The building is several **centuries** *old.*
- **sent**-yoo-ree

cereal
cereals *noun*
1 a grain crop grown on farms. Wheat, rye, barley, and oats are cereals.

wheat

rye

oats

barley

2 a breakfast food made from the grains of a cereal crop.
- say **seer**-ree-al

breakfast **cereal**

certain
adjective
sure, or definite.
Are you **certain** *this is the right train?*
- opposite **uncertain**

certificate
certificates *noun*
a piece of paper that proves certain facts.
She received a **certificate** *for passing her maths exam.*

chain
chains *noun*
metal loops joined together to make a strong cable.

chair
chairs *noun*
a piece of furniture for sitting on.

chalk
chalks *noun*
a soft, white rock made from the fossils of tiny seashells.

challenge
challenges challenging challenged *verb*
to ask someone to try to do something better than you.
He **challenged** *her to a race.*

chameleon
chameleons *noun*
a type of lizard that lives in trees in hot regions and eats insects, rodents, and small birds. Chameleons can change colour to match their surroundings.

- say ka-**mee**-lee-on

a b c d e f g h i j k l m n o p q r s t u v w x y z

A B **C** D E F G H I J K L M N O P Q R S T U V W X Y Z

champion
champions *noun*
someone who is the best at a sport.

chance
chances *noun*
an opportunity, or possibility. *He was given the **chance** to study abroad.*

change
changes changing changed *verb*
1 to become different or to make something different.

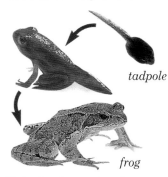

tadpole

frog

*Tadpoles **change** into frogs.*
2 to give up something in return for something else. *He **changed** seats.*
change *noun*

change
noun
small amounts of money.

channel
channels *noun*
1 a passage or track for water to flow along.
2 a television or radio station. *What's on the other **channel**?*

chaos
noun
complete confusion.
■ say **kay**-os

chapter
chapters *noun*
a section of a book.

character
characters *noun*
1 what a person is like. *A miserable **character**.*
2 a person in a play or film. *He played the **character** of the young king.*

charity
charities *noun*
an organization that gives aid to those who need it. *The Red Cross is a **charity**.*

chart
charts *noun*
a map or diagram that provides information.

*A pie **chart** showing popular forms of transport.*

chase
chases chasing chased *verb*
to run after something or somebody.

cheap
adjective
not costing much money.
■ opposite **expensive**

an expensive ring

£250

a cheap ring

50p

cheat
cheats cheating cheated *verb*
to trick someone, or to be dishonest so that you have an advantage over them.

check
checks checking checked *verb*
to look at something to make sure it is all right.
check *noun*

check
checks *noun*
a pattern of regular squares in different colours, often on cloth or paper.

cheek
cheeks *noun*
the side of your face below your eye.

cheek

cheer
cheers cheering cheered *verb*
to shout out loudly and happily.

cheer noun

cheese
cheeses *noun*
a food made from the thickened parts of milk.

cheetah
cheetahs *noun*
a spotted mammal that belongs to the cat family. Cheetahs live on the dry plains of Africa and prey on other animals. They are extremely fast runners.

chef
chefs *noun*
a person whose job it is to cook and prepare food.
■ say **shef**

chemical
chemicals *noun*
any substance that can change when joined or mixed with another. Chemicals can be natural or manufactured.
■ say **kem**-ik-al

cheque
cheques *noun*
a piece of paper from a bank that you can use to pay for things.
■ say **check**

cherry
cherries *noun*
a round, soft fruit with a small stone in its centre.

chess
noun
a board game for two people. The winner is the person who takes the other player's king.

chest
chests *noun*
1 the front of your body below your shoulders and above your stomach.

chest

2 a wooden box with a lid for keeping things in.

chew
chews chewing chewed *verb*
to use your teeth to break up food.
■ say **choo**

chick
chicks *noun*
a young bird.

child
children *noun*
a young person. A child legally becomes an adult at the age of 18.
■ opposite **adult**

chimney
chimneys *noun*
a pipe above a fire that takes smoke out of a building.

chimpanzee
chimpanzees *noun*
a mammal that lives in groups in forests in central Africa. Chimpanzees are related to the ape family. Their main diet is fruit and nuts, though sometimes they eat small animals.

chin
chins *noun*
the part of your face between your mouth and your neck.

chin

china
noun
a type of delicate pottery made from fine, white clay.

chip
chips *noun*
1 a small piece of something that has broken off something larger.

wood **chips**

2 a gap or mark on something, showing the place where a small part has broken off.

chip

3 a fried piece of potato.
4 a small piece of material with many tiny electronic circuits printed on it. Chips are used in electronic devices for storing information.

silicon
chip

chocolate
chocolates *noun*
a sweet food made from crushed and roasted cocoa beans, milk, and sugar.

choir
choirs *noun*
a group of singers.
■ say **kwire**

choke
chokes choking choked *verb*
to stop or almost stop breathing.
The fire-fighters almost **choked** *in the dense smoke.*

choose
chooses choosing chose chosen *verb*
to decide that you want one thing and not another.
I **chose** *the blue trousers, instead of the red ones.*
choice *noun*

chop
chops chopping chopped *verb*
to cut up something with a sharp tool.

a b c d e f g h i j k l m n o p q r s t u v w x y z

A B **C** D E F G H I J K L M N O P Q R S T U V W X Y Z

chop-stick
chop-sticks *noun*
a thin piece of wood or plastic, used in pairs for eating food.

chorus
choruses *noun*
lines in a song that are repeated at the end of each verse.
■ say **kor**-us

Christian
Christians *noun*
a person who believes in and follows the teachings of Jesus Christ and believes that Jesus is the son of God.

church
churches *noun*
a building where Christians hold religious services.

chute
chutes *noun*
a sloping channel for sliding things down.
Water chute.
■ say **shoot**

cigarette
cigarettes *noun*
a rolled-up piece of paper filled with tobacco, which can be lit and smoked. Cigarettes can harm your heart and lungs.

cinema
cinemas *noun*
a building where people pay to watch films.

circle
circles *noun*
a flat, exactly round shape.
circular *adjective*

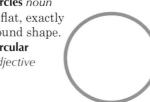

circuit
circuits *noun*
1 any completed path or track.
2 the completed path of an electric current.

electrical **circuit**
■ say **sir**-kit

circus
circuses *noun*
a show with clowns, jugglers, and acrobats that travels around the country.

citizen
citizens *noun*
a person who lives in, and belongs to, a particular place.
A British citizen.

city
cities *noun*
a very large, important town.
London, Glasgow, and Cardiff are British cities.

civilization
civilizations *noun*
a large group of people living in a well-organized way.
The Aztec civilization.
■ say siv-il-ize-**ay**-shun

claim
claims claiming claimed *verb*
to say that something is yours.
She claimed first prize in the competition.

clang
clangs clanging clanged *verb*
to make a deep, loud, ringing sound.
Bells clang.

clank
clanks clanking clanked *verb*
to make a short, metallic sound.

Chains clank.

clap
claps clapping clapped *verb*
to make a short, sharp sound with your hands.

Clap your hands.
clap *noun*

clash
clashes *noun*
a loud, metallic sound.
Cymbals clash.

class
classes *noun*
1 a group of pupils who are taught together.
My class is learning French.
2 a group of people, animals, or things that are similar to each other in some way.
Butterflies belong to the class of insects.

classify
classifies classifying classified *verb*
to sort things out into groups of different types.
Books can be classified as fiction or non-fiction.

clatter
clatters clattering clattered *verb*
to make a repeated rattling sound.

The plates clattered to the floor.

claw
claws *noun*
one of the long, curved, pointed nails that many animals and birds have on their feet.
owl's claw

clay
noun
a type of earth that is soft and sticky when wet, and hard when dried or heated. Clay is used to make pots and bricks.

modelling clay

clean
cleans cleaning cleaned *verb*
to remove dirt or stains.

clean
adjective
without any dirt
or stains.
Clean silver.
■ comparisons **cleaner**
cleanest

clear
clears clearing cleared *verb*
to move things that are in
the way.
*The walkers **cleared** a path
through the bushes.*

clear
adjective
1 easy to see through.
*The water was so **clear** that
I could see the fish.*

2 easy to understand.
*A **clear** explanation.*
■ comparisons **clearer clearest**

clench
**clenches clenching
clenched** *verb*
to curl up
your hand or
hands tightly.

*She
clenched
her fists.*

clever
adjective
able to learn and understand
things easily.
■ comparisons **cleverer cleverest**

click
clicks clicking clicked *verb*
to make a short, sharp sound
with your fingers.
Clicking your fingers.

cliff
cliffs *noun*
the high, steep side of
a mountain or rock.

climate
climates *noun*
the type of weather that
a place has over a long time.
*The **climate** in southern Africa
is hot and dry.*

climb
climbs climbing climbed *verb*
to move upwards, using your
hands and feet.

climb *noun*

cling
clings clinging clung *verb*
to hold onto something
very tightly.

*Clinging
upside-down.*

clink
clinks clinking clinked *verb*
to make a soft, ringing sound.
*The ice **clinked** in the glass.*

clip
noun
1 a small metal or
plastic object to fasten
something together.
*A paper **clip**.*
2 a short section of film.

clock
clocks *noun*
an instrument that shows
the time.

clockwise
adverb
moving in the same direction
as the hands on a clock.
■ opposite **anti-clockwise**

close
closes closing closed *verb*
to shut something.
■ say **kloze**

close
adjective
near to something.
Close to the house.
■ say **klose**
■ comparisons **closer closest**

clot
clots *noun*
a soft lump in a liquid.
*A blood **clot**.*

cloth
noun
woven material that is
used to make clothes and
other things.

clothes
noun
the things that we wear.
clothing *noun*

cloud
clouds *noun*
a mass of tiny drops of water,
or pieces of ice, floating high
in the air. The water falls as
rain, and the ice falls as hail
or snow.

cloudy *adjective*

clown
clowns *noun*
a circus performer who wears
funny clothes
and makes
people laugh.

club
clubs *noun*
1 a group of people who meet
together for a purpose, and
the place where they meet.
*A drama **club**.*
2 a thick, heavy stick that is
used as a weapon.
3 a stick with a shaped head
that is used to hit balls in
golf (see **sport** on page 197).

clue
clues *noun*
a piece of information that
helps to solve a mystery.

A B **C** D E F G H I J K L M N O P Q R S T U V W X Y Z

clumsy

adjective

moving awkwardly, or without skill.

*The big shoes made her walk in a **clumsy** way.*

■ comparisons **clumsier clumsiest**

coach

coaches *noun*

1 a long-distance bus.

2 a person who teaches people a special skill. *An athletics **coach**.*

coach

coaches coaching coached *verb*

to teach somebody how to do something. *She **coaches** the hockey team every Saturday.*

coal

noun

a hard, brittle, brown or black rock that is burned as a fuel. Coal is made from fossilized plants that died millions of years ago.

coast

coasts *noun*

the seashore.
coastal *adjective*

coat

coats *noun*

1 an item of clothing you wear over your clothes to keep warm outside.

2 an animal's fur.
3 a layer of paint.

cobra

cobras *noun*

a large, poisonous snake that lives in hot regions. Cobras can flatten the bones of their neck into a hood shape when threatened. They kill their prey with a bite that paralyses them.

cobweb

cobwebs *noun*

a very fine, sticky net made by spiders to trap flies.

cockatoo

cockatoos *noun*

a parrot with head feathers that it can lift up or flatten. Cockatoos eat fruit, nuts, and plant roots (see **bird** on page 28).

cockerel

cockerels *noun*

a young, male chicken.

cocoa

noun

a powder made from cocoa beans, the dried seeds of the cacao tree. Cocoa is used to make chocolate and as a flavour in food and drink.

■ say **koe**-koe

cocoa beans   *cocoa* drink

coconut

coconuts *noun*

the fruit of the coconut palm tree. The hard, outer shell has a layer of sweet, white, edible flesh inside, and contains a thin liquid known as coconut milk.

cod

noun

a large sea fish that lives in shoals close to the ocean floor. Cod use their sharp teeth to eat smaller fish, shellfish, and worms.

code

codes *noun*

1 a set of rules.
*The highway **code**.*
2 a series of signs, symbols, or letters for sending messages secretly or quickly.

● ● ● ▬ ▬ ▬ ● ● ●

*SOS message in Morse **code***

coffee

noun

a drink made from the roasted and crushed seeds of the coffee plant. When roasted, the seeds are called beans.

coffee

*roasted **coffee** beans*

cog

cogs *noun*

1 a wheel with shapes cut out around its edge. Cogs are used together in machines to turn other things round.

2 the tooth-shaped, metal parts around such a wheel.

coil

coils *noun*

something that is twisted around into circles.

coil of metal

coin

coins *noun*

a piece of money made of metal.

cold
adjective
having a low temperature.
A cold day.
■ opposite **hot**

cold
colds *noun*
an infection that often makes you sneeze and cough and may give you a sore throat.

collapse
collapses collapsing collapsed *verb*
1 to fall down suddenly.
The tent collapsed.
2 to fold up.
My umbrella collapses so I can put it in my bag.
collapsible *adjective*

collect
collects collecting collected *verb*
to bring together.
I collect autographs.
collection *noun*

collide
collides colliding collided *verb*
to crash into something.

Our cars collided.
collision *noun*

colour
colours *noun*
what something looks like when light is shining on it. Yellow, green, red, and blue are the names of some colours.

fruits of different colours
colourful *adjective*

column
columns *noun*
1 a tall, vertical, round post that is used as a support or to decorate buildings.

2 a list where things are written underneath each other.

33
27
46
58
19
183

Adding up a column of figures.

comb
combs *noun*
a piece of wood, metal, or plastic with teeth. A comb is used to arrange hair.

combine
combines combining combined *verb*
to bring things together to make something else.

Blue and yellow paint combine to make green.
combination *noun*

come
comes coming came *verb*
to move towards, or arrive at, one place from another.
Hurry up! The train is coming.

comedy
comedies *noun*
a film, play, or radio or television show that makes you laugh.

comet
comets *noun*
a huge ball of dust, ice, and gases that travels around the Sun, often followed by a luminous trail of gases.

comfortable
adjective
pleasant and easy to sit in or wear.
A comfortable chair.
■ opposite **uncomfortable**

comic
comics *noun*
a magazine that contains stories told in pictures.

command
commands commanding commanded *verb*
to order someone to do what you want.
The teacher commanded them to sit down.
command *noun*

common
adjective
often seen, or normal.
Seagulls are a common sight along the coast.

common sense
noun
the ability to act sensibly in different situations.
Common sense stopped us from driving in the fog.

communicate
communicates communicating communicated *verb*
to talk, write, or send a message to someone else.

Communicating by telephone.
■ say kom-**yoo**-ni-kate
communication *noun*

community
communities *noun*
a group of people who live together in the same place.
■ say kom-**yoo**-ni-tee

commuter
commuters *noun*
a person who travels a long distance to and from work every day.
commute *verb*

compact disc
compact discs *noun*
a small, flat circle of plastic that can have sound, or sound, words, and pictures, recorded on it. Compact disc is shortened to CD.

a b c d e f g h i j k l m n o p q r s t u v w x y z

A
B
C
D
E
F
G
H
I
J
K
L
M
N
O
P
Q
R
S
T
U
V
W
X
Y
Z

company
noun

1 a group of people who work together to make or sell something.
A computer company.
2 people or animals with whom you spend time.
My cat is good company.

compare
compares comparing compared *verb*

to look at several things to see how they are the same and how they are different.
My teacher compares me with my sister all the time.
comparison *noun*

compass
compasses *noun*

1 an instrument that shows the direction you are facing.
The magnetic compass needle always points north.

magnetic needle

2 a tool with one fixed leg and one movable leg, which is used for drawing circles.

competition
competitions *noun*

an event where one person or a team of people try to do better than their opponents.
Our team came second in the swimming competition.
compete *verb*

complain
complains complaining complained *verb*

to say that you are not happy about something.
The passengers complained about the late train.

complete
completes completing completed *verb*

to finish something.

Completing the jigsaw.
complete *adjective*

complicated
adjective

hard to understand, or difficult.

a complicated knot
■ opposite **simple**

composer
composers *noun*

a person who writes music.
compose *verb*

compromise
compromises compromising compromised *verb*

to end an argument by both sides deciding to give up part of what they want.
They both wanted to ride the bike, but had to compromise by taking turns.
■ say **kom**-pro-mize
compromise *noun*

compulsory
adjective

that must be done.
Maths is a compulsory subject at school.

computer
computers *noun*

an electronic machine that arranges and stores information digitally, using a set of instructions called a program. Used for communication.

laptop computer

concentrate
concentrates concentrating concentrated *verb*

to think carefully about something.

Concentrating on a puzzle.
■ say **kon**-sen-trate
concentration *noun*

concert
concerts *noun*

an event where people sing or play music for an audience to listen to.

conclusion
conclusions *noun*

1 the end of something.
The story's conclusion was a happy one.
2 a decision that is based on all the things you know.
She came to the conclusion that it was a sensible idea.
conclude *verb*

concrete
noun

a mixture of sand, cement, stones, and water, which is used for building.

concrete paving stones

condition
noun

1 the state that something is in.

Grooming helps to keep a horse in good condition.
2 a rule.
He went out on the condition that he was back before dark.

confident
adjective

believing you can do something, or being sure something will happen.
I'm confident I'll win.
confidence *noun*

confiscate
confiscates confiscating confiscated *verb*

to punish by taking something away from someone.
I had my football confiscated.

confuse
confuses confusing confused verb
1 to make someone puzzled because of some difficulty in understanding. *The instructions confused me.*
2 to find it difficult to tell one thing from another. *I always confuse the twins.*

congratulate
congratulates congratulating congratulated verb
to say to someone that they have done well.

Congratulating the winner.
congratulations noun

conifer
conifers noun
a tree that has needles instead of leaves. Conifers stay green all year round, and have cones instead of flowers.

Scotch pine

connect
connects connecting connected verb
to link up two things.

Connecting the digital camera to the computer.
connection noun

conscience
consciences noun
a feeling inside you that tells you what is right and wrong. *A guilty conscience.*
■ say **kon**-shuns

conscious
adjective
awake and aware of what is happening. *The man was still conscious after the accident.*
■ say **kon**-shus
■ opposite **unconscious**

conservation
noun
the protection and careful use of something. Conservation groups try to protect animals, plants, and the environment.

consider
considers considering considered verb
to think about something carefully. *She considered going out, but decided not to.*

considerate
adjective
thoughtful towards other people.

He is very considerate.

consonant
consonants noun
any letter of the alphabet that is not a vowel (see **alphabet** on page 16).

constant
adjective
going on without stopping. *A constant problem.*
constantly adverb

constellation
constellations noun
a group of stars.

The Plough

construct
constructs constructing constructed verb
to build.

Constructing a model.
construction noun

contact
contacts contacting contacted verb
to communicate with someone. *You can contact me by phone while I'm away.*
contact noun

contain
contains containing contained verb
to have something inside.

The box contains tools.
container noun

content
contents noun
an object inside something, such as a box, bag, or book.
■ say **kon**-tent

lunch box contents

content
adjective
happy and satisfied.
■ say kon-**tent**
contented adjective

contest
contests noun
a match or competition between people. *A juggling contest.*

continent
continents noun
one of seven very large areas of land that usually includes several countries.

the continent of Africa

continual
adjective
happening often, or without stopping. *Continual noise.*
continually adverb

continue
continues continuing continued verb
to carry on. *The match continued after the rain had stopped.*
continuous adjective

A
B
C
D
E
F
G
H
I
J
K
L
M
N
O
P
Q
R
S
T
U
V
W
X
Y
Z

contract

contracts contracting contracted
verb
to shrink or make smaller.
Your eye pupils **contract** *when light is shone on them.*

contradict

contradicts contradicting contradicted *verb*
to say the opposite of what someone else has said.
The politicians **contradicted** *each other.*
contradiction *noun*

contribute

contributes contributing contributed *verb*
to give a part of something.
We all **contributed** *to the meal.*
contribution *noun*

control

controls controlling controlled *verb*
to have the power to make something or someone do what you want.

These toy planes are **controlled** *from the ground.*

convenient

adjective
useful, or easy for you.
A **convenient** *time.*
■ say kon-**vee**-nee-ent
■ opposite **inconvenient**

conversation

conversations *noun*
talk between two or more people.

A friendly **conversation**.

convince

convinces convincing convinced
verb
to persuade somebody to believe something.
■ say kon-**vins**

cook

cooks cooking cooked *verb*
to prepare and heat food so that it can be eaten.
cookery *noun*

cook

cooks *noun*
someone who prepares food.

cool

adjective
slightly cold.

This box keeps drinks **cool**.
■ opposite **warm**

co-operate

co-operates co-operating co-operated *verb*
to work with someone in a helpful way.
We **co-operated** *on a project.*
co-operation *noun*

copper

noun
a red-brown coloured metal that goes green when it comes into contact with moist air.

copper ore   *copper* pipe

copy

copies copying copied *verb*
to do the same thing as someone else.
Copy me! I'll show you how to do it.
copy *noun*

coral

corals *noun*
a hard substance that is made of the skeletons of small sea animals. Coral is found in warm seas.

core

cores *noun*
the middle part of something.
An apple **core**.

cork

noun
the soft, springy bark of the cork oak tree, which is used to make mats, tiles, and seals for bottles.

cork oak bark

wine **cork**

corn

noun
a general name for the seeds or the plants of wheat, barley, rye, and oats.

corner

corners *noun*
the place where two lines or surfaces meet at an angle.
A street **corner**.

correct

adjective
right, with no mistakes.
■ opposite **incorrect**
correction *noun*

corridor

corridors *noun*
a long indoor passage, with doors leading off it into rooms.

cosmetics

noun
the things that people use to change the way their skin or hair looks.

lipstick   *eye pencil*

cost

costs costing cost *verb*
to have a price.
A computer **costs** *hundreds of pounds.*
cost *noun*

costume

costumes *noun*

1 an outfit worn in a particular period of time. *Historical* **costume**.

2 an outfit worn for a special reason. *Theatrical* **costume**.

gauntlets

silk stockings

ruff

doublet

hose

16th-century **costume**

chemise

corset

petticoat

drawers

crinoline frame

19th-century lingerie

tunic (chiton)

sandals

Ancient Greek **costume**

wig

beauty patch

cravat

waistcoat

cuff

handbag

mules

headdress

trimming

pendant

girdle

cloche hat

brim

breeches

stockings

buckle

petticoat

pantaloons

pumps

19th-century **costume**

18th-century **costume**

braces

14th-century **costume**

cotton
noun
1 soft, white hairs that surround the seeds on a cotton plant.
2 thread or cloth woven from cotton plants.
cotton thread

cough
coughs coughing coughed *verb*
to force air out of your lungs with a sharp noise.
■ say **kof**

council
councils *noun*
a group of people who are chosen to make decisions for an organization or community.

counter
counters *noun*
a flat surface in a shop or bank where you are served.
The cheese counter.

country
countries *noun*
1 an area of land with its own borders, people, and laws.

China is one of the biggest countries in the world.
2 land outside towns and cities.

courage
noun
being brave when you are in danger or difficulty.
It takes courage to admit that you are wrong.
■ say **kur**-rij
courageous *adjective*

course
courses *noun*
1 the plan of lessons that students must follow in a school or college subject.
Our history course starts on Monday.
2 the ground where many outdoor sports, such as golf and horse-racing, take place.

horse-racing course

court
courts *noun*
1 the place where it is decided whether people have broken the law and what punishment they should receive.
2 a piece of ground, marked with lines, on which some sports are played.
A badminton court.

cousin
cousins *noun*
a child of the sister or brother of someone's parent.

cover
covers covering covered *verb*
to put something over or on something else.

Cover your mouth.
cover *noun*

cow
cows *noun*
1 a female mammal that eats grass and is reared on farms to produce milk and beef.

2 the female of some large animals, such as elephants and whales.

coward
cowards *noun*
a person who is easily scared.

crab
crabs *noun*
a shellfish with 10 legs and a soft body protected by a hard covering. The front pair of legs end in claws which the crab uses to catch its prey.

coral crab

crack
cracks cracking cracked *verb*
to become damaged so that it splits, but does not break.
The mirror cracked when he dropped it.
crack *noun*

cracker
crackers *noun*
1 a thin, dry biscuit often eaten with cheese.
2 a long, round package of coloured paper containing a small present. Crackers are used at parties and make a loud noise when pulled apart.

craft
crafts *noun*
1 an activity that requires skill.

paper craft

2 a boat, aeroplane, or spaceship.

crane
cranes *noun*
1 a machine that lifts and moves heavy objects.

2 a large bird that lives near marshes and lakes, and feeds on plants, small insects, and animals. Cranes have a loud, echoing cry.

crowned crane

crash
crashes crashing crashed *verb*
to fall or collide with a loud noise.
The tray of china crashed to the floor.
crash *noun*

crate
crates *noun*
an open container for storing and carrying things, usually bottles.

crawl
crawls crawling crawled *verb*
to move along on your hands and knees.

*Most babies **crawl** before they learn to walk.*

crayfish
noun
a spiny shellfish that looks like a small lobster. Crayfish live under stones during the day and hunt for small fish and insects at night.

crazy
adjective
foolish or strange.
■ comparisons **crazier craziest**

creak
creaks creaking creaked *verb*
to make a low, squeaking sound.
*The door **creaked** open.*

cream
noun
1 the oily part of milk that rises to the top. Cream is often used to make sweets and puddings.

*a jug of **cream***

2 a yellow-white colour.

crease
creases *noun*
a line or fold, usually made in cloth or paper.

crease

crease *verb*

create
creates creating created *verb*
to design and make something.
*She **created** a beautiful painting.*
■ say kree-**ate**

creature
creatures *noun*
any living thing.

creek
creeks *noun*
a small, narrow inlet or bay in the coast.

creep
creeps creeping crept *verb*
to walk forwards very slowly and quietly.

*The cat **crept** up on the birds.*

crew
crews *noun*
1 the people who work on a ship or aeroplane.
2 a team of people who work together in a job.
*The film **crew** was ready to begin shooting.*

cricket
crickets *noun*
1 a jumping insect that eats plants. Crickets rub their wings together to make a singing sound. They have long back legs for jumping.

2 a team game played with 11 players in each team. The winning team is the one with the most points, called runs. Runs are scored by the person batting (see **sport** on page 197).

cried
*from the verb **to cry***
*The baby **cried** all last night.*

crime
crimes *noun*
an activity that is against the law.
*Murder is a very serious **crime**.*

criminal
criminals *noun*
a person who carries out a crime.

crisp
adjective
dry and easily broken into pieces.

crisp biscuits

■ comparisons **crisper crispest**

criticize
criticizes criticizing criticized *verb*
to say what you think is wrong with something.
*He was upset when I **criticized** his painting.*
■ say **krit**-i-size
criticism *noun*

crocodile
crocodiles *noun*
a reptile that lives on land and in water. Crocodiles are fierce hunters, and hunt at night for fish, mammals, and frogs (see **skeleton** on page 188).

crop
crops *noun*
a vegetable or plant that is grown on a farm for food.
*The potato **crop**.*

cross
crosses crossing crossed *verb*
1 to go over something, from one side to another.
***Crossing** the street.*
2 to place two things across each other in a cross shape.

*He **crossed** his fingers.*

a b c d e f g h i j k l m n o p q r s t u v w x y z

A B C D E F G H I J K L M N O P Q R S T U V W X Y Z

cross
crosses *noun*
an object or sign made by two lines crossing each other.

cross
adjective
angry.

*I get **cross** when people drop litter.*
crossly *adverb*

crossword
crosswords *noun*
a word puzzle with clues. You write down the answers by putting each letter of the answer into a separate square.

b	e	a	n	
u		w		s
s	h	a	r	p
y		r		o
	w	e	s	t

crouch
crouches crouching crouched *verb*
to bend down low, with your legs curled underneath you.

crowd
crowds *noun*
a large number of people gathered close together.

crown
crowns *noun*
a circle of precious metals and jewels. Kings and queens wear crowns on their heads on special occasions.

cruel
adjective
unkind and hurtful.

crumb
crumbs *noun*
a very small piece of food, such as bread, cake, or biscuits.

crunch
crunches crunching crunched *verb*
to crush or chew something noisily.
*She **crunched** a juicy apple.*

crush
crushes crushing crushed *verb*
to damage something by squeezing it very hard.

***Crushing** a can.*

crust
crusts *noun*
1 a hard covering.

*pie **crust***

2 the thick, hard outer covering of Earth.

crutch
crutches *noun*
a support for someone who has difficulty walking.

cry
cries crying cried *verb*
to have tears falling from your eyes because you are upset or frightened.

crystal
crystals *noun*
a piece of clear quartz with flat sides that has been formed naturally.

■ say **kris**-tal

cub
cubs *noun*
a young mammal, such as a fox, lion, or bear.

*fox **cub***

cube
cubes *noun*
a solid shape with six square sides.

cucumber
cucumbers *noun*
a green vegetable with a crisp, white flesh that grows on vines. Cucumbers are a popular vegetable to use in salads.

cuddle
cuddles cuddling cuddled *verb*
to hug someone in a loving way.

*A mother **cuddling** her daughter.*

culprit
culprits *noun*
a person who has done something wrong.
*The **culprit** had the stolen money in his pocket.*

cunning
adjective
able to trick people.

cup

cups *noun*

a container used for drinking liquids out of.

cure

cures curing cured *verb*

to make somebody well again after they have been ill.

curious

adjective

1 eager to find out about things.
*She was **curious** to see what was behind the door.*
2 strange but interesting.
*I saw a very **curious** animal the other day.*
■ say **kew**-ree-us

curl

curls *noun*

a small, curved piece of hair.
*Her hair is a mass of **curls**.*
curly *adjective*

currency

currencies *noun*

the money of a country.
*The **currency** of France is the Euro.*

current

currents noun

1 a flow of water or air moving in a certain direction.
*The **current** carried the boat out to sea.*
2 the flow of electricity through a wire.
*Switch off the **current** when you change a light bulb.*

curry

curries *noun*

1 a hot, spicy dish made of meat, fish, or vegetables, usually served with rice.

*vegetable **curry***

2 a mixture of hot spices used to flavour food.

curry powder

curtain

curtains *noun*

pieces of material that are hung from a bar and can be pulled across a window or space.

curtsy

curtsies *noun*

a formal way for women to greet someone.

■ also spelt **curtsey**

curve

curves *noun*

a line that bends smoothly.

curve *verb*

cushion

cushions *noun*

a type of pillow used for sitting or leaning on.

customer

customers *noun*

a person who buys something from a shop or a company.

cut

cuts cutting cut *verb*

to divide something into parts, using a sharp tool.

Cutting with scissors.

cut

cuts *noun*

a wound, often made by something sharp.

cutlery

noun

knives, forks, and spoons.

cycle

cycles cycling cycled *verb*

to ride a bicycle.

cyclist

cycle

cycles *noun*

changes that happen regularly in a particular order.
*The life-**cycle** of a butterfly.*

cyclone

cyclones *noun*

a tropical storm with very strong winds.
■ say **sye**-klone

cylinder

cylinders *noun*

a solid or hollow object with circular ends and straight sides (see **shape** on page 182).
■ say **sil**-in-der

cymbal

cymbals *noun*

a round, hollow, brass musical instrument, which makes a loud, clashing sound when hit.

A B C D E F G H I J K L M N O P Q R S T U V W X Y Z

Dd

daffodil
daffodils *noun*
a plant that grows from a bulb and has a large, trumpet-shaped flower at the end of each stem.

dagger
daggers *noun*
a knife with a short, sharp, pointed blade, that is used as a weapon.

daily
adverb
every day.
*Letters are delivered **daily**.*
daily *adjective*

dairy
dairies *noun*
a place where milk and cream are stored and butter and cheese are made.

daisy
daisies *noun*
a common plant with white or pink flowers. Daisies close their petals when it is dark. Some kinds of daisy are wild, while others are grown as garden plants.

dam
dams *noun*
a wall built across a river or stream to hold back the flow of water.

damage
damages damaging damaged *verb*
to harm something.

*The collision **damaged** the front of the boat.*
■ say **dam**-ij
damage *noun*

damp
adjective
slightly wet or moist.
*A **damp** towel.*
■ comparisons **damper dampest**
damp *noun*

dance
dances dancing danced *verb*
to move about to music.

dance *noun*

dandelion
dandelions *noun*
a common, wild plant with a thick root and a single yellow flower on each stem. Fine hairs attached to the seeds mean that the seeds are easily blown away by the wind.

seeds

danger
dangers *noun*
a situation that might be harmful to you.

***Danger** – falling rocks.*
dangerous *adjective*

dare
dares daring dared *verb*
1 to challenge someone to do something frightening to show they are not afraid.
2 to be bold or foolish enough to do something frightening or dangerous.

dark
adjective
1 not much light, or no light.

*The street was **dark** away from the street lights.*
dark *noun*
2 with a lot of black in it.
Dark blue.
■ comparisons **darker darkest**
■ opposite **light**

dash
dashes dashing dashed *verb*
to run very quickly for a short distance.
*I **dashed** onto the platform, but the train had just left.*

data
noun
facts and figures about something.
■ say **day**-ter

database
databases *noun*
a large amount of information stored in a computer.

date
dates *noun*
1 the day, month, and year.
2 a sweet, sticky fruit with a stone in the middle.

daughter

daughters *noun*

a person's female child.

■ say **daw**-ter

dawdle

dawdles dawdling dawdled *verb*

to move or do things slowly.

*Stop **dawdling**!*

dawn

dawns *noun*

the early part of the day when it starts to become light.

■ opposite **dusk**

day

days *noun*

1 the part of the day when it is light.

■ opposite **night**

2 a period of 24 hours, starting and ending at midnight.

dazed

adjective

not able to think clearly.

*He has a **dazed** look in his eyes.*

■ say **day**-zd

dazzle

dazzles dazzling dazzled *verb*

to shine a bright light into someone's eyes so that they find it difficult to see.

dazzling *adjective*

dead

adjective

no longer living.

dead leaves

■ opposite **alive**

dead

noun

a time when everything is still and quiet.

*The **dead** of night.*

deadly

adjective

able to kill.

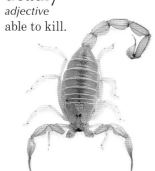

*A scorpion's sting is **deadly**.*

deaf

adjective

not able to hear well or not able to hear at all.

deafness *noun*

dear

adjective

1 expensive.

*The café prices are very **dear**.*

2 loved very much.

*A **dear** friend.*

■ comparisons **dearer dearest**

debt

debts *noun*

money or a favour that you owe to someone.

■ say **det**

decade

decades *noun*

a period of 10 years.

*The **decade** of 1920 to 1929.*

decay

decays decaying decayed *verb*

to rot away.

*Your teeth will **decay** if you don't look after them.*

decay *noun*

deceive

deceives deceiving deceived *verb*

to trick a person into thinking something is true when it isn't.

deceit *noun*

decibel

decibels *noun*

a unit of measurement that shows how loud a sound is.

■ say **des**-ee-bel

decide

decides deciding decided *verb*

to make up your mind.

*He couldn't **decide** what to eat.*

decision *noun*

deciduous

adjective

losing leaves every year.

■ opposite **evergreen**

■ say dis-**id**-yoo-us

decimal

adjective

counting numbers and parts of numbers in tens.

3.752

*A **decimal** number.*

decimal *noun*

deck

decks *noun*

one of the floors of a ship.

deck

declare

declares declaring declared *verb*

to say something to everyone.

*The judges **declared** the winner at the end of the competition.*

decline

declines declining declined *verb*

to decrease or get worse.

*His health **declined** steadily.*

decline *noun*

decorate

decorates decorating decorated *verb*

to make something look better by painting it or by adding extra things to it.

Decorating a room for a party.

decoration *noun*

a
b
c
d
e
f
g
h
i
j
k
l
m
n
o
p
q
r
s
t
u
v
w
x
y
z

A
B
C
D
E
F
G
H
I
J
K
L
M
N
O
P
Q
R
S
T
U
V
W
X
Y
Z

decrease
decreases decreasing decreased
verb
to become smaller.
*The number of whales
in the world is **decreasing**.*
■ opposite **increase**

deep
adjective
going down
a long way.

*A **deep** well.*
■ comparisons **deeper deepest**

deer
noun
a mammal with hooves that
eats grass and leaves. A male
deer is called a stag and has
large, branching horns called
antlers. A female
deer is called
a doe.

stag

defeat
defeats defeating defeated *verb*
to win a game or a battle
against someone.
*She **defeated** her brother
at chess.*

defend
defends defending defended
verb
to protect or guard.
*Birds stay with their eggs to
defend them from attackers.*
defence *noun*

define
defines defining defined *verb*
to describe accurately what
something means.
definition *noun*

definite
adjective
certain and clear.
*Are you **definite** about that?*
definitely *adverb*

degree
degrees *noun*
1 a unit used to measure
temperature and angles.
The symbol for a degree is °.
2 a certificate awarded by
a college or university.

delay
delays delaying delayed *verb*
to take place later
than expected.
*The aeroplane's departure was
delayed for seven hours.*
delay *noun*

delete
deletes deleting deleted *verb*
to remove something.

\ *word **deleted***

deliberately
adverb
on purpose.
*He **deliberately** pushed me.*
deliberate *adjective*

delicate
adjective
easily broken or damaged.

***Delicate** butterfly wings.*

delicious
adjective
tasting very nice.
*The ice-cream was **delicious**.*

delighted
adjective
very pleased.

*He was **delighted** with his
birthday present.*

deliver
delivers delivering delivered
verb
to bring something to
someone.

*They **delivered** the new sofa
this morning.*
delivery *noun*

demand
demands demanding demanded
verb
to ask someone for something
firmly, not expecting them
to refuse.
*She **demanded** to know
the truth.*
demand *noun*

demolish
**demolishes demolishing
demolished** *verb*
to destroy something.

*They started **demolishing**
the house yesterday.*

demonstrate
**demonstrates demonstrating
demonstrated** *verb*
1 to show someone how to
do something.
*He **demonstrated** the new
food mixer.*
2 to take part in a public
rally or meeting to show
that you feel very strongly
about something.
*The marchers **demonstrated**
against the new road.*
demonstration *noun*

denim
noun
a type of strong,
cotton cloth that
is often
dyed blue.

dense
adjective
thick.
*A **dense** fog.*

dent
dents *noun*
a hollow left in the surface of
something after it has been
hit or pressed.
*The car had a **dent** in
its bonnet.*
dent *verb*

dentist
dentists *noun*
a person who examines and
repairs your teeth.

depart

departs departing departed *verb*
to leave.

*The boat **departs** for the island every hour.*
departure *noun*

depend

depends depending depended *verb*
to need or rely on someone or something.
*I'm **depending** on you to be there on time.*

describe

describes describing described *verb*
to say or write what something or someone is like.
***Describe** your house to me.*
description *noun*

desert

deserts deserting deserted *verb*
to leave without permission, not planning to return.
*He **deserted** the army.*
■ say de-**zert**

desert

deserts *noun*
a large, dry, sandy or stony area of land, with few plants.
■ say **dez**-ert

deserve

deserves deserving deserved *verb*
to have earned some reward because of something you have done.
*He **deserved** a rest after working so hard.*

design

designs designing designed *verb*
to plan what something is going to look like.

Designing a book.
design *noun*

desire

desires *noun*
a strong wish.
desire *verb*

desk

desks *noun*
a table that you use for working on, often with drawers in it.

desperate

adjective
1 ready to do anything without thinking of the risks.
*A **desperate** escape plan.*
2 very serious or hopeless.
*A **desperate** situation.*

dessert

desserts *noun*
a sweet dish eaten at the end of a meal.

■ say de-**zert**

destination

destinations *noun*
the place someone or something is going to.

*The plane's **destination** is Australia.*

destroy

destroys destroying destroyed *verb*
to completely ruin something.
*The fire **destroyed** the hut.*
destruction *noun*

detail

details *noun*
a small part of something.
*The news report gave few **details** of the robbery.*
detailed *adjective*

detective

detectives *noun*
a person who investigates crimes.

detergent

detergents *noun*
a soapy powder or liquid that is used for cleaning things such as clothes or dishes.
■ say de-**ter**-jent

*bottle of **detergent***

determined

adjective
not letting anything stop you from doing something.

*He was **determined** to reach the top of the mountain.*
determination *noun*

develop

develops developing developed *verb*
to grow and become more complete.
*The bud **developed** into a beautiful flower.*
development *noun*

device

devices *noun*
a machine or tool invented for a special purpose.

*A corkscrew is a **device** for pulling corks out of bottles.*

dew

noun
small drops of water that form on cool surfaces outside during the night.

a b c d e f g h i j k l m n o p q r s t u v w x y z

diagonal
adjective
sloping at an angle from one edge to another.

diagonal stripes

diagram
diagrams *noun*
a drawing or plan that shows or explains something.

A diagram of the inside of a volcano.

dial
dials *noun*
the face of a measuring device that has numbers on it.

dial

diameter
diameters *noun*
the width of a circle, measured by a straight line.

diameter

diary
diaries *noun*
a book in which you write down your thoughts and daily events (see **time** on page 216).

dice
noun
cubes with a different number of dots, from one to six, on each side. Dice are used in indoor games. A single cube is sometimes called a die.

dictionary
dictionaries *noun*
a book that contains an alphabetical list of words with their meanings.

die
dies dying died *verb*
to stop living.
death *noun*

diet
diets *noun*
the food that you usually eat.

Fruit and vegetables are part of a healthy diet.

different
adjective
not like something else.

Two different shells.
■ opposite **same**
difference *noun*

difficult
adjective
hard to do.
It was difficult to cut the string with blunt scissors.
■ opposite **easy**

dig
digs digging dug *verb*
to make a hole in the earth.

digest
digests digesting digested *verb*
to break food down so that the body can use it.
■ say die-**jest**
digestion *noun*

digit
digits *noun*
1 a number from nought to nine, shown as a figure rather than written in words.
2 a finger or toe.

digital
adjective
1 showing number information in figures.
2 storing information using the digits zero and one.

digital camera

dilute
dilutes diluting diluted *verb*
to make thinner or weaker, often by adding water.
dilution *noun*

dim
adjective
not bright.
A dim light bulb.
■ comparisons **dimmer dimmest**

dinghy
dinghies *noun*
a small, open sailing boat (see **boat** on page 31).
■ say ding-ee

dingo
dingoes *noun*
a wild dog that lives in Australia. Dingoes hunt alone or in small packs and eat birds, reptiles, and small animals.

dinner
dinners *noun*
the main meal of the day.

A B C D E F G H I J K L M N O P Q R S T U V W X Y Z

dinosaur

dinosaurs *noun*
one of a group of land
reptiles that lived on Earth,
at different times, for more
than 150 million years.
The last dinosaurs died out
65 million years ago.

beak

brow horn

nose horn

beak

frilled crest

Triceratops
■ say **try-ser-**a-tops

plates

tail spikes

Stegosaurus
■ say **steg-**oh-**saw-**rus

Gallimimus
■ say **gal-**i-**mime-**us

neck

snout

hand

claw

armour plating

Euoplocephalus
■ say **yoo-**oh-plo-**sef-**al-us

Troodon
■ say **troe-**o-don

Barosaurus
■ say **bar-**oh-**saw-**rus

tail

claw

Deinonychus
■ say **die-**no-**nike-**us

Heterodontosaurus
■ say **het-**er-oh-**dont-**oh-**saw-**rus

crest

padded toes

scaly skin

teeth

claw

leg

Corythosaurus
■ say **kor-**ith-oh-**saw-**rus

toe

Tyrannosaurus rex
■ say tie-**ran-**oh-**saw-**rus **reks**

a b c **d** e f g h i j k l m n o p q r s t u v w x y z

61

A B C D E F G H I J K L M N O P Q R S T U V W X Y Z

dip
dips dipping dipped *verb*
1 to put something into a liquid or a soft substance and then take it out again immediately.

*Fruit **dipped** in chocolate.*
2 to slope downwards.
*The road **dips** slightly here.*

direct
directs directing directed *verb*
1 to show or tell someone how to get to a particular place.

*He **directed** the tourist to the castle.*
direction *noun*
2 to be in charge of the making of a play or a film.

Directing a film.

direct
adjective
going the shortest way.
*A **direct** route.*

directory
directories *noun*
a book that contains information about people and organizations, usually listed in alphabetical order.
*A telephone **directory**.*

dirty
adjective
not clean.

■ comparisons **dirtier dirtiest**
■ opposite **clean**

disabled
adjective
not having a limb, or being without power or strength, especially of movement, in part of your body because of injury or disease.
disability *noun*

disagree
disagrees disagreeing disagreed *verb*
to think differently from someone about something.
*We always **disagree**.*
■ opposite **agree**
disagreement *noun*

disappear
disappears disappearing disappeared *verb*
to go out of sight.

*The rabbit **disappeared** into its burrow.*
■ opposite **appear**
disappearance *noun*

disappoint
disappoints disappointing disappointed *verb*
to make someone sad by not doing something they expected.
*I **disappointed** my friends by not going to the match with them.*
disappointed *adjective*

disaster
disasters *noun*
a terrible event that may cause damage and suffering.

*Floods are natural **disasters**.*
■ say di-**zah**-ster
disastrous *adjective*

disc
discs *noun*
any thin, flat, circular object.
*A compact **disc**.*

discover
discovers discovering discovered *verb*
to find or find out.

*The pirates **discovered** a chest of buried treasure on the island.*

discuss
discusses discussing discussed *verb*
to talk about something with someone else.
*We **discussed** where to go for our holiday.*
discussion *noun*

disease
diseases *noun*
an illness.
*Measles is an infectious **disease**.*

disgraceful
adjective
so bad that the person involved should be ashamed.
*Do this work again – it's **disgraceful**!*

disguise
disguises *noun*
an outfit that you wear to hide who you really are.

■ say dis-**gize**
disguise *verb*

disgusting
adjective
very unpleasant.
*There was a **disgusting** smell coming from the drains.*

dish
dishes *noun*
1 a plate or bowl that is used to hold food.

*A **dish** for serving vegetables.*

2 one part of a meal.

*The main **dish**.*

dishonest

adjective

telling lies or stealing.

■ opposite **honest**

disinfectant

disinfectants *noun*

a chemical that is used for killing germs.

disinfect *verb*

dislike

dislikes disliking disliked *verb*

to think someone or something is not very nice.

She **disliked** the smell of the perfume.

■ opposite **like**

disobey

disobeys disobeying disobeyed *verb*

to refuse to do something that someone tells you to do. *You mustn't **disobey** orders.*

■ opposite **obey**

disobedient *adjective*

disperse

verb

to scatter widely. *The dandelion seeds were **dispersed** by the wind.*

dispersal *noun*

display

displays displaying displayed *verb*

to put something in a place where people can look at it.

Displaying paintings.

disposable

adjective

for throwing away after use.

dissolve

dissolves dissolving dissolved *verb*

to mix something with water or another liquid so it becomes part of the liquid.

A tablet **dissolving** in water.

distance

distances *noun*

the space measured between two places.

The signpost shows the **distance** between London and Edinburgh.

distinguish

distinguishes distinguishing distinguished *verb*

to be able to tell the difference between things. *Can you **distinguish** between the twins?*

■ say dis-**ting**-gwish

distract

distracts distracting distracted *verb*

to take someone's attention away from what they are doing. *The noise outside **distracted** her from her work.*

distribute

distributes distributing distributed *verb*

to give something out.

The teacher **distributed** the books to the children.

district

districts *noun*

an area in a town, city, county, or country, which is sometimes marked out for a particular purpose. *Postal **district**.*

disturb

disturbs disturbing disturbed *verb*

to interrupt the peace and quiet of a place or person.

The noise of the drill **disturbed** her.

disturbance *noun*

ditch

ditches *noun*

a long channel that drains away water.

dive

dives diving dived *verb*

to jump head first into water.

diver

divers *noun*

a person who swims beneath the water, often taking an air supply to breathe with.

scuba **diver**

divide

divides dividing divided *verb*

1 to split something up into parts.

The cheese is **divided** into eight portions.

2 to separate a number into equal parts.

8÷2=4

Eight **divided** by two equals four.

division *noun*

a b c d e f g h i j k l m n o p q r s t u v w x y z

A
B
C
D
E
F
G
H
I
J
K
L
M
N
O
P
Q
R
S
T
U
V
W
X
Y
Z

divorce
divorces divorcing divorced
verb
to end a marriage legally.
divorce *noun*

dock
docks *noun*
1 a place where ships load
and unload cargo.
dock *verb*

2 the place in a courtroom
where the person on trial
stands or sits.

doctor
doctors *noun*
a person who is trained to
treat sick or injured people.

dodge
dodges dodging dodged *verb*
to avoid being hit by
something by moving out
of the way very quickly.
*She **dodged** the ball coming
towards her.*

dog
dogs *noun*
a mammal that is often
kept as a pet. Dogs
mainly eat meat and can
be trained to carry out
certain tasks, such as
herding sheep. Dogs are
related to wolves and foxes
(see **pet** on page 148).

*collie **dog***

doll
dolls *noun*
a toy that is made to look
like a human being.

dolphin
dolphins *noun*
a fish-eating sea mammal.
Dolphins breathe air, so they
must swim to the surface
often. They are friendly
animals and are known for
their intelligence. Dolphins
are a type of small whale.

■ say **doll**-fin

domino
dominoes *noun*
a small, flat piece of wood
or plastic with dots marked
on it. Dominoes are used
in a table game, also
called dominoes.

donation
donations *noun*
a gift, usually of money, that
is made to a charity or
another organization.
*He made a large **donation**.*

donkey
donkeys *noun*
a member of the horse family
that has long ears and a soft,
furry coat. Donkeys eat grass
and in some countries are
used for carrying
people and goods.

door
doors *noun*
a piece of wood, glass, or
metal that opens and shuts
to provide a way into a room,
cupboard, building, or vehicle.

dot
dots *noun*
a very small, round spot.
*A full stop is a **dot**.*

double
adjective
twice
as much.

*A **double** six.*
■ say **dub**-ul

doubtful
adjective
not sure, or unlikely.
*He was **doubtful** about
his chances of winning.*
■ say **dowt**-ful
doubt *verb*

dough
noun
a mixture of flour and either
milk or water that is used
to make bread or cakes.
■ say **doh**

doughnut
doughnuts *noun*
a sweet, round cake made
from dough, which is fried
in fat and
covered
in sugar.

■ say **doh**-nut

dove
doves *noun*
a bird that
is a member of
the pigeon family.
Doves are
often used
as a symbol
of peace.

down
adverb
to a lower
place.

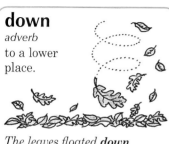

*The leaves floated **down**.*
■ opposite **up**

downcast
adjective
sad and upset.
*He looked
downcast.*

downhill
adjective
sloping down.

***downhill** skiing*

downpour
downpours *noun*
a large, heavy
amount
of rain.

downstairs
adverb
to a lower floor.

*He ran
downstairs
to answer
the phone.*

downstairs
adjective
on a lower floor than the one
you are on.

*A party in a **downstairs** flat.*

doze
dozes dozing dozed *verb*
to sleep lightly for
a short time.
*She **dozed** in the chair.*

dozen
dozens *noun*
12 of something.

*A **dozen** candles.*

drag
drags dragging dragged *verb*
to pull something along
the ground.

*He **dragged** his schoolbag
behind him.*

dragon
dragons *noun*
a fierce, imaginary animal in
myths and fairy tales, that
breathes fire and has a large,
scaly body and wings.

dragonfly
dragonflies *noun*
a long, thin insect with two pairs of
wings, often found near ponds and
rivers. Dragonflies feed on small
flying insects, which they catch with
their legs while flying.

drain
drains *noun*
a pipe or channel that takes
away waste
water and
other liquids.

drain
drains draining drained *verb*
to flow away slowly.
*The water **drained** away.*

drama
dramas *noun*
1 a play.
*My favourite **drama** is
Shakespeare's* Hamlet.
2 plays, or the theatre
in general.
3 an exciting or
frightening event.
*There was **drama** today when
the school caught fire.*

draw
draws drawing drew drawn *verb*
1 to make a picture or
diagram with a pencil
or crayon.

2 to move together by pulling.
*He **drew** the curtains.*

drawer
drawers *noun*
a box-shaped container that
slides in and out of a piece of
furniture. Drawers are used
to store things in.

*A chest of **drawers**.*

dream
dreams dreaming dreamed or
dreamt *verb*
1 to have thoughts and
pictures going through your
mind while you are asleep.

*I **dreamt** that I was stroking
a lion.*
2 to hope for something.
*She **dreamed** of travelling
around the world.*
dream *noun*

drench
drenches drenching drenched
verb
to soak with water.
*The rain **drenched** her.*

dress
**dresses dressing
dressed** *verb*
to put
on clothes.

*My little
sister can
dress herself.*
■ opposite
undress

a
b
c
d
e
f
g
h
i
j
k
l
m
n
o
p
q
r
s
t
u
v
w
x
y
z

dress

dresses noun

a piece of clothing that has a top joined to a skirt.

dried

from the verb **to dry**
He **dried** his clothes outside.

dried

adjective

with water or liquid removed.

dried
apricots

drift

drifts drifting drifted verb

1 to move slowly without control.
The boat **drifted** along.
2 to be carried along by water or air.

drift

drifts noun

a pile of snow or sand made by the wind.

drill

drills drilling drilled verb

to bore a hole in something using a drill.

electric
drill

drill

drills noun

1 a tool used to make holes.
2 a practice.
Fire **drill**.

drink

drinks drinking drank drunk
verb

to swallow liquid.

drink noun

drip

drips dripping dripped verb

to fall slowly, drop by drop.
Water **dripped** from the tap.

drip noun
dripping adjective

drive

drives driving drove driven verb

to make a car, train, or other vehicle move.
They **drove** along the country roads.
drive noun

drizzle

drizzles drizzling drizzled verb

to rain in small, fine drops, like a mist.
drizzle noun

droop

droops drooping drooped verb

to hang down in a weak or tired way.

The tulip **drooped** over the edge of the vase.
■ rhymes with **hoop**

drop

drops noun

1 a small amount of liquid.

— a **drop** of ink

2 a long way down.
It was a big **drop** from the bridge to the river below.

drop

drops dropping dropped verb

to let something fall.

He **dropped** his sunglasses.

drought

droughts noun

a period of time when there is not enough rain.

Many crops died during the **drought**.
■ say **drowt**

drown

drowns drowning drowned verb

to die because you have gone under water and have not been able to breathe.

drowsy

adjective

sleepy.

drug

drugs noun

1 a chemical substance used as a medicine to treat people who are ill or in pain.
2 an illegal chemical substance which people take to make them feel different. Taking this kind of drug is dangerous and can kill you.

drum

drums noun

a hollow musical instrument that has a covering across one or both ends. You hit the drum with sticks, special wire brushes, or your hands to make different sounds.

Japanese **drum**

drum
drums drumming drummed *verb*
to tap or hit continuously,
or to play a drum.

dry
adjective
not wet.
*They came in from the rain
and changed into **dry** clothes.*
■ comparisons **drier driest**
■ opposite **wet**
dry *verb*

duck
ducks *noun*
a water bird that has oily,
waterproof feathers, and
webbed feet for swimming.
Ducks eat fish, small plants,
and small animals. Male
ducks are called drakes.

*duck
(female)*

*drake
(male)*

duet
duets *noun*
a piece of music to be played
or sung by two people.

*A violin **duet**.*
■ say dew-**et**

dug
*from the verb **to dig***
*Our dog **dug** up part of
the lawn this morning.*

dull
adjective
1 not bright.
*It was a **dull** day.*
2 not exciting.
*I thought the film was
very **dull**.*
■ comparisons **duller dullest**

dummy
dummies *noun*
a model of a
person's body,
for making or
displaying
clothes on.

*dressmaker's
dummy*

dump
dumps dumping dumped *verb*
to put something down,
or throw it away carelessly.
*They **dumped** the shopping
bags on the floor.*

dune
dunes *noun*
a hill of sand, near the sea
or in a desert, which is made
by the wind.

dungeon
dungeons *noun*
an underground prison cell
in an old building, such as
a castle.

■ say **dun**-jun

duplicate
duplicates *noun*
an exact copy.

*One key is
a **duplicate**
of the other.*
■ say **dew**-pli-kate

during
preposition
1 at some time in.
*I fell asleep **during** the film.*
2 the whole time of.
***During** the summer months
we go swimming in the sea.*

dusk
noun
the time of evening when
it starts to get dark.
■ opposite **dawn**

dust
noun
tiny pieces of dirt that
float in the air and settle
on surfaces.
dusty *adjective*

duty
duties *noun*
things that you ought to do
or feel you should do.
*It is the guard's **duty** to make
sure the doors are locked.*

dvd
noun
a plastic disc that contains
digital recordings of sounds
and images (see **abbreviations**
on page 246).

dye
dyes dyeing dyed *verb*
to change the colour of
something by soaking
it in coloured liquids.

*These balls of wool have been
dyed different colours.*
dye *noun*

dynamite
noun
a powerful substance that
explodes when it is burnt.

dynasty
dynasties *noun*
a series of rulers from
the same family.
■ say **din**-as-tee

dyslexia
noun
a learning difficulty that
can affect reading, writing,
or spelling.
■ say dis-**lek**-see-a
dyslexic *adjective*

a
b
c
d
e
f
g
h
i
j
k
l
m
n
o
p
q
r
s
t
u
v
w
x
y
z

Ee

each
adjective
every single one.
*They **each** received a present.*

eager
adjective
wanting to do or have
something very much.
*The riders were **eager** to start
the race.*
eagerly *adverb*

eagle
eagles *noun*
a large bird of prey that lives
in mountainous areas. Eagles
eat animals and birds, and
have good eyesight for
spotting prey a long way off.

*golden
eagle*

ear
ears *noun*
1 the part
of your body
that you
hear with.

ear

earlobe

early
adverb
1 near the beginning.
*The hero dies **early** in the film.*
2 before the expected time.
*He arrived **early** for the show.*
■ comparisons **earlier earliest**
■ opposite **late**

earn
earns earning earned *verb*
to get something because
you have worked for it or
deserve it.
*They **earned** some pocket
money by cleaning cars.*

earring
earrings *noun*
a piece of jewellery that
can be attached to,
or hung from,
the earlobe (see
jewellery on
page 112).

2 the top of a cereal stalk
where the seeds grow.

ear of wheat

Earth
noun
the planet
that we
live on.

earth
noun
1 the surface of the land
or ground.
2 the material that plants
grow in.

earthquake
earthquakes *noun*
a violent shaking of the
ground, because of movement
from within Earth.

east
noun
one of the four main
compass directions. East
is the direction in which
the Sun rises.

north

west   *east*

eastern
adjective   *south*

easy
adjective
simple, not difficult.
■ comparisons **easier easiest**
■ opposite **difficult**

eat
eats eating ate eaten *verb*
to take in food
through
your mouth.

echo
echoes *noun*
a sound that bounces off a
surface and repeats itself.
*My voice **echoed** in the cave.*
■ say **eh**-ko
echo *verb*

eclipse
eclipses *noun*
1 a time when the Moon comes
between Earth and the Sun,
hiding the Sun's light.

*An **eclipse** of the Sun.*

2 a time when Earth comes
between the Sun
and the Moon, hiding
the Moon's light.
*An **eclipse** of the Moon.*

ecology
noun
the study of how animals,
plants, and humans affect
one another and how they
live in their environment.
■ say ee-**kol**-o-jee

edge
edges *noun*
the border of something.

*Flowers lined the path's **edge**.*

edible
adjective
safe to eat.
*Are these mushrooms **edible**?*

A B C D E F G H I J K L M N O P Q R S T U V W X Y Z

educate
educates educating educated
verb

to teach someone so that they learn and understand things.
education *noun*

eel
eels *noun*

a long, thin fish that lives in rivers and the sea. Eels eat tiny sea plants, animals called plankton, and other fish.

ribbon eel

effect
effects *noun*

the result of an action or event on another person or thing.
Seeing the crash on the news had a bad effect on me.

effort
efforts *noun*

the energy you need to do something.

It took a lot of effort to lift the suitcase.

egg
eggs *noun*

a rounded object that is produced by some female animals. Eggs contain the animal's babies, which hatch when developed.

crow's egg

egg *yolk*
egg *white*
egg *shell*
egg *cup*
hen's egg

elastic
noun
a stretchy fabric.

Braces made from elastic.

elbow
elbows *noun*
the joint in the middle of your arm.

elbow

elderly
adjective
rather old.

elect
elects electing elected *verb*
to choose someone to do something by voting for them.

election
elections *noun*
the time when people vote for someone to be in charge.
Council elections.

electric
adjective
powered by electricity.

electric razor

electricity
noun
a form of energy that is used for heating and lighting, and for making machines work. Electricity is produced at a power station and carried along cables and wires.
electrical *adjective*

elephant
elephants *noun*
a huge mammal that lives in southern Asia and Africa. Elephants eat tree bark, roots, leaves, grass, and other plants. They use their trunks like hands to pick up or hold their food.

African elephant

elevator
elevators *noun*
a large box or cage that carries people and goods between the floors of a building. Elevators are also called lifts.

email
noun
messages sent electronically between computers.

embarrass
embarrasses embarrassing embarrassed *verb*
to make someone feel ashamed or shy.
It embarrasses me to have to speak in public.
embarrassment *noun*

emergency
emergencies *noun*
a sudden, dangerous event.

Helicopters are sometimes used in emergencies.
■ say ee-**mer**-jen-see

emigrate
emigrates emigrating emigrated *verb*
to leave your own country to go to live in another.
My best friend is emigrating to New Zealand.
emigration *noun*

emotion
emotions *noun*
a strong feeling people have.
Love and hate are emotions.

employ
employs employing employed *verb*
to pay somebody to do a job.
I employ six people in my office.

empty
adjective
having nothing inside.

an empty bottle

a b c d e f g h i j k l m n o p q r s t u v w x y z

69

emu
emus *noun*
a large bird that lives on the hot, grassy plains of Australia and eats leaves and insects. Emus can't fly, but they can run very fast.

■ say **ee**-mew

encourage
encourages encouraging encouraged *verb*
to help someone feel happy and confident about what they are doing.

*Cheerleaders **encourage** their team.*
■ say en-**kur**-rij

encyclopedia
encyclopedias *noun*
a book, or set of books, that contains facts and information about lots of different things.
■ say en-sye-kloh-**pee**-dee-a

end
ends ending ended *verb*
to finish.
*The film **ends** at 8.30 pm.*

end
ends *noun*
the place where something finishes.

*There is a rubber at the **end** of this pencil.*

endangered
adjective
in danger of becoming extinct.

*Turtles are **endangered** animals.*

enemy
enemies *noun*
1 a person who dislikes you or would like to harm you.
2 the opposing country or army during a time of war.

energy
noun
1 the strength that makes a person or animal lively and active.

*She has lots of **energy**.*
energetic *adjective*

2 the power or ability of something to make something else work.

*Wind **energy**.*

engine
engines *noun*
a machine that uses fuel to make something move.

*jet **engine***

engineer
engineers *noun*
a person who is trained to design, build, or repair things such as machines, buildings, or bridges.

enjoy
enjoys enjoying enjoyed *verb*
to like doing something.

enormous
adjective
very large.

*An **enormous** umbrella.*

enough
adjective
as much as is needed.
*Do you have **enough** money?*
enough *noun*

enter
enters entering entered *verb*
1 to go into a place.

*The train **entered** the tunnel.*
entrance *noun*
2 to take part in.
*She **entered** the diving competition with her friends.*
3 to write down a name or some other information.
*I **entered** my name at the top of the test paper.*

entertain
entertains entertaining entertained *verb*
to amuse people or provide a pleasant way to pass the time.

*The juggler **entertained** the children all afternoon.*
entertainment *noun*

enthusiastic
adjective
very interested in something.
*He is an **enthusiastic** skier.*
■ say en-**thyoo**-zee-as-tik
enthusiasm *noun*

entire
adjective
whole.
*The **entire** class came to my party.*
entirely *adverb*

envelope
envelopes *noun*
a folded paper container for letters or cards.

environment

environments *noun*

the surroundings in which a person, plant, or animal lives.
*A city **environment** is often noisy and polluted.*
environmental *adjective*

■ say en-**vire**-o-ment

envy

envies envying envied *verb*

to feel unhappy because you want something that someone else has.
*I **envy** her long holidays.*
envious *adjective*
envy *noun*

episode

episodes *noun*

one part of a television or radio series.
*The first **episode** was so exciting, that he couldn't wait to see the next one.*

equal

adjective
the same.

Equal in length.
■ say **ee**-kwul

equator

noun

an imaginary line around the middle of Earth that divides the northern half of the world from the southern half. The equator is drawn onto maps and globes.
■ say ee-**kway**-tor

equator

equipment

noun

the things that you need for a job or an activity.

*snorkelling **equipment***

error

errors *noun*

a mistake.
*She failed the exam because her paper was full of **errors**.*

erupt

erupts erupting erupted *verb*
to explode suddenly.

*The volcano **erupted**.*
eruption *noun*

escalator

escalators *noun*

a moving staircase that carries people between levels or floors.

escape

escapes escaping escaped *verb*
to run away from somewhere or someone.

*The tiger **escaped** from his cage.*

establish

establishes establishing established *verb*

to organize or set up.
*They **established** a camp at the foot of the mountain.*

estimate

estimates estimating estimated *verb*

to make a thoughtful guess about something.
*We **estimated** that the journey would take 10 hours.*
estimate *noun*

evaporate

evaporates evaporating evaporated *verb*

to dry up gradually, changing from a liquid to a gas.
*The water slowly **evaporated**.*
evaporation *noun*

even

adjective
1 flat or level.

*Smooth and **even** grass.*
■ opposite **uneven**
2 a number that can be divided by two.
■ opposite **odd**

evening

evenings *noun*

the end of the day when the Sun sets and it grows dark.

event

events *noun*

something important that happens or is organized.

*The fireworks display is a big **event** each year.*

eventually

adverb
in the end or finally.
*After arguing for hours we **eventually** reached an agreement.*

evergreen

adjective
having green leaves all year round.

Nobel pine tree

Nobel pine branch

■ opposite **deciduous**

every

adjective
all, or each one.
♦ *We couldn't use the car park as **every** space was full.*
♦ ***Every**body in the family loves chocolate.*
♦ *We can't take **every**one with us, as there are only four places on the bus.*
♦ ***Every**thing in the house was stolen.*
♦ *There were daffodils **every**where they looked.*

a b c d e f g h i j k l m n o p q r s t u v w x y z

evidence

noun

proof that something
has happened.

*The detectives looked for
evidence at the scene of
the crime.*

evil

adjective

wicked.

evolution

noun

the gradual development
of animals and plants over
a very long time.

Mesohippus

Pliohippus

Equus

Evolution *of the horse.*

ewe

ewes *noun*

a female sheep.

■ say **you**

ewe

lamb

exact

adjective

accurate or precise.

*She pointed to the **exact** place
on the map.*

■ say egg-**zact**

■ opposite **approximate**

exactly *adverb*

exaggerate

**exaggerates exaggerating
exaggerated** *verb*

to say more about something
than is really true.

*She **exaggerated** the size
of her catch.*

■ say egg-**za**-jur-rate

exaggeration *noun*

exam

exams *noun*

an important test to find out
how much you know about
something. Exam is short
for examination.

examine

examines examining examined
verb

to look at
an object
closely and
carefully.

■ say egg-**za**-min

example

examples *noun*

something that is typical of
other similar things, or how
a rule works.

*Can you think of an **example** of
a plant that has blue flowers?*

excellent

adjective

extremely good.

*The **excellent** flower
arrangement won first prize.*

except

preposition

but, or other than.

*All the sheep were in the pen
except one.*

exception *noun*

exciting

adjective

thrilling.

*The roller coaster ride was
very **exciting**.*

excitement *noun*

excuse

excuses *noun*

a reason you give for not
doing what you should
have done.

*He had a good **excuse** for not
washing up.*

■ say ex-**kew**-s

excuse *verb*

exercise

exercises *noun*

1 activities or
training that
you do to
become fit or
to stay fit.

exercise *verb*

2 a piece of work that
practises a skill or
a person's knowledge
of something.

*A maths **exercise**.*

exhausted

adjective

extremely tired.

*She was **exhausted** after her
long run.*

exhaustion *noun*

exhibition
exhibitions *noun*
an event where things are
displayed for people to look at.

*A sculpture **exhibition**.*
■ say ex-i-**bish**-un

exist
exists existing existed *verb*
to be or to live.
*Dinosaurs **existed** long
before humans.*
existence *noun*

exit
exits *noun*
a way out of a building.

*We left by the nearest fire **exit**.*

expand
expands expanding expanded
verb
to become larger.
*Water **expands** as it freezes.*
■ opposite **contract**
expansion *noun*

expect
expects expecting expected *verb*
to think that something is
likely to happen.

*He was **expecting** rain.*

expedition
expeditions *noun*
an adventurous journey that
is made for a special reason,
such as exploring.

*They set off on an **expedition**
to cross the Antarctic.*

expensive
adjective
costing a lot of money.
■ opposite **cheap**

*an **expensive** watch*
£300

£2   *a cheap
watch*

experience
experiences *noun*
1 an important event
that you remember for
a long time.
*Travelling around the world
was a fantastic **experience**.*
experience *verb*
2 knowledge or skill gained
from doing something for
a long time.
*She has years of **experience**.*
■ say ex-**peer**-ree-ens
experienced *adjective*

experiment
experiments *noun*
a test that you do in order
to find out something.

expert
experts *noun*
a person who knows a lot
about a subject.
*The space shuttle was designed
by **experts**.*
expert *adjective*

explain
explains explaining explained
verb
to help somebody to
understand something.
*Our teacher **explained**
how rainbows occur.*
explanation *noun*

explode
explodes exploding exploded
verb
to burst apart suddenly,
often into many pieces.

explosion
noun

explore
explores exploring explored *verb*
to look around somewhere
carefully for the first time.
*After we arrived on the island,
we set off to **explore**.*
exploration *noun*

extinct
adjective
no longer existing.

*The dodo is
an **extinct** bird.*

extra
adjective
more than
is usual.

*An **extra** scoop of ice-cream.*
extra *adverb*

extraordinary
adjective
very unusual.
*What an **extraordinary** car.
It must be 10 metres long!*

extreme
adjective
very great, or much more
than usual.
*He was in **extreme** danger.*

eye
eyes *noun*
the part of the body that
you see with.

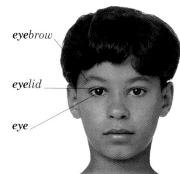

eyebrow
eyelid
eye

A B C D E **F** G H I J K L M N O P Q R S T U V W X Y Z

Ff

fable
fables noun
a story, often with animal characters, that tries to teach us in an amusing way.

fabric
fabrics noun
cloth.

façade
façades noun
the front of a building.

■ say fa-**sard**

face
faces noun
the front of your head, where your nose, eyes, and mouth are.

fact
facts noun
a piece of information that is known to be true.

factory
factories noun
a building where people make things using machines.

fade
fades fading faded verb
1 to lose colour or strength.

The photograph was old and had **faded**.
2 to disappear slowly.
The music **faded** away.

fail
fails failing failed verb
to be unsuccessful at doing something.
He **failed** his driving test.
failure noun

faint
adjective
not very strong.
She heard a **faint** noise coming from the cupboard.

faint
faints fainting fainted verb
to become unconscious for a short time.

He **fainted** in the heat.
faint noun

fair
adjective
1 light in colour.

Fair hair.
■ opposite **dark**
2 done in a way that is right and honest.
Everyone gets a **fair** share.
■ opposite **unfair**
3 dry and sunny.
Fair weather.
■ comparisons **fairer fairest**

fair
fairs noun
an outdoor event with stalls, competitions, games, and other entertainments.

fairy
fairies noun
a small, imaginary creature from stories. Fairies often have magical powers.

faith
noun
a strong feeling of trust in someone or something.
I have **faith** in my doctor.

faithful
adjective
trustworthy or reliable.
A **faithful** friend.

fake
adjective
imitation, not real.

fake jewels
fake noun

falcon
falcons noun
a bird with a sharp beak and claws that is related to the eagle. Falcons are good hunters and can fly very fast. They eat birds, reptiles, and small mammals.

■ say **fol**-kon

fall

falls falling fell fallen *verb*
to drop from a higher
place to a lower place.

*She was thrown from the horse
and **fell** into the water.*
fall *noun*

fall

falls *noun*
the American name
for autumn.

false

adjective
not real or true.
*He wore
a **false** beard.*

familiar

adjective
well-known to you.
*I saw a **familiar** face
in the crowd.*
■ opposite **unfamiliar**

family

families *noun*
1 a group of people who are
closely related to each other.
*I come from a large **family** of
five brothers and sisters.*
2 a group of animals or
plants that are related
to each other.

*These butterflies belong to
the same **family**.*

famine

famines *noun*
a time when there is not
enough to eat, usually
because of a drought or a war.

famous

adjective
well-known to many people.

*A **famous** film star.*

fan

fans *noun*
1 a device that moves air
around to make you
feel cooler.

*electric
fan*

2 a person who is very
interested and enthusiastic
about something.

*They played to their **fans**.*

fanatic

fanatics *noun*
someone who believes in
something so strongly that
it controls their life.
*A football **fanatic**.*

fang

fangs *noun*
1 a long, pointed
tooth that
meat-eating
animals use
for tearing up
their food.

fang

2 a snake's long, sharp
tooth that can give a
poisonous bite.

fantastic

adjective
1 difficult to believe.
*A **fantastic** tale about giants.*
2 very pleasing or wonderful.
*We had a **fantastic** holiday.*

fantasy

fantasies *noun*
something that is imaginary
and not real.

far

adverb
1 to or from a long way away.
*Have you come **far**?*
2 how distant something is.

*A quiet road **far** from the city.*
■ comparisons **farther farthest**
or **further furthest**
■ opposite **near**

fare

fares *noun*
the money that you must
pay to travel on a bus, train,
or aeroplane.
*What is the **fare** to Glasgow?*

farm

farms *noun*
a place where crops
are grown or animals are
reared for food.

*sheep **farm***
farm *verb*

fascinate

fascinates fascinating fascinated
verb
to interest someone so
much that they think of
nothing else.
*Dinosaurs **fascinate** me.*
■ say **fas**-in-ate
fascination *noun*

fashion

fashions *noun*
a way of
dressing that
people like and
want to copy at
a particular time.

*Long, straight
dresses were the
fashion in the 1920s.*
fashionable *adjective*

fast

adjective
at great speed.
■ comparisons **faster fastest**
■ opposite **slow**
fast *adverb*

fast

adverb
firmly held.

*Stuck **fast** in the mud.*

a b c d e f g h i j k l m n o p q r s t u v w x y z

A
B
C
D
E
F
G
H
I
J
K
L
M
N
O
P
Q
R
S
T
U
V
W
X
Y
Z

fast
fasts fasting fasted *verb*
to go without food for
a special reason.
*Muslims **fast** during
the festival of Ramadan.*
fast *noun*

fasten
fastens fastening fastened *verb*
to join something together so
that it holds.

***Fastening** her collar.*

fat
fats *noun*
1 the oily substance that
is stored under the skin
and in the cells of animals
and people.
2 an oily, solid substance that
is used in cooking. Lard, oil,
butter, and margarine are
all fats.

margarine

fat
adjective
having a lot of fat or flesh.

■ comparisons **fatter fattest**

fatal
adjective
resulting in death.
Fatal injuries.
■ say **fay**-tal
fatally *adverb*

father
fathers *noun*
a male
parent.

fault
faults *noun*
1 something that is wrong.
*A **fault** in the computer.*
2 a mistake that someone
has made.
*It was my **fault** we were late.*
3 a split in Earth's crust.
*The San Andreas **Fault** is
in California.*
■ say **folt**

favour
favours *noun*
a kind and helpful action.
*Will you do me a **favour**?*

favourite
adjective
liked the best.

*Red is her **favourite** colour.*
favourite *noun*

fawn
fawns *noun*
a young deer.

fax
faxes *noun*
a picture or message, that
is recorded electronically on
a fax machine. A fax is sent
by telephone lines to another
fax machine where it is
printed out.
fax *verb*

fear
fears *noun*
the feeling of being afraid.
*He had a **fear** of spiders.*
fear *verb*

feather
feathers *noun*
part of the soft,
light covering
that a bird
has on its
body (see
bird on
page 28).

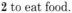

fee
fees *noun*
money that you pay to
a person or organization
for a service.

feed
**feeds feeding
fed** *verb*
1 to give
someone or
something food.

2 to eat food.

*Caterpillars
feed on leaves.*

feel
feels feeling felt *verb*
1 to experience an emotion.
*I **feel** happy today.*
2 to experience
something
through
touch.

feeling
noun

fell
*from the verb **to fall***
*I **fell** off my bike last week.*

female
adjective
belonging to the sex that can
give birth to babies, or
produce eggs or seeds.
■ opposite **male**
female *noun*

feminine
adjective
of or like women or girls.
■ say **fem**-in-nin
■ opposite **masculine**

fence
fences *noun*
a barrier that separates one
piece of land from another.

fern
ferns *noun*
a type of plant that has feathery leaves and doesn't produce flowers (see **plant** on page 151).

ferocious
adjective
fierce, dangerous, and cruel.
ferociously *adverb*

ferry
ferries *noun*
a boat or ship that regularly sails a short distance between two places, carrying vehicles, passengers, or cargo.

fertile
adjective
where something grows well.
Fertile farmland.

festival
festivals *noun*
a celebration or special event, often with music, dancing, and plays.

A dance festival.

fetch
fetches fetching fetched *verb*
to go and get something and bring it back.

The dog fetched the stick.

fever
fevers *noun*
an illness when your body temperature is very high and your pulse is fast.

few
adjective
not many, or a small number of something.

There are a few pencils in the jar.
■ opposite **many**

fiancé / fiancée
fiancés / fiancées *noun*
someone who is engaged to be married.
■ say fee-**on**-say
■ a **fiancé** is a man and a **fiancée** is a woman

fibre
fibres *noun*
a fine thread of something.

rope **fibre**

fiction
noun
a story or poem that has been made up and is not about real events.
I read a lot of crime fiction.
■ opposite **non-fiction**

field
fields *noun*
an area of land where grass grows, crops are grown, or animals graze.

fierce
adjective
violent or dangerous.

A fierce dog.
■ comparisons **fiercer fiercest**
fiercely *adverb*

fig
figs *noun*
a small, soft fruit with a tough skin and sweet flesh, which is full of tiny seeds. Figs can be eaten fresh or dried.

fight
fights fighting fought *verb*
to struggle against a person or animal.

Fighting with swords.
fight *noun*

figure
figures *noun*
1 a symbol that represents a written number.

2 the shape of the human body.
He saw a shadowy figure walking through the mist.
■ say **fig**-gur

file
files *noun*
1 a folder for keeping paper and other pieces of information together.

2 a metal tool with rough sides that is used to smooth edges.

3 a line of people, animals, or vehicles.

The ducklings walked in single file.

a b c d e **f** g h i j k l m n o p q r s t u v w x y z

A
B
C
D
E
F
G
H
I
J
K
L
M
N
O
P
Q
R
S
T
U
V
W
X
Y
Z

fill
fills filling filled *verb*
to put as much of
something into
a container as it
can hold.

film
films filming filmed *verb*
to use a movie or video
camera to take moving
pictures of something.

film
films *noun*
1 a series of moving pictures
shown on a screen.
*We went to see a film
at the cinema.*
2 a long, thin piece of special
plastic that is used in
cameras for taking
photographs.

3 a thin layer of something.
A film of oil.

filter
filters *noun*
a device that only allows
some things, such as water
or air, to pass through it.

coffee
filter

filter
verb

fin
fins *noun*
1 the part of a fish that sticks
out from its body and helps it
to swim and keep its balance
(see **fish** on page 79).
2 a device that helps vehicles
keep steady while going fast
(see **universe** on page 229).

fin

Bluebird racing car

final
adjective
last in a series.
*This is the final call for
the flight to Paris.*
finally *adverb*

find
**finds finding
found** *verb*
to discover
something.

*He found the key under
the mat.*

fine
fines *noun*
money you have to pay as
a punishment.
A parking fine.

fine
adjective
1 all right.
I feel fine.
2 dry and sunny.
Fine weather.
3 very thin or
delicate.
*The pen has
a fine tip.*

4 having many
small parts.
Fine sand.
5 very good.
Fine food.
■ comparisons **finer finest**

finger
fingers *noun*
one of the separate parts
at the end of your hand.

fingernail

finger

thumb

fingerprint
fingerprints *noun*
the mark that
your finger or
thumb makes
when it touches
something.

finish
finishes finishing finished *verb*
to come to the end
of something.

*She finished the race ahead
of him.*

fire
fires *noun*
the heat, light, and flames of
something
burning.

fire alarm
fire alarms *noun*
a bell that rings to warn
people of a fire.

fire engine
fire engines *noun*
the vehicle that fire-fighters
travel in to get to a fire.

fire extinguisher
fire extinguishers *noun*
a device filled with
water, powder, or
chemicals that is
used for putting
out fires.

fire-fighter
fire-fighters *noun*
someone whose job is to
put out fires and rescue
people in danger.

firework
fireworks *noun*
a device that burns or
explodes when lit, creating
a colourful display.

firm
adjective
1 solid.
A firm mattress.
2 fixed so it cannot move.
3 determined and definite.
A firm decision.
firmly *adverb*

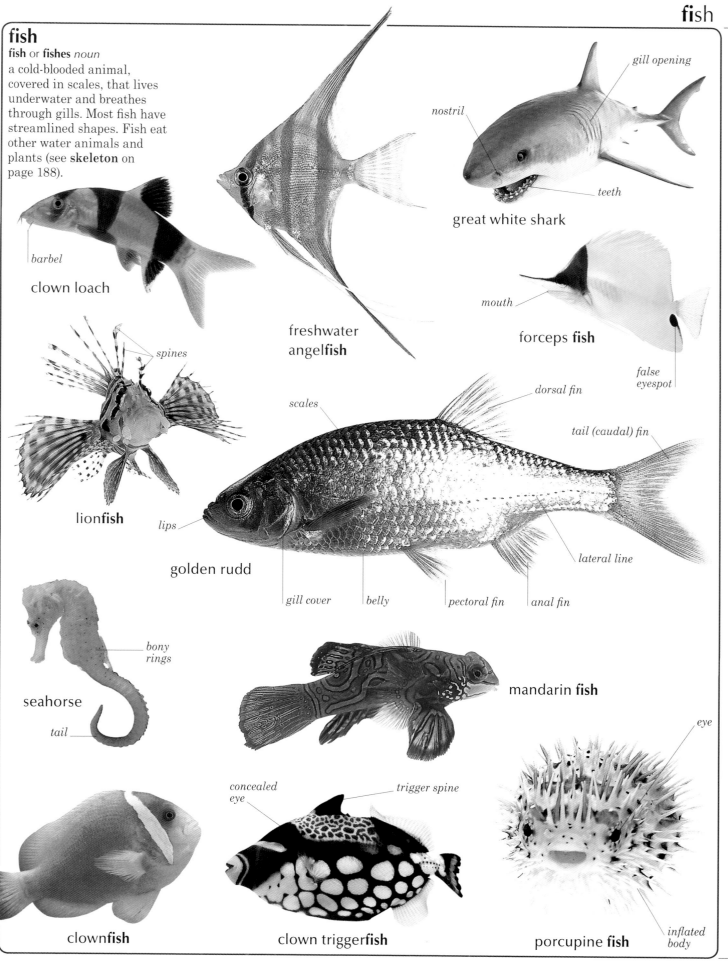

fish

fish or fishes *noun*
a cold-blooded animal, covered in scales, that lives underwater and breathes through gills. Most fish have streamlined shapes. Fish eat other water animals and plants (see **skeleton** on page 188).

barbel

clown loach

freshwater angel**fish**

nostril

gill opening

teeth

great white shark

mouth

forceps **fish**

false eyespot

spines

lion**fish**

scales

dorsal fin

tail (caudal) fin

lateral line

lips

golden rudd

gill cover

belly

pectoral fin

anal fin

bony rings

seahorse

tail

mandarin **fish**

concealed eye

trigger spine

eye

clown**fish**

clown trigger**fish**

porcupine **fish**

inflated body

A B C D E **F** G H I J K L M N O P Q R S T U V W X Y Z

fish
fishes fishing fished *verb*
to try to catch fish.
fishing *noun*

fist
fists *noun*
the shape your hand makes when you curl up your fingers and thumb tightly.

fit
fits fitting fitted or **fit** *verb*
1 to be the right size or shape.

*She checked to see if the skirt **fitted** her.*

2 to put something in place.
*I **fitted** a lock to the door.*

fit
adjective
healthy.
■ comparisons **fitter fittest**

fix
fixes fixing fixed *verb*
1 to mend something.

***Fixing** a car engine.*
2 to make something secure.
*They **fixed** the shelf to the wall.*

fizzy
adjective
full of bubbles.

*A **fizzy** drink.*
fizz *verb*

flag
flags *noun*
a piece of cloth with a design that represents a country or an organization. Flags are often flown from flag-poles.

└─ *flag-pole*
United Nations **flag**

flake
flakes *noun*
a small, thin piece of something.

***flakes** of pastry*
flake *verb*

flame
flames *noun*
a bright point of burning gas in a fire.

flammable
adjective
catching fire easily.
■ opposite **non-flammable**

flap
flaps flapping flapped *verb*
1 to hang or swing loosely.
*The washing **flapped** in the wind.*
2 to move up and down.
*Birds **flap** their wings in order to fly.*

flash
flashes *noun*
1 a sudden, bright light.
*A **flash** of lightning.*
flash *verb*
2 a short period of time.
*It was all over in a **flash**.*

flask
flasks *noun*
a container for liquids that usually has a narrow top and a tight-fitting lid.

laboratory *flask*

flat
adjective
1 level or even.
*A **flat** roof.*
2 without air inside it.

*A **flat** beach ball.*

flat
flats *noun*
a home with several rooms that is part of a larger building.

flavour
flavours *noun*
the taste of food or drink.

*This dessert has an orange **flavour**.*

flea
fleas *noun*
a very small, jumping insect without wings that sucks the blood of humans and animals.

flew
from the verb **to fly**
*He **flew** to France yesterday.*

flexible
adjective
easy to bend.

*A **flexible** ruler.*

flick

flicks flicking flicked *verb*
to touch or hit something in a quick, light way.

*The horse **flicked** the flies away with its tail.*
flick *noun*

flight

noun
1 the action of flying.

*A parakeet in **flight**.*
2 a journey through the air.
■ say **flite**

fling

flings flinging flung *verb*
to throw something suddenly and forcefully.
*He **flung** his shoes into the corner.*

float

floats floating floated *verb*
to rest on the surface of water or another liquid without sinking.

floating *adjective*

flock

flocks *noun*
a group of birds, or animals such as sheep or goats.
*A **flock** of geese.*

flood

floods flooding flooded *verb*
to cover an area that is normally dry with a large amount of water.
*The river burst its banks, **flooding** the town.*
flood *noun*

floodlight

floodlights *noun*
a large, bright lamp that is used at night to light up an open area, such as a sports ground.

floodlit *adjective*

floor

floors *noun*
1 a surface that you walk on inside a building.
*A marble **floor**.*
2 a level of a building.
*I live on the sixth **floor** of our block of flats.*

florist

florists *noun*
a person who sells and arranges flowers.

flour

noun
a powder made by crushing grain such as wheat. Flour is used in foods such as bread and cakes.
■ say **flower**

flow

flows flowing flowed *verb*
to move along steadily.
*A steady **flow** of traffic.*

flower

flowers *noun*
the part of a plant that contains the seeds. Flowers often have colourful petals (see **plant** on page 151).

petal

flu

noun
an infectious illness, caused by a virus, which often affects the nose and throat. Flu is short for influenza.

fluff

noun
soft fibres or threads from a material.
fluffy *adjective*

fluid

fluids *noun*
a substance that flows. Gases and liquids are fluids.

fluorescent

adjective
giving off light.

*His **fluorescent** top made him visible in the dark.*
■ say flooer-**es**-ent

flush

flushes flushing flushed *verb*
1 to become red in the face.
*She **flushed** with anger when her friend shouted at her.*
2 to clean with a sudden and quick flow of water.
*He **flushed** the dirty water away.*

flute

flutes *noun*
a wind instrument made of wood or metal. You play it by covering holes with your fingers or special pads and blowing across a hole at one end.

flutter

flutters fluttering fluttered *verb*
to move or flap quickly.

*The butterflies **fluttered** around the bush.*

A
B
C
D
E
F
G
H
I
J
K
L
M
N
O
P
Q
R
S
T
U
V
W
X
Y
Z

fly
flies *noun*
a flying insect with two wings and six legs. Most flies feed on rotting plants and animals. There are many different kinds of fly.

bluebottle **fly**

fly
flies flying flew *verb*
to travel through the air.

foal
foals *noun*
a young horse.

foam
noun
lots of very small air bubbles. Foam can be liquid or solid.

shaving **foam**

focus
focuses focusing focused *verb*
to adjust something to make a clearer and sharper image.
He **focused** *his camera on the flower.*
focus *noun*

fog
noun
a thick cloud of tiny water droplets and dust that hangs in the air, close to the ground.
foggy *adjective*

fold
folds folding folded *verb*
to bend one part of something over another.

a **fold**

fold *noun*

follow
follows following followed *verb*
to go behind or after someone or something.
The dog **followed** *him all the way home.*

food
noun
all the things that humans and animals eat to help them live and grow.

Pasta is an Italian **food**.

foolish
adjective
not sensible.

He was **foolish** *to walk under the ladder.*
foolishly *adverb*

foot
feet *noun*
the part of your body that you stand on.

football
noun
1 a game for two teams of 11 players. The winning team is the one that scores the most goals by heading or kicking a large ball into a net. Football is also called soccer.

2 a ball used in American football and football games.

an American **football**

footprint
footprints *noun*
the mark left by a foot or shoe.

footstep
footsteps *noun*
the sound of somebody walking.
I heard **footsteps** *behind me.*

forbid
forbids forbidding forbade forbidden *verb*
to tell a person that they must not do something.
I **forbid** *you to drive.*
■ opposite **allow**
forbidden *adjective*

force
forces forcing forced *verb*
1 to make a person do something.
I was **forced** *to make a choice.*
2 to push strongly.
They **forced** *the safe open.*

force
forces *noun*
1 a power.

The **force** *of the wind blew her hat off.*
2 a group of people who together have power.
The armed **forces**.

forearm
forearms *noun*
the part of your arm between your elbow and your wrist.

forearm

forecast
forecasts forecasting forecast *verb*
to predict that something will happen in the future.

Forecasting the weather.
forecast *noun*

forehead

foreheads *noun*

the part of your face above your eyes and below your hair.

forehead

foreign

adjective

belonging to another country. *Foreign languages.*
- say **for**-in
foreigner *noun*

forest

forests *noun*

a very large area of trees.

forget

forgets forgetting forgot forgotten *verb*

to not remember something. *I forgot my sister's birthday.*
- opposite **remember**

forgive

forgives forgiving forgave forgiven *verb*

to stop blaming or being angry with somebody for something they said or did. *I forgave my brother for losing my favourite CD.*
forgiveness *noun*

fork

forks *noun*

1 a tool with two or more narrow spikes that is used for lifting things.

table fork

2 the place where something divides into two parts.

A fork in the road.

form

forms *noun*

1 the shape or the type of something. *Trains are a form of transport.*
2 a printed piece of paper with spaces in which you write information. *I filled in a form to join the library.*

formula

formulas or **formulae** *noun*

1 a type of recipe or code that shows chemists what chemicals are made of.

$$H_2O$$

chemical formula for water
2 instructions or a recipe for making or doing something.

fortnight

noun

a period of time lasting two weeks.
fortnightly *adjective*
fortnightly *adverb*

fortune

noun

1 luck. *He had the good fortune to be rescued from the wreck.*
- opposite **misfortune**
2 a lot of money.

She won a fortune.

forwards

adverb

moving towards the front. *He fell forwards onto his hands.*

fossil

fossils *noun*

the remains or print of a plant or animal that died many years ago. Fossils are found preserved in rocks.
fossilized *adjective*

foster

fosters fostering fostered *verb*

to give a home for a period of time to a child who comes from another family. *They have fostered three children in the past two years.*

fought

from the verb **to fight**
The team fought back, but in the end they lost the game.
- say **fort**

found

from the verb **to find**
She found her wallet this morning.

fountain

fountains *noun*

a statue or structure that sprays water up into the air.

fox

foxes *noun*

a mammal that belongs to the dog family and lives in the countryside and in towns. Foxes eat small animals, birds, and scraps from dustbins.

fraction

fractions *noun*

1 a number that is part of a whole number.

One-third is a fraction.
2 a very small part of something. *You can fly there in a fraction of the time it takes to drive.*

fracture

fractures fracturing fractured *verb*

to break.

fracture

The X-ray showed where the bone had fractured.
fracture *noun*

fragile

adjective

delicate and easily broken.

fragile coral
- say **fra**-jile

a
b
c
d
e
f
g
h
i
j
k
l
m
n
o
p
q
r
s
t
u
v
w
x
y
z

A B C D E **F** G H I J K L M N O P Q R S T U V W X Y Z

frame
frames *noun*
a structure that surrounds the edge of something, holding it in place.

A picture frame.

frantic
adjective
very upset and excited, because of fear, worry, or pain.
The frantic animal tried to escape from its cage.
frantically *adverb*

freckle
freckles *noun*
a small, light brown spot on the skin.

freckles

free
adjective
1 costing no money.
Please accept this free gift.
2 not restricted by rules or limits.
Have you any free time this week?
free *adverb*
free *verb*

freedom
noun
being free.
The freedom to do as you like.

freeze
freezes freezing froze frozen
verb
to reach such a low, cold temperature that a liquid becomes a solid.

The lake froze in winter.

freezer
freezers *noun*
a machine that freezes food so that it can be stored for a long time without going bad.

freight
noun
goods that are carried by road, rail, sea, or air.
■ rhymes with **mate**

freight train

frequent
adjective
happening often.
There is a frequent train service to the city.
■ say **free**-kwent
frequently *adverb*

fresh
adjective
new, not stale or preserved.

fresh parsley   *dried parsley*

friend
friends *noun*
somebody that you like and who likes you.
friendly *adjective*

frighten
frightens frightening frightened
verb
to make somebody feel afraid.
She was always trying to frighten her brother.
frightening *adjective*

fringe
fringes *noun*
1 a border made up of loose, hanging pieces of material or thread.

fringe

2 the hair that hangs over your forehead.

frog
frogs *noun*
an amphibian that lives in or near water. Frogs eat spiders, worms, small fish, and insects.

front
fronts *noun*
the part of something that faces forwards.

front of a truck

frontier
frontiers *noun*
the border between two regions or countries, especially if one of them is wild and unknown.
■ say **frun**-teer

frost
frosts *noun*
tiny ice crystals that form on surfaces outside in very cold weather.
frosty *adjective*

frown
frowns frowning frowned *verb*
to pull your eyebrows together and wrinkle your forehead to show that you are not happy about something.

frozen
adjective
preserved by being kept very cold.

frozen peas

fruit

fruits *noun*
the part of a plant
that contains
the seeds. Many
fruits are edible.

■ rhymes with **boot**

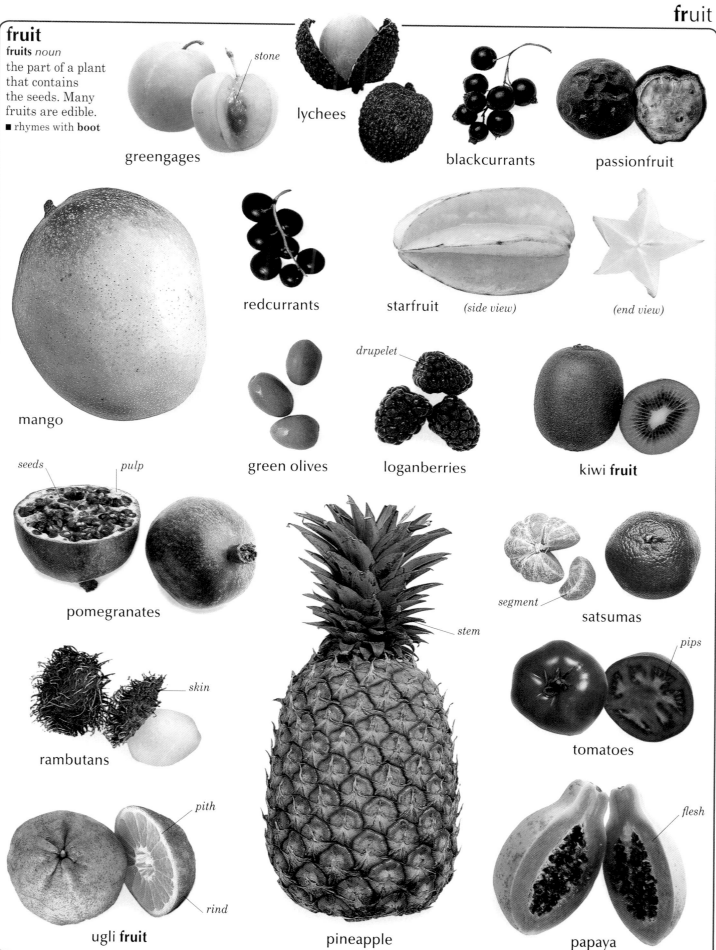

greengages

stone

lychees

blackcurrants

passionfruit

mango

redcurrants

starfruit   *(side view)*   *(end view)*

green olives

drupelet

loganberries

kiwi **fruit**

seeds   *pulp*

pomegranates

segment

satsumas

rambutans

skin

stem

tomatoes

pips

ugli **fruit**

pith

rind

pineapple

papaya

flesh

a
b
c
d
e
g
h
i
j
k
l
m
n
o
p
q
r
s
t
u
v
w
x
y
z

A B C D E **F** G H I J K L M N O P Q R S T U V W X Y Z

frustrate
frustrates frustrating frustrated
verb
to upset someone by keeping them from doing something they want to do.
It was frustrating that the last tickets for the concert had already been sold.
frustration *noun*

fry
fries frying fried *verb*
to cook something in hot fat.

frying pan

fuel
fuels *noun*
something that is burnt to give heat or power.
Wood, coal, and petrol are types of fuel.

full
adjective
without space for any more.

This box is full of beads.

fumes
noun
smoke or gas that is often strong-smelling and unpleasant. Some fumes are poisonous.
Exhaust fumes.

fun
noun
an enjoyable activity.
The treasure hunt was great fun.

fund
funds *noun*
an amount of money collected for a special reason.

The church has started a fund to repair the roof.

funeral
funerals *noun*
a formal occasion during which the body of someone who has died is buried or burned.

fungus
fungi or **funguses** *noun*
a plant with no flowers or leaves. Fungus grows in damp places, and has seeds called spores.

fly agaric

funnel
funnels *noun*
1 a tube that is wide at one end and narrow at the other. Funnels are used for pouring liquids through small openings.

2 the chimney on a ship.

funnel

funny
adjective
1 making you laugh or smile.

2 strange or odd.
What's that funny noise?
■ comparisons **funnier funniest**

fur
noun
the soft, hairy covering that some animals have on their bodies.

furry *adjective*

furious
adjective
very angry.
She was furious to discover that her wallet was missing.
■ say **fyoor**-ree-us

furnace
furnaces *noun*
an oven that heats metals to a very high temperature, so that they melt.
■ say **fur**-nis

steel-making furnace

furniture
noun
chairs, beds, cupboards, and other movable things that you have in the place where you live or work.

cupboard

armchair

double bed

furrow
furrows *noun*
a groove in the earth made by a plough.

fuse
fuses *noun*
a safety device for electrical machines that stops the current from flowing if it is too strong.

fuss
fusses fussing fussed *verb*
to be more anxious than is necessary about something.
Don't fuss!
fussy *adjective*

future
noun
the time that is to come.
In the future, people might travel to Mars.
■ opposite **past**

Gg

gadget
gadgets *noun*
a small, useful tool.
- say **ga**-jit

galaxy
galaxies *noun*
a large group of stars.
The Milky Way is a galaxy.

gale
gales *noun*
a strong wind.

gallop
gallops galloping galloped *verb*
to move in the way that
a horse does when it runs
as fast as it can.

gamble
gambles gambling gambled *verb*
to bet money on the result of
a race, game, or competition.

game
games *noun*
an activity that you play
for fun, or a sport. Many
games have rules and
a scoring system.

skittles

gang
gangs *noun*
a group of people who do
things together.
A gang of road workers.

gaol
gaols *noun*
another spelling
of the word "jail".
- say **jayl**

gap
gaps *noun*
a space between two things.

A gap in the hedge.

gape
gapes gaping gaped *verb*
to stare at something with
your mouth open.
*They gaped at the acrobat
on the tightrope.*

garage
garages *noun*
1 a place where cars and
other vehicles are stored.

2 a place where cars and
other vehicles are mended.
- say **ga**-rarj or **ga**-rij

garbage
noun
things that have been
thrown away.
- say **gar**-bij

garden
gardens *noun*
a piece of ground where fruit,
flowers, vegetables, and other
plants are grown.

*The garden looked beautiful
in the summer.*

garlic
noun
a plant with
an onion-shaped bulb,
made up of sections
called cloves. Garlic is
used in cooking to add
flavour to food.

*garlic
cloves*

string of garlic

gas
gases *noun*
a substance that is
not a liquid or a solid.

*This camping
stove is
powered by
a gas called
butane.*

gash
gashes *noun*
a long, deep cut.

gasp
gasps gasping gasped *verb*
to struggle to breathe, taking
in air in short, quick breaths.
*He rose to the surface of
the water, gasping for air.*
gasp *noun*

gate
gates *noun*
a type of outside door that
is fitted into walls or fences.

gather
gathers gathering gathered *verb*
to collect together.

Gathering leaves.

a b c d e f g h i j k l m n o p q r s t u v w x y z

gave
from the verb **to give**
She **gave** me a kite for
my birthday last week.

gaze
gazes gazing gazed verb
to stare at something
for a long time.
He **gazed** out of the window.

gem
gems noun
a jewel or
precious stone.

emerald

aquamarine

fire opal

heliodor

yellow sapphire

general
adjective
1 usual, or to do with
most people.
The **general** opinion is that
exercise is good for you.
2 having to do with the main
parts, but not the details.
The newspaper reported the
general points of the
President's speech.
generally adverb

generation
generations noun
all the people who
are in approximately
the same age group.
There is usually
a period of about
30 years between
one generation
and the next.

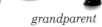

Three
different
generations.   child   parent   grandparent

generous
adjective
kind and ready to give.
It was **generous** of him
to lend us the car.
generously adverb

genius
geniuses noun
a person who is
extremely intelligent.
Many people think that
Albert Einstein was a **genius**.
■ say **jee**-nee-us

gentle
adjective
kind and
careful.

Be **gentle** with the kitten.
■ comparisons **gentler gentlest**
gently adverb

genuine
adjective
real, or not imitation.
A **genuine** leather bag.
■ say **jen**-yoo-in

geography
noun
the study of Earth's surface
and its inhabitants.
■ say jee-**og**-raf-ee

geometry
noun
the study of shapes, surfaces,
and angles.
■ say jee-**om**-met-ree

germ
germs noun
a tiny plant or animal that
can cause illness.

germinate
germinates
germinating
germinated verb
to start to grow.

a seed **germinating**

gesture
gestures noun
a sign that
you make
with your
hands
or body.

ghost
ghosts noun
the spirit of
a dead person.
Some people
believe they
can see ghosts.
■ say **goest**
ghostly adjective

giant
giants noun
a huge, imaginary person
from fairy tales
or legends.

giant
adjective
very large.

gift
gifts noun
a present.

gigantic
adjective
huge or enormous.
A **gigantic** house with
20 bedrooms.
■ say jie-**gan**-tik

giggle
giggles giggling giggled verb
to laugh in a nervous
or silly way.

gill
gills *noun*
the organ that a fish uses to breathe (see **fish** on page 79).

gimmick
gimmicks *noun*
a way of making people aware of something or somebody.
*Free gifts are often given away as a **gimmick** to draw attention to a new product.*

ginger
noun
a spicy root that is used to add flavour to food.

*ground **ginger***

*root **ginger***

giraffe
giraffes *noun*
a very tall mammal that lives on dry plains in Africa. Giraffes eat leaves on trees, which they can reach with their long necks.

girl
girls *noun*
a young female person.

give
gives giving gave given *verb*
to let somebody have something.

*He **gave** her a book as a prize.*

glacier
glaciers *noun*
a huge river of ice that moves very slowly.

glad
adjective
pleased and happy.
*I am **glad** to be back home.*

gladiator
gladiators *noun*
a man who was trained to fight for entertainment in ancient Rome.

glance
glances glancing glanced *verb*
to take a quick look at something.
*She **glanced** at the clock to see if it was time to go out.*

gland
glands *noun*
one of the parts of your body that makes the chemicals your body needs.
Glands near your eyes make tears.

glare
glares glaring glared *verb*
1 to look at someone in an angry way.
2 to shine very brightly.
*The sun **glared** down.*
glare *noun*

glass
noun
1 a transparent, fragile substance that is used to make things such as windows and bottles.

stained glass

2 a container that is used to drink from.

*wine **glass***

glasses
noun
a pair of lenses in frames. People wear glasses to help them see better.

gleam
gleams gleaming gleamed *verb*
to shine or glow.

glider
gliders *noun*
a very light aircraft with no motor that flies using air currents.

glimpse
glimpses glimpsing glimpsed *verb*
to see something or someone for just a few moments.
*He **glimpsed** his friend in the crowd.*

glitter
glitters glittering glittered *verb*
to shine with a bright, sparkling light.

a b c d e f **g** h i j k l m n o p q r s t u v w x y z

A B C D E F **G** H I J K L M N O P Q R S T U V W X Y Z

globe
globes *noun*
the world, or a model of the world.

gloomy
adjective
dull and dark.
*A **gloomy** winter day.*

glossy
adjective
shiny.
Glossy paper.
■ comparisons **glossier glossiest**

glove
gloves *noun*
a piece of clothing that you wear on your hands.

glow
glows glowing glowed *verb*
to give off a steady light.

*The fire **glowed** brightly in the dark.*

glue
glues *noun*
a substance that is used to stick things together.

glue *verb*

gnat
gnats *noun*
a small, biting insect with wings and long, fine legs.
*A mosquito is a type of **gnat**.*
■ say **nat**

gnaw
gnaws gnawing gnawed *verb*
to chew something.

*The mouse **gnawed** the wood.*
■ say **naw**

goal
goals *noun*
1 the target that you have to aim the ball at in some games.
*An ice hockey **goal**.*
2 a point scored for sending a ball into a net.

*She scored a **goal** in the last minute of the game.*
3 an aim or an ambition.
*My **goal** in life is to become a doctor.*

goat
goats *noun*
a mammal with horns from the same animal group as sheep. Goats eat grass and other plants and are often kept on farms for their milk. A baby goat is called a kid.

gobble
gobbles gobbling gobbled *verb*
to eat something quickly and in a greedy way.

God
noun
the being that Christians, Jews, and Muslims worship and believe made the world.

god
gods *noun*
a being that people worship and believe has power over their lives.

*Shiva, a Hindu **god***

*Vishnu, a Hindu **god***

goggles
noun
special glasses worn to protect the eyes.

*swimming **goggles***

gold
noun
a soft, bright, yellow metal that is very valuable.

gold ore

gold ring

goldfish
noun
an orange fish that is often kept in aquariums and ponds as a pet.

golf
noun
a game played on a grass course, with a ball, and sticks called clubs. Players hit the ball into holes around the course. The player who completes the course in the fewest shots is the winner.

gong
gongs noun
a metal disc that you hit to make a loud noise.

good
adjective
1 pleasant or of high quality.
*That was a **good** film!*
2 useful.
*This knife is **good** for cutting.*
3 kind or well-behaved.
*A **good** child.*
4 skilful.
*She's very **good** at maths.*
■ comparisons **better best**

goodbye
interjection
a word that you say when someone leaves.

goods
noun
things that can be bought and sold.

goose
geese noun
a large bird that lives on or near water. Geese eat grasses and grain. A male goose is called a gander. Some types of geese are kept by farmers for their eggs, meat, and feathers.

gorge
gorges noun
a deep, narrow valley.

gorgeous
adjective
very nice to look at or taste.
*The long, sandy beach looked **gorgeous** in the photograph.*
■ say **gor**-jus

gorilla
gorillas noun
a large mammal covered in dark hair that lives in rainforests in Africa. Gorillas eat fruits, nuts, and leaves. They are the largest and strongest apes in the world.

*baby **gorilla***

gossip
gossips gossiping gossiped verb
to talk about someone or something without always knowing whether what you say is true or not.
*People often **gossip** about film stars.*

government
governments noun
a group of people who run a country.
■ say **guv**-er-ment
govern verb

grab
grabs grabbing grabbed verb
to take hold of something in a quick, rough way.

*He **grabbed** his coat and ran to the station.*

graceful
adjective
moving in a beautiful way.

*Ballet dancers are very **graceful**.*
gracefully adverb

gradually
adverb
happening slowly, little by little.
*The path **gradually** became steeper.*
gradual adjective

graffiti
noun
writing and drawing on walls in public places.

■ say gra-**fee**-tee

grain
grains noun
1 a seed of a cereal crop such as wheat or barley, or a quantity of these seeds.

*barley **grains***

2 a small, hard piece of something.
*Sand is made up of many tiny **grains**.*
3 the pattern in wood.

*different wood **grains***

grammar
noun
the rules for writing and speaking a language.

grand
adjective
large and impressive.
*The **grand** house had a huge, iron gate.*
■ comparisons **grander grandest**

a b c d e f g h i j k l m n o p q r s t u v w x y z

91

grandchild
grandchildren *noun*
a son or daughter's child.
*A **grandchild** can be a
granddaughter or a grandson.*

grandfather
grandfathers *noun*
the father of a parent.
*A **grandfather** can also be
called granddad or grandpa.*

grandmother
grandmothers *noun*
the mother of a parent.
*A **grandmother** can also be
called grandma or granny.*

grandfather
grandmother

grandchild

grape
grapes *noun*
a small, round
fruit with a smooth
green or black
skin and
soft, juicy
flesh.
Grapes can
be used to
make wine.

*bunch of **grapes***

grapefruit
grapefruit or **grapefruits** *noun*
a large, round, juicy fruit
with a thick
skin and
a sour taste.

graph
graphs *noun*
a diagram that shows
how amounts and numbers
of things compare with
each other.

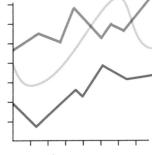

■ say **grarf**

grasp
grasps grasping grasped *verb*
1 to take hold of something
firmly.

2 to understand something.
*They couldn't **grasp** how
the computer worked.*

grass
grasses *noun*
a plant with long, thin, green
leaves. Grass is an important
food for many animals.

grasshopper
grasshoppers *noun*
a jumping insect that
feeds on plants.
Grasshoppers have
two sets of wings
and strong
back legs.

grateful
adjective
feeling thankful to
someone because they
have done something
for you.

*She was **grateful** for
one of his sandwiches.*
gratefully *adverb*

grave
graves *noun*
a hole in the ground in
which a dead body is buried.

grave
adjective
very serious and important.

gravel
noun
a mixture of tiny pieces of
stone, used for covering paths
and roads.

gravity
noun
1 the natural
force that pulls
everything down
towards Earth.

*Apples fall downwards
rather than upwards because
of **gravity**.*
2 seriousness.
*The **gravity** of a crime.*
■ say **grav**-it-ee

gravy
noun
the juice that comes out
of meat when it is cooked.
Gravy is served as a sauce.
■ say **gray**-vee

graze
grazes grazing grazed *verb*
1 to move around eating
grass and plants, in the
way that cattle and other
animals do.

grazing antelopes
2 to scrape your skin.
*When I **grazed** my knee
it was very painful.*

grease
noun
a soft, thick oil or fat.
greasy *adjective*

great
adjective
1 very big.
*The **great** trees grew
over the road.*

2 important or powerful.
*A **great** leader.*
■ say **grayt**
■ comparisons **greater greatest**

greedy
adjective
wanting much more of
something than you need.
*A **greedy** person.*
■ comparisons **greedier greediest**

green
noun
a colour.

greenhouse
greenhouses *noun*
a building made mainly
of glass, used for
growing plants.

greet
greets greeting greeted *verb*
to welcome someone.

greeting
greetings
noun
an action,
or words,
used when
meeting
someone.

grey
noun
a colour that is a mixture of
black and white.

grief
noun
great unhappiness.

grill
grills *noun*
a set of
metal bars
for cooking
food on.
grill *verb*

barbecue
grill

grin
grins grinning grinned *verb*
to have a big smile.

grin *noun*

grind
grinds grinding ground *verb*
to crush something into
a powder by
rubbing it.

Grinding spices.

grip
grips gripping gripped *verb*
to hold on to something
very firmly.
*She **gripped** her briefcase.*

groan
groans groaning groaned *verb*
to make a long, deep sound
because you are unhappy
or in pain.

groceries
noun
food, cleaning
materials, and
other things that
you buy regularly
to use at home.

■ say **grow**-sir-eez

groom
grooms grooming groomed *verb*
to make an animal clean by
brushing it.

groove
grooves *noun*
a long, fine line that is cut
into a flat surface.

grotesque
adjective
ugly and strange.
■ say grow-**tesk**

ground
noun
1 the surface of Earth.

*You could see the **ground** from
the top of the tower.*
2 a place where some sports
are played.
*A cricket **ground**.*

group
groups *noun*
people, animals, or things
that are connected in
some way.

*A **group** of schoolchildren.*

grow
grows growing grew grown *verb*
1 to become bigger.

*The plant **grew**
a little more
every day.*

2 to gradually become
something.
Growing older.

growl
growls growling growled *verb*
to make a long, low, angry
sound deep down in
the throat.
*The dog **growled** every time
I came near.*

a b c d e f g h i j k l m n o p q r s t u v w x y z

growth
noun

the way in which things change as they become older and bigger. The growth of animals and plants happens in many different ways.

Snake

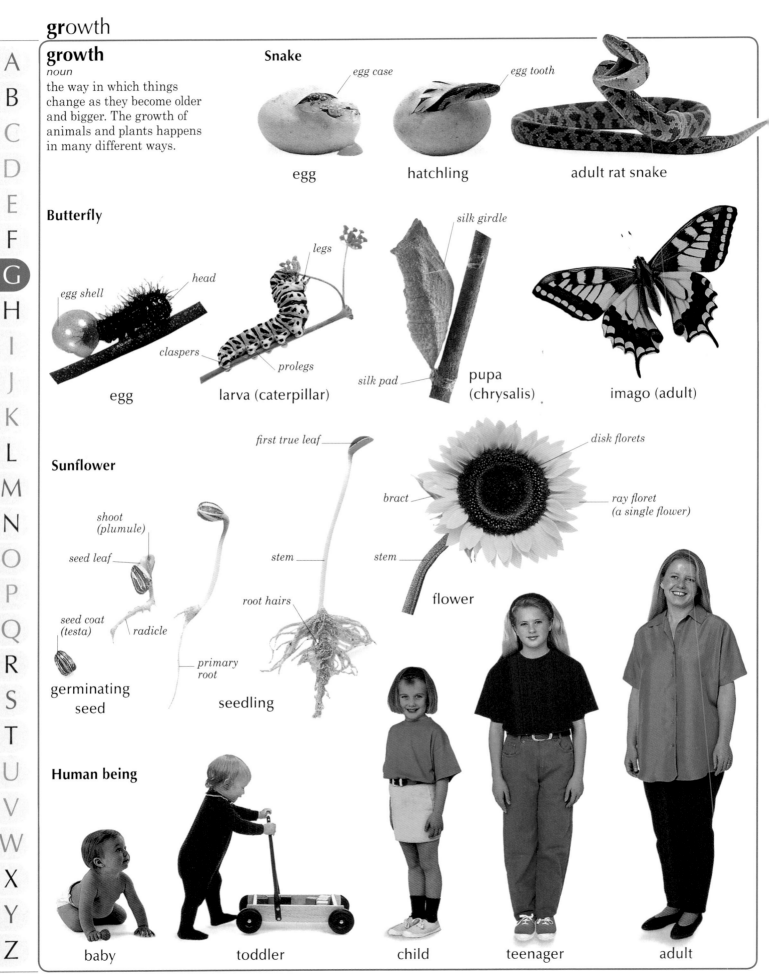

egg case

egg

egg tooth

hatchling

adult rat snake

Butterfly

egg shell

head

egg

legs

claspers

prolegs

larva (caterpillar)

silk girdle

silk pad

pupa (chrysalis)

imago (adult)

Sunflower

first true leaf

disk florets

shoot (plumule)

seed leaf

bract

ray floret (a single flower)

stem

stem

seed coat (testa)

radicle

root hairs

flower

germinating seed

primary root

seedling

Human being

baby

toddler

child

teenager

adult

grub
grubs *noun*
the larva of a newly hatched insect before it becomes an adult. A grub looks like a thick, soft worm.

grumble
grumbles grumbling grumbled *verb*
to complain crossly, usually in a quiet voice.

grunt
grunts grunting grunted *verb*
to make a short sound like the noise a pig makes.

guarantee
guarantees *noun*
1 a promise from a company that if one of their products goes wrong they will mend or replace it.
*A one-year **guarantee**.*
2 a promise that something will happen.
■ say ga-ran-**tee**

guard
guards guarding guarded *verb*
to watch over something to keep it safe.
*The building was **guarded** at night.*
■ say **gard**

guard
guards *noun*
1 someone who watches over and protects something or someone.

security guard

guess
guesses guessing guessed *verb*
to suggest an answer to a question, without being sure it is the right one.

*She had to **guess** what she was holding.*
guess *noun*

guest
guests *noun*
someone who stays at a house or a hotel.
■ rhymes with **best**

guide
guides *noun*
1 someone whose job is to show people around places.
*The **guide** took us around the museum.*
2 a book with maps and information about a place.
guide *verb*

2 something that prevents damage or injury.

face guard

guilty
adjective
having done something wrong.

guilt *noun*

guitar
guitars *noun*
a musical instrument with six or twelve strings. You pull the strings with your fingers to make different sounds.

electric guitar

gulp
gulps gulping gulped *verb*
to swallow something fast or in large amounts.
*He **gulped** the drink quickly.*

gum
gums *noun*
1 the firm part inside your mouth around your teeth.
2 a sticky substance that is usually made from plants.
3 Chewing-gum.

gun
guns *noun*
a weapon that shoots bullets.

*18th-century **gun***

gurgle
gurgles gurgling gurgled *verb*
to make small bubbling sounds in the throat.
*The baby **gurgled** when his mother tickled him.*

gust
gusts *noun*
a sudden, strong rush of wind.
*A **gust** of wind blew off his hat.*

gym
gyms *noun*
a large room or building where people can play sports or exercise, often using special equipment. Gym is short for gymnasium.
■ say **jim**

gymnast
gymnasts *noun*
a person who is skilled in gymnastics.
■ say **jim**-nast

gymnastics
noun
a sport in which people perform exercises that develop physical strength and ability.
■ say jim-**nass**-ticks

a
b
c
d
e
f
g
h
i
j
k
l
m
n
o
p
q
r
s
t
u
v
w
x
y
z

A B C D E F G **H** I J K L M N O P Q R S T U V W X Y Z

Hh

habit
habits *noun*
1 something that you usually do without thinking.

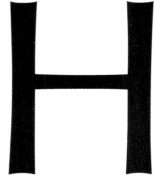

*Biting your nails is a bad **habit**.*

2 a type of clothing worn by monks and nuns.

*monk's **habit***

habitat
habitats *noun*
the natural place where an animal, bird, or plant lives and grows.

hail
noun
frozen rain that falls in small, hard balls.

hair
noun
1 thin strands that grow on the skin of animals and people.
2 a mass of thin strands that covers your head.

plaited
hair

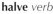

hairy *adjective*

hairbrush
hairbrushes *noun*
a brush for hair.

haircut
haircuts *noun*
a style in which hair is cut.
*Have you seen his new **haircut**?*

hairdresser
hairdressers *noun*
someone whose job it is to cut hair.

half
halves *noun*
one of two equal parts of something.

halve *verb*

hall
halls *noun*
1 a corridor or small room at the entrance of a house.
2 a large, open room in a building, used for meetings or other group activities.

halt
halts halting halted *verb*
to stop walking or moving forwards.
■ say **holt**

ham
noun
meat from the leg of a pig that has been preserved with salt or smoke.

hamburger
hamburgers *noun*
a flat piece of chopped beef, grilled and served in a roll.

hammer
hammers *noun*
a tool with a metal end, that is used to knock nails into wood and to hit things.

hammer *verb*

hammock
hammocks *noun*
a bed made of cloth or net, hung by rope and fastened at two ends.

hand
hands *noun*
the part of your body at the end of your arm that has four fingers and one thumb.

hand
hands handing handed *verb*
to give something to someone with your hand.
Hand the hammer to me.

handkerchief
handkerchiefs *noun*
a small piece of cloth or paper, used for blowing your nose.

handle
handles *noun*
a part of something that is designed to be grasped or held by the hand.

*door **handle***

handle
handles handling handled *verb*
to touch or hold something.
*Please **handle** that vase carefully!*

handlebar

handlebars *noun*

a bar at the front of a bicycle that you turn to steer (see **transport** on page 221).

handsome

adjective

attractive and pleasant to look at.

*A **handsome** man.*

handstand

handstands *noun*

an upside-down position, standing on your hands, with your legs in the air.

handwriting

noun

writing done by hand, not typed or printed.

hang

hangs hanging hung *verb*

to support something from above.

Hanging up her clothes.

hangar

hangars *noun*

a very large building where aircraft are stored.

hang-glider

hang-gliders *noun*

a huge kite that a person can hang from. The hang-glider rides on currents of air, in the same way as a glider.

happen

happens happening happened *verb*

to take place.

*What **happened** to your car?*

happy

adjective

pleased and content.

*He felt **happy** on his birthday.*

■ comparisons **happier happiest**
happiness *noun*

harbour

harbours *noun*

a sheltered place where ships can anchor and unload safely.

hard

adjective

1 solid and firm to touch.

***Hard** ground.*

2 difficult to understand or do.

*These sums are **hard**.*

■ comparisons **harder hardest**
hard *adverb*

hare

hares *noun*

a furry, plant-eating mammal that belongs to the same animal group as rabbits. Hares can run fast and have very good hearing. Males are called jacks and females are called jills.

harm

harms harming harmed *verb*

to damage or injure something or somebody.

harmful

adjective

able to damage or injure someone or something.

■ opposite **harmless**

harmony

harmonies *noun*

a collection of musical notes played or sung together to make a pleasant sound.

*They sang in perfect **harmony**.*

harp

harps *noun*

a musical instrument that has a large frame with strings stretched across it. Harps are played by pulling the strings with your fingers.

frame
harp

harvest

harvests harvesting harvested *verb*

to gather a crop, such as fruit or wheat, when it is ready to be used or eaten.

combine
harvester

Harvesting wheat.
harvest *noun*

hat

hats *noun*

something that is worn on the head.

hatch

hatches hatching hatched *verb*

to be born by coming out of an egg.

hate

hates hating hated *verb*

to dislike something or someone very much.
hatred *noun*

haul

hauls hauling hauled *verb*

to pull with force.

Hauling a boat.

a b c d e f g h i j k l m n o p q r s t u v w x y z

unted

haunted

adjective

having ghosts or other spirits in it.

*A **haunted** house.*

hawk

hawks *noun*

one of a group of birds that hunt animals for food. Falcons, buzzards, and vultures are all hawks.

long-legged buzzard

hay

noun

grass that has been cut and dried to be fed to animals. Hay is often stored in large heaps called haystacks.

Hay is often hung in a net for horses to eat.

hazard

hazards *noun*

a risk or dangerous obstacle.

*Icy pavements are a **hazard** to pedestrians in winter.*

hazardous *adjective*

head

heads *noun*

1 the part of your body that contains your brain, and is where your ears, eyes, nose, and mouth are.

2 a leader of a group.

*She is the **head** of a large company.*

headache

headaches *noun*

a pain in your head.

headlamp

headlamps *noun*

a light at the front of a vehicle, used when driving at night.

headlamp

headline

headlines *noun*

the title of a report in a newspaper.

*Have you seen the **headlines** today?*

headphones

noun

a device worn over the ears that is used for listening to the radio or to recorded music.

healthy

adjective

well and strong.

■ say **hell**-thee

■ comparisons **healthier healthiest**

health *noun*

heap

heaps *noun*

a collection of things lying on top of each other.

*She left her clothes in a **heap** on the chair.*

hear

hears hearing heard *verb*

1 to notice a sound.

*Did you **hear** that bird?*

2 to listen to.

*I'd like to **hear** you play the piano.*

heart

hearts *noun*

1 the organ in your chest that pumps blood around your body.

heart

2 a shape.

■ say **hart**

heat

heats heating heated *verb*

to make or become warmer.

*We **heated** some water.*

heat *noun*

heave

heaves heaving heaved *verb*

to lift, pull, or throw something with a lot of effort.

*He **heaved** the sack onto the back of the truck.*

heavy

adjective

weighing a large amount.

*a **heavy** stone*

a light feather

■ say **hev**-ee

■ comparisons **heavier heaviest**

■ opposite **light**

hedge

hedges *noun*

a line of bushes grown so that they make a boundary between two places.

hedgehog

hedgehogs *noun*

a small, nocturnal mammal covered in spines. Hedgehogs hunt for insects and small animals. They roll into a ball when they feel threatened.

heel
heels noun
1 the back part of your foot.

heel

2 the higher back part of a shoe.

heel

height
heights noun
the measurement of how tall or high someone or something is.

*He measured his **height**.*
■ say **hite**

held
*from the verb **to hold***
*I **held** a snake when we went to the zoo yesterday.*

helicopter
helicopters noun
a type of aircraft that uses rotating blades to make it fly and hover.

helmet
helmets noun
a strong hat, worn to protect the head.

cycling helmet

help
helps helping helped verb
to make something easier or better for someone.
help noun

helpless
adjective
unable to take care of yourself.
*A baby is completely **helpless**.*

hemisphere
hemispheres noun
one half of the world.

*northern **hemisphere***

*southern **hemisphere***

herb
herbs noun
a plant that is used fresh or dried to flavour food or to make medicines.
*Two different types of **herb**.*

herbal adjective

rosemary   *oregano*

herd
herds noun
a group of large, grazing animals.

*A **herd** of bison.*

here
adverb
in this place.
*Is there a doctor **here**?*

hero / heroine
heroes / heroines noun
1 a very brave person.
2 the main character in a story, film, or play.
■ **hero** is male and **heroine** is female

hesitate
hesitates hesitating hesitated verb
to pause because you are not sure what to do.

*He **hesitated** before jumping into the icy pool.*
hesitation noun

hexagon
hexagons noun
a shape with six sides (see **shape** on page 182).

hibernate
hibernates hibernating hibernated verb
to go to sleep for the winter.

*A fieldmouse **hibernating**.*
■ say **hie**-ber-nate
hibernation noun

hiccup
hiccups noun
a sudden movement in your chest that causes a quick breath and a short gulp.
■ also spelt **hiccough**
hiccup verb

hide
hides hiding hid hidden verb
to put yourself or something out of sight.

hieroglyphics
noun
a type of writing which uses pictures to represent sounds, words, and letters.

*ancient Egyptian **hieroglyphics***
■ say **hie**-roh-**gli**-fiks

a b c d e f g h i j k l m n o p q r s t u v w x y z

A B C D E F G **H** I J K L M N O P Q R S T U V W X Y Z

high

adjective
tall or a long
way up.

***High** above the ground.*
■ say **hye**
■ comparisons **higher highest**

highway

highways *noun*
a main road.

hi-jack

hi-jacks *noun*
a crime in which a vehicle or
an aircraft is seized by force,
and people are held prisoner.
hi-jack *verb*

hill

hills *noun*
an area of high ground.
hilly *adjective*

Hindu

Hindus *noun*
a follower of Hinduism
(cultural and religious beliefs
and practices that originated
in India centuries ago).

hinge

hinges *noun*
a metal device that
holds doors and
gates in place,
allowing them to
open and close.

hint

hints hinting hinted *verb*
to suggest something
in a vague way.
*He **hinted** that he knew
about my secret.*

hip

hips *noun*
a joint at
the top of each
of your legs,
between your
waist and
your thigh.

hip

hippopotamus

hippopotamuses or **hippopotami**
noun
a large mammal that lives
in Africa. Hippopotamuses
spend most of the time in
lakes or rivers, and eat
water plants.

hire

hires hiring hired *verb*
to pay money so you can
borrow something or use
someone's services.
*They **hired** a car for two weeks.*

hiss

hisses hissing hissed *verb*
to make a noise
like air escaping
from a tyre.

*Snakes **hiss**.*
hiss *noun*

history

noun
the study of things that
have happened to people
in the past.
*We are studying the **history**
of the USA.*
historical *adjective*

hit

hits hitting hit *verb*
to come into contact
with someone or
something in
a forceful way.

*The tennis player **hit** the ball
over the net.*

hit

hits *noun*
a success.
*The song was a big **hit**.*

hoax

hoaxes *noun*
an unpleasant trick or a joke
where a person tries to make
someone believe something
that isn't really true.
*A **hoax** phone call.*
■ say **hoe-ks**

hobble

hobbles hobbling hobbled *verb*
to walk with difficulty
and pain.

hobby

hobbies *noun*
an activity that you do
for enjoyment in your
spare time.

*Stamp-collecting is
a popular **hobby**.*

hold

holds holding held *verb*
1 to keep something in
a certain position.

***Holding** a cup and saucer.*
2 to contain.

*This container
holds kitchen
utensils.*

hold

holds *noun*
a place inside a ship or
an aircraft where cargo
is stored.
*The cars were driven
into the ferry's **hold**.*

hole
holes *noun*
a hollow place or gap
in something.

holiday
holidays *noun*
a period of time off from
school or work.

hollow
adjective
with a space inside.

*The mouse ran
through the **hollow** pipe.*

home
homes *noun*
the place where a person
or an animal lives or
comes from.

honest
adjective
truthful or able to be trusted.
- say **on**-nist
- opposite **dishonest**
honesty *noun*

honey
noun
a sweet,
sticky food,
made by bees
from the nectar
of flowers.
- say **hun**-ee

*jar of **honey***

honeycomb

hood
hoods *noun*
a part of a coat, jacket, or
sweatshirt that covers
your head.

hood

hoof
hoofs or **hooves** *noun*
the hard, nail-like
part of the foot of
a horse, deer, or
similar animal.

*horse's **hoof***

hook
hooks *noun*
a curved metal object used
for hanging things on or for
catching things.

*clothes
hook*

hoop
hoops *noun*
a round strip of plastic, wood,
or metal.

hoot
hoots hooting hooted *verb*
1 to make a sound like
the noise an owl makes.
2 to blow a horn or whistle.
hoot *noun*

hop
**hops hopping
hopped** *verb*
to jump on
one leg.

hop *noun*

hope
hopes hoping hoped *verb*
to want something to happen,
and think that it might.
*I **hope** I'll be in the team.*
hopeful *adjective*

horizon
horizons *noun*
the line in the distance
where the land or the sea
seems to meet the sky.

- say hor-**ize**-on

horizontal
adjective
parallel to the ground.
*A table top is **horizontal**.*
- opposite **vertical**
horizontally *adverb*

horn
horns *noun*
1 a tough, pointed, bony part
on the head of some animals.

*goat's **horn***

2 a brass wind instrument
that you play by holding
down valves with your
fingers and blowing through
the narrow end of the tube.

*French **horn***

3 a device that is used to
make a warning signal.

*old-fashioned car **horn***

horoscope
horoscopes *noun*
a prediction of what might
happen to you in the future,
made from the position of the
stars and your date of birth.

horrible
adjective
very unpleasant
or frightening.
horribly *adverb*

horror
noun
a feeling of shock and fear.
*They watched in **horror** as
the house burned down.*

a
b
c
d
e
f
g
h
i
j
k
l
m
n
o
p
q
r
s
t
u
v
w
x
y
z

horse

horses *noun*

a large, plant-eating mammal that is often used for riding and pulling equipment. There are many different breeds of horse, and their coats can be a variety of colours.

headcollar

ovaro coat (chestnut and white)

pinto

mane

palomino coat

palomino

nostril · halter · lip · neck · knee · hoof · bay coat · belly · tail

Arab

stripe · grey coat · black coat · horseshoe · docked tail · feathers

Shetland pony · shire

hard hat · jodhpurs · pommel · saddle · numnah · dappled grey coat · stirrup · girth · boot · bridle · bit · reins

thoroughbred

ring · bit · joint

snaffle bit

forelock · throat · muzzle · shoulder · breast · forearm · chestnut · fetlock joint · ergot · pastern

croup · loins · back · withers · quarters · bay coat · hock · shank · heel · elbow · nail · horseshoe

thoroughbred

liver-chestnut coat · dun coat

falabella foals (miniature **horses**)

hose
hoses *noun*
a long, narrow tube, through which liquids can be sent.

garden hose

hospital
hospitals *noun*
a place where sick or injured people are treated.

hostage
hostages *noun*
a person who is taken prisoner by someone who demands something in return for the prisoner's safety.

hot
adjective
1 very warm.

*The bars of the heater are very **hot**.*
2 very spicy.

*Chilli peppers taste very **hot**.*
■ comparisons **hotter hottest**

hotel
hotels *noun*
a building with bedrooms that people pay to stay in. Most hotels have a restaurant and a bar.

***hotel** building*

hour
hours *noun*
a period of time lasting 60 minutes. There are 24 hours in a day.
■ say **ow**-er
hourly *adjective*

house
houses *noun*
a building that people live in.

houseboat
houseboats *noun*
a small boat that people live on.

household
households *noun*
all the people that live together in one home.

hover
hovers hovering hovered *verb*
to stay in one place in the air.

*A hummingbird **hovers** by beating its wings very fast.*

hovercraft
hovercraft *noun*
a vehicle that rides on a cushion of air. A hovercraft can travel across land and sea.

how
adverb
in what way.
***How** does this work?*

howl
howls howling howled *verb*
to make a long, whining sound like a wolf.

huddle
huddles huddling huddled *verb*
to push or squeeze together.
*They **huddled** under the shelter.*

hug
hugs hugging hugged *verb*
to hold someone close in a loving way.

huge
adjective
very large or enormous.
*He was so hungry that he ate a **huge** plateful of food.*

hum
hums humming hummed *verb*
to make a musical sound with your lips closed.
humming *noun*

human being
human beings *noun*
a man, woman, or child.

■ say **hew**-mun
human *adjective*

humane
adjective
kind and merciful.
■ say hew-**mane**
humanely *adverb*

A
B
C
D
E
F
G
H
I
J
K
L
M
N
O
P
Q
R
S
T
U
V
W
X
Y
Z

humid
adjective
warm and damp.
The weather was **humid**.

humiliate
humiliates humiliating humiliated *verb*
to make someone feel ridiculous or ashamed.
■ say hew-**mil**-lee-ate

humour
noun
the ability to see or show that something is funny.
A good sense of **humour**.
■ say **hew**-mer
humorous *adjective*

hump
humps *noun*
a large, round lump.

This camel has two **humps**.

hung
from the verb **to hang**
I **hung** *my coat up when I arrived this morning.*

hungry
adjective
wanting or needing something to eat.

hungry chicks
■ comparisons **hungrier**
hungriest
hunger *noun*

hunt
hunts hunting hunted *verb*
1 to chase an animal, often to kill it for food.

Lions **hunt** *in packs.*
2 to search for something in many places.

I **hunted** *all over the house for my key.*
hunt *noun*

hurl
hurls hurling hurled *verb*
to throw something as hard as you can.

She **hurled** *the cushion across the room.*

hurricane
hurricanes *noun*
a violent storm with very strong winds.

hurry
hurries hurrying hurried *verb*
to act quickly, because there is not a lot of time.

He had to **hurry** *to deliver the parcel on time.*

hurt
hurts hurting hurt *verb*
1 to cause pain or injury.
I **hurt** *my leg when I fell.*
2 to be painful.
My broken arm **hurts**.

husband
husbands *noun*
a married man.
■ opposite **wife**

hush
noun
silence.
There was a **hush** *as the teacher came into the room.*

hut
huts *noun*
a small shelter.

Tourists stayed in **huts** *on the beach.*

hutch
hutches *noun*
a large box made of wood and wire for a small pet to live in.

rabbit **hutch**

hydrogen
noun
a gas that is lighter than air, burns easily, and has no taste, colour, or smell.
■ say **hye**-dro-jen

hyena
hyenas *noun*
a fierce mammal from Africa and Asia that looks like a large dog. Hyenas hunt for food and have a strange bark which sounds like a laugh.

■ say hye-**ee**-na

hygiene
noun
cleanliness and health.

Good **hygiene** *is important in the kitchen.*
■ say **hye**-jeen

hysterical
adjective
crying or laughing wildly.
■ say his-**ter**-rik-al

Ii

ice
noun
frozen water.

iceberg
icebergs *noun*
a huge piece of ice floating in cold seas.

ice-cream
ice-creams *noun*
a sweet, frozen food made mainly from cream or milk.

ice-cube
ice-cubes *noun*
a small block of ice used in drinks.

ice-rink
ice-rinks *noun*
a surface of ice, either inside or outside a building, that people skate on.

ice-skate
ice-skates *noun*
a boot with a metal blade on the sole, used for skating on ice.

icicle
icicles *noun*
a hanging piece of ice, formed by dripping water that has frozen.

idea
ideas *noun*
a thought or suggestion about something.
*Do you have any better **ideas**?*

ideal
adjective
perfect in every way.
*That's an **ideal** solution.*
ideal *noun*

identical
adjective
exactly the same.

identical candles

identify
identifies identifying identified *verb*
to recognize something or someone by name.

*Can you **identify** which tree these leaves come from?*
identification *noun*

identity
identities *noun*
who someone is or what something is.

*The card around his neck shows his **identity**.*

idle
adjective
lazy, or doing nothing.

igloo
igloos *noun*
a round building made of snow and ice.

ignorant
adjective
not knowing about something.
ignorance *noun*

ignore
ignores ignoring ignored *verb*
to take no notice of someone or something.

iguana
iguanas *noun*
a large lizard found mainly in Central and South America. The common iguana lives near rivers and streams. It eats plants, insects, and small animals.

*common **iguana***

ill
adjective
feeling sick or unwell.
illness *noun*

illegal
adjective
not allowed by law.
*It is **illegal** to park there.*
■ opposite **legal**
illegally *adverb*

illustrate
illustrates illustrating illustrated *verb*
to supply with pictures.

Illustrating a book.
illustration *noun*

image
images *noun*
a picture of something or someone, or a picture in your mind.

imaginary

adjective

not real.

*The unicorn is an **imaginary** animal.*

■ say i-**mag**-in-ery

imagine

imagines imagining imagined
verb

to create a picture of something in your mind.

■ say i-**ma**-jin
imagination *noun*

imitate

imitates imitating imitated *verb*
to copy the way that someone talks or does something.

imitation

imitations *noun*
a copy.

*These **imitations** of fruit don't look real.*
imitation *adjective*

immediately

adverb
without delay.
*Go home **immediately**!*
immediate *adjective*

immigrate

immigrates immigrating immigrated *verb*

to go to a country in order to live there permanently.
immigration *noun*

impact

impacts *noun*

1 the action of one object hitting another with force.

*The **impact** of the crash wrecked both cars.*
2 something that has enough power to create strong feelings in someone.
*Travelling abroad had a great **impact** on me.*

impatient

adjective

1 not willing to wait.

*He became **impatient** when the bus didn't come.*
2 easily annoyed.
*She was often **impatient** with her little brother.*
impatience *noun*

important

adjective

1 meaning a lot.
*Winning this competition is very **important** to me.*
2 having great power or influence.
*An **important** visitor.*
importance *noun*

impossible

adjective

not able to be done.

*It is **impossible** for people to fly like birds.*
■ opposite **possible**

impress

impresses impressing impressed
verb

to make someone have a good opinion of something.
*His cooking skills **impressed** the judges.*

improve

improves improving improved
verb

to make or become better.

*We **improved** the flower pot by decorating it.*
improvement *noun*

include

includes including included *verb*
to put something in as part of a whole.
*The travel brochure **includes** pictures of the hotels.*
inclusion *noun*

inconvenient

adjective

not easy or not suitable.
*Steep stairs are **inconvenient** for a lot of people.*
■ say in-kon-**vee**-nee-ent
■ opposite **convenient**
inconvenience *noun*

increase

increases increasing increased *verb*
to become bigger in size or number.
■ opposite **decrease**
increase *noun*

incredible

adjective

difficult to believe.
*He tells some **incredible** stories.*

independent

adjective

not controlled by anyone or anything.
■ opposite **dependent**
independently *adverb*

index

indexes or **indices** *noun*
an alphabetical list of subjects and page numbers, usually found at the back of a book.

indignant

adjective

upset and annoyed because something is unfair.
*They were **indignant** about the way they were treated.*
indignantly *adverb*

individual

adjective

separate or for just one person.

Individual teaching.
individual *noun*

indoors
adverb
inside a building.
*Let's go **indoors** now.*
■ opposite **outdoors**

industry
industries *noun*
a trade or business, and all the people and processes involved in it.

*The food **industry**.*
industrial *adjective*

infant
infants *noun*
a very young child.

infancy *noun*

infection
infections *noun*
a disease caused by germs, which can be passed from one person to another.
infect *verb*
infectious *adjective*

infinite
adjective
with no end.
infinity *noun*

inflate
inflates inflating inflated *verb*
to make something bigger by filling it with air or gas.

inflatable *adjective*

influence
influences influencing influenced *verb*
to have an effect on someone so that they change their ideas or behaviour.
■ say **in**-floo-ens
influence *noun*

information
noun
useful facts about something.

*The board gave **information** about the birds in the area.*

infuriate
infuriates infuriating infuriated *verb*
to make someone very angry.
■ say in-**fyoo**-ree-ate

ingredient
ingredients *noun*
one of the parts of a mixture.

***Ingredients** for a salad.*
■ say in-**gree**-dee-ent

inhabitant
inhabitants *noun*
a person who lives in a place.
*The desert has very few **inhabitants**.*
inhabit *verb*

initial
initials *noun*
the first letter of a word or name.

*Robert Anderson's **initials**.*
■ say i-**nish**-al

inject
injects injecting injected *verb*
to put a substance into your body using a hollow needle and a syringe.
injection *noun*

injure
injures injuring injured *verb*
to hurt yourself or somebody else.

*He **injured** his leg when he fell down the stairs.*
injured *adjective*
injury *noun*

ink
inks *noun*
a black or coloured liquid used for writing or drawing.

inland
adjective
away from the sea, towards the middle of the country.

inlet
inlets *noun*
a small opening or bay along the coast.

*An **inlet**.*

innocent
adjective
not guilty.
*He was arrested for stealing, but was found to be **innocent**.*
innocence *noun*
innocently *adverb*

inquire
inquires inquiring inquired *verb*
to ask for information.

*He **inquired** at the stand about the way to the museum.*
■ also spelt **enquire**
inquiry *noun*

a b c d e f g h i j k l m n o p q r s t u v w x y z

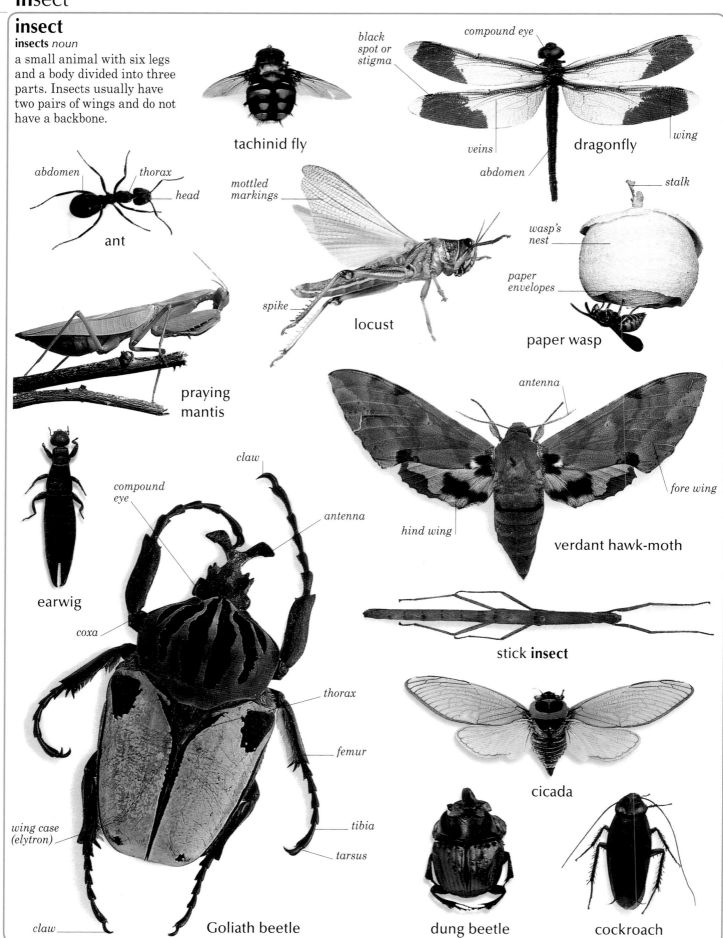

insect

insects *noun*
a small animal with six legs and a body divided into three parts. Insects usually have two pairs of wings and do not have a backbone.

tachinid fly

black spot or stigma

compound eye

veins

wing

abdomen

dragonfly

abdomen   *thorax*

head

ant

mottled markings

stalk

wasp's nest

paper envelopes

spike

locust

paper wasp

praying mantis

antenna

claw

compound eye

antenna

earwig

coxa

hind wing

fore wing

verdant hawk-moth

stick **insect**

thorax

femur

cicada

wing case (elytron)

tibia

tarsus

claw

Goliath beetle

dung beetle

cockroach

insert

inserts inserting inserted *verb*
to put one thing
inside another.

inside

preposition
in the interior of.

Inside the box.

inside

adverb
in or into something.
Come **inside**!
inside *noun*

insist

insists insisting insisted *verb*
to say something very firmly.
*She **insisted** that she had seen
a ghost.*
insistence *noun*
insistent *adjective*

inspect

inspects inspecting inspected
verb
to check something carefully.

*Cars are **inspected** for faults
before leaving the factory.*
inspection *noun*

instant

adjective
immediate.
*She was an **instant** success.*

instead

adverb
in place of.
*I chose the red pen **instead**
of the blue one.*

instinct

instincts *noun*
a strong, natural feeling that makes
animals or people do things that
they haven't learnt.
*Birds have a pecking **instinct**.*

instruction

instructions *noun*
information about something.
*Read the **instructions** before
you use the machine.*
instruct *verb*

instrument

instruments *noun*
a device or tool that
has a special use.

*A navigational **instrument**.*

insult

insults insulting insulted *verb*
to upset someone by saying
unpleasant things to them
or about them.
insult *noun*

intelligent

adjective
quick to learn, think,
and understand.

*She was **intelligent**, so she
solved the puzzle quickly.*
intelligence *noun*

interest

interests interesting interested
verb
to hold the attention of.
*Anything to do with space
interests me.*
interesting *adjective*

interfere

interferes interfering interfered
verb
to involve yourself in
something that isn't anything
to do with you.

*She kept **interfering** as
he tried to prepare lunch.*

interior

interiors *noun*
the part that is inside
something.

interior of a doll's house
interior *adjective*

interjection

interjections *noun*
a word such as "goodbye"
or "please" that can be
used on its own.

internal

adjective
on the inside.

*The **internal** workings
of a pocket watch.*
■ opposite **external**
internally *adverb*

international

adjective
involving several countries.
*An **international** event.*

internet

noun
a worldwide computer
network for sharing
information and
sending messages.

interrupt

**interrupts interrupting
interrupted** *verb*

1 to stop someone from
talking by breaking into
the conversation.
*Please don't **interrupt** while
I'm speaking!*
2 to stop something
happening temporarily.
*The tennis match was
interrupted by rain.*

intersection

intersections *noun*
a place where lines or
roads cross each other.

*A busy road **intersection**.*

a b c d e f g h i j k l m n o p q r s t u v w x y z

A B C D E F G H I J K L M N O P Q R S T U V W X Y Z

interval
intervals *noun*
a period of time
between events.
*There was a short interval
between the two acts.*

interview
interviews *noun*
a meeting where someone
is questioned.

A job interview.
interview *verb*

intestine
intestines *noun*
an organ that leads from
the stomach. Food is digested
in the intestine as well as in
the stomach.
■ say in-**tes**-tin

introduce
introduces introducing
introduced *verb*
to present a person or idea to
someone for the first time.
Introduce me to your friend.
introduction *noun*

invade
invades invading invaded *verb*
to enter a place as an enemy.
invasion *noun*

invent
invents inventing invented *verb*
to design an original device
or process.
*This device was invented
to record sound
and play
it back.*
invention
noun

investigate
investigates investigating
investigated *verb*
to look at a situation
carefully to find out what
is happening or what
has happened.
*The police are investigating
yesterday's robbery.*
investigation *noun*

invisible
adjective
unable to be seen.
■ opposite **visible**

invitation
invitations *noun*
a written or spoken request
asking someone to come
and be with you.

A party invitation.
invite *verb*

involve
involves involving involved *verb*
to include or affect
something.
*Two cars were involved in
the accident.*

involved
adjective
complicated.
An involved plan.

iris
irises *noun*
1 a tall,
flowering
plant that
grows from
a bulb or a
root-like stem.

iron
noun
1 a strong, heavy metal
found in rocks, which is used
to make things such as tools
and gates.

wrought iron gate

2 a piece of electrical
equipment that heats up and
is used to remove creases
in clothing.

irrigate
irrigates irrigating
irrigated *verb*
to supply land with water.
irrigation *noun*

irritate
irritates irritating irritated *verb*
to annoy someone.
irritation *noun*

2 the round,
coloured
part of
the eye.

iris

■ say **eye**-ris

Islam
noun
the Muslim religion. Muslims
believe there is one God,
Allah, and that Mohammed
is his prophet.
Islamic *adjective*

island
islands *noun*
a piece of land completely
surrounded by water.

■ say **eye**-land

itch
itches itching itched *verb*
to have a feeling in your
skin that makes you want
to scratch.

*She scratched her hand
because it was itching.*
itch *noun*

ivy
ivies *noun*
an evergreen
climbing plant.

■ say **eye**-vee

Jj

jab
jabs jabbing jabbed *verb*
to push a finger or a pointed tool into something in a quick, sharp way.
*He **jabbed** his finger into his friend's ribs.*
jab *noun*

jacket
jackets *noun*
a short coat.

jagged
adjective
having rough, sharp edges.
***Jagged** rocks.*

jaguar
jaguars *noun*
a meat-eating mammal that belongs to the cat family. Jaguars live in forests and marshes of North and South America.

jail
jails *noun*
a place where criminals are kept locked up.

jam
jams *noun*
1 a sweet food made from boiled fruit and sugar.   *strawberry **jam***
2 a group of people or things that are squashed together.

*traffic **jam***

jar
jars jarring jarred *verb*
to make an unpleasant sound or a jolt.
jarring *adjective*

jar
jars *noun*
a glass container with a wide top, used for storing foods.

javelin
javelins *noun*
a long, pointed stick that is thrown like a spear in athletic competitions.

jaw
jaws *noun*
the U-shaped bone that supports your mouth, allowing it to open and close.

jaw

jazz
noun
a type of popular music with strong rhythms, first played in the USA.

jealous
adjective
annoyed and unhappy because others have something you would like.
*He was **jealous** of his friend's computer.*
■ say **jel**-lus
jealousy *noun*

jeans
noun
trousers made of denim.

jeep
jeeps *noun*
a small, open vehicle for driving over rough ground (see **car** on page 39).

jelly
jellies *noun*
a soft, firm, clear food made from fruit juice and sugar.

jellyfish
jellyfish or jellyfishes *noun*
a sea animal that has a transparent, soft body. Jellyfish feed on fish and tiny sea animals, which they catch by stinging them with their long tentacles.

*mangrove **jellyfish***

jet
jets *noun*
1 a sudden spray or stream of liquid or gas.
*The water was thrown up in a huge **jet**.*
2 a fast aircraft that is powered by an engine that sucks in air, heats it, and then pushes it out again.

*supersonic **jet***

Jew
Jews *noun*
a person whose ancestors were Hebrew or whose religion is Judaism.
Jewish *adjective*

jewel
jewels *noun*
1 a precious stone that has been cut and polished. Diamonds, rubies, and emeralds are all jewels.
2 an ornament made of gems and precious metals that people wear.

a b c d e f g h i j k l m n o p q r s t u v w x y z

jewellery

noun

ornaments that people wear. Jewellery is usually made from metals and decorated with jewels.

silver

hook

filigree bead

gold chain

Viking armband

earrings

lapis lazuli

gold amulet

turquoise

cornelian

amethyst

diamond

amethyst

Egyptian necklace

pendant

peridot

red garnet

drop earrings

heliodor

solitaire ring

spacer

pearl

choker

scarf pin

emerald

setting

green garnet

citrine

sapphires

fire opal

ruby

amethyst

cufflinks

eternity ring

opal

malachite

pearl

pearl

diamond

tourmaline

cameo brooch

diamanté

clasp

collar

jigsaw puzzle
jigsaw puzzles *noun*
a puzzle with oddly shaped pieces that fit together to make a picture.

job
jobs *noun*
1 a task or some work that you have to do.
Jobs to do around the house.
2 work that someone is paid to do.
I have an outdoor job.

jockey
jockeys *noun*
a person who rides a horse in races.

jog
jogs jogging jogged *verb*
to run steadily and slowly.

join
joins joining joined *verb*
1 to put two things together.

Joining the two ends of a strip of paper.
2 to become a member of something, such as a club.

joint
joints *noun*
the place where two pieces of something join together.
The bones in your body meet at joints to help you move around.

ankle joint

joke
jokes *noun*
something that someone says or does to make people laugh.
joke *verb*

jolt
jolts jolting jolted *verb*
to shake or move in a bumpy way.

Jolting along a bumpy track.
jolt *noun*

journalist
journalists *noun*
a person who gathers and writes news.
■ say **jer**-nal-list

journey
journeys *noun*
a distance travelled.
■ say **jer**-nee

Judaism
noun
the religion of Jewish people. Jews believe in one God, and in the teachings of the Old Testament and the Talmud, the Jewish holy books.
■ say **joo**-day-izm

judge
judges judging judged *verb*
to decide whether something is right or wrong, good or bad.
judgement *noun*

judge
judges *noun*
1 a person in charge of a court, who decides the punishment of those people that the jury finds guilty.
2 a person who decides the winner of a competition or contest.

judo
noun
a sport from Japan, in which two people fight using special movements to try and throw the other player to the ground.

jug
jugs *noun*
an open container that is used to hold liquids, and that has a handle and a spout.

juggle
juggles juggling juggled *verb*
to keep several objects in the air at the same time by throwing and catching.

juice
juices *noun*
a liquid from fruit or meat.
juicy *adjective*

jump
jumps jumping jumped *verb*
to throw yourself into the air.

junction
junctions *noun*
a place where several things join, such as roads or railways.

jungle
jungles *noun*
a dense, tropical forest.

junior
adjective
younger or less experienced.

jury
juries *noun*
a group of 12 people, chosen from the public, who sit in court and decide whether the person on trial is guilty or not guilty.

justice
noun
a fair and honest judgement.
■ say **jus**-tis

a b c d e f g h i j k l m n o p q r s t u v w x y z

A B C D E F G H I J **K** L M N O P Q R S T U V W X Y Z

kaleidoscope

kaleidoscopes *noun*

a tube with mirrors and small pieces of colourful plastic inside that you can look through. When the tube is turned, the pieces move, making a pattern of colours.

■ say kal-**eye**-do-skope

kangaroo

kangaroos *noun*

a marsupial mammal from Australia that eats leaves and plants. Kangaroos can hop fast on their strong back legs. The females carry their young in a stomach pouch.

karate

noun

a sport from Southeast Asia, in which people fight with their hands and feet, using special movements.

■ say ka-**rah**-tee

kayak

kayaks *noun*

a covered canoe for one person, originally made from sealskins.

■ say **kie**-ak

kebab

kebabs *noun*

pieces of meat and vegetables, usually cooked over a grill on a sharp spike of wood or metal called a skewer.

keep

keeps keeping kept *verb*

1 to have something and not give it away.
*She **keeps** a goldfish as a pet.*
2 to remain.
***Keep** still!*
3 to continue.
*He **kept** walking.*

kennel

kennels *noun*

a shelter outdoors for a dog.

key

keys *noun*

1 a piece of metal that has been cut so that it will lock and unlock a door or padlock.

***key**hole*

2 a small lever that you press with your finger.
*Computer **keys**.*

keyboard

keyboards *noun*

a row of keys that you use to play a musical instrument, or to use a computer or a typewriter.

*computer **keyboard***

kick

kicks kicking kicked *verb*

to hit something or someone with your foot.

kick *noun*

kidnap

kidnaps kidnapping kidnapped *verb*

to take someone away against their will and keep them prisoner.
kidnapping *noun*

kidney

kidneys *noun*

one of two organs in your body that filters your blood and helps to keep it clean.

kidney

kill

kills killing killed *verb*

to make someone or something die.
*She **killed** the wasp with a rolled-up newspaper.*

kind

kinds *noun*

a type or sort of something.

nailbrush   *pastry brush*   *floor brush*

*Different **kinds** of brush.*

kind

adjective

helpful and generous to other people.

■ comparisons **kinder kindest**
■ opposite **unkind**

king

kings *noun*

a male ruler of a country.

kingfisher

kingfishers *noun*

a bird with a long, straight bill and a small body. Kingfishers eat insects or fish and live in river banks or holes in trees.

kiss
kisses kissing kissed *verb*
to touch someone with your lips in an affectionate way.

kiss *noun*

kitchen
kitchens *noun*
a room in which food is prepared and cooked.

kite
kites *noun*
a light, material-covered frame that is flown in the air. Kites are attached to a string held by a person on the ground.

kitten
kittens *noun*
a young cat.

kiwi
kiwis *noun*
a nocturnal bird from New Zealand. Kiwis have hair-like feathers but they cannot fly. They have long, curved bills, which they use to hunt for insects and worms (see **bird** on page 28).
- say **kee**-wee

knee
knees *noun*
the joint between the upper and lower bones of your leg.

knee

- say **nee**

kneel
kneels kneeling kneeled or **knelt** *verb*
to go down on your knees.
- say **neel**

knew
from the verb **to know**
I knew the answers to the test this morning.
- say **new**

knife
knives *noun*
a sharp blade with a handle, that is used for cutting.
- say **nife**

knight
knights *noun*
a soldier from medieval times who rode a horse. A knight fought on behalf of a lord, or for the king or queen.
- say **nite**

knit
knits knitting knitted *verb*
to make clothes and blankets from wool, using large plastic or metal needles.
- say **nit**
knitting *noun*

knob
knobs *noun*
a round handle made of metal, china, plastic, or wood that is fitted to a piece of furniture.
- say **nob**

knock
knocks knocking knocked *verb*
to strike something sharply and quickly.
She knocked at the door.
- say **nok**

knot
knots *noun*
a twisted or tied piece of string, rope, or other cord.

- say **not**
knot *verb*

know
knows knowing knew known *verb*
1 to understand something or be sure about something.
Do you know her name?
2 to have met somebody before.
I have known him for years.
- say **no**

knowledge
noun
the things that someone knows, or all the things that are known.
- say **nol**-lidj
knowledgeable *adjective*

knuckle
knuckles *noun*
one of the bony joints at the base of your fingers.

knuckle

- say **nuk**-ul

koala
koalas *noun*
a marsupial from Australia. Koalas eat the leaves and bark of the eucalyptus trees, in which they live.

kosher
adjective
food that is prepared so that it satisfies the rules of the Jewish religion.
Kosher meat.
- say **koh**-shur

a b c d e f g h i j k l m n o p q r s t u v w x y z

Ll

label
labels *noun*
a small notice attached to something that gives you information about it.

laboratory
laboratories *noun*
a place where scientists work.

lace
noun
1 a material with a pattern of small holes.

lace border

2 a cord that is used to fasten things.

lace
laces lacing laced *verb*
to thread a lace through holes.

shoelace

lack
noun
a state of not having enough or any of something.
*The plants died from **lack** of water.*
lack *verb*

ladder
ladders *noun*
a wooden or metal frame with rungs or steps, which you use for climbing up or down.

rung

ladle
ladles *noun*
a large, deep, round spoon used to serve soup and other liquids.

ladybird
ladybirds *noun*
a small, flying insect with spotted wing covers. Ladybirds eat other small insects.

lagoon
lagoons *noun*
a shallow lake, cut off from the sea or a larger lake by coral, rocks, or sand banks.

laid
*from the verb **to lay***
1 He **laid** his paintings on the table, so we could see them.
2 Our hen **laid** two eggs this morning.

lake
lakes *noun*
a large area of water surrounded by land.

lamb
lambs *noun*
1 a young sheep.

2 meat from a young sheep.

lamp
lamps *noun*
a light that works by using electricity, oil, or gas.

land
lands landing landed *verb*
to arrive on the ground after flying.

*The plane **landed** on the runway.*

land
lands *noun*
1 the parts of the world that are not covered by sea.
2 a country, or an area of ground.
*The farmer owns all the **land** around the village.*

language
languages *noun*
the words or movements that people use to communicate with each other.

*The word "language" in sign **language**.*
■ say **lang**-gwij

lantern
lanterns *noun*
a light that is inside a transparent case to protect it from winds.

lap
laps *noun*
1 the top of your legs when you are sitting down.

*The books were on his **lap**.*
2 one circuit of a race track.
*The runners were on the last **lap** of the race.*

lap

laps lapping lapped *verb*
1 to splash gently
against something.
*The waves **lapped**
against the beach.*
2 to drink using the tongue,
in the way an animal does.

*The kittens **lapped** up the milk.*

large

adjective
great in size.

*a small tomato   a **large** tomato*

■ comparisons **larger largest**
■ opposite **small**

larva

larvae *noun*
an insect after it has hatched
out of its egg, but before
it has become an adult
(see **growth** on page 94).

laser

lasers *noun*
a machine that produces a
beam of powerful light.
Lasers are used
to cut metal, to
perform surgery,
or for light shows.

last

adjective
1 the only one left.
*The **last** roll on the plate.*
■ opposite **first**
2 the most recent.
*We stayed in **last** night.*

last

lasts lasting lasted *verb*
to take a certain amount
of time.
*My riding lesson **lasts** an hour.*

late

adjective
after the correct time.
*They were **late** for dinner.*
■ comparisons **later latest**
■ opposite **early**

laugh

laughs laughing
laughed *verb*
to make
a noise with
your voice
because you
think that
something
is funny.

■ say **larf**
laughter *noun*

launch

launches launching launched
verb
1 to put a boat or ship into
the water.

2 to start
something off.

*They **launched** the space
shuttle successfully.*

law

laws *noun*
a set of rules that people
live by, usually made by
the government of a country.
*It is against the **law** to
drop litter.*

lawn

lawns *noun*
an area of grass that
is regularly cut in a park
or a garden.

lay

lays laying laid *verb*
1 to arrange or
put something
down on
a surface
carefully.

Lay the cards on the table.
2 to produce an egg.

lay

*from the verb **to lie***
*He **lay** down on the bed.*

layer

layers *noun*
a single thickness
of something.

*There is a **layer** of nuts
on top of the cake.*

lazy

adjective
not wanting to work
or do anything energetic.
■ comparisons **lazier laziest**

lead

leads leading led *verb*
1 to go first to show someone
the way.
*Our tour guide **led** us
to the coach.*
■ opposite **follow**
2 to be in charge of something.
*She **led** the expedition
to the South Pole.*

lead

leads *noun*
1 a thin strap or chain
attached to a dog's collar and
used to control it.
2 the first place in a race.
*She was in the **lead** all the way
around the race track.*
3 a clue.
*The police followed up
every **lead**.*
■ rhymes with **feed**

lead

noun
a soft, heavy metal used
in building and for
making weights.

diving belt

*lead
weight*

■ rhymes with **bed**

leaf

leaves *noun*
one of the thin,
flat, green parts
of a plant that
grows out from
the stem
or shoots.

leak

leaks *noun*
a hole or crack in a container
through which liquid or gas
can escape.
*There is a **leak** in this bottle.*
leak *verb*

lean

lean
leans leaning leaned
or **leant** verb
to rest on something or tilt to one side.

leap
leaps leaping leaped or **leapt** verb
to jump a long distance, or to jump high into the air.

leap year
leap years noun
a year that has 366 days, instead of 365. A leap year happens once in every four years. The extra date in a leap year is 29th February.

learn
learns learning learned or **learnt** verb
to find out about something, and to understand it.
*We **learnt** about magnetism at school today.*
learning noun

leather
noun
a material made from the skin of an animal, usually a cow. **leather bag**

leave
leaves leaving left verb
1 to go away.
*We'll **leave** after lunch.*
2 to let something stay as it is.
***Leave** those cakes alone!*

lecture
lectures noun
a talk given by one person to an audience.

leek
leeks noun
a long vegetable with layers of tight leaves. Leeks are part of the onion family.

left
adjective
the side that is opposite to the right.

*She writes with her **left** hand.*
left noun

leg
legs noun
1 the part of your body between your hip and your foot.

leg

2 a support for furniture.

*table **leg***

legal
adjective
allowed by law, or to do with the law.
■ say **lee**-gal
■ opposite **illegal**

legend
legends noun
a well-known old story which may or may not be true.
■ say **lej**-und

leisure
noun
a time when you don't have to work.
■ say **lezh**-ur

lemon
lemons noun
a sour, juicy fruit with a tough, yellow skin.

lend
lends lending lent verb
to give something to someone for a short time.
*He **lent** me his umbrella because it was raining.*
■ opposite **borrow**

length
lengths noun
1 the measurement of something from one end to the other.
*Thirty centimetres in **length**.*
2 a piece cut from a longer piece.

*A **length** of ribbon.*

lens
lenses noun
a curved piece of plastic or glass that is used to help you to see things in a clearer way. Lenses are an important part of telescopes, cameras, and spectacles.

*contact **lens***
***lens** case*
■ say **lenz**

leopard
leopards noun
a large mammal that lives in Africa and Asia and belongs to the cat family. Leopards hunt at night, and are good at climbing trees.

■ say **lep**-ard

leotard
leotards noun
a tight piece of clothing worn for dancing and other kinds of exercise.

■ say **lee**-o-tard

less
adjective
not as much.
*Three is **less** than four.*
■ opposite **more**

118

lesson
lessons *noun*
a period of time for teaching
and learning.
*A piano **lesson**.*

let
lets letting let *verb*
to allow someone to
do something.
*The farmer **let** the children
stroke the donkey.*

letter
letters *noun*
1 a written symbol that
is part of the alphabet
(see **alphabet** on page 16).
2 a written message that
you send to
someone
by post.

lettuce
lettuces *noun*
a green vegetable with large
leaves around a short, central
stem. Lettuce is often used
in salads.

■ say **let**-iss

level
adjective
smooth and flat.
*A sports field should be **level**.*

lever
levers *noun*
1 a bar that is used to lift heavy
weights or to force things open.
2 a long bar or handle for
operating a machine.

lever

espresso coffee machine

liberty
liberties *noun*
freedom.
*The prisoner's relatives
campaigned for his **liberty**.*

library
libraries *noun*
a place where books and
other sources of information
are collected and may
be borrowed.

licence
licences *noun*
an official certificate that
shows you have permission
to do something.
*A driving **licence**.*
■ say **lie**-sens
license *verb*

lick
licks licking licked *verb*
to touch something with your
tongue to eat it
or make it wet.

***Licking** an
ice-lolly.*

lid
lids *noun*
the top of a container.

*saucepan **lid***

lie
lies lying lied *verb*
to say something that you
know is untrue.
lie *noun*

lie
lies lying lay lain *verb*
to be in a horizontal position.
***Lying** down.*

life
lives *noun*
1 all things that are living.
Life on Earth.
2 the time that you are alive.
*My grandma had a long,
happy **life**.*

lifeboat
lifeboats *noun*
a boat for rescuing people
who are in trouble at sea.

lifeguard
lifeguards *noun*
a person whose job it is
to rescue people who are
in trouble in the sea or in
a swimming pool.

lift
lifts lifting lifted *verb*
to pick something up.

lift
lifts *noun*
1 a machine that carries
people up to or down from
high places, either in
a building or outside.

*A ski **lift**.*
2 a ride in a vehicle that you
don't have to pay for.
*Can I give you a **lift** into town?*

light
lights lighting lit *verb*
to make something catch fire,
or to turn on a light.
***Lighting** a candle.*

light
lights *noun*
something that shines to help
you see in the dark.
*I had to turn on the **light**
so I could see the way.*

a
b
c
d
e
f
g
h
i
j
k
l
m
n
o
p
q
r
s
t
u
v
w
x
y
z

A
B
C
D
E
F
G
H
I
J
K
L
M
N
O
P
Q
R
S
T
U
V
W
X
Y
Z

light
adjective
1 weighing little.

*a **light** balloon*   *a heavy bucket*

■ comparisons **lighter lightest**
■ opposite **heavy**
2 not dark in colour.
*Her dress was **light** blue.*

lighthouse
lighthouses *noun*
a tall tower
with a bright,
flashing light
that guides or
warns ships
around dangerous
areas of coast.

lightning
noun
a flash of light in the sky
during a thunderstorm.

like
likes liking liked *verb*
to think that someone
or something is pleasant.
■ opposite **dislike**
likeable *adjective*

like
adjective
similar to.
*He looks **like** his brother.*

lily
lilies *noun*
a tall plant that grows
from a bulb, with large,
trumpet-shaped blooms.

lime
limes *noun*
a juicy fruit
with a sour
flavour, similar
to that of a lemon.

limit
limits *noun*
the point where
something ends.
*The **limits** of the town.*

limp
limps limping limped *verb*
to walk with difficulty
because your leg or your
foot is injured or stiff.
*The dog **limped** because it
had a thorn in its paw.*
limp *noun*

limp
adjective
not stiff.
*A **limp** flag.*

line
lines *noun*
1 a piece of rope or thread.
*A fishing **line**.*
2 a long, thin mark.

*A wavy **line**.*

3 a straight row of something.

*A **line** of cars.*

liner
liners *noun*
a large passenger ship.

link
links *noun*
1 one of the individual
sections that make
up a chain.

link

2 a connection between
two things.
*The motorway will provide
a **link** between the two cities.*

lion
lions *noun*
a large mammal that is found
in Africa and India. Lions
belong to the cat family. They
live together in groups called
prides. The females, called
lionesses, hunt at night for
large animals such as
antelope and zebra.

lioness

lip
lips *noun*
1 one of the two soft,
pink edges of
your mouth.

lips

2 the top edge of a container.

lip

liquid
liquids *noun*
a substance that
flows and is
not a gas.

list
lists *noun*
the names of several people
or things written in columns.
*A shopping **list**.*

listen
listens listening listened *verb*
to hear and pay attention to
something, such as music.

lit
from the verb **to light**
*They **lit** a fire last night.*

literature
noun
novels, plays, poems, and other written material.

litter
noun
1 rubbish left lying around.
2 baby animals born to the same mother at one time.

*A **litter** of puppies.*

little
adjective
1 small in size.

*a **little** ball*   *a big ball*

■ comparisons **littler littlest**
■ opposite **big**
2 not much.
*I only have a **little** time.*
■ comparisons **less least**

live
lives living lived *verb*
1 to be alive.
*He **lived** to an old age.*
2 to stay in a place.

*Hermit crabs **live** in shells.*
■ rhymes with **give**
living *adjective*

live
adjective
1 having life.
*A **live** snake.*
2 shown while the event is taking place.
*A **live** television show.*
■ rhymes with **dive**

liver
livers *noun*
an organ in the body that cleans the blood and helps to digest food.

liver

living
noun
the way a person lives or earns money.
*He earns his **living** as a chef.*

lizard
lizards *noun*
a reptile with scales. Most types of lizard have four legs and a long tail. Many lizards live in warm regions and eat insects.

*A gecko is a type of **lizard**.*

load
loads *noun*
an amount of something that is carried.

*A **load** of gravel.*

load
loads loading loaded *verb*
to put things into a vehicle.
***Loading** the ship with cargo.*

loaf
loaves *noun*
a lump of bread baked as one piece that can be cut into slices.

***loaf** of bread*

lobster
lobsters *noun*
a large shellfish that lives in the sea and has five pairs of legs. One pair of legs are claws, which lobsters use for cutting up dead fish and crushing shellfish to eat.

*European **lobster***

local
adjective
having to do with the area near to a place.
*The **local** paper showed a picture of the flood.*
locally *adjective*

locate
locates locating located *verb*
1 to be in a particular place.
*The company is **located** in the north.*
2 to find where something is.
*He finally **located** the garage down a side street.*

location
locations *noun*
the place or position of something.

lock
locks *noun*
1 a device that keeps something shut.

combination lock

lock *verb*
2 a device on a canal that raises or lowers the water level, so that boats can move up and down.

locker
lockers *noun*
a small, narrow cupboard with a lock, which is used for storing clothes or books.

log
logs *noun*
a thick piece of tree trunk or branch.

lonely
adjective
feeling sad and alone.
*He was **lonely** with no one to play with.*
■ comparisons **lonelier loneliest**
loneliness *noun*

a b c d e f g h i j k l m n o p q r s t u v w x y z

121

A
B
C
D
E
F
G
H
I
J
K
L
M
N
O
P
Q
R
S
T
U
V
W
X
Y
Z

long
adjective
1 having
great length.

*a short
string
of beads*

*a **long**
string
of beads*

■ comparisons **longer longest**
■ opposite **short**
2 being a certain length.
*The fish was one metre **long**.*

look
looks looking looked *verb*
1 to use your eyes
to see something.

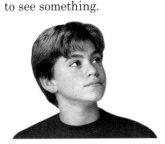

***Looking** up.*
2 to appear a certain way.
*He **looked** tired after
a sleepless night.*

loose
adjective
not firmly
fastened
or held.

***loose**
scarf*

■ say **loos**
■ comparisons **looser loosest**
loosely *adverb*
loosen *verb*

lose
loses losing lost *verb*
1 to no longer
have something.

*She has **lost**
her shoe.*
■ opposite **find**
2 to be defeated in a game
or battle.
*He **lost** the match.*
■ say **looz**
■ opposite **win**

loud
adjective
noisy.
Loud music.
■ comparisons **louder loudest**

loudspeaker
loudspeakers *noun*
a device
that turns
electrical
signals
into sound.

love
loves loving loved *verb*
to like someone or something
very much.
love *noun*

low
adjective
near the ground.

*A **low** table.*
■ comparisons **lower lowest**

lower
lowers lowering lowered *verb*
to let something down to
the ground carefully.

*The load was **lowered**
onto the pile.*

luck
noun
something that happens
to you by chance, without
being planned.
*I had the good **luck** to win
a free holiday.*
lucky *adjective*

luggage
noun
cases and bags containing
your clothes and other
things that you carry when
you travel.

■ say **lug**-ij

lukewarm
adjective
not very warm.
*The hot water system wasn't
working properly, so he had
to have a **lukewarm** shower.*

lull
lulls lulling lulled *verb*
to calm someone.
*He **lulled** the baby to sleep.*

lullaby
lullabies *noun*
a song that is sung to help
children to fall asleep.

luminous
adjective
glowing in the dark.

*A deep-sea fish with
luminous markings.*
■ say **loo**-min-us

lump
lumps *noun*
a rough piece of something.
*A **lump** of coal.*

lunch
lunches *noun*
a meal eaten in the middle of
the day.

lung
lungs *noun*
one of a pair of organs
inside your body that you use
for breathing.

lung

luxury
luxuries *noun*
something that is expensive.
*The new car was a **luxury**.*
■ say **luk**-sher-ee
luxurious *adjective*

lyrics
noun
the words to a song.
■ say **lir**-iks

Mm

machine
machines *noun*
a piece of equipment that is made up of several parts. The parts move together to do a particular job.

*A food mixer is a useful **machine**.*

machinery
noun
machines in general.

mad
adjective
1 crazy or foolish.
*She is **mad** to swim in the sea during winter.*
2 very angry.
■ comparisons **madder maddest**

magazine
magazines *noun*
a collection of news, stories, pictures, and advertisements with a paper cover.

magic
noun
tricks that a person performs that seem to make impossible and surprising things happen.
magical *adjective*

magician
magicians *noun*
someone who performs magic tricks.

magnet
magnets *noun*
a piece of iron that attracts metals with iron or steel in them.

magnetic *adjective*
magnetism *noun*

magnificent
adjective
grand and wonderful.
*A **magnificent** fountain.*

magnify
magnifies magnifying magnified *verb*
to make something look bigger than it really is.

***magnifying** glass*

mail
noun
letters, cards, and parcels that are collected and delivered.

mail *verb*

main
adjective
most important.
*The **main** road.*
mainly *adverb*

major
adjective
big or important.
*Scientists have made a **major** discovery.*
■ opposite **minor**
majority *noun*

make
makes making made *verb*
1 to create, produce, build, or do something.

*She **made** some musical pipes out of straws and tape.*

2 to cause something to happen.

*The stone **made** ripples in the pond.*
3 to force someone to do something.
*Our teacher **made** us tidy the classroom.*

make-up
noun
a substance that people put on their faces to change the way that they look.

male
adjective
belonging to the sex that can be a father, but cannot give birth to babies, or produce eggs or seeds.
■ opposite **female**
male *noun*

male

a b c d e f g h i j k l m n o p q r s t u v w x y z

123

mammal

mammals *noun*
one of a group of animals that usually have hair or fur and a backbone, and are warm-blooded. Most female mammals give birth to live babies and feed them on milk.

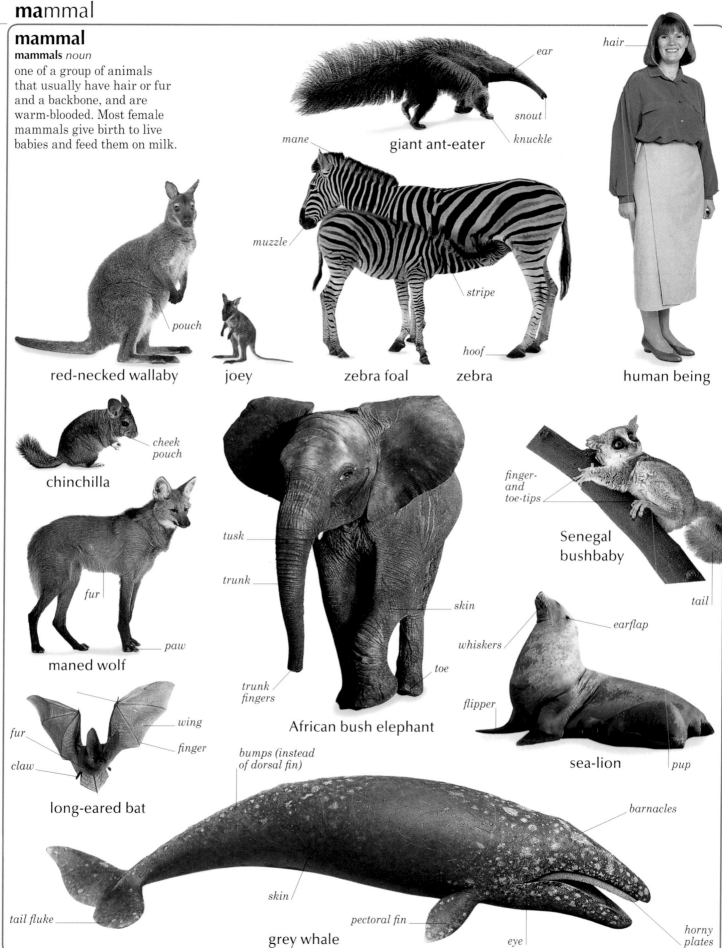

ear
snout
knuckle
giant ant-eater

hair

mane
muzzle
stripe
hoof

pouch
red-necked wallaby

joey

zebra foal

zebra

human being

cheek pouch
chinchilla

finger- and toe-tips
Senegal bushbaby

tail

fur
paw
maned wolf

tusk
trunk
skin
trunk fingers
toe
African bush elephant

whiskers
earflap
flipper
sea-lion
pup

fur
claw
wing
finger
long-eared bat

bumps (instead of dorsal fin)
barnacles
skin
tail fluke
pectoral fin
eye
horny plates
grey whale

A B C D E F G H I J K L M N O P Q R S T U V W X Y Z

man
men *noun*
an adult
male person.

man
noun
people in general.
*Apes are related to **man**.*

manage
**manages managing
managed** *verb*
1 to be in charge of a business
or part of a business.
*She **manages** a shop, and has
two assistants to help her.*
2 to be able to do something
that is difficult.
*She **managed** to swim right
across the bay.*

manner
noun
a way that a person acts,
or a way something is done.
*She always greets us in
a friendly **manner**.*

manners
noun
the way a person behaves.

*He has good **manners**.*

manufacture
**manufactures manufacturing
manufactured** *verb*
to make something in large
quantities with a machine.
***Manufacturing** cars.*
■ say man-yoo-**fak**-chur

many
adjective
a large number.
*There were so **many** people,
that I couldn't find her.*
■ comparisons **more most**
■ opposite **few**

map
maps *noun*
a drawing of all, or part of,
Earth's surface. Maps often
show where towns, rivers,
and other geographical
features are.

*road **map***

marathon
marathons *noun*
a very long running race.
A marathon is 42.195 km
(26.2 miles) long.

marble
noun
1 a hard rock that is used in
buildings to make floors or
for decoration.

***marble** slab*
2 a small, glass ball that
is used to play a children's
game, called marbles.

march
marches marching marched *verb*
to walk with quick,
regular steps.

***march** noun*

margarine
noun
a food made of vegetable
oil that is used for spreading
on bread, or in baking.
■ say mar-jer-**een**

margin
margins *noun*
a space that forms a border at
the edge of a piece of paper.

margin

marine
adjective
living in the sea, or having
something to do with the sea.

***marine** life*
■ say ma-**reen**

mark
marks *noun*
1 a line or a stain
on something.
*A chalk **mark**.*
2 a score that shows how well
you have done at something.
*I got high **marks** in French.*

market
markets *noun*
a place with stalls for
buying and selling goods,
often outside.

*open **market***

marmalade
marmalades *noun*
a type of jam made from fruit
such as oranges or limes.

*orange **marmalade***

marry
marries marrying married *verb*
to become someone's husband
or wife at a wedding.
marriage *noun*

marsh
marshes *noun*
a low area of land that
is always very wet.

a b c d e f g h i j k l m n o p q r s t u v w x y z

A B C D E F G H I J K L **M** N O P Q R S T U V W X Y Z

marsupial

marsupials *noun*

one of a group of mammals that carry their babies in pouches. Kangaroos and koalas are marsupials (see **mammal** on page 124).

■ say mar-**soo**-pee-al

masculine

adjective

of, or like, men or boys.

■ say **mas**-kul-lin
■ opposite **feminine**

mask

masks *noun*

something that hides or protects the face.

party
mask
mask *verb*

mass

masses *noun*

a very large number of people or things.

*A **mass** of bees gathered around the hive.*

mast

masts *noun*

an upright pole that holds the sails on a boat or ship (see **boat** on page 31).

mat

mats *noun*

a covering for a floor, or to put under dishes on a table.

match

matches matching matched *verb*

to be similar to, or to go well with, something else.

*His trousers **matched** his hat and scarf.*
matching *adjective*

match

matches *noun*

1 a sports competition between two people or teams. *A football **match**.*
2 a small stick of wood or card that you strike against a rough surface to make a flame.

mate

mates mating mated *verb*

to join together as males and females to produce babies. *Many animals **mate** in the spring, and have their babies in the summer.*
mate *noun*

material

materials *noun*

1 cloth.

*woven **material***

mathematics

noun

the study of numbers, quantities, shapes, and sizes. Mathematics is often shortened to maths.

*Symbols that are used in **mathematics**.*
mathematical *adjective*

matter

noun

1 any substance that takes up space and has weight, such as solids, liquids, and gases. *Everything is made up of **matter**.*
2 a subject that needs to be discussed or decided. *It was an urgent **matter**.*

mattress

mattresses *noun*

a soft, thick pad that you lie on in a bed.

mature

adjective

fully grown or developed.
mature *verb*
maturity *noun*

2 things that are used to make or do something.

*building **materials***

maximum

noun

the greatest possible amount.

*This box holds a **maximum** of 12 pencils.*

■ opposite **minimum**

may

might *verb*

1 to ask or have permission to do something. *May I go now?*
2 to suggest that something is possible. *It **may** rain later.*

■ always used with another verb

mayonnaise

noun

a creamy sauce made from eggs, vegetable oil, and vinegar, and eaten with salads.

■ say may-on-**ayz**

maze

mazes *noun*

a system of paths in which it is difficult to find your way around.

meadow

meadows *noun*

a field of grass, often with wild flowers growing in it.

■ say med-oh

meal
meals *noun*
food eaten at
a particular
time of the day.

*An evening **meal**.*

mean
adjective
1 unkind or unpleasant.
*That was a **mean** trick!*
2 not generous with money
or other things.
*He was too **mean** to buy us
an ice-cream.*
■ comparisons **meaner meanest**

meaning
meanings *noun*
the explanation behind what
something says or what
it is about.
*She didn't understand
the **meaning** of the joke.*
mean *verb*

meanwhile
adverb
at the same time.
*Put the pasta on to boil, and
meanwhile make the sauce.*

measure
measures measuring measured
verb
to find out how big or how
heavy something is.

■ say **mezh**-ur
measurement *noun*

meat
noun
the parts of an animal that
can be eaten.

*meat
kebabs*

mechanic
mechanics *noun*
a person who makes and
repairs engines
and machines.

mechanical
adjective
worked by a machine.

*A **mechanical** toy.*

medal
medals *noun*
a piece of metal that looks
like a large coin hanging on
a ribbon. Medals are awarded
to people for
something
special that
they have done.

*war **medal***

medical
adjective
having to do with medicine
or doctors.
***Medical** school.*

medicine
medicines *noun*
a substance given
to a sick person
to help make
them better.

■ say **med**-i-sin

medieval
adjective
coming from the historical
period between
the 12th and
15th centuries.

*medieval
costume*

■ say
med-ee-**ee**-val

medium
adjective
an average size, not
particularly large or small.

small ***medium*** *large*

meet
meets meeting met *verb*
to come face-to-face with
another person.
*I **meet** my friend at
the bus-stop every day.*
meeting *noun*

melody
melodies *noun*
a tune.
*Do you recognize this **melody**?*
melodic *adjective*

melon
melons *noun*
a round yellow or green fruit
with a tough skin, soft flesh,
and many seeds.

melt
melts melting melted *verb*
to turn from a solid to
a liquid when heated.

*The butter **melted** quickly
in the hot pan.*

A B C D E F G H I J K L **M** N O P Q R S T U V W X Y Z

member
members *noun*
a person who belongs
to a club or an organization.

memorial
memorials *noun*
a structure
that is built
to remind us
of people who
have died.

A war **memorial**.

memorize
**memorizes memorizing
memorized** *verb*
to learn something so that
you can remember it in detail.
*Memorize the directions before
you set off.*

memory
memories *noun*
1 the ability to
remember things.
I've got a terrible **memory**
for people's names.
2 what you remember of
something that has happened
in the past.
*The photos brought back
happy* **memories**.

mend
mends mending mended *verb*
to repair something that
is broken.

mental
adjective
having to do with the mind.
Mental arithmetic.

menu
menus *noun*
a list of dishes
in a restaurant.

■ say **men**-yoo

mercury
noun
a heavy, silver-coloured
metal that is usually
in a liquid form.
Mercury is often used
in thermometers.

mercury _____

mercy
noun
the ability to forgive someone
or to treat them
sympathetically.
The prisoners were shown
mercy *and released.*
merciful *adjective*

merit
merits meriting merited *verb*
to deserve something.
She **merited** *a special award
for bravery.*
merit *noun*

mermaid
mermaids *noun*
a sea creature from
legends that has the upper
body of a woman and
the tail of a fish.

merry
adjective
happy and cheerful.
■ comparisons **merrier merriest**

mess
messes *noun*
things that are dirty or in the
wrong place and look untidy.
There was a lot of **mess** *after
they had finished cooking.*
messy *adjective*

message
messages *noun*
a piece of information or an
instruction that you send to
someone or leave for them.

met
from the verb **to meet**
I **met** *my friend in
town yesterday.*

metal
metals *noun*
a substance that is found in
rocks and can be hammered
or stretched into a shape.
Iron, gold, and copper are
all metals. Electricity and
heat can be passed
through metals.

tin can

gold watch

metallic *adjective*

meteorite
meteorites *noun*
a piece of rock that falls to
Earth from space without
burning up. Pieces of rock
that burn up as they enter
Earth's atmosphere are
called meteors.

meteorite
■ say **meet**-ee-or-ite

method
methods *noun*
a way of doing something.
Organic farming **methods**.

microphone
microphones *noun*
a device that is
used to send sound
over a distance
or to make
it louder.

microscope
microscopes *noun*
an instrument that
magnifies very
tiny things so
that they can be
seen in detail.

microwave oven
microwave ovens *noun*
an oven that cooks food very
quickly by passing electrical
signals through it.

midday

noun

12 o'clock in the middle of the day.
- opposite **midnight**

middle

middles *noun*

the centre, or the part between the outer edges of something.

*She sat in the **middle** of the bench, between her two friends.*

midnight

noun

12 o'clock at night.
- opposite **midday**

might

*from the verb **may***
*It **might** snow later.*
- say **mite**

migrate

migrates migrating migrated *verb*

1 to go from one place to another to live there.
***Migrating** from the country to the city.*
2 to go from one place to another every year at the same time.

*Birds **migrate** huge distances.*
- say my-**grate**
migration *noun*

military

adjective

to do with an army, navy, or air force.

***military** hat*

milk

noun

the liquid that female mammals produce to feed their babies. People also drink goat's and cow's milk.

mill

mills *noun*

1 a building where materials are manufactured.

*saw**mill***

2 a device that grinds or crushes.

*pepper **mill***

millionaire

millionaires *noun*

a very rich person with money and property worth more than a million pounds or dollars.

mime

mimes *noun*

a type of acting that uses movements instead of words.

mime *verb*

mimic

mimics mimicking mimicked *verb*

to imitate what someone says or does.

*Parrots can **mimic** lots of noises.*

mind

minds minding minded *verb*

1 to object to something.
*Do you **mind** if I sit here?*
2 to take care of someone for a time.
*I had to **mind** the baby while my sister went out.*

mind

minds *noun*

1 the thoughts, feelings, and memory of a person.
*I've changed my **mind**.*
2 intelligence.
*She has a quick **mind**.*

mine

mines *noun*

1 a deep hole in the ground from which minerals are dug out of rock.
miner *noun*
2 a type of bomb that can float in the sea or be buried in the ground.

*coal **mine***

mineral

minerals *noun*

a natural substance, such as coal or gold, that is found in rocks and in the ground.

lapis lazuli

miniature

adjective

very small, or made to a small scale.

***miniature** china*
- say **min**-it-cher
miniature *noun*

minimum

noun

the smallest possible amount or number.
*The **minimum** age for driving a car is 17.*
- opposite **maximum**

minister

ministers *noun*

1 a person who holds religious services in a church.
2 someone in charge of a government department.
*The health **minister**.*

a b c d e f g h i j k l **m** n o p q r s t u v w x y z

A B C D E F G H I J K L **M** N O P Q R S T U V W X Y Z

minor

adjective

small or unimportant.
*A **minor** fault delayed
the plane's departure.*

■ opposite **major**
minority *noun*

minus

preposition

subtract or less.
*8 **minus** 5 equals 3.*

■ opposite **plus**

minus

minuses *noun*

a symbol in mathematics
that means
subtract.
minus *adjective*

minute

minutes *noun*

a measurement of time that
lasts 60 seconds. There are
60 minutes in an hour.

■ say **min**-it

minute

adjective

extremely small.

*A **minute** bead.*
■ say my-**newt**

miracle

miracles *noun*

a sudden, wonderful event
that sometimes makes a bad
situation better.
*Her recovery after the accident
was a **miracle**.*

■ say **mir**-i-kul
miraculous *adjective*

mirage

mirages *noun*

something that looks real
from far away, but is not
there when you get closer to it.
*The lake that they saw in the
desert was only a **mirage**.*

■ say mi-**razh**

mirror

mirrors *noun*

a shiny surface,
usually made
of glass. Mirrors
reflect the images
of things placed
in front of them.

mischievous

adjective

playful in a way that can
be annoying.

*The **mischievous** cat knocked
over the plant.*
■ say **mis**-chi-vus
mischievously *adverb*

miserable

adjective

very sad or unhappy.

miss

misses missing missed *verb*

1 to fail to meet, reach,
or hit something that you
are aiming at.
*He threw the ball at the target,
but **missed** it.*

2 to be sad because someone
is not there.
*I will **miss** you.*

3 to fail to keep, have, or
attend something.
*She has **missed** school for three
weeks now.*

mist

mists *noun*

a cloud of tiny water drops
in the air.
misty *adjective*

mistake

mistakes *noun*

something that someone
does wrong.

$$8-5=1$$

mistaken *adjective*

mix

mixes mixing mixed *verb*

to combine two
or more things
together.

mixture *noun*

moan

moans moaning moaned *verb*

to complain or to make
a long, low, groaning noise
because of pain or sadness.

moat

moats *noun*

a deep ditch filled with water
that surrounds a castle.

mobile

adjective

able to move or be
carried about.
*A **mobile** phone.*

mobile

mobiles *noun*

a decoration made of small
objects hanging
on strings.

model

models *noun*

1 a small copy of something
larger.

*A **model** of an aeroplane.*
model *adjective*

2 a person who demonstrates
clothes or other things that
are for sale.

*A fashion **model**.*

3 a person who poses for
photographs or for an artist.

modern
adjective
of the present time.
*A **modern** house.*

modest
adjective
not boasting about your talents and actions.
*He was too **modest** to say he had won the first prize.*

moist
adjective
slightly wet.
moisture *noun*

mole
moles *noun*
1 a small, furry mammal that lives in underground tunnels. Moles eat worms and insects and they are almost blind.

2 a small, dark patch on your skin.

moment
moments *noun*
a short time.
*I'll be back in a **moment**.*

money
noun
the coins and notes used to buy things.

mongrel
mongrels *noun*
a dog that is a mixture of more than one breed.

monk
monks *noun*
a man who lives in a religious community.

Buddhist monk

■ say **munk**

monkey
monkeys *noun*
a furry mammal that usually lives in hot regions. Most monkeys live in trees and eat fruit, although some eat small insects and mammals. There are many different species of monkey.

macaque

■ say **munk**-ee

monster
monsters *noun*
a fierce, frightening creature from myths and fairy tales.

month
months *noun*
a period of between 28 and 31 days. A year is divided into 12 months.

mood
moods *noun*
a way you feel at a particular time.
*The sunny day put us all in a good **mood**.*

moon
moons *noun*
a ball-shaped natural satellite made of rock that revolves around a planet (see **universe** on page 229).

mop
mops *noun*
a tool for cleaning floors, used with water and a bucket.

more
adjective
greater in number or quantity.
■ opposite **less**

morning
mornings *noun*
the early part of the day, ending at noon.
*School starts at 8.30 in the **morning**.*

mosaic
mosaics *noun*
a picture or pattern made of small squares of coloured stone.

■ say mo-**zay**-ik

mosque
mosques *noun*
a building where Muslims go to pray.
■ say **mosk**

mosquito
mosquitoes or **mosquitos** *noun*
a small, flying insect found in hot, wet regions. Female mosquitoes bite and feed on the blood of people and animals, and can infect them with serious illnesses, such as malaria.

■ say moss-**kee**-toe

most
adjective
greatest in number or quantity.
■ opposite **least**

motel
motels *noun*
a hotel specially built for motorists.

moth
moths *noun*
a flying insect with wings covered in fine scales. Moths belong to the same animal group as butterflies, but they usually fly at night.

*pine emperor **moth***

mother
mothers *noun*
a female parent.

motion
motions *noun*
movement.
*The rocking **motion** of the boat made me feel sick.*

a b c d e f g h i j k l m n o p q r s t u v w x y z

131

motor

motors *noun*

a machine that supplies power to objects to move them or make them work.

motorbike

motorbikes *noun*

a two-wheeled vehicle that is powered by a motor.

motorist

motorists *noun*

a person who drives a car regularly.

motorway

motorways *noun*

a road that is specially designed for cars to travel along quickly.

mountain

mountains *noun*

an area of land that rises up to a great height.
mountainous *adjective*

mourn

mourns mourning mourned *verb*

to be sad because someone has died.

■ say **morn**

mouse

mice *noun*

1 a small, furry mammal from the rodent family. Mice have large front teeth which they use to gnaw food. Mice mainly eat plants, but sometimes they eat small animals and insects too.

2 a control switch for a computer that can be used to move things around on a computer screen.

mouth

mouths *noun*

1 the opening in your face that you use for eating and talking.

mouth

2 the end of a river where it meets the sea.

move

moves moving moved *verb*

to go from one place to another, or to make something change position.
movement *noun*

moving

adjective

1 making you feel very sad.
*The film was very **moving**.*
2 able to move.
*Keep your fingers away from all **moving** parts.*

mow

mows mowing mowed *verb*

to cut down grass.

Mowing the lawn.
■ rhymes with **go**

mud

noun

soft, wet earth.
muddy *adjective*

muddle

muddles *noun*

a confusing or untidy situation.
muddle *verb*

mug

mugs *noun*

a large cup without a saucer.

multiply

multiplies multiplying multiplied *verb*

to increase a number or an amount of something by adding it to itself several times.

9x5=45

*Nine **multiplied** by five equals forty-five.*
multiplication *noun*

munch

munches munching munched *verb*

to make a crunching noise while eating something.
***Munching** a lettuce.*

murder

murders murdering murdered *verb*

to kill someone deliberately.

murmur

murmurs *noun*

a quiet, whispering sound.
murmur *verb*

muscle

muscles *noun*

the fleshy parts of your body that help it to move.

*biceps **muscle***

■ say **mus**-ul
muscular *adjective*

museum

museums *noun*

a place where objects from other times and places, or of special interest, are displayed.
■ say mew-**zee**-um

mushroom

mushrooms *noun*

a common fungus that grows in warm, damp areas. Some mushrooms can be eaten, but others are poisonous.

*field **mushrooms***

music

noun

the sound that people make when they sing, or play musical instruments.

musical instrument

musical instruments *noun*
an instrument for making music, usually played by hitting, blowing, or pulling or hitting strings.

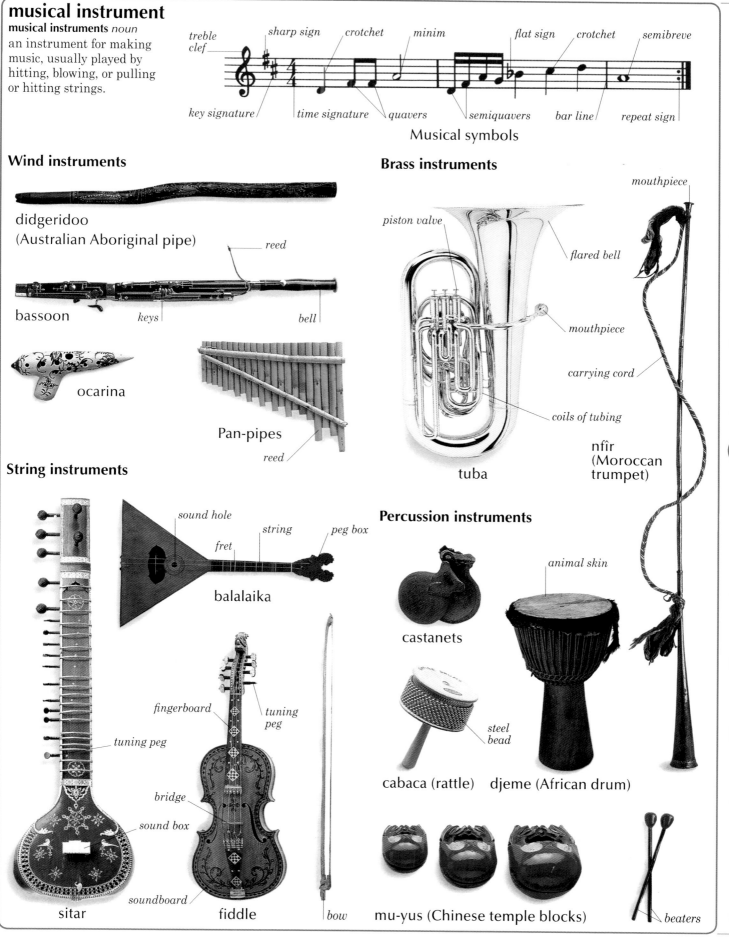

Musical symbols

treble clef · sharp sign · crotchet · minim · flat sign · crotchet · semibreve
key signature · time signature · quavers · semiquavers · bar line · repeat sign

Wind instruments

didgeridoo
(Australian Aboriginal pipe)

bassoon — reed, keys, bell

ocarina

Pan-pipes — reed

String instruments

sitar — tuning peg

balalaika — sound hole, fret, string, peg box

fiddle — fingerboard, tuning peg, bridge, sound box, soundboard

bow

Brass instruments

tuba — piston valve, flared bell, mouthpiece, carrying cord, coils of tubing

nfîr
(Moroccan trumpet) — mouthpiece

Percussion instruments

castanets

cabaca (rattle) — steel bead

djeme (African drum) — animal skin

mu-yus (Chinese temple blocks)

beaters

a b c d e f g h i j k l **m** n o p q r s t u v w x y z

A B C D E F G H I J K L **M** N O P Q R S T U V W X Y Z

musician
musicians *noun*
a person who sings,
plays a musical instrument,
or writes music.

■ say myoo-**zish**-un

Muslim
Muslims *noun*
a person who believes in and
follows the Islamic religion.
■ also spelt **Moslem**

mussel
mussels *noun*
a type of shellfish, which
is edible. Some mussels live
in the sea, while
others live
in lakes
and streams.

must
verb
to have to do something.
*I must post her birthday
present today.*
■ opposite **must not** or **mustn't**
■ always used with another verb

mustard
noun
a spicy powder
or sauce, made
from mustard
seeds and
used to
add flavour
to food.

mutiny
mutinies *noun*
a rebellion by the crew of a
ship or by soldiers in an army
against the people in charge.
■ say **myoo**-tin-ee
mutiny *verb*

mutter
mutters muttering muttered *verb*
to talk in a low voice.
*I can't hear when you **mutter**.*

mutual
adjective
shared by two or more.
*A **mutual** friend.*
■ say **myoo**-tyoo-al

muzzle
muzzles *noun*   *muzzle*
1 the mouth and
nose of an animal.
2 a cage or straps
put over an
animal's mouth
to stop
it biting.

mystery
mysteries *noun*
an unusual and
puzzling event.
*His disappearance is
still a **mystery**.*
mysterious *adjective*

myth
myths *noun*
an ancient story that tries
to explain how the world
became the way it is.

*Zeus was the god of light,
clear skies, and thunder
in Greek **myths**.*
mythical *adjective*

nail
nails *noun*
1 a long, thin, pointed
metal spike that is
hammered into
pieces of wood
to fasten
them together.
nail *verb*

2 a hard substance that
grows at the ends of
your fingers
and toes.

*finger**nail***

naked
adjective
not wearing any clothes.
■ say **nay**-kid

name
names *noun*
a word that a person or thing
is known by.
*My dog's **name** is Rover.*

nap
naps *noun*
a short sleep.

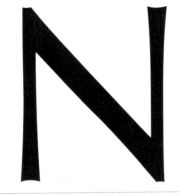

*He had a quick **nap**
before supper.*

narrator
narrators *noun*
someone who tells
a story, either by
writing it or
by reading
it aloud.

narrate *verb*

narrow
adjective
with sides or
edges that
are very
close together.

*The path was very **narrow**.*
■ comparisons **narrower
narrowest**
■ opposite **wide**

nasty
adjective
unpleasant or cruel.
■ comparisons **nastier nastiest**

nation
nations *noun*
a group of people who usually
share the same history,
language, and way of life,
and live in the same country.
national *adjective*

natural
adjective
produced by nature.

natural sponge

nature
noun
all the things in the world that are not made by humans, such as the weather, animals, plants, and the sea.
■ say **nay**-cher

naughty
adjective
disobedient or badly behaved.

*It is very **naughty** to draw on walls.*
■ say **nor**-tee
■ comparisons **naughtier naughtiest**

nautical
adjective
relating to ships, sailors, or sailing.

ship's register

map dividers

Nautical instruments.   *sextant*

navigate
navigates navigating navigated
verb
to steer a boat, ship, or aircraft in a particular direction using special instruments and maps.

navigation *noun*

navy
noun
1 a country's warships and sailors.
2 a dark blue colour.

near
preposition
close to or not far from.

*They lived **near** the airport.*
■ opposite **far**
near *adjective*
near *adverb*

nearby
adverb
not far away.
*Do you live **nearby**?*

nearly
adverb
not quite, but almost.
*It's **nearly** bedtime.*

necessary
adjective
needed.
***Necessary** equipment for survival at sea.*
■ say **nes**-es-er-ee
■ opposite **unnecessary**
necessarily *adverb*

hand-held flare

parachute flare

life jacket

neck
necks *noun*
the part of the body that supports your head and joins it to the rest of your body.

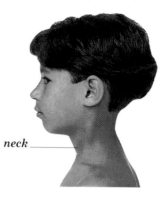

neck

necklace
necklaces *noun*
a chain or beads worn around the neck as a piece of jewellery.

nectar
noun
a sweet liquid that bees and some birds collect from flowers. Bees use nectar to make honey.

need
needs needing needed *verb*
to want something because you have to have it.
*Do you **need** anything from the shops?*

needle
needles *noun*
1 a small, thin piece of pointed steel.

*sewing **needle***
2 a plastic or metal stick used for knitting.

3 a thin, pointed leaf of some plants, such as pine trees.
4 a part that points on a dial.
*A compass **needle**.*

negative
adjective
1 saying or meaning no.
*A **negative** answer.*
2 smaller than zero.
*A **negative** number.*
■ opposite **positive**

neglect
neglects neglecting neglected
verb
to pay too little or no attention to someone or something.

*They **neglected** their garden.*
neglect *noun*

negotiate
negotiates negotiating negotiated *verb*
to discuss something in order to reach an agreement.
■ say neg-**oh**-she-ate
negotiation *noun*

neighbour
neighbours *noun*
someone who lives near you.
■ say **nay**-ber

neighbourhood
neighbourhoods *noun*
the people and the area where you live.
■ say **nay**-ber-hood

a b c d e f g h i j k l m **n** o p q r s t u v w x y z

A B C D E F G H I J K L M **N** O P Q R S T U V W X Y Z

nephew
nephews noun
the son of a person's brother, sister, brother-in-law, or sister-in-law.
- say **nef**-few

nerve
nerves noun
1 a thin fibre that connects your brain to all parts of your body. Nerves carry messages to and from your brain so that you can feel and move.

nerve

2 courage.
*To lose your **nerve**.*

nervous
adjective
slightly worried or frightened about what is happening or going to happen.

*He was **nervous** about speaking in public.*
nervously adverb

nest
nests noun
the home that a bird or animal builds out of leaves, grass, and other materials.

nest verb

squirrel's **nest**

net
nets noun
a material made of knotted threads, string, or rope. Nets are often used to catch fish.

nettle
nettles noun
a plant with stinging hairs on its stems and leaves. These hairs can cause a rash on your skin if you touch the plant.

network
networks noun
1 a system of connected lines, roads, people, computers, or organizations.

*Plan of a rail **network**.*

2 a group of connected radio or television stations that can broadcast the same programmes.

neutral
adjective
1 not being on anyone's side.
*A **neutral** country.*
2 not very definite.
*Grey is a **neutral** colour.*
- say **new**-trul

never
adverb
not ever.
*I've **never** been here before.*

new
adjective
1 recently made, or unused.

*I bought a **new** shirt today.*
2 unfamiliar or recently changed.
*A **new** job.*
- comparisons **newer newest**
- opposite **old**

news
noun
information about recent events around the country or around the world.
*Have you heard the **news**?*

newspaper
newspapers noun
large sheets of paper, printed with pictures and news reports.

*daily **newspapers***

next
adjective
1 coming immediately after.
*The **next** day.*
2 nearest.
*It's in the **next** room.*
next adverb

nib
nibs noun
the point at the end of an ink pen where the ink comes out.

nib

nibble
nibbles nibbling nibbled verb
to eat by taking quick, small bites out of something.

Nibbling some nuts.
nibble noun

nice
adjective
1 pleasant or delightful.
*A **nice** day.*
2 kind.
*He is a **nice** person.*
- comparisons **nicer nicest**

nickel
noun
a strong, silvery-white metal. Nickel is often used as a covering for metal objects because it doesn't rust easily.

nickel ore

nickname
nicknames *noun*
a shortened form of a name or an extra name that people may use instead of a person's proper name.
*She was so clever that she earned the **nickname** Brains.*

niece
nieces *noun*
the daughter of a person's brother, sister, brother-in-law, or sister-in-law.
■ say **neess**

night
nights *noun*
the time between sunset and sunrise, when the sky is dark.

■ opposite **day**

nightmare
nightmares *noun*
an unpleasant and frightening dream.

*A **nightmare** about a ghost.*

nimble
adjective
able to move quickly and easily.
Nimble fingers.

nitrogen
noun
a gas with no taste or smell. All living things contain nitrogen, and air is mainly made of nitrogen.
■ say **nite**-tro-jen

nobody
noun
no person.
Nobody came to the party.

nocturnal
adjective
active at night.

*Bats are **nocturnal** animals.*

nod
nods nodding nodded *verb*
to move your head up and down.
nod *noun*

noise
noises *noun*
any kind of sound, especially a sound that is too loud or unpleasant.

*He was making a lot of **noise**.*

noisy
adjective
making loud sounds.
noisily *adverb*

non-fiction
noun
information that is written about real events, things, and people.
■ opposite **fiction**

nonsense
noun
words that are silly or do not make sense.

noodle
noodles *noun*
a type of pasta that is made in long, flat, narrow strips.

noon
noun
12 o'clock midday.

noose
nooses *noun*
a circle of rope with a sliding knot. The loop tightens when the rope is pulled.

normal
adjective
usual or ordinary.
*Come at the **normal** time.*
normally *adverb*

north
noun
one of the four main compass directions. North is to your right when you are facing the setting Sun.

northern *adjective*

nose
noses *noun*
the part of your face that you smell and breathe with through two openings called nostrils.

nose
nostril

note
notes *noun*
1 a short, written message to remind you of something, or a short letter.

2 a piece of paper money.

3 a single sound in a piece of music.

nothing
noun
1 not anything.
*There's **nothing** to worry about.*
2 zero.

notice
notices noticing noticed *verb*
to see or be aware of something and pay attention to it.

*He **noticed** that he had a mark on his sleeve.*
noticeable *adjective*

a b c d e f g h i j k l m **n** o p q r s t u v w x y z

137

A B C D E F G H I J K L M **N** O P Q R S T U V W X Y Z

notice
notices *noun*
1 a written or printed sign that provides information.

Notices on a board.
2 attention.
Take no notice of them.

noun
nouns *noun*
a word that is used as a name. A noun can name a person, a place, a thing, or an idea.

novel
novels *noun*
a fictional written story in book form.

nowhere
adverb
not in any place.

His dog was nowhere to be seen.

nozzle
nozzles *noun*
a spout fitted to the open end of a pipe or hose, through which water or other liquids are sprayed.

nozzle

nuclear energy
noun
energy that is released by splitting the centre, or nucleus, of particular atoms.
■ say **new**-klee-er

nude
adjective
with no clothes on.

nudge
nudges nudging nudged *verb*
to push or poke someone gently to draw their attention to something.

nudge *noun*

nugget
nuggets *noun*
a lump of something, usually used for minerals.

A gold nugget.

nuisance
nuisances *noun*
an annoying person or thing.

The cat was being a nuisance.
■ say **new**-sans

numb
adjective
unable to feel anything.
His fingers were numb with cold.
■ say **num**

number
numbers *noun*
a figure used in counting that shows the quantity or total of something.

848

848 is a three-figure number.

numeral
numerals *noun*
a symbol that stands for a number. *VI is the Roman numeral for 6.*

numerous
adjective
very many.
Too numerous to count.

nun
nuns *noun*
a woman who lives in a religious community.

nurse
nurses *noun*
a person who is trained to care for and treat sick people, usually in a hospital.

nursery
nurseries *noun*
1 a room or building where young children are looked after.

nut
nuts *noun*
1 a tree fruit that consists of a seed, or kernel, surrounded by a hard shell.

almond   *kernel*

brazil nut   *kernel*

2 a small piece of metal with a hole in it that is screwed onto a bolt.

bolt

nut

nutmeg
nutmegs *noun*
the hard seed of the tropical, evergreen nutmeg tree. Nutmegs can be used as a spice in cooking.

nutrient
nutrients *noun*
a part of a food that gives living things what they need to be healthy or to grow.

2 a place where trees and plants are grown and sold.

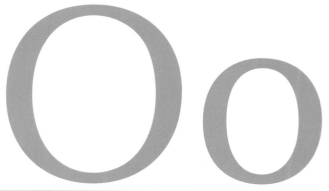

oak
oaks noun

a large deciduous tree that has fruit called acorns. Oak wood is often used for making furniture (see **tree** on page 223).

oak leaf

oar
oars noun

a long pole with a wide, flat end used for rowing a boat.
■ say **or**

oasis
oases noun

a place in the desert where there is water and where plants and trees can grow.

■ say oh-**ay**-sis

oats
noun

a type of cereal grown on farms. Oats are used to make food and to feed cattle, horses, and other animals.

obey
obeys obeying obeyed verb

to do something that someone tells or orders you to do.

*She taught the dog to **obey** her commands.*
■ opposite **disobey**
obedient adjective

object
objects noun

anything you can see or touch that isn't alive.
■ say **ob**-jekt

object
objects objecting objected verb

to dislike or disagree with something.
*He **objected** to people dropping litter in the street.*
■ say ob-**jekt**

oblong
adjective

longer than it is wide, with sides nearly parallel.

*An **oblong** box.*
oblong noun

observatory
observatories noun

a building from which people observe stars, the planets, and the weather, using powerful telescopes.

observe
observes observing observed verb

to watch something.
observation noun

obstacle
obstacles noun

a thing that blocks your way. *He had to jump over 10 **obstacles** to win the race.*

obstinate
adjective

difficult to persuade.

*He was very **obstinate** and refused to tidy up his bedroom.*
obstinately adverb

obstruct
obstructs obstructing obstructed verb

to block or to prevent something or someone from passing.

*She **obstructed** his path.*
obstruction noun

obvious
adjective

easy to see or understand.
■ say ob-vee-us
obviously adverb

occasion
occasions noun

1 a special event.

*The park opening was a grand **occasion.***
2 a time when something happens.
*I have flown in an aeroplane on two **occasions.***

occupation
occupations noun

the work that someone does to earn a living.

occupy
occupies occupying occupied verb

1 to keep someone busy.
*Sport **occupies** my time for most of the weekend.*
2 to take up a space or live in a place.
*The company **occupied** the top two floors of the building.*
3 to control a place by force.
*The army **occupied** the city.*

occur
occurs occurring occurred verb

1 to happen or exist.
*When did the problem **occur**?*
2 to come into your mind.
*That never **occurred** to me.*

a
b
c
d
e
f
g
h
i
j
k
l
m
n
o
p
q
r
s
t
u
v
w
x
y
z

ocean
oceans *noun*
a very large area of sea, usually separating continents.

Pacific Ocean

octagon
octagons *noun*
a flat shape with eight straight sides (see **shape** on page 182).

octopus
octopuses or octopi *noun*
a sea animal that does not have a backbone. Octopuses have eight arms, which they use for catching crabs, shellfish, and fish. They have good eyesight and are thought to have the ability to learn things.

odd
adjective
1 strange or unusual. *That's a very odd thing to do!*
■ comparisons **odder oddest**
2 not belonging to a pair or a set of things.

Wearing odd socks.
3 any number that cannot be divided exactly by two.
■ opposite **even**

odour
odours *noun*
a strong smell.

There was a strange odour coming from the dustbin.
■ say **oh-der**

offend
offends offending offended *verb*
1 to upset or annoy someone. **offensive** *adjective*
2 to break a law.

offer
offers offering offered *verb*
to ask someone if they would like something, or if you can do something for them.

He offered her some grapes.
offer *noun*

office
offices *noun*
a place where people organize and run a business.

official
adjective
properly approved by someone in charge.
■ say **o-fish-al**
officially *adverb*

often
adverb
many times.
I often go to school by bus.

oil
noun
1 a thick liquid that occurs naturally underground. Oil is used to make products such as fuel and plastics.
2 a greasy substance that is found in the seeds and fruits of some plants. This type of oil is often used for cooking.

oily *adjective*   *Sunflower oil.*

oil rig
oil rigs *noun*
a structure and machinery used for drilling into the ground in search of oil and gas. Some oil rigs are used at sea, while others are used on land.

oil slick
oil slicks *noun*
a patch of oil, usually spilt accidentally, that floats on the surface of the sea.

oil-tanker
oil-tankers *noun*
a ship that transports huge amounts of oil.

ointment
ointments *noun*
a substance that you put on your skin or on a wound to make it better.

old
adjective
1 having been in use for a long time.

An old teddy bear.
■ opposite **new**
2 having existed for a long time.
■ opposite **young**
■ comparisons **older oldest**

olive
olives *noun*
a small, oval fruit that grows in countries near the Mediterranean Sea. Olives are eaten in salads and crushed to make olive oil.

Olympic Games
noun
a sporting competition for athletes from countries all over the world, held every four years.

omit
omits omitting omitted *verb*
to leave something out, or not to do something. *His name was omitted from the list.*

onion
onions *noun*
a small, round root vegetable with a strong taste. Onions have a thin, papery skin with many layers inside.

only
adjective
without any others.
*He's the **only** person wearing green.*

only
adverb
1 just.

*There were **only** a few beads left in the box.*
2 no more than.
***Only** five of us went to the park.*

open
adjective
1 not closed or shut, so that people or things can go in and out.

***Open** car doors.*
■ opposite **shut**
2 with plenty of space, or not closed in.
***Open** fields.*

opera
operas *noun*
a musical play where the words are sung instead of spoken.

opera singer

operate
operates operating operated
verb
1 to work a piece of machinery.

*You must take care when **operating** machinery.*
2 to carry out surgery in a hospital.

operating *adjective*
operation *noun*

opinion
opinions *noun*
a person's belief or judgement about something.
*Who is the best football player, in your **opinion**?*

opponent
opponents *noun*
someone who is on the opposite side in a fight or competition.

*Chess **opponents**.*

opportunity
opportunities *noun*
a chance, or a suitable time to do something.
*He had the **opportunity** to go to Europe for a year.*

oppose
opposes opposing opposed *verb*
to argue or fight against someone or something.
*They **opposed** the decision to close the park.*
opposition *noun*

opposite
adjective
1 on the other side.

*He saw his friend on the **opposite** side of the river.*
2 completely different.
*Tall is the **opposite** of short.*
opposite *noun*

optician
opticians *noun*
a person whose job is to test peoples' sight and to sell spectacles and contact lenses.
■ say op-**tish**-un

optimistic
adjective
expecting or hoping that things will go well.
***Optimistic** about the future.*
■ opposite **pessimistic**
optimism *noun*

option
options *noun*
a choice.
*You have several **options**: you can travel by car, train, or plane.*
optional *adjective*

orange
oranges *noun*
1 a colour made by mixing red and yellow together.

orang-utan
orang-utans *noun*
a large ape that lives in tropical forests in Southeast Asia. Orang-utans eat mainly fruit, but also eat leaves, bark, and birds' eggs. They live in nests called platforms, which they build in trees.

■ say or-**rang**-a-tan

orbit
orbits orbiting orbited *verb*
to move around a planet, a moon, or the Sun in space.
*The Earth **orbits** the Sun.*
orbit *noun*

orchard
orchards *noun*
an area of land where fruit trees are grown.

*They were picking apples in the **orchard**.*

2 a juicy fruit with a tough skin.

A B C D E F G H I J K L M N O P Q R S T U V W X Y Z

orchestra

orchestras *noun*

a large group of musicians who play together.

■ say **or**-kes-tra

orchid

orchids *noun*

a type of plant with flowers that are an unusual shape.

■ say **or**-kid

order

orders *noun*

1 an instruction telling someone to do something.

*He gave them **orders** to stop.*

2 a request for something in a shop or restaurant.

order *verb*

3 a way that things are placed or arranged. *Alphabetical **order**.*

4 a peaceful, lawful state. *Law and **order**.*

ordinary

adjective

not different or unusual in any way.

*His sandwich was rather **ordinary**, but she had a special one.*

organ

organs *noun*

1 a musical instrument with a keyboard and large air pipes. The pipes make a noise when air is forced into them.

2 a part inside your body that does a particular job. Your heart is an organ.

organism

organisms *noun*

any living animal or plant.

organization

organizations *noun*

a group of people with common aims or business.

organize

organizes organizing organized *verb*

to arrange or plan something.

***Organizing** work into folders.*
organization *noun*

origin

origins *noun*

the beginning of something, or where something or someone comes from. *The pot was of Roman **origin**.*

■ say **o**-rij-in

original

adjective

earliest or first. *An **original** design.*

■ say or-**rij**-in-nal

ornament

ornaments *noun*

an object that is used as a decoration.

orphan

orphans *noun*

someone whose parents have died.

■ say **or**-fan

ostrich

ostriches *noun*

a tall bird from Africa that can run very fast, but cannot fly. Ostriches live in dry, open countryside and eat plants, fruit, insects, and small animals.

other

adjective

the remaining one, usually of two.

*She tried the **other** hat on.*

ought

verb

to do something because it is necessary or should be done. *You **ought** to be in bed.*

■ say ort

■ always used with another verb

out

adverb

1 away from a place or not in a place.

*The bird pulled the worm **out** with its beak.*

2 into view. *The sun came **out** from behind the cloud.*

■ opposite **in**

3 no longer lit. *Blow the candle **out**.*

outcome

outcomes *noun*

the result of something. *What was the **outcome** of the match?*

outdoors

adverb

not inside a building. *Shall we eat **outdoors** today?*

■ opposite **indoors**

outfit

outfits *noun*

a set of clothes worn for a particular occasion.

outgrow

outgrows outgrowing outgrew outgrown *verb*

to grow too big for something. *He had **outgrown** his clothes.*

outline

outlines *noun*

a line that shows the shape of something. ***Outline** of a leaf.*

outside

outsides *noun*

a part of something that faces out. *They painted the **outside** of the house green.*
outside *adverb*

oval

ovals noun

a flat, round shape like a zero.

oval adjective

oven

ovens noun

a space for cooking food, heating, or drying things, usually inside a stove.

over

preposition

above or across.
*She threw the ball **over** the wall.*

overboard

adverb

over the side of a ship or boat.

*The fishermen threw their nets **overboard**.*

overgrown

adjective

covered in plants that have been left to grow wild.
*An **overgrown** garden.*

overhear

overhears overhearing overheard verb

to hear people talking about things accidently.

overlap

overlaps overlapping overlapped verb

to cover the edge of something.
*Fish scales **overlap** each other.*

overtake

overtakes overtaking overtaken overtook verb

to catch up with and pass by.
*The car **overtook** the lorry.*

owe

owes owing owed verb

to have to pay back money or something else you have borrowed.
*You **owe** me £5.*

owl

owls noun

a nocturnal bird that hunts for mice, and other small animals. Owls have good hearing and can see well in the dark. They can turn their heads around to see behind them.

own

owns owning owned verb

to have something that belongs to you.

ox

oxen noun

a bull used for carrying or pulling things.
*A zebu is a type of **ox**.*

oxygen

noun

a gas found in air and water. You cannot see, smell, or taste oxygen. All living things need oxygen in order to live.

■ say **ox**-i-jen

oyster

oysters noun

a shellfish that lives in shallow water. Oysters feed on tiny bits of food that they filter through the edge of their shells.

ozone layer

noun

a layer of ozone gas in Earth's atmosphere that protects Earth from the more harmful rays of the Sun.

Pp

pack

packs packing packed verb

to put things into a suitcase, box, or other container.

■ opposite **unpack**
2 to fit in as much as possible.
*The hall was **packed** with people.*

pack

packs noun

1 a bundle that you carry.
2 a group of similar animals or objects.
Pack of cards.

package

packages noun

a wrapped parcel or bundle.

pad

pads noun

1 a pile of sheets of paper joined at one end.
2 a thick piece of soft material.
3 the soft, fleshy parts on an animal's paw.
4 a place where helicopters land and take off.

paddle

paddles noun

a pole with a flat blade at one or both ends. You hold the paddle and use it to move a boat or canoe through water (see **boat** on page 31).

paddle

paddles paddling paddled verb

1 to move a boat through water using a paddle.

2 to walk around in shallow water.

paddock

paddocks noun

a fenced area of grass, often where animals are kept.

padlock

padlocks noun

a type of portable lock often used on gates.

page

pages noun

one side of a single piece of paper forming part of a book, newspaper, or magazine.

a b c d e f g h i j k l m n o p q r s t u v w x y z

paid
from the verb **to pay**
*I **paid** for the cinema tickets.*

pail
pails *noun*
a bucket, usually made of wood or metal.

pain
pains *noun*
suffering caused by an injury, disease, or sadness.
painful *adjective*

paint
paints *noun*
a coloured liquid used for decorating or for making pictures.

*paint*brush

paint
paints painting painted *verb*
to cover a surface with colour, either for decoration or to create a picture.

painting
paintings *noun*
a painted picture.

pair
pairs *noun*
a set of two things that match each other, or belong together.
*A **pair** of socks.*

palace
palaces *noun*
a large, grand home belonging to an important person.

pale
adjective
of faint colour, almost white.
*He painted the hall **pale** blue.*
■ comparisons **paler palest**

palm
palms *noun*
1 the flat, middle part on the inside of your hand.

2 a tree without branches that grows in hot regions. Palms have long leaves that grow from the top of the trunk (see **tree** on page 223).

pan
pans *noun*
a metal container with a handle, used for cooking.

pancake
pancakes *noun*
a flat, fried cake made of eggs, flour, and milk.

panda
pandas *noun*
a large, bear-like mammal that lives in the mountain forests of China. Pandas mainly eat bamboo shoots, but sometimes eat other plants and small animals.

panic
panics panicking panicked *verb*
to lose control suddenly because you are frightened or do not know what to do.
*The chickens **panicked** when they saw the fox.*
panic *noun*

pant
pants panting panted *verb*
to breathe quickly through your mouth because you are hot or out of breath.

panther
panthers *noun*
a black leopard.

pantomime
pantomimes *noun*
a traditional children's play with music, songs, and dancing.

paper
papers *noun*
a material made from wood, and mainly used for writing, printing, and drawing on.

parachute
parachutes *noun*
an apparatus made of material, which helps people and objects fall to the ground safely from an aircraft.

■ say **pa**-ra-shoot

parade
parades *noun*
a procession of people, animals, or vehicles, either for display or inspection.

paragraph
paragraphs *noun*
a section in a piece of writing. Paragraphs start on a new line.

parallel
adjective
being side by side and at the same distance from each other.

parallel lines

paralyse
paralyses paralysing paralysed *verb*
to be unable to move a part of the body because of an injury or disease.
paralysis *noun*

parcel
parcels *noun*
an object wrapped up with paper.

parent
parents *noun*
a father or mother.

park
parks *noun*
an area of grass and trees, that the public may use.

park
parks parking parked *verb*
to drive a vehicle into a position where it can be left.

parliament
parliaments *noun*
a group of people who have been elected to govern and make the laws of their nation.
■ say **par**-li-ment

parrot
parrots *noun*
a large bird that lives in tropical forests and eats fruit and seeds. Parrots are often kept as pets. In the wild, parrots live in large flocks.

part
parts *noun*
1 a piece of something.

The parts of an electric guitar.
2 a role in a play.

She played the part of the queen in the play.

particular
adjective
1 a specific one.
Which particular one do you mean?
2 special, or careful.
Take particular care of that!

partner
partners *noun*
one of a pair of people who do something together, such as dancing or playing a game.
A business partner.

party
parties *noun*
1 a group of people invited to celebrate a special occasion.
2 an organized group of people who have the same political beliefs.

pass
passes passing passed *verb*
1 to go by someone or something.
2 to give something to someone with your hand.

He passed the bowl to her.
3 to be successful in an examination.

passenger
passengers *noun*
someone travelling in or on a vehicle that is controlled by another person.

motorcycle passenger

passport
passports *noun*
an official certificate that you need for travelling to other countries.

past
noun
the time before now.
past *adjective*

past
adverb
by or beyond.
He walked past the shop.

pasta
noun
an Italian food, usually made from wheat flour and water.

Different shapes of pasta.

paste
pastes *noun*
1 a soft, moist, or sticky substance.
2 a type of glue made of flour and water.

pasteurize
pasteurizes pasteurizing pasteurized *verb*
to heat and then cool something to kill the bacteria in it. Milk is usually pasteurized.
■ say **past**-yoor-ize

pastry
pastries *noun*
a dough made of flour, water, and fat that is baked to make small cakes called pastries, or cases for pies and tarts.

cheese pastries

pasture
pastures *noun*
a field of grass where animals graze.

patch
patches *noun*
1 a small piece of material that is placed over a hole to repair it.

patch

2 a small area of something.
A patch of grass.

path
paths *noun*
a narrow track for walking along, or a route.

patient
adjective
able to wait calmly.
■ say **pay**-shunt
patience *noun*

patient
patients *noun*
a person being treated by a doctor, nurse, or dentist.

patrol
patrols patrolling patrolled *verb*
to guard a place by moving around it and checking it regularly.
patrol *noun*

A B C D E F G H I J K L M N O P Q R S T U V W X Y Z

pattern
patterns noun
1 a decorative shape or design.

patterned adjective

2 a guide for making things, such as toys or clothes.

teddy bear **pattern**

pause
pauses pausing paused verb
to stop what you are doing for a short time.
■ say **porz**
pause noun

pavement
pavements noun
a hard path for pedestrians usually at the side of a road.

paw
paws noun
a soft, padded animal foot with claws or nails.

cat's **paw**

pay
pays paying paid verb
to give money in return for something.
payment noun

pea
peas noun
a small, round, sweet-tasting vegetable that grows in a pod.

pea pod

peace
noun
a period of quietness and calm.
peaceful adjective

peach
peaches noun
a round fruit with a velvety skin and a large stone inside.

peacock
peacocks noun
a large bird that is also called a peafowl. Peacocks live in forests in Africa and India and eat insects, grains, plants, and small animals. The males are known for their beautiful tail-feathers (see **bird** on page 28).

peak
peaks noun
the pointed top of a mountain.

peanut
peanuts noun
a small, edible nut that grows in pods under the ground.

pear
pears noun
a pale green or brown fruit with a thin skin, pale, juicy flesh, and pips.

■ rhymes with **hair**

pearl
pearls noun
a smooth, shiny, rounded object that grows inside an oyster. Pearls are often used for making jewellery.

pearl

■ say **purl**

pebble
pebbles noun
a small, smooth, rounded stone.

peck
pecks pecking pecked verb
to bite or strike with a beak.

The bird **pecked** *at the food.*

peculiar
adjective
strange, odd, or queer.

pedal
pedals noun
a lever that you work with your foot to move or control something (see **transport** on page 221).

pedestrian
pedestrians noun
a person travelling on foot.

peel
peels peeling peeled verb
to remove or strip something off.

Peeling a banana.

peep
peeps peeping peeped verb
to look quickly and secretly at something or someone.

peer
peers peering peered verb
to look closely at something or someone.

peg
pegs noun
a wooden or plastic object used to hang clothes on a washing-line.

pelican
pelicans noun
a large bird that lives in or near water in warm regions. It has a pouch beneath its bill which it uses to catch and hold fish.

pen
pens *noun*
1 a tool filled with ink, used for writing.

2 a small area with a fence, for keeping animals in. *A pig **pen**.*

penalty
penalties *noun*
a fine or a punishment for breaking a law or rule, or for breaking a rule during a sports game.
*The **penalty** for cheating in an exam is severe.*

pencil
pencils *noun*
a tool with grey or coloured graphite inside, used for writing and drawing.

penguin
penguins *noun*
a large, fish-eating seabird found in the cold seas of the southern hemisphere. Penguins cannot fly, but are good underwater swimmers (see **bird** on page 28).

penknife
penknives *noun*
a small knife that folds into a case.

pentagon
pentagons *noun*
a flat shape with five sides of equal length (see **shape** on page 182).

people
noun
1 human beings in general.
2 members of a particular race or nation.

pepper
peppers *noun*
1 the dried berries of the pepper plant used to flavour foods.

pepper**corns*   *ground **pepper

2 a bright green, yellow, orange, or red vegetable (see **vegetable** on page 233).

per cent
noun
a fraction of a whole written as part of 100. 50 per cent means 50 parts of 100. Per cent is also written as percentage. The sign for per cent is %.

*27% (**per cent**) of 100 is 27.*

perch
perches perching perched *verb*
to sit on a branch or other place like a bird.

***Perching** on a branch.*
perch *noun*

perfect
adjective
having nothing wrong, or just right.
perfectly *adverb*

perform
performs performing performed *verb*
to put on a show for other people.

Performing in the street.
performance *noun*

perfume
perfumes *noun*
1 a sweet-smelling liquid that you put on your skin.

2 any sweet or pleasant smell.

perhaps
adverb
maybe or possibly.

perimeter
perimeters *noun*
the outer edge or boundary of something.
■ say per-**rim**-it-ter

period
periods *noun*
a length or portion of time.
*A fortnight is a **period** of two weeks.*

permanent
adjective
lasting a long time or for ever.
*A **permanent** job.*
■ opposite **temporary**

permission
noun
the act of allowing someone to do something.

*He put his hand up to ask for **permission** to leave the room.*
permit *verb*

perpendicular
adjective
crossing at or forming a right angle.
■ say pur-pen-**dik**-yoo-lar

person
persons or **people** *noun*
a human being.

personal
adjective
belonging to, or meant for one person.

Personal belongings.

personality
personalities *noun*
1 your character or the sort of person you are.
*My sister has a friendly **personality**.*
2 someone famous.
*A sports **personality**.*

persuade
persuades persuading persuaded *verb*
to make someone believe or do something by giving good reasons.
*She **persuaded** me to go skiing with her.*
persuasion *noun*
■ say pur-**swade**

pest
pests *noun*
an insect or animal that is harmful or a nuisance.

Colorado beetle

a b c d e f g h i j k l m n o p q r s t u v w x y z

pet
pets *noun*
a tame animal that is kept because it is loved rather than because it is useful. Pets are often kept in the home.

paw

Siamese cat

seed hopper

cere

green budgerigar

male (cock)

female (hen)

zebra finches

identity tag

Jack Russell puppy

scut

giant Flemish rabbit

Abyssinian guinea pig

Peruvian guinea pig

grooming brush

tortoiseshell-and-white coat

rumpy

Manx cat

golden retriever

golden coat

Persian cat

water bottle

ear tuft

Angora rabbit

self golden guinea pig

wiry coat

fox terrier

lead

sleek coat

clipping scissors

fur

whiskers

tabby coat

dew claw

whippet

lop-eared French rabbit

shorthaired cat

petal

petals *noun*

the coloured outer parts of a flower that are not green (see **plant** on page 151).

petrol

noun

a liquid fuel made from oil, used for powering vehicles.

photocopy

photocopies *noun*

an exact copy of words or pictures, made by a machine.

photocopy *verb*

photograph

photographs *noun*

a picture made using a camera. Photograph can be shortened to photo.

*Taking a **photograph**.*

photographer

photographers *noun*

a person who takes photographs.

physical

adjective

to do with the body. ***Physical** exercise.*

■ say **fiz**-i-kal

pianist

pianists *noun*

a person who plays the piano.

■ say **pee**-an-ist

piano

pianos *noun*

a large, stringed, musical instrument with black and white keys. Different musical notes are produced by pressing the keys.

*grand **piano***

pick

picks picking picked *verb*

1 to choose something.

*She asked him to **pick** a card.*
2 to remove a flower, fruit, or leaf from a plant.

Picking a flower.

picnic

picnics *noun*

a meal that is eaten in the open air, away from home.

picnic *verb*

picture

pictures *noun*

an image of something, such as a painting or a photograph.

pie

pies *noun*

a pastry case filled with vegetables, meat, fish, or fruit and baked in an oven.

*apple **pie***

piece

pieces *noun*

a bit or a part of something.

*A **piece** of cheese.*

pier

piers *noun*

a long platform built out into the sea for people to walk along or to tie boats to.

pig

pigs *noun*

an animal with a blunt snout and a curly tail, which is kept on farms to provide meat, such as pork, ham, and bacon.

*sow (female **pig**)*   *piglets*

pigeon

pigeons *noun*

a bird that is common in the town and countryside. Pigeons mainly eat berries, fruits, and seeds. Some pigeons can be trained to deliver messages.

■ say **pij**-in

pigment

pigments *noun*

1 a coloured powder that is mixed with other substances to make paint.

windsor red   cadmium yellow

2 the substance that gives colouring to the skin of animals and vegetables.

pile

piles *noun*

a group of things resting or lying one on top of the other.

pill

pills *noun*

a small piece of medicine that is swallowed whole.

a b c d e f g h i j k l m n o p q r s t u v w x y z

A B C D E F G H I J K L M N O P Q R S T U V W X Y Z

pillow
pillows *noun*
a soft pad for resting your
head on in bed.

pilot
pilots *noun*
a person who controls and
flies an aircraft.

pin
pins *noun*
a small piece of metal
with a sharp point at one
end, used to fasten pieces
of cloth together.

pin cushion

pinch
pinches pinching pinched *verb*
to squeeze someone's skin
between your finger
and thumb.

pine
pines *noun*
an evergreen
tree that has
needle-shaped
leaves and
produces cones.

Arolla pine

pineapple
pineapples *noun*
a tropical fruit with a tough,
scaly skin and a sprout of
spiky, green leaves at the top
(see **fruit** on page 85).

pink
noun
a colour made by
mixing red and
white together.

pipe
pipes *noun*
a tube through which liquids
and gases can flow.

pipeline

pirate
pirates *noun*
someone who
attacks and
robs ships or
boats at sea.

pit
pits *noun*
1 a deep hole in the ground.
2 a coal mine.

pitch
pitches *noun*
1 an area where some games
or sports are played.
*We went to the cricket **pitch** to
watch the game.*
2 how high or low a musical
note, a musical instrument,
or a human voice is.

pitiful
adjective
making you feel sad or
full of pity.
*A **pitiful** sight.*

pity
noun
a feeling of sadness for
someone because they are
unhappy or in pain.
pity *verb*

pizza
pizzas *noun*
a round, flat piece of dough
with tomato, cheese, and
other foods on top, which
is baked in an oven.

■ say **peet**-sa

place
places *noun*
1 a particular area.
2 a position in
a competition
or race.

*They won the first, second, and
third **places** in the race.*

place
places placing placed *verb*
to put something in
a position.
*He **placed** the vase in
the centre of the table.*

plain
adjective
1 ordinary, or not fancy.
*Her dress was very **plain**.*
2 understandable or clear.
*His meaning was **plain**.*

plain
plains *noun*
a large area of flat land.

plan
plans *noun*
a map or drawing of
an area, such as a room,
building, or town.

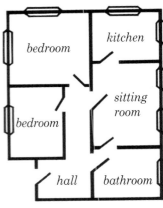

*A **plan** of a flat.*

plan
plans planning planned *verb*
to decide how you are
going to do something.
plan *noun*

planet
planets *noun*
one of the huge spheres of
rock and gas that revolve
around the Sun. The eight
planets in our solar system
are Mercury, Venus, Earth,
Mars, Jupiter, Saturn,
Uranus, and Neptune (see
universe on page 229).

plant
plants planting planted *verb*
to put a seed,
bulb, or plant
into the soil
so that it
will grow.

***Planting** a window box.*

plant

plants *noun*

a living thing that cannot move around like animals do, and that makes its own food. Some plants grow in the ground, while others grow in water. Plants usually have a stem, leaves, flowers, and roots.

capsule

poppy seedheads

frond

pinna

fern

spine (leaf)

stigma

stamen

style

petal

sepal

pedicel (flower stalk)

flower bud

stem

leaf

hibiscus

flower head

spike

bract

thistle

magnified pollen grains

bulb

root

tulip

frond

green seaweed

rock

bract

calla lily

pitcher

flower

stalk

stalk

capsule

moss

stalk

lily pad

waterlily

cactus

pitcher **plant**

plaster
plasters *noun*

1 a powder mixed with water that is spread on walls and ceilings to make them smooth.
2 a small piece of sticky material that is put over a wound to keep it clean.

plastic
plastics *noun*

a light, manufactured material made from chemicals. Many types of plastic can be heated up and moulded into different shapes and products.

plastic duck

plate
plates *noun*

a flat dish that is used for serving food on.

dinner plate

plateau
plateaus or **plateaux** *noun*

a high, wide, flat area of ground.

■ say **plat**-oh

platform
platforms *noun*

1 the flat, raised area at a station where passengers get on and off trains.
2 a flat, raised area in a hall where speakers or performers stand so they can be seen.

platypus
platypuses or **platypi** *noun*

an Australian mammal with a bill like a duck's, webbed feet, and a long, flat tail. Platypuses live in water and, unusually for a mammal, lay eggs. They eat plants, worms, insects, and water animals.

■ say **plat**-ee-pus

play
plays playing played *verb*

1 to take part in a game, usually with other people.

Playing with a balloon.
2 to make music on a musical instrument.

Playing a concertina.
3 to act a part.
*She **played** the fairy.*
play *noun*

pleasant
adjective

enjoyable or well-liked.
*A **pleasant** evening.*

■ opposite **unpleasant**

please
interjection

a word used when you ask for something politely.

pleasure
pleasures *noun*

enjoyment or satisfaction.

■ say **plezh**-er

pleat
pleats *noun*

a fold that is pressed or sewn into cloth.

pleat

pleat *verb*

plenty
noun

a large amount of something. *Do you want some sweets? I've got **plenty**.*
plentiful *adjective*

plot
plots plotting plotted *verb*

to make a secret plan. *The thieves **plotted** to rob the bank.*
plot *noun*

plot
plots *noun*

1 the story of a book, play, or film.
*The book has a complicated **plot**.*
2 a small piece of ground.

plough
ploughs *noun*

a farm tool that has large blades for cutting and turning the soil. Ploughs are used to prepare the soil for planting crops and are pulled by a tractor or an animal.

plough

■ rhymes with **now**
plough *verb*

plug
plugs *noun*

1 a circular piece of plastic or other material used to keep water in a bath or sink.
2 an electrical device that connects the wire from a piece of electrical equipment to a source of electricity.

plum
plums *noun*

a fruit that grows on trees, and has a smooth, thin skin and soft, juicy flesh.

plumber
plumbers *noun*

a person who fits water and heating pipes into buildings and repairs them when they go wrong.

plunge
plunges plunging plunged *verb*
to fall or dive very quickly.

The bridge broke in two and **plunged** *into the river.*
plunge *noun*

plural
plurals *noun*
a word used to describe two or more things or people.
The **plural** *of baby is babies.*

plus
preposition
added to.
4 **plus** *2 equals 6.*
■ opposite **minus**

plus
pluses *noun*
a symbol in mathematics that means add.

pocket
pockets *noun*
a small pouch or fold sewn into clothing or a bag where you can put your belongings.

pocket

pod
pods *noun*
a long seed-case that holds the seeds of some plants.

bean **pod**

poem
poems *noun*
a piece of writing, set out in lines which sometimes rhyme. Poems describe things in a thoughtful and imaginative way.

poet
poets *noun*
a person who writes poetry.

poetry
noun
a general name for poems.

point
points *noun*
1 the sharp end of an object.

Each star has six **points**.
2 a score in a game or competition.
How many **points** *did you get?*
3 the main aim or purpose.
What's the **point** *of this story?*
4 the level, time, or place at which something happens.
The freezing **point** *of water is 0°C.*
5 a dot or speck.

point
points pointing pointed *verb*
to show where something is with your finger.

poison
poisons *noun*
a substance that can kill or harm animals or plants.
poison arrow frog

A deadly **poison** *can be made from this frog's skin.*
poisonous *adjective*

poke
pokes poking poked *verb*
to push something with a stick, your finger, or another pointed object.

He **poked** *the fire with a stick.*

polar bear
polar bears *noun*
a large mammal that lives in Arctic regions. Polar bears eat animals such as seals and fish. Their white fur camouflages them against the snow and ice where they live.

pole
poles *noun*
1 a long, rounded rod made from wood, metal, or plastic.

A row of flag **poles**.

police
noun
an organization that is responsible for keeping law and order and making sure that a country's laws are not broken.

polish
polishes polishing polished *verb*
to rub something so that it shines.

Polishing *shoes.*

polish
polishes *noun*
a substance that is rubbed into something to make it shine.

furniture **polish**

polite
adjective
well-mannered and pleasant to other people.
■ opposite **rude**
politely *adverb*

2 the most northern and southern end of an imaginary line, or axis, that passes through Earth's centre.
North **Pole**

South **Pole**
3 either end of a magnet.

a b c d e f g h i j k l m n o p q r s t u v w x y z

153

A B C D E F G H I J K L M N O P Q R S T U V W X Y Z

politics

noun

the work of government.
political *adjective*

pollen

noun

a fine, yellow powder found in the middle of flowers. Pollen is made by the male parts of a flower.

pollinate

pollinates pollinating pollinated
verb

to transfer pollen from the male to the female parts of a plant so that a seed can grow.

*The bee **pollinated** the flower.*

pollute

pollutes polluting polluted *verb*
to make a thing or a place dirty, unclean, or harmful.
*Chemicals from the factory **polluted** the river.*
pollution *noun*

pond

ponds *noun*

an area of fresh water that is smaller than a lake.

*duck **pond***

pony

ponies *noun*

a small horse (see **horse** on page 102).

pool

pools *noun*

a small area of water, especially one that is made for people to swim in.

*swimming **pool***

poor

adjective

1 not having enough money to live on.
*The family was very **poor**.*
■ opposite **rich**
2 of low or bad quality.
*The house was in a **poor** condition.*
3 unfortunate.
*The **poor** child was soaking wet.*
poor *noun*

popcorn

noun

a snack made by heating grains from the maize plant until they burst open and puff up.

poppy

poppies *noun*

a wild flower with delicate, petals. When the flowers die, they leave behind a round seed-head (see **plant** on page 151).

popular

adjective

liked by many people.

population

populations *noun*

all the people living in a district or country.

porch

porches *noun*

a shelter built around the entrance to a building.

porcupine

porcupines *noun*

a large rodent that is covered in lots of sharp spines called quills. A porcupine can raise the quills to protect itself from its enemies. Porcupines eat bark, buds, twigs, and leaves.

pork

noun

meat from a pig.

porpoise

porpoises *noun*

a sea mammal that belongs to the whale family. Porpoises eat shrimp, fish, squid, and other sea animals.

■ say **por**-pus

port

ports *noun*

a place on a coast or river, where ships load and unload.

portable

adjective

easily carried or moved about.

portable
DVD player

portion

portions *noun*

a part or share of something.

*A **portion** of fish pie.*

portrait

portraits *noun*

a picture of a person or animal, especially their face.

pose

poses posing posed *verb*

to arrange yourself or a thing in a particular position, especially for a painting or a photograph.
pose *noun*

position

positions *noun*

1 the way in which a person or thing is placed or arranged.
*A sitting **position**.*
2 a place or location.
*He found the **position** of his house on the map.*

positive
adjective
definite or certain.
■ opposite **negative**

possess
possesses possessing possessed
verb
to own or have something.
possession *noun*

possible
adjective
able to be done or happen.
*Is it **possible** to walk there?*
■ opposite **impossible**
possibly *adverb*

post
noun
1 the delivery of letters and other mail, or the letters themselves.
2 an upright pole of wood, stone, or metal set in the ground.

gate-**post**

3 a job or duty and the place where it is done.

poster
posters *noun*
a large notice or picture that is displayed on a wall as an advert or for decoration.

post office
post offices *noun*
a place where you go to buy stamps, and to send letters and parcels.

postpone
postpones postponing postponed *verb*
to put something off until later.
*The game was **postponed** because of the rain.*

posy
posies *noun*
a small bunch of flowers.

pot
pots *noun*
a container with high sides.

coffee **pot**

potato
potatoes *noun*
a common root vegetable that can be boiled, roasted, fried, or baked.

pottery
noun
a general name for containers and ornaments made from clay, then baked in a kiln.
*kitchen **pottery***

pouch
pouches *noun*
1 a small, open bag or sack that is used for carrying things like money.
2 a part of the body that is shaped like a bag or pocket (see **mammal** on page 124).

pounce
pounces pouncing pounced *verb*
to spring forward suddenly and grab hold of something.

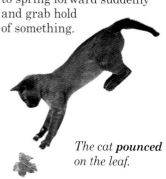
*The cat **pounced** on the leaf.*

pour
pours pouring poured *verb*
to tip a container up so that its contents flow out.

poverty
noun
the situation of not having enough money to live on.
*The family lived in **poverty**.*

powder
noun
a mass of very fine, dry grains of a substance.

washing **powder**

power
powers *noun*
1 the ability to do something.
2 the ability to control what someone else does.
3 energy or force.

*Batteries provide the **power** for this torch.*
■ rhymes with **our**

practical
adjective
1 sensible and useful.
*Gloves are very **practical** in cold weather.*
■ opposite **impractical**
2 having practice at doing something.
*You need **practical** experience for this job.*

practise
practises practising practised *verb*
to do something over and over again in order to be good at it.

***Practising** the piano.*
practice *noun*

a b c d e f g h i j k l m n o p q r s t u v w x y z

praise

praises praising praised *verb*
to tell someone that what they have done is very good.
praise *noun*

pray

prays praying prayed *verb*
to talk to a god, prophet, or saint.
prayer *noun*

precaution

precautions *noun*
care or action taken in advance to prevent something from happening.
*Locks are a **precaution** against theft.*

■ say pri-**kor**-shun

precious

adjective
very valuable or special to someone.

*The ring was very **precious**.*
■ say **presh**-us

precise

adjective
exact or accurate.

*Stopwatches measure the **precise** time.*
■ say pri-**sise**

predict

predicts predicting predicted *verb*
to say what is going to happen in the future.
prediction *noun*

preen

preens preening preened *verb*
to clean and arrange feathers with the beak. Birds preen themselves.

prefer

prefers preferring preferred *verb*
to like something or someone better than another.

*She pointed to the pair of skates she **preferred**.*
preferable *adjective*

pregnant

adjective
expecting a baby.
pregnancy *noun*

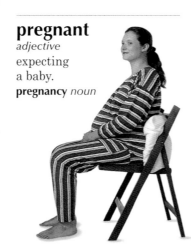

prehistoric

adjective
belonging to the time before any records were written.

prejudice

prejudices *noun*
a strong feeling about something, which has been formed unfairly or before all the facts are known.
■ say pre-joo-dis

prepare

prepares preparing prepared *verb*
to make something or yourself ready.

Preparing sandwiches for lunch.

preposition

prepositions *noun*
a word that shows how one person or thing relates to another.
*The bird was **on** the chair **in** the garden.*

prescription

prescriptions *noun*
an order for medicine written by a doctor.

present

noun
1 the time now.
*The story takes place in the **present**.*
present *adjective*
2 a gift to someone.

■ say **prez**-ent

present

presents presenting presented *verb*
to award or give something to someone.
*The judge **presented** the rider with a cup.*
■ say pri-**zent**

preserve

preserves preserving preserved *verb*
1 to keep something the way it is.
2 to keep food so that it lasts.
*Fruit **preserved** in a jar.*

press

presses pressing pressed *verb*
to squeeze or push something down, often in order to flatten it.

Pressing flowers.

pretend

pretends pretending pretended *verb*
1 to try to make people believe something that isn't true.
2 to believe something for fun.

*He **pretended** to be a cowboy.*
pretence *noun*

pretty

adjective
nice to look at.
■ comparisons **prettier prettiest**

prevent
prevents preventing prevented
verb
to stop something
from happening.
*The barrier **prevented** anyone
from falling down the hole.*
prevention *noun*

previous
adjective
happening or existing before.
*The **previous** day.*
■ say **pree**-vee-us

prey
noun
creatures that are hunted
and eaten by other animals.

*The owl swooped
down on its **prey**.*
■ say **pray**
prey *verb*

price
prices *noun*
the amount of money needed
to buy something.

prickly
adjective
having many
little sharp
points or
needles.

*A **prickly** cactus.*
■ comparisons **pricklier**
prickliest
prick *verb*

priest
priests *noun*
a person who is trained
to lead religious services.

prince / princess
princes / princesses *noun*
a son or daughter of a king
or queen. The wife of a prince
is also a princess.
■ **prince** is male and **princess**
is female

principle
principles *noun*
a general rule, belief, or truth.
*Scientific **principles**.*

print
prints printing printed *verb*
1 to write the letters of words
separately, rather than
joining them up.

2 to put words, pictures,
or patterns onto paper,
using paint or ink,
and printing blocks.

Printing a picture.
printed *adjective*

printer
noun
a machine that prints on
paper, usually linked to
a computer.

prison
prisons *noun*
a secure place in which
criminals are kept
as punishment.

private
adjective
belonging only to one person
or a few people, or not open
to the public.
*My diary is **private**.*
■ say **pry**-vit
privately *adverb*

prize
prizes *noun*
a reward
for winning
something.

*The **prize** was a silver cup.*

probable
adjective
likely to happen.
probably *adverb*

problem
problems *noun*
something that is difficult to
do or hard to understand.

process
processes *noun*
the method of making or
doing something.
■ say **proh**-sess

procession
processions *noun*
a line of people or vehicles
following each other.

*A **procession** of musicians.*

prod
prods prodding prodded *verb*
to poke or push something,
often with something sharp.

produce
produces producing produced
verb
1 to make something happen.
*The magician **produced**
a rabbit out of his hat.*
2 to make, grow, manufacture,
or create something.

*The orange trees **produced**
a large crop of fruit this year.*
■ say pro-**juce**
product *noun*
production *noun*

produce
noun
things that
are grown
or made.

*farm **produce***
■ say **prod**-yoos

profession
professions *noun*
1 a job or occupation where
special knowledge of
a subject is needed.
2 all the people who do such
a job.
*The medical **profession**.*

professional
adjective
1 having to do with
a profession.
*He took **professional** advice.*
2 earning a living from
an occupation that is not
usually thought of as a job.
*A **professional** footballer.*

a b c d e f g h i j k l m n o **p** q r s t u v w x y z

profile

profile
profiles *noun*
the side view of a face or object.

profit
profits *noun*
the extra money made when something is sold for more than it cost to make or buy.
- opposite **loss**
profitable *adjective*

program
programs *noun*
a set of instructions that tells a computer how to do something.

programme
programmes *noun*
1 a television or radio show.
2 a list of planned events.
3 a small book of information about a play or concert.

progress
noun
the process of moving forwards or improving.

*She made slow **progress** through the swamp.*
progress *verb*

prohibit
prohibits prohibiting prohibited *verb*
to ban, or to forbid someone to do something.

*Smoking is **prohibited**.*

project
projects *noun*
a piece of work involving research and study of a particular subject.

*He is doing a **project** on plants.*
- say pro-**jekt**

project
projects projecting projected *verb*
to stick out or throw outwards.

*The rock **projected** over the valley.*
- say pro-**jekt**

promise
promises promising promised *verb*
to say, and mean that you will, or will not, do something.
promise *noun*

promotion
promotions *noun*
1 a campaign to improve the sale of a product or event by advertising it.

*The **promotion** for a new yoghurt.*
2 a change to a more important job or position.
promote verb

prompt
prompts prompting prompted *verb*
to encourage someone to do or say something.

prompt
adjective
on time, or without delay.

*A **prompt** delivery.*

pronoun
pronouns *noun*
a word such as "he" or "she" that is used in a sentence to replace a noun.
*Jane was ill today, so **she** didn't go to school.*

pronunciation
pronunciations *noun*
the way a word is said.
- say pro-nun-see-**ay**-shun
pronounce *verb*

proof
noun
a thing or happening that shows something is true.

*The footprint was **proof** that someone had been there.*

propeller
propellers *noun*
a device with revolving blades. Propellers spin round to move a boat through the water, or to power an aeroplane through the air (see **boat** on page 31 and **transport** on page 221).

proper
adjective
suitable and correct.

*This is the **proper** way to hit a golf ball so that it rolls along the ground.*
properly *adverb*

property
noun
1 the things that belong to a person.
2 a general name for the buildings and land owned by someone.

prosecute
prosecutes prosecuting prosecuted *verb*
to accuse someone of a crime in a law court.
- say **pros**-i-kyoot
prosecution *noun*

protect
protects protecting protected *verb*
to keep someone or something from being harmed.

*Gardening gloves **protect** your hands from thorns.*
protection *noun*

158

protest
protests protesting protested *verb*

to say very clearly that you disagree with something.

*They **protested** against the building of a new road.*
■ say pro-**test**
protest *noun*

proud
adjective
feeling very pleased or satisfied.

*She was **proud** of her new outfit.*
■ say **prowd**
proudly *adverb*

prove
proves proving proved *verb*
to show that something is true.
■ say **proov**

proverb
proverbs *noun*
a short common saying that comments on life.
*"Many hands make light work" is a **proverb**.*

provide
provides providing provided *verb*
to supply something that is useful or needed.

*The runners were **provided** with drinks along the route.*

prowl
prowls prowling prowled *verb*
to move around quietly while searching for something.

*The tiger **prowled** around the tree.*

public
adjective
open to everybody.

publish
publishes publishing published *verb*
to produce and print a book, newspaper, or magazine.

puddle
puddles *noun*
a shallow pool of rain-water or other liquid on the ground.

puff
puffs *noun*
a small, sudden gust of smoke, air or breath.

*a **puff** of smoke*

pull
pulls pulling pulled *verb*
to move something with force towards you or in the same direction as you are going.

*Pulling** on a rope.*

pulley
pulleys *noun*
a device made of a wheel with a rope or a chain round it that is used for lifting heavy objects.

pulp
noun
the soft, inside part of a plant, particularly fruits (see **fruit** on page 85).

pulse
pulses *noun*
the regular sound of your blood as the heart pumps it through your body.

*Feeling her **pulse**.*

pump
pumps pumping pumped *verb*
to fill or inflate something by forcing air or liquids into it.

***Pumping** up a balloon.*

pump
pumps *noun*
a device that pushes liquids or gases into or out of something.

*bicycle **pump***

punch
punches *noun*
1 a hard blow made with your fist.

punch *verb*
2 a machine that stamps holes, letters, or patterns in something.

*hole **punch***
3 a sweet drink made by mixing fruit juices and other liquids together. Punch is usually served from a large bowl.

puncture
punctures *noun*
a hole, often made by a sharp point, that lets the air out of something.
*My tyre has a **puncture**.*
puncture *verb*

a b c d e f g h i j k l m n o p q r s t u v w x y z

A B C D E F G H I J K L M N O P Q R S T U V W X Y Z

punish
punishes punishing punished
verb

to make someone suffer in some way for things they have done wrong.
punishment *noun*

pupa
pupae *noun*

the stage of an insect's development when it changes from a larva to a winged insect inside a rounded case (see **growth** on page 94).

■ say **pew**-pa

ladybird
pupa

pupil
pupils *noun*

1 a student at school.

2 the small, dark part at the centre of your eye, which expands or contracts to let in the right amount of light.

pupil

puppet
puppets *noun*

a doll or animal figure that is moved by pulling on its strings or by making hand movements inside it.

finger **puppet**

string **puppet**

puppy
puppies *noun*

a young dog (see **pet** on page 148).

purchase
purchases purchasing purchased *verb*

to buy something.

■ say **pur**-chis

pure
adjective

clean, or not mixed with anything.
***Pure** gold.*

■ comparisons **purer purest**

purple
noun

a colour made by mixing red and blue together.

purpose
purposes *noun*

a reason for doing something, or an aim.

purr
purrs purring purred *verb*

to make a low, rumbling noise like a cat makes.

purse
purses *noun*

a small bag for carrying money.

push
pushes pushing pushed *verb*

to move something away from you by pressing hard against it.

*He had to **push** the car to a garage when it broke down.*

put
puts putting put *verb*

to place or position something somewhere.

*She **put** her books into her school bag.*

puzzle
puzzles *noun*

1 a problem or question that it is difficult to find the answer to.
2 a game in which you have to find the answers to a problem.

puzzle
puzzles puzzling puzzled *verb*

to try to work out something you do not understand.

pyjamas
noun

a matching jacket and trousers that are worn in bed.

pyramid
pyramids *noun*

1 a solid shape with a square base and four triangular faces which meet in a point (see **shape** on page 182).
2 an ancient tomb or temple, shaped like a pyramid.

*The **pyramids** of Egypt.*
■ say **pir**-a-mid

python
pythons *noun*

a large snake that is found in hot regions. Pythons kill by wrapping themselves around their prey and squeezing. They eat small mammals.

■ say **pie**-thun

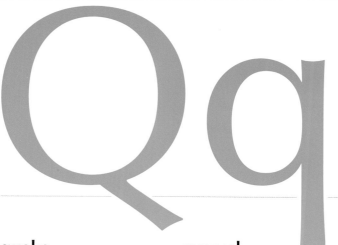

Qq

quake
quakes quaking quaked *verb*
to shake or tremble.

He quaked with fear when he saw the crocodile.
■ say **kwake**

qualify
qualifies qualifying qualified *verb*
to prove that you are fit or suitable for something.
I hope I qualify for the team!
■ say **kwol**-i-fie
qualification *noun*

quality
qualities *noun*
1 a judgement of how good or bad something is.
High quality.
2 something that is special about someone or something.
She has many good qualities.
■ say **kwol**-i-tee

quantity
quantities *noun*
an amount or number.

A large quantity of crates.
■ say **kwon**-ti-tee

quarrel
quarrels quarrelling quarrelled *verb*
to have an argument or disagreement with someone.
■ say **kwor**-rul
quarrel *noun*

quarry
quarries *noun*
a place where stone, sand, or gravel is cut out of the ground.

A stone quarry.
■ say **kwor**-ee

quarter
quarters *noun*
one of four equal pieces of a whole.

four orange quarters
■ say **kwor**-ter

quartz
noun
a hard mineral, often found in crystal form.

■ say **kworts**

quay
quays *noun*
an area by a harbour where ships are loaded and unloaded.
■ say **kee**

queen
queens *noun*
a female ruler of a country or the wife of a king.

query
queries *noun*
a question or inquiry, because you have a doubt or problem about something.

The teacher helped to answer the student's query.
■ say **kweer**-ree
query *verb*

question
questions questioning questioned *verb*
to ask someone for information or an answer.
■ opposite **answer**
question *noun*

queue
queues *noun*
a line of people or vehicles that are waiting for something.
■ say **kew**
queue *verb*

quick
adjective
fast or sudden.
A quick movement.
■ comparisons **quicker quickest**
■ opposite **slow**
quickly *adverb*

quiet
adjective
silent and peaceful.
■ comparisons **quieter quietest**

quill
quills *noun*
a large feather, especially one that has been made into an ink pen.
■ say **kwil**

quill pen

quilt
quilts *noun*
a thick, soft cover for a bed.

patchwork quilt

quite
adverb
1 fairly.
I am quite good at running.
2 completely.
You are quite right.

quiz
quizzes *noun*
a game in which you are asked questions to find out how much you know.

quote
quotes quoting quoted *verb*
to repeat something that someone else has said or written.
quotation *noun*

a b c d e f g h i j k l m n o p q r s t u v w x y z

161

Rr

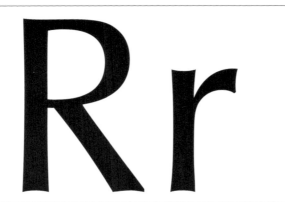

rabbi
rabbis *noun*
a teacher of the Jewish
religion and law.
■ say **rab**-eye

rabbit
rabbits *noun*
a small mammal with long
front teeth that lives
underground in burrows.
Rabbits are normally active in
the evening or at night. They
eat grass, roots, and leaves.

race
races *noun*
1 a competition of speed.

*A swimming **race**.*
race *verb*
2 a group of people who
share the same ancestors
and may share some
physical characteristics.
racial *adjective*

racket
rackets *noun*
1 a bat with
strings used
for playing
sports such
as tennis and
badminton (see
sport on page 197).

*badminton **racket***

2 a loud,
annoying noise.
*He was making
a **racket** with
his drums.*

radar
noun
a device that tells you
the position and speed of
ships, cars, and aircraft
by sending out radio waves.

*An airport **radar** screen.*
■ say **ray**-dar

radiator
radiators *noun*
1 a thin, metal tank with hot
water flowing through it,
which heats a room.
2 a metal tank that allows
air to cool the hot water in
the engine of a vehicle.
■ say **ray**-dee-ay-tor

radio
radios *noun*
a device that sends or
receives electrical signals
and changes them
into sound.

radioactivity
noun
the energy released by the
centre of atoms breaking
up in some substances. High
amounts of radioactivity can
be harmful to living things.

*They tested for **radioactivity**
outside the nuclear
power station.*
■ say **ray**-dee-oh-ak-**tiv**-i-tee
radioactive *adjective*

radius
radii or **radiuses** *noun*
a straight line drawn
from the centre
of a circle to
its outer
edge.

radius

raft
rafts *noun*
1 a floating platform
made of logs that
have been tied
tightly together.

rag
rags *noun*
a small, torn piece of cloth.

rage
rages *noun*
anger or uncontrolled temper.
*In her **rage**, she slammed
the door shut.*

raid
raids *noun*
a sudden surprise attack
by a group of people.
*The police made a **raid** on the
house, arresting two women.*
raid *verb*

rail
rails *noun*
1 a long bar for holding on to,
or for hanging clothes on.
*Use the **rail** to help you climb
the stairs.*
2 a long line of metal track
that trains run along.

3 the railway.
*We travelled by **rail**
around Europe.*

2 a hollow mat made of rubber
or plastic and filled with
air, which can
be used as
a boat.

*life **raft***

railway
railways *noun*
1 a network of tracks that trains run on.
2 a transport system that uses rail tracks, together with trains, stations, and land.

rain
rains *noun*
water that falls from the clouds in drops.

rain *verb*
rainy *adjective*

rainbow
rainbows *noun*
an arch of colours that appears in the sky when the sun shines during rain.

raindrop
raindrops *noun*
a single drop of rain.

rainfall
noun
the amount of rain that falls over a particular area.
The chart shows the annual **rainfall** *in South America.*

rainforest
rainforests *noun*
a dense, hot, wet jungle that grows in tropical areas.

rake
rakes raking raked *verb*
to gather up leaves into a pile or to smooth over soil.

rake

rally
rallies *noun*
1 a large, public meeting held to discuss something that is important or worrying to people.

The party held a political **rally** *in the park.*
2 a long-distance car race that tests drivers' skills.

ram
rams *noun*
1 a male sheep.

2 a device for pushing against something with force.

They used the log as a **ram** *to break down the door.*
ram *verb*

ran
from the verb **to run**
1 *Last week, he* **ran** *a 400 metre race.*
2 *She* **ran** *a bookshop.*

ranch
ranches *noun*
a huge farm where cattle or other animals are reared, usually found in America.

rang
from the verb **to ring**
1 *He* **rang** *the doorbell.*
2 *She* **rang** *me twice today.*

ranger
rangers *noun*
a person who looks after a forest or a wildlife park.

rapid
adjective
quick or swift.

rare
adjective
unusual or not common.
A **rare** *blue morpho butterfly.*

■ comparisons **rarer rarest**
■ opposite **common**

rascal
rascals *noun*
a mischievous person.

rash
rashes *noun*
a patch of red, itchy spots on your skin.

raspberry
raspberries *noun*
a juicy, red fruit that grows on a bush with thorns.

■ say **rarz**-bur-ree

rat
rats *noun*
a common rodent that looks like a large mouse. Some kinds of rats eat plants, while others eat small animals. They can gnaw through stone, wood, and even metal with their strong front teeth.

rate
rates *noun*
1 a speed.
Ostriches can run at a **rate** *of 50 kilometres per hour.*
2 a level of payment.
The holiday company charges high **rates** *for its apartments.*

a b c d e f g h i j k l m n o p q r s t u v w x y z

A B C D E F G H I J K L M N O P Q **R** S T U V W X Y Z

rather
adverb
1 fairly or quite.
*It was **rather** hot the other day.*
2 preferably.

*She'd **rather** have fruit than cake.*

ration
rations *noun*
a fixed amount of something that someone is allowed.
*Food **rations**.*
■ say **rash**-un
ration *verb*

raw
adjective
1 in its natural condition, not processed or cooked.

raw carrot
2 not experienced.
*A **raw** recruit.*
3 painful to touch.
*A **raw** wound.*

ray
rays *noun*
a long, narrow beam of light, heat, or other powerful force.

rays of light

react
reacts reacting reacted *verb*
to say or do something in response to an event.
*He **reacted** badly to the news.*
■ say ree-**akt**
reaction *noun*

razor
razors *noun*
a device with a blade that people use to shave.

reach
reaches reaching reached *verb*
1 to stretch out your hand and arm to touch something.

2 to arrive at a place.
*After a long trek they **reached** the other side of the island.*

read
reads reading read *verb*
to look at and understand written words.
■ rhymes with **seed**

ready
adjective
prepared, or able to start.
■ say **red**-ee

real
adjective
actually existing, or genuine.

realize
realizes realizing realized *verb*
to become aware, or to understand completely.

*She did not **realize** the puddle was so deep.*

really
adverb
very, or actually.
*The trip was **really** good fun.*

rear
rears rearing reared *verb*
1 to feed and care for young animals as they grow up.
*Our cat has **reared** 10 kittens.*
2 to rise up on the back legs.
*A **rearing** horse.*

rear
noun
the back of something, or the part that is opposite or behind the front.

*The **rear** of a car.*
rear *adjective*

reason
reasons *noun*
an explanation of why or how something has happened.

rebel
rebels *noun*
someone who fights against those in charge.
■ say **reb**-ul
rebellion *noun*

receipt
receipts *noun*
a written or printed piece of paper that shows you have received and paid for something.
■ say re-**seet**

receive
receives receiving received *verb*
to take something given or sent to you.

*She **received** lots of presents for her birthday.*

recent
adjective
not long ago.
*A **recent** storm.*
■ say **ree**-sunt
recently *adverb*

recipe
recipes noun

instructions that tell you how to make and cook food, or how to make a drink.

recipe book
■ say **res**-i-pee

recite
recites reciting recited verb

to say aloud something that you have learned by heart.

reckon
reckons reckoning reckoned verb

1 to suppose or think something.
*What do you **reckon** that is?*
2 to work out the amount of something.
■ say **rek**-un

recognize
recognizes recognizing recognized verb

to see someone or something and know who they are or what it is.

*He **recognized** his friend's bike because of the red bags.*
recognition noun

record
records recording recorded verb

1 to store sounds or pictures, on tape, film, record, compact disc (CD), or digital versatile/video disc (DVD).
2 to write down information on paper.
■ say ri-**cord**

record
records noun

1 a round plastic disc with tiny grooves in the surface, on which sounds are recorded.
2 information that is written or printed.

*She kept a **record** of the day's events in her diary.*
3 the fastest or best performance in an activity or sport.
*They tried to beat the **record** for the number of people who can stand on a chair.*
■ say **rek**-ord

recorder
recorders noun

a small wooden or plastic wind instrument that you blow into. The air is forced out through holes, which you cover with your fingers to make different sounds.

recover
recovers recovering recovered verb

1 to get better after being ill.
2 to get something back.

*He **recovered** his hat from the lake.*

Recording a song.

recreation
noun

the things we like to do in our spare time, such as playing sports and having hobbies.

recruit
recruits noun

a new member of an organization or group.
■ say ri-**krute**

rectangle
rectangles noun

a flat four-sided shape with four right angles in its corners (see **shape** on page 182).

recycle
recycles recycling recycled verb

to use things again, often by turning rubbish into new products. Glass, plastics, paper, and metal can all be recycled.

*materials for **recycling***

red
noun

a colour.

reduce
reduces reducing reduced verb

to make something smaller in size or amount.
*The shop **reduced** the price of hats by half.*
■ say ri-**dews**
reduction noun

reed
reeds noun

a tall plant with a long, stiff, straight stem that grows in wet areas. Reeds are used to make house roofs and paper.
*common **reed***

reef
reefs noun

a raised, narrow ridge of rock, sand, or coral, just above or below the surface of the sea.

*coral **reef***

referee
referees noun

someone who watches over a game or contest to see that people keep to the rules.

reference
adjective

providing information.
*The **reference** book was full of interesting facts.*
reference noun

refinery
refineries noun

a large factory where natural substances are processed into other products. Oil is made into petrol at a refinery.

*oil **refinery***

A
B
C
D
E
F
G
H
I
J
K
L
M
N
O
P
Q
R
S
T
U
V
W
X
Y
Z

reflect
reflects reflecting reflected *verb*
1 to throw back light, heat, or sound that has come from somewhere else.
Shiny surfaces **reflect** *light.*
2 to give back, or show, an image of something or someone.

His face was **reflected** *in the mirror.*
reflection *noun*

refrigerator
refrigerators *noun*
a machine that keeps food and drink cool and fresh. Refrigerator can be shortened to fridge.

refugee
refugees *noun*
someone who leaves their home and belongings and escapes to another place, usually because he or she is in danger.
■ say ref-yoo-**jee**

refuse
refuses refusing refused *verb*
to say that you will not do something.

He **refused** *to give her the ball.*

region
regions *noun*
an area or district of a country.

A mountain **region***.*
■ say **ree**-jun

regret
regrets regretting regretted *verb*
to be sorry or sad about something that has happened.
He **regretted** *being angry with his sister.*

regular
adjective
1 normal, or happening at certain times.
A **regular** *bus service.*
2 even in shape or sound.

These wooden cubes are **regular** *shapes.*
■ opposite **irregular**
regularly *adverb*

rehearse
rehearses rehearsing rehearsed *verb*
to practise doing something before giving a performance in public.

Rehearsing for a play.
■ say re-**herss**
rehearsal *noun*

reign
reigns reigning reigned *verb*
to rule a country or region as a queen or king.
■ say **rain**
reign *noun*

rein
reins *noun*
a long, thin, leather strap that a rider uses to control a horse (see **horse** on page 102).
■ say **rain**

reindeer
reindeer or **reindeers** *noun*
a deer with large antlers that lives in cold, Arctic regions. Reindeer herds migrate great distances every summer and winter in search of plants to eat. Some reindeer are tamed and used to pull sledges.

relative
relatives *noun*
a member of someone's family.

relax
relaxes relaxing relaxed *verb*
to rest and feel comfortable.

She **relaxed** *with her favourite book.*

relay
relays *noun*
a team race in which runners carrying a baton take it in turns to run part of the distance.

release
releases releasing released *verb*
to let someone or something go free.

They **released** *balloons in the park to celebrate the event.*

reliable
adjective
able to be trusted.

relief

noun

1 the removal of worry, pain, or unhappiness.
It was a relief when the exam was over.
2 help given to people who need it.

■ say ri-**leef**

religion

religions *noun*

a belief in God or gods, and the way people express this belief in their life and worship.
religious *adjective*

reluctant

adjective

unsure or unhappy about doing something.

He was reluctant to cross the old bridge.

rely

relies relying relied *verb*

to depend on someone for something with complete trust.
Young birds rely on their mothers for food.

■ say ri-**lie**

remain

remains remaining remained *verb*

1 to stay behind.

He remained there alone.
2 to be left behind.
remains *noun*
3 to stay unchanged.
She remained calm while everyone else panicked.

remember

remembers remembering remembered *verb*

to think about a place, person, object, or past event again.
She suddenly remembered she had left her bag on the bus.

remind

reminds reminding reminded *verb*

to make someone remember something.

A calendar reminds you of future events.

remote

adjective

far away, distant.
A remote farmhouse.

remove

removes removing removed *verb*
to take something off or away.

She removed her shoe to get a stone out.

renew

renews renewing renewed *verb*
to begin, make, or get again.
He renewed his bus pass.

rent

rents *noun*

a regular payment that you make to the owner of something so that you can use it.
rent *verb*

repair

repairs repairing repaired *verb*
to mend something that is broken.

Repairing a bicycle.
repair *noun*

repeat

repeats repeating repeated *verb*
to say or do something again.
repetition *noun*

replace

replaces replacing replaced *verb*
1 to put something back where it came from.

She replaced the book on the shelf.
2 to exchange or renew.
He replaced his bicycle with a bigger, more expensive one.
replacement *noun*

replay

replays replaying replayed *verb*
1 to play a sports match again.
2 to play a recording of something again.

replica

replicas *noun*

an exact copy of something.
She made a replica of the ship out of matchsticks.

reply

replies replying replied *verb*
to answer.
He replied to the invitation immediately.
reply *noun*

report

reports *noun*

a spoken or written account of a situation or event.

reporter

reporters *noun*

a person who gathers information on events and writes or speaks about them for a television programme, newspaper, or radio station.

represent

represents representing represented *verb*
to mean or show something.

Sailors use this flag to represent the word "yes" when they signal to other ships.

a
b
c
d
e
f
g
h
i
j
k
l
m
n
o
p
q
r
s
t
u
v
w
x
y
z

reptile

reptiles *noun*

one of a group of cold-blooded animals that have a backbone, lungs for breathing, dry, scaly skin, and clawed fingers or toes. Reptiles lay their eggs on dry land.

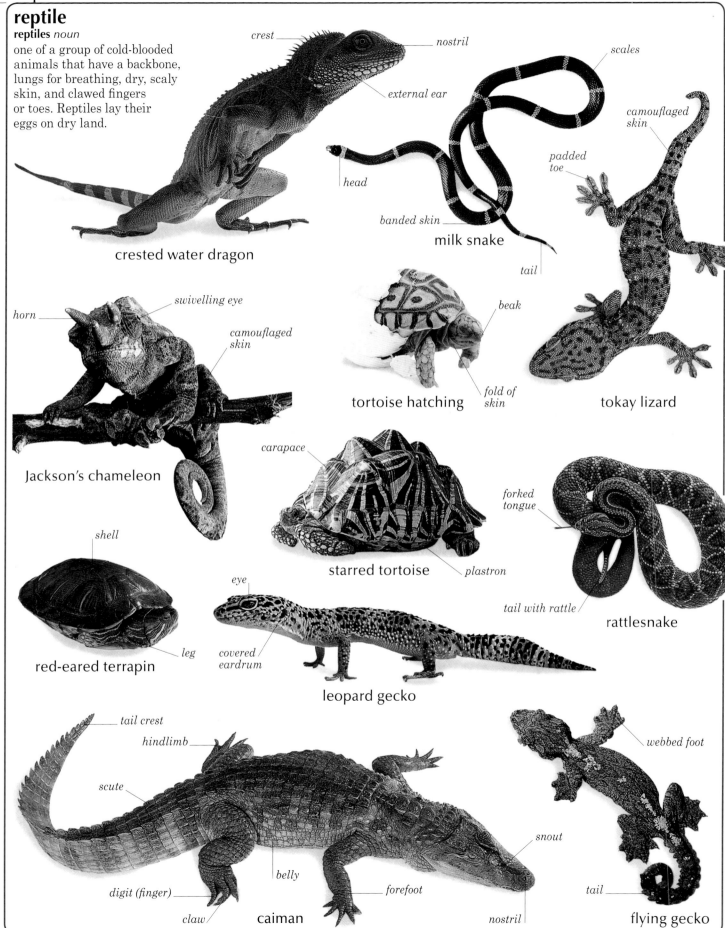

crest

nostril

external ear

crested water dragon

scales

head

banded skin

milk snake

tail

camouflaged skin

padded toe

horn

swivelling eye

camouflaged skin

Jackson's chameleon

beak

tortoise hatching

fold of skin

tokay lizard

carapace

shell

leg

red-eared terrapin

starred tortoise

plastron

forked tongue

tail with rattle

rattlesnake

eye

covered eardrum

leopard gecko

tail crest

hindlimb

scute

webbed foot

digit (finger)

belly

claw

caiman

forefoot

snout

nostril

tail

flying gecko

request

requests requesting requested
verb

to ask for something formally.
*The prisoner **requested** a visit
to his mother.*
■ say ri-**kwest**
request *noun*

rescue

rescues rescuing rescued *verb*
to save someone who is
injured or in danger.

■ say **res**-kew

research

**researches researching
researched** *verb*
to study
a subject in
order to learn
new facts
or develop
new ideas.

***Researching** objects found
on the seashore.*
research *noun*

reserve

reserves reserving reserved *verb*
to arrange to have something
kept for a later time.
*They **reserved** a table at
the restaurant for 8 o'clock.*
reservation *noun*

reservoir

reservoirs *noun*
a large storage area
where water is
collected and stored
for future use.
■ say **rez**-ur-vwah

resign

resigns resigning resigned *verb*
to give up your job.
■ say ri-**zine**

resist

resists resisting resisted *verb*
to try to stop something
from happening.
*He **resisted** temptation.*

resort

resorts *noun*
a place where many people
go for a holiday.

*A ski **resort**.*

resource

resources *noun*
a supply of something useful
or valuable, such as oil or gas.
*The country is rich in
natural **resources**.*
■ say ri-**zorse**

respect

noun
1 admiration for someone.
*I have great **respect** for her.*
2 politeness.
respect *verb*
respectful *adjective*

response

responses *noun*
a reply, in actions or words,
to something.
respond *verb*
responsive *adjective*

responsible

adjective
1 sensible and dependable.
2 in charge of something.

*The boy was
responsible for
feeding his dog.*

rest

noun
1 the time when you
are relaxing.
rest *verb*
2 something that is left over.
*Most people left yesterday, but
the **rest** went this morning.*
3 when something is still.
*The ball came to **rest**
at the teacher's feet.*

restaurant

restaurants *noun*
a place where people go to
buy and eat a meal.

■ say **rest**-er-ront

restless

adjective
unable to stay still or relax.

*The baby had a **restless** night.*

restore

restores restoring restored *verb*
to mend something old or
worn, so that it looks new
or can be used again.

result

results *noun*
the effect of certain actions
or events.
*What was the **result**
of the experiment?*
result *verb*

retire

retires retiring retired *verb*
to give up working, usually
because of old age or illness.

return

returns returning returned *verb*
1 to come back
from somewhere.

*The boomerang **returned** easily
to his hand.*
2 to give something back
to a person.
*She **returned** the book
he had lent her.*
return *noun*

a
b
c
d
e
f
g
h
i
j
k
l
m
n
o
p
q
r
s
t
u
v
w
x
y
z

A B C D E F G H I J K L M N O P Q **R** S T U V W X Y Z

revenge
noun
harm or injury that a person does to another, in return for something unpleasant previously done to them.

reverse
reverses reversing reversed *verb*
to go backwards, usually in a vehicle.

*She **reversed** her motorbike into the parking space.*

reverse
adjective
at the opposite side, inside, or back of an object.

*The **reverse** side of the coat is lined with white material.*
reverse *noun*

revise
revises revising revised *verb*
to look back over work, either to check for mistakes, or to prepare for a test.
revision *noun*

revolution
revolutions *noun*
1 one complete turn.
2 a time when people fight to change the government of their country.
*The French **Revolution**.*

reward
rewards *noun*
a prize given because of a good thing someone has done.

LOST
£50 reward

*They offered a **reward** to anyone who found their cat.*

rhinoceros
rhinoceroses *noun*
a heavy mammal that lives in hot regions. Rhinoceroses have one or two horns and thick skin with hardly any hair.

■ say ry-**noss**-er-rus

rhubarb
noun
a large-leaved plant. Its long stems can be cooked and eaten as a dessert.

■ say roo-**barb**

rhyme
rhymes *noun*
words which have the same or similar sound and are often found in a poem.
■ say **rime**

rhythm
rhythms *noun*
a regular pattern of sound, such as beats in music.
■ say **rith**-um

rib
ribs *noun*
one of the bones that curves round from your spine to the front of your chest. Ribs protect your internal organs (see **skeleton** on page 188).

ribbon
ribbons *noun*
a thin strip of decorative material often used for tying hair or wrapping up presents.

rice
noun
a grass-like plant that grows in warm, wet regions. The small white or brown grains can be cooked and eaten.

*cooked **rice***

rich
adjective
1 having a lot of money.
2 having a lot of something.
*Milk is **rich** in calcium.*
■ comparisons **richer richest**
■ opposite **poor**

riddle
riddles *noun*
a word puzzle in which you have to guess the answer from clues, often in a rhyme.

rhythm
rhythms *noun*

ride
rides riding rode ridden *verb*
1 to travel on the back of a horse.

2 to travel on anything that moves.

Riding on a Ferris wheel.
ride *noun*

ridiculous
adjective
crazy, funny, or not making sense.

*She looked **ridiculous**.*
■ say ri-**dik**-yoo-lus

right
adjective
1 the opposite direction to left.
*My **right** hand.*
2 correct or lawful.
*The **right** answer.*
right *noun*

right-angle

right-angles *noun*

an angle that measures 90 degrees, formed by two lines that are perpendicular to one another (see **shape** on page 182).
The four inside corners of a square are **right-angles**.

rim

rims *noun*

the edge or border of something.

He looked over the **rim** *of the volcano into the crater.*

ring

rings ringing rang rung *verb*

1 to strike metal or play a bell so that it makes a pleasant sound.

2 to make a telephone call.
I have tried to **ring** *her three times today.*

ring

rings *noun*

a piece of jewellery that is worn on your finger (see **jewellery** on page 112).

rinse

rinses rinsing rinsed *verb*

to wash something in water with no soap in it.

riot

riots *noun*

uncontrolled fighting among a crowd of people who are angry or protesting about something.
■ say **ry**-ut

rip

rips ripping ripped *verb*

to tear something, usually cloth or paper.

He **ripped** *the piece of paper in half.*

ripe

adjective

ready to pick or eat, usually used about fruit.
■ comparisons **riper ripest**
■ opposite **unripe**

ripple

ripples *noun*

a small wave on the surface of water.

When the duck dived, it made **ripples** *on the water's surface.*

rise

rises rising rose risen *verb*

to go upwards or become higher.
Heat **rises**.
rising *adjective*

risk

risks risking risked *verb*

to take the chance of harming or losing something.
He **risked** *his life to save her.*
risk *noun*
risky *adjective*

river

rivers *noun*

a large stream of water that flows into another river, a lake, or the ocean.

road

roads *noun*

a path for vehicles to travel on, usually with a hard, smooth surface.

roar

roars roaring roared *verb*

to make a loud, deep, rumbling noise like the noise a lion makes.

roast

roasts roasting roasted *verb*

to cook food in a hot oven or over a fire.

rob

robs robbing robbed *verb*

to steal from someone, often by using violence.
They **robbed** *the bank.*
robbery *noun*

robber

robbers *noun*

a person who robs you of something, usually money or goods.

robot

robots *noun*

a machine that can imitate some human actions. Robots are often used in factories, but can also be used in homes.

A toy **robot** *runs on batteries.*

rock

rocks *noun*

a hard, stony substance that covers most of Earth's surface, or a large lump of this substance.

granite **rock**
rocky *adjective*

rock

rocks rocking rocked *verb*

to move gently backwards and forwards, or from side to side.

rocking *chair*

rocket
rockets noun
1 an engine that powers a spacecraft. Hot gases are released from the rear of the engine, causing the craft to move forwards.

2 a type of firework that shoots into the sky and explodes.

rode
from the verb **to ride**
*She **rode** her horse last week.*

rodent
rodents noun
a small, usually nocturnal mammal with long front teeth for gnawing food. Some rodents eat insects and plants, while others only eat plants. Rats, mice, and squirrels are rodents.
■ say **roh**-dent

roll
rolls rolling rolled verb
1 to move by turning over and over.

*The logs **rolled** down the hill.*
2 to move along on wheels.
3 to tilt from side to side, like a ship on a rough sea.

4 to flatten something by moving a tool over it.

roll
rolls noun
1 paper, cloth, film, or other material that has been wound onto a tube.

rolls of wrapping paper

2 a rounded piece of bread, cake, or pastry.

bread rolls

roof
roofs noun
1 the outside covering on top of a vehicle or a building.
2 the highest surface inside your mouth or a cave.

room
rooms noun
1 one of the separate areas inside a building.

bathroom
2 space.
*Is there any **room** in the car for me?*

roost
roosts roosting roosted verb
to settle down for the night, used about birds.

root
roots noun
the part of a plant that usually grows underground. A plant's roots supply it with water and minerals from the soil (see **plant** on page 151).

rope
ropes noun
a strong, thick piece of twisted string or wire.

*coil of **rope***

rose
roses noun
a plant with thorns along its stem and flowers with many petals.

rose
from the verb **to rise**
*The Sun **rose** in the sky.*

rot
rots rotting rotted verb
to go bad, or to weaken and break down.
rotten adjective

rotate
rotates rotating rotated verb
to turn around a central point like a wheel does.

axis
*The Earth **rotates** on its axis.*
rotation noun

rough
adjective
1 uneven, or not smooth.
*A **rough** sea.*
2 approximate, or not exact.
*A **rough** guess.*
■ comparisons **rougher roughest**

round
adjective
shaped like a circle, with no corners.

route
routes noun
the way you go to get from one place to another.

*We drew our **route** on the map in red.*
■ say **root**

row
rows noun
an argument or quarrel.
■ rhymes with **now**

row
rows noun
a line of several things next to each other.

■ rhymes with **toe**

row
rows rowing rowed verb
to make a boat move forwards by pulling it through the water with oars.

royal
adjective
to do with a king, queen, or members of his or her family.

rub
rubs rubbing rubbed *verb*
to press something backwards and forwards over the surface of something else.

*She **rubbed** her wet hair with a towel.*

rubbish
noun
the things that people throw away because they no longer have use for them.

rude
adjective
speaking or behaving in a way that does not show respect.
■ opposite **polite**

rug
rugs *noun*
1 a small carpet made of thick material.

2 a soft blanket.

rugby
noun
a sport in which two teams, of 15 players each, throw and kick an oval ball, trying to score points by running over a line with it or kicking it between the goal posts.

*a **rugby** union game*

ruin
ruins *noun*
the broken remains of a building.

ruined *adjective*

ruin
ruins ruining ruined *verb*
to spoil or damage something.

*She **ruined** her top by spilling ink on it.*

rule
rules *noun*
an instruction of what must or must not be done, for example in a game.

rule
rules ruling ruled *verb*
to govern a country or a group of people.

ruler
rulers *noun*
1 a straight piece of wood, metal, or plastic that is used for measuring and drawing straight lines.
2 a person, such as a king or queen, who rules a country.

rumble
rumbles rumbling rumbled *verb*
to make a long, low sound, like the noise thunder makes.
rumble *noun*

rumour
rumours *noun*
a tale passed from one person to another, about something that may not be true.

run
runs running ran *verb*
1 to move quickly on your legs.

2 to organize something.
*He **runs** a swimming club.*

runway
runways *noun*
a long, flat strip of ground with a hard surface from which aircraft take off and land.

runway

rural
adjective
to do with the countryside or farms.
*A **rural** village.*
■ say **roo**-ral

rush
rushes rushing rushed *verb*
to hurry, or to do something quickly.

rust
noun
the red-brown coating that forms on some metals when they get wet.

*The sickle was covered with **rust**.*

rustle
rustles rustling rustled *verb*
to make a soft, whispering sound.
*The leaves on the tree **rustled** in the wind.*

rye
noun
a grass with light-brown grains, grown to make bread, and as cattle food.

Ss

sack

sacks *noun*

a large, strong bag made of cloth, plastic, or paper, which is used for carrying or storing things.

sacred

adjective

holy, or connected with the worship of God or gods. *The Qur'an is the **sacred** book of Muslims.*

■ say **say**-krid

sad

adjective

not feeling happy.

■ comparisons **sadder saddest**

■ opposite **happy**

saddle

saddles *noun*

a seat for a rider on a horse or a bicycle (see **horse** on page 102 and **transport** on page 221).

*horse **saddle***

safari

safaris *noun*

an expedition to hunt or observe wild animals, usually in Africa.

■ say sa-**far**-ree

safe

adjective

1 protected from harm or danger.
***Safe** on dry land.*
2 not dangerous.
*A **safe** driver.*

■ comparisons **safer safest**

safety *noun*

safe

safes *noun*

a lockable metal box that is used for storing money and valuable things.

sag

sags sagging sagged *verb*

to bend or sink, especially in the middle.

*The sofa **sagged** in the middle.*

said

*from the verb **to say***

1 *She **said** "Good morning".*
2 *The clock **said** half past four.*

sail

sails sailing sailed *verb*

to travel across water in a ship or boat.

sail

sails *noun*

a piece of material attached to the mast of a boat or ship that catches the wind and helps to move the vessel along (see **boat** on page 31).

salad

salads *noun*

a mixture of vegetables, fruit, or other foods, usually served cold.

mixed salad

salary

salaries *noun*

an amount of money regularly paid to someone for work they have done.
*A monthly **salary**.*

sale

sales *noun*

1 the act of offering something to be sold.

*The house is for **sale**.*
2 an event where things are sold at reduced prices.
*Half-price **sale**!*

saliva

noun

the fluid that is produced in your mouth to help you to chew and digest food.

salmon

noun

a large, edible fish. Salmon hatch in rivers, but then swim to the sea to live. They swim back up rivers to lay their eggs.

■ say **sam**-un

salt

noun

a substance made of small, white crystals that we put on food in order to add flavour.

*salt **mill***

salty *adjective*

salute

salutes saluting saluted *verb*

to give a sign of respect by raising the right hand to the forehead or by firing guns into the air.

salute *noun*

same

adjective

1 matching exactly.
*She was wearing the **same** dress as me.*
2 mentioned or seen before.
*He looks like the **same** person who was there yesterday.*

■ opposite **different**

sample

samples noun

a small part of something that shows what the rest is like.

The supermarket was giving away free samples of cheese.
sample verb

sand

noun

very small grains of broken rock, found on beaches or in deserts.

sandal

sandals noun

a shoe with a top made of straps, usually worn in warm weather.

sandwich

sandwiches noun

slices of bread with another food in between.

sang

from the verb **to sing**
The blackbird sang loudly outside my window.

sank

from the verb **to sink**
1 *The ship sank at sea.*
2 *The balloon sank slowly.*

sari

saris noun

a long, light cloth wrapped around the body and shoulder that is worn mainly by women of India, Bangladesh, Nepal, and Sri Lanka.

sarong

sarongs noun

a traditional Asian skirt worn by men and women and made from a piece of cloth wrapped around the waist or chest.

sash

sashes noun

a band of fabric worn around the waist or over the shoulder.

sash

sat

from the verb **to sit**
1 *I sat down on the floor.*
2 *She sat an English exam.*

satellite

satellites noun

1 an object in orbit around a larger object in space. Planet satellites are called moons.
2 an artificial device in space that receives and transmits information around the world.
An Earth observation satellite.

■ say **sat**-a-lite

satisfy

satisfies satisfying satisfied verb

to please someone, or give someone what they want or need.
His answer didn't satisfy the teacher.
satisfaction noun

sauce

sauces noun

a liquid or soft food that is eaten with a meal.

raspberry sauce

■ say **sors**

saucepan

saucepans noun

a metal container with a handle, used for cooking.

■ say **sors**-pan

saucer

saucers noun

a small, shallow plate that is placed beneath a cup.

■ say **sor**-ser

sausage

sausages noun

a food made from a mixture of chopped meat, fat, and cereal inside a tube of thin skin.

■ say **sos**-ij

save

saves saving saved verb

1 to rescue.
The fire-fighter saved him from the burning house.
2 to not waste.
Save power – turn off the light!
3 to keep something to use later.
He saved all his pocket money.

saw

saws noun

a tool for cutting wood, which has a handle and a blade with sharp teeth.

saw

saws sawing sawed verb

to use a saw.

Sawing a plank of wood.

saw

from the verb **to see**
I saw my face in the mirror.

say

says saying said verb

1 to speak words out loud.
"Hurry up!" I said.
2 to give a message or some information.
The sign says "No Entry".

scald

scalds scalding scalded *verb*
to burn with hot liquid
or steam.
- say **skold**

scale

scales *noun*
1 a series of regular
marks along a line used
for measuring.
*Thermometers have a scale
for measuring temperature.*
2 a set sequence of musical
notes going from the highest
to the lowest, or from
the lowest to the highest.

3 a small, hard plate on
the skin of a fish, insect,
or reptile (see **fish** on
page 79, **insect** on page 108,
reptile on page 168).
4 the size of a map or a model
compared with the actual
size of the object.

*This model of a building has
been made to scale.*

scales

noun
a machine that is used
to weigh things.

kitchen scales

scar

scars *noun*
a mark left on the skin
after a wound has healed.
scar *verb*

scarce

adjective
not great in amount,
or not often found.
Snow is scarce in May.
- say **skairs**

scare

scares scaring scared *verb*
1 to become frightened.
2 to make someone
else frightened.

*The bear appeared suddenly
and scared him.*

scarecrow

scarecrows *noun*
a figure made from sticks and
old clothes, which is used to
scare birds away from crops.

scarf

scarves *noun*
a piece of cloth that you wear
around your shoulders, neck,
or head for decoration or to
keep warm.

scatter

scatters scattering scattered *verb*
to spread in many
different directions.
The wind scattered the seeds.

scavenger

scavengers *noun*
an animal or person who
searches through rubbish.

scavenge *verb*

scene

scenes *noun*
1 the place where
something happened.
The scene of the crime.
2 a part of a play or film, set
in a particular time or place.
3 a view.

A winter scene.
- say **seen**

scenery

noun
1 the way a place looks.
*The scenery in the mountains
was amazing.*
2 an artificial background
used in a play or a film.

- say **seen**-er-ree

scent

scents *noun*
1 a trail of smell left by
an animal or a person.
The dog followed the scent.
2 perfume.

- say **sent**

scheme

schemes *noun*
1 a secret plan.
2 a way of arranging things.
A colour scheme.
- say **skeem**

school

schools *noun*
a place where children
go to learn.
- say **skool**

science

sciences *noun*
the study of things
in the world, which involves
observing, measuring, and
experimenting to test ideas.
- say **sye**-ens
scientific *adjective*

scientist

scientists *noun*
someone who does
scientific work.
- say **sye**-en-tist

scissors

noun
a tool with handles
and two blades joined
together. Scissors are
used for cutting
things, such as
paper and hair.

- say **siz**-ers

scold

scolds scolding scolded *verb*
to speak to someone angrily
because they have done
something wrong.
*My father scolded me
for being late.*

scoop
scoops scooping scooped *verb*
to lift something up using your hand or a tool shaped like a deep spoon.

scoop

Scooping pasta out of a jar.

score
scores scoring scored *verb*
to win points in a game.

scorn
scorns scorning scorned *verb*
to show by words or your expression that you do not think much of something or someone.
*The journalist **scorned** the plans for the power station.*
scornful *adjective*

scorpion
scorpions *noun*
a small, nocturnal animal that is part of the same animal group as spiders. Scorpions usually live in hot regions. They eat insects and spiders which they kill with the poisonous stingers on their tails.

*imperial **scorpion***

scowl
scowls scowling scowled *verb*
to frown in an angry or bad-tempered way.
*She **scowled** when she was given extra homework.*
scowl *noun*

scramble
scrambles scrambling scrambled *verb*
1 to crawl or climb fast, using your hands.

*He **scrambled** back up the river bank.*
2 to mix together.
Scrambling an egg.

scrap
noun
1 a small piece of something.

scraps *of paper*

2 anything that is worn out or no longer of any use.

*The cars were sold as **scrap**.*
scrap *verb*

scrape
scrapes scraping scraped *verb*
to drag an object across something, often removing part of the surface.

***Scraping** wallpaper off the walls.*

scratch
scratches scratching scratched *verb*
1 to make a mark on the surface of something with a sharp object.

*The cat **scratched** the tree trunk with its claws.*
2 to rub skin with fingernails or claws to stop it itching.
scratch *noun*

scream
screams screaming screamed *verb*
to cry out in a loud, high voice because you are frightened or in pain.
scream *noun*

screen
screens *noun*
1 a flat surface onto which moving images are projected. *Some cinemas have six **screens**.*
2 a barrier that is used to hide, separate, or protect something.

*She dressed behind a **screen**.*
3 the part of a computer or television on which the picture or text appears.

screw
screws *noun*
a metal pin used for fastening things together.

screwdriver
screwdrivers *noun*
a tool for turning screws.

script
scripts *noun*
1 a written version of a play, film, radio, or television show.
2 handwriting.

scrub
scrubs scrubbing scrubbed *verb*
to clean by rubbing hard.

Scrubbing a rabbit hutch.

sculpture
sculptures *noun*
a piece of art made from wood, stone, metal, or another solid material.

sea
seas *noun*
the salt water that covers two-thirds of Earth's surface.

sea life

noun

all the plants and animals
that live in the sea or
on the seashore.

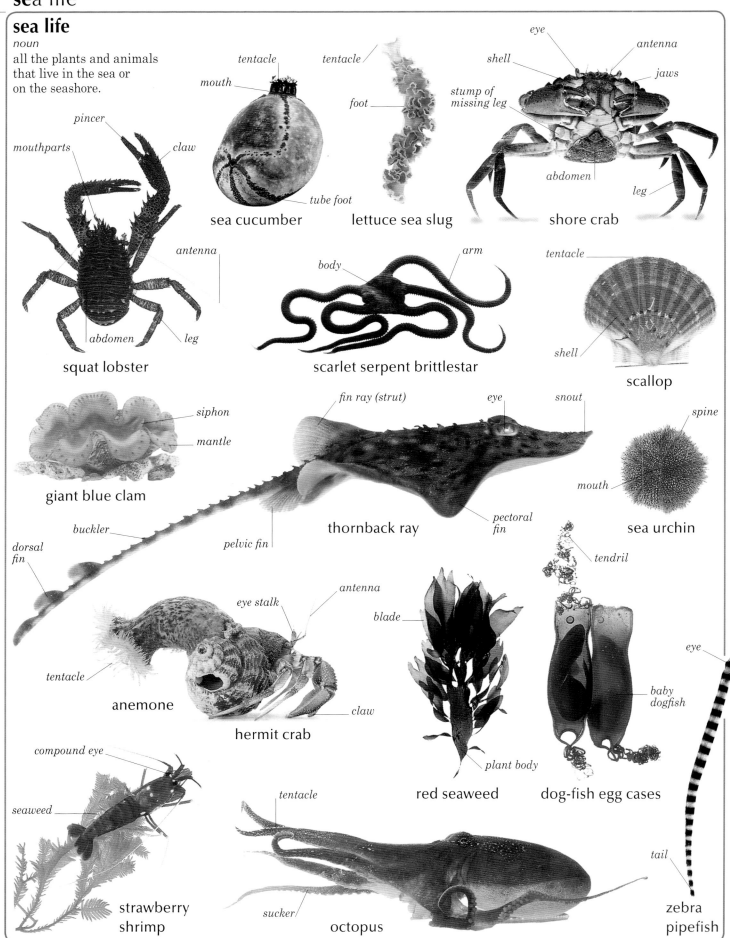

pincer

mouthparts

claw

tentacle

mouth

tentacle

foot

eye

antenna

shell

jaws

stump of
missing leg

tube foot

abdomen

leg

sea cucumber

lettuce sea slug

shore crab

antenna

body

arm

tentacle

abdomen

leg

shell

squat lobster

scarlet serpent brittlestar

scallop

siphon

mantle

fin ray (strut)

eye

snout

spine

mouth

giant blue clam

buckler

dorsal
fin

pelvic fin

thornback ray

pectoral
fin

sea urchin

tendril

eye stalk

antenna

blade

baby
dogfish

eye

tentacle

anemone

claw

hermit crab

plant body

red seaweed

dog-fish egg cases

compound eye

seaweed

tentacle

tail

strawberry
shrimp

sucker

octopus

zebra
pipefish

seal
seals *noun*

1 a sea mammal usually found in cold seas. Seals eat fish and are excellent swimmers. Some seals are clumsy on land, where they move by rolling or sliding along.

2 a piece of paper or wax that is used to mark something or to close it so that you can tell whether it has been opened.

*wax **seal***

seal
seals sealing sealed *verb*

to close something securely or tightly.
***Seal** the envelope.*

search
searches searching searched *verb*

to look hard for something.

*He **searched** for his ball in the long grass.*
search *noun*

season
seasons *noun*

1 one of the four divisions of the year marked by particular kinds of weather.
*Our **seasons** are spring, summer, autumn, and winter.*
2 a particular part of the year.
*The football **season** starts next week.*

seat
seats *noun*

anything that is used for sitting on.

*child's car safety **seat*** | ***seat**-belt*

second
seconds *noun*

a very short period of time. There are 60 seconds in one minute.

secret
secrets *noun*

something that is not known by everyone.
*Can you keep a **secret**?*
secret *adjective*

secretary
secretaries *noun*

a person whose job is to assist other people by making business appointments, writing letters, and keeping records.

section
sections *noun*

a separate part or portion of something.
*The library has a children's **section**.*

secure
adjective
1 well fastened.

*A **secure** door.*
secure *verb*

see
sees seeing saw seen *verb*

to notice something with your eyes.

*You can **see** a long way with binoculars.*

seed
seeds *noun*

a small, hard part of some flowering plants, from which new plants may grow (see **growth** on page 94).

*sunflower **seeds***

seek
seeks seeking sought *verb*

to search for something, or try to achieve something.
***Seeking** help.*

seem
seems seeming seemed *verb*

to appear to be.
*She **seems** worried about something.*

2 safe and confident.
*My baby brother needs his teddy to make him feel **secure**.*

seesaw
seesaws *noun*

a balancing toy. Children play on a seesaw by sitting at either end of a board and rocking up and down.

seize
seizes seizing seized *verb*

to take hold of something suddenly.
*The thief **seized** her bag.*
■ say **seez**

seldom
adverb

not often, or rarely.
*I **seldom** get home before six.*

select
selects selecting selected *verb*

to choose something you want from a number of things.

*She **selected** a pot of paint from the tray.*
selection *noun*

selfish
adjective

only caring about yourself.
*He was very **selfish** and never shared his toys.*

sell
sells selling sold *verb*

to give something to someone in return for money.
*They **sell** all sorts of vegetables in the market.*

a b c d e f g h i j k l m n o p q r **s** t u v w x y z

A B C D E F G H I J K L M N O P Q R **S** T U V W X Y Z

semaphore

noun

a way of sending messages by signalling with two flags. The flags are held in different positions to represent each letter of the alphabet.

The letter "x" in semaphore.

■ say **sem**-a-for

send

sends sending sent *verb*

to make someone or something go to another place. *Send me a postcard!*

senior

adjective

older, more experienced, or more important. *The headteacher is senior to the other teachers.*

■ say **seen**-ee-or

sense

senses *noun*

1 one of the five ways in which we can receive information about the world. The five senses are sight, hearing, touch, smell, and taste.

You need your sense of hearing to use a telephone.
2 a feeling.
A sense of disappointment.
3 reasonable decisions or good judgement.
She has a lot of sense.
4 a meaning that can be understood.
It makes sense.

sensible

adjective

thinking clearly or in a practical way.

She was sensible about dressing for the cold weather.
sensibly *adverb*

sensitive

adjective

1 quick to feel, understand, or react to something.

Sensitive hairs on this plant make the leaves close when they are touched.
2 easily upset or hurt.
His skin was very sensitive where he had been burnt.

sentence

sentences *noun*

1 a group of words that make sense together. Sentences start with a capital letter and end with a full stop. They usually include a verb.
2 a punishment decided by a judge in a law court.
He received a four-year prison sentence.

separate

separates separating separated *verb*

to set apart from each other.

He separated the yellow marbles from the green ones.
separate *adjective*
separately *adverb*

sequel

sequels *noun*

something that follows an earlier event, or continues a story from a previous book or film.
A film sequel.

■ say **see**-kwul

sequence

sequences *noun*

a number of things that follow in a particular order.

■ say **see**-kwens

sequin

sequins *noun*

a small, shiny, metal or plastic disc that is sewn onto material as a decoration.

■ say **see**-kwin

serial

serials *noun*

a story that is broadcast or published in a series of parts.

series

noun

1 a group of similar things that follow one another in order.
A series of books on nature.

2 a television or radio show that is broadcast in regular episodes, or a set of novels about the same characters.

serious

adjective

1 requiring careful thought.
A serious question.
2 not smiling or laughing.
A serious expression.
3 worrying or dangerous.

The fallen tree caused serious damage to the roof.

servant

servants *noun*

a person whose job it is to work for someone in that person's home.

serve

serves serving served *verb*

1 to help someone, usually by giving them something they want or need.
2 to start play in games like tennis by hitting the ball to your opponent.

service

services *noun*

1 the act of serving.
Good restaurant **service**.
2 employment in the armed forces or in a public organization.
Military **service**.
3 the supply of something that helps or serves people.
A telephone **service**.
4 religious worship.
A church **service**.
5 the act of checking and repairing machinery so that it continues to work well.
A car **service**.

set

sets *noun*

a group of things that belong together.

A toy construction **set**.

set

sets setting set *verb*

1 to put in position or arrange something.
She **set** *the vase on the table.*
2 to give someone a task to do.
The teacher **set** *the class some homework.*
3 to go below the horizon.
The Sun **sets** *in the west.*
4 to go hard.
The cement took a long time to **set**.

settle

settles settling settled *verb*

1 to calm down, or stop moving.

The dog **settled** *down to sleep.*

2 to decide or agree about something without any doubts.
Settle *an argument.*

several

adjective

a number, usually three or more, but not many more.
Several *people waved as they walked past.*

severe

adjective

1 extremely bad.
A **severe** *accident.*
2 strict or hard.
The rock face was a **severe** *test for the climbers.*
severely *adverb*

sew

sews sewing sewn *verb*

to join something together using a needle and thread.

Sewing on a shirt button.

■ say **so**

sewer

sewers *noun*

a large, underground pipe or channel that takes dirty water and waste matter away.

■ say **soo**-er

sex

sexes *noun*

one of two groups, male or female, that people, animals, and plants are divided into.

shade

shades *noun*

1 a cool place where the Sun's direct light doesn't reach.

She sat in the **shade** *to read.*
shady *adjective*
2 a slight difference in colour.

Different **shades** *of paint.*

shadow

shadows *noun*

a dark shape made by something that is blocking the light.

shadow

shaft

shafts *noun*

1 a long, vertical passageway.
A lift **shaft**.
2 a long, straight part of something.
A **shaft** *of light.*

shaggy

adjective

having long, rough, untidy hair.

■ comparisons **shaggier shaggiest**

shake

shakes shaking shook shaken *verb*

1 to move something rapidly up and down, or from side to side.

Shaking hands.
2 to tremble with fear, shock, or cold.

shall

verb

a word used to show that something will happen in the future.
I **shall** *go shopping later.*

■ always used with another verb

shallow

adjective

not deep.

They played in **shallow** *water.*

shame

shames *noun*

1 a sad thing that happens.
It's a **shame** *you can't come.*
2 an uncomfortable, guilty feeling about something you have done.
ashamed *adjective*

shampoo

shampoos *noun*

a soapy liquid that is used for washing hair.

shampoo *verb*

shape

shapes *noun*

the outline or form of an object. Everything has a shape. Some shapes are two-dimensional, because they have width and length, but no height. Some shapes are three-dimensional, because they have width, length, and height.

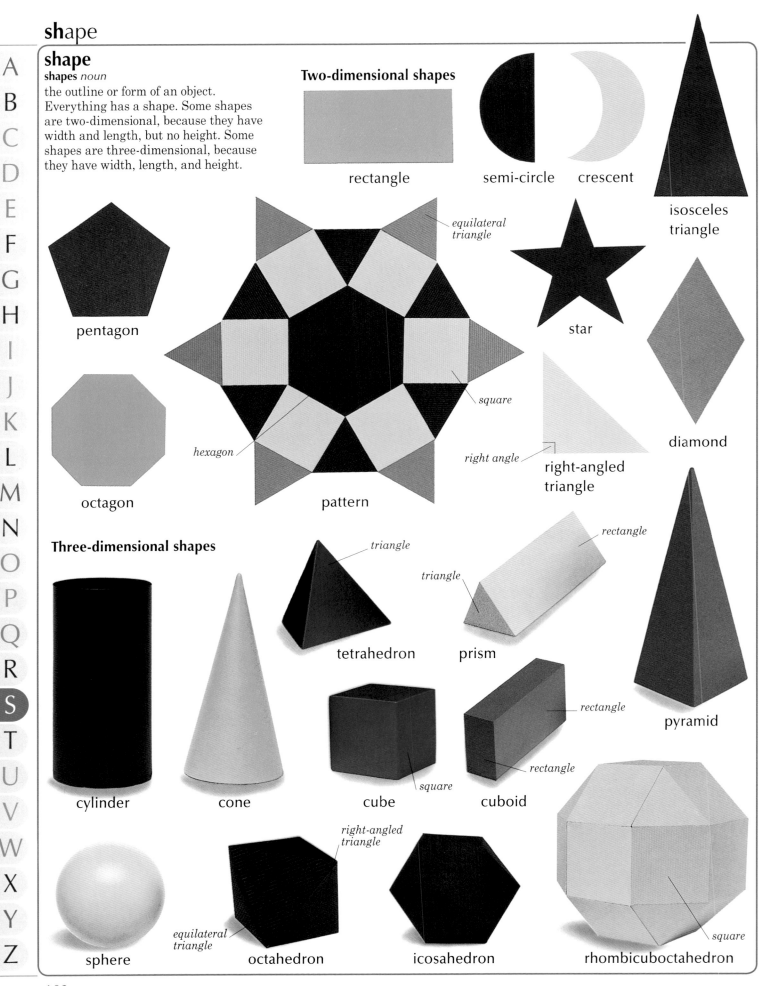

Two-dimensional shapes

rectangle

semi-circle

crescent

isosceles triangle

equilateral triangle

star

pentagon

square

diamond

octagon

hexagon

pattern

right angle

right-angled triangle

Three-dimensional shapes

triangle

rectangle

triangle

tetrahedron

prism

rectangle

pyramid

cylinder

cone

cube

square

cuboid

rectangle

rectangle

right-angled triangle

sphere

equilateral triangle

octahedron

icosahedron

rhombicuboctahedron

square

share

shares sharing shared *verb*
1 to have or use together.
2 to divide something into parts to give to others.

*They **shared** the melon.*

shark

sharks *noun*
a large fish with rows of sharp teeth, which lives in both cold and warm seas. Sharks eat fish or small water animals and are able to detect smells and sounds at great distances.

*leopard **shark***

sharp

adjective
with a thin edge or a fine point that may be used for cutting things.
*Careful – that knife is **sharp**!*
■ comparisons **sharper sharpest**

shatter

shatters shattering shattered *verb*
1 to break into many pieces.

*When she sang the top notes, the glass **shattered**.*
2 to ruin someone's plans, or to make someone upset.
*The loss of their jobs **shattered** their dreams of buying a home.*

shave

shaves shaving shaved *verb*
to remove hair from the skin with a razor.

shawl

shawls *noun*
a large piece of cloth worn over the shoulders.

shear

shears shearing sheared shorn *verb*
to cut off wool or fur.
*We **shear** sheep for their wool.*

shed

sheds *noun*
a small building for storing things such as garden tools.

shed

sheds shedding shed *verb*
to drop, lose, or separate from something.

*Snakes **shed** their skins.*

sheep

sheep *noun*
a farm animal reared for its wool and meat.

sheer

adjective
1 very steep.
*It was a **sheer** drop.*
2 complete or absolute.
***Sheer** exhaustion.*

sheet

sheets *noun*
a large, thin, flat piece of cloth, paper, plastic, or metal.
*A **sheet** of steel.*

shelf

shelves *noun*
a horizontal piece of wood or metal for storing things on.

shell

shells *noun*
the hard, outer covering that protects some living things. Eggs, nuts, and animals such as snails, crabs, and tortoises have shells (see **reptile** on page 168).

*egg **shell***   *nut **shell***

*crab's **shell***

shellfish

noun
any small, edible water animal that has a shell.

shield

shelter

shelters *noun*
a thing that protects someone or something from the weather or from danger.

*The doorway was a **shelter** from the rain.*
shelter *verb*
sheltered *adjective*

sheriff

sheriffs *noun*
1 in Scotland, a senior judge of a particular area.
2 in America, a person who is elected to keep the law and order in a particular area.

shield

shields *noun*
a strong piece of metal or leather that soldiers used to carry in battle to protect their bodies from their opponents' weapons.

*an ancient Indian **shield***

shield

shields shielding shielded *verb*
to protect.

*She **shielded** her eyes from the sun.*

a b c d e f g h i j k l m n o p q r **s** t u v w x y z

183

A
B
C
D
E
F
G
H
I
J
K
L
M
N
O
P
Q
R
S
T
U
V
W
X
Y
Z

shin
shins noun
the front part
of your leg below
the knee.

shin

shine
shines shining shone verb
to give out or reflect light.

The car headlights **shone**
on the road ahead.
shiny adjective

ship
ships noun
a large vessel for
transporting people and
cargo by sea. A ship is
powered by a motor or sails,
and is bigger than a boat.

shipwreck
shipwrecks noun
1 the destruction of a ship
at sea.
*The whole of the ship's cargo
was lost in the* **shipwreck**.
2 the remains of a ship that
was destroyed at sea.

■ say **ship**-rek

shirt
shirts noun
a piece of clothing
for covering the top
half of your body. Shirts
have sleeves and usually
have a collar and buttons
down the front.

shiver
shivers shivering shivered verb
to tremble with cold or fear.

He **shivered** *in the cold wind.*

shock
shocks noun
1 an unpleasant experience.
shock verb
shocking adjective
2 pain and injury caused
by a flow of electricity
through a person's body.
3 a state of weakness caused
by injury or pain, or by an
unpleasant experience.
He was in **shock** *after
the accident.*

shoe
shoes noun
a protective covering worn
on your feet, often
made of leather.

shook
from the verb **to shake**
The dog **shook** *himself dry.*

shoot
shoots shooting shot verb
1 to fire a bullet from a gun
or another weapon.

She **shot** *at the ducks in
the fairground booth, hoping
she would win a prize.*
2 to wound or kill with
a bullet or other weapon.
The hunters **shot** *the birds.*
3 to take pictures with
a camera.
She **shoots** *lots of
animal photographs.*

shop
shops noun
a place where people can
go to buy things they need
or want.
shop verb

shore
shores noun
the edge of an ocean, sea,
or lake.

*sea***shore**

short
adjective
1 not long in
measurement.

short hair

2 not lasting a long time.
The film was very **short**.
■ comparisons **shorter shortest**
■ opposite **long**
3 not having enough
of something.
We are **short** *of milk.*

shortage
shortages noun
a situation where there is
not enough of something.
There is a **shortage** *of bread
in the supermarket.*

shorten
**shortens shortening
shortened** verb
to make
something shorter.

She **shortened** *the little girl's
skirt for her.*

shorts
noun
a pair of short trousers
that usually finish above
the knees (see **sport** on
page 197).

shot
shots noun
the act of shooting.
She fired a **shot** *at the target.*

should
verb

a word used to show that
something must be done,
ought to be done, or is
expected to happen.
*I **should** do my homework.*

■ opposite **should not /
shouldn't**
■ always used with another verb

shoulder
shoulders *noun*

the place below your neck
where your
arms join
your body.

shoulder

shout
shouts shouting shouted *verb*
to call out loudly.
shout *noun*

shovel
shovels *noun*

a broad tool like a spade
that you use to scoop up
material such as earth,
sand, or rubbish.

show
shows showing showed *verb*
to allow something to be
seen, or to make something
clear to other people.

*He **showed** the class
his favourite photograph
in the book.*

show
shows *noun*

a public performance
or exhibition.

shower
showers *noun*

1 a device that sends out
a fine spray of water, used
for washing your body.

2 a short, sudden fall of rain.
3 a sudden fall of something
in large quantities.
*A **shower** of sparks.*

■ rhymes with **our**
shower *verb*

shred
shreds *noun*

a small, narrow strip
that has been cut or torn
off something.

*_**shreds** of paper_*

shriek
shrieks shrieking shrieked *verb*
to cry out in a high-pitched
voice because you are
excited or afraid.
*He **shrieked** when he saw
the mouse.*

■ say **shreek**
shriek *noun*

shrill
adjective

making a sharp, high sound.
*A **shrill** whistle.*

■ comparisons **shriller shrillest**

shrink
**shrinks shrinking shrank
shrunk** *verb*

to become
smaller.

*His jumper had **shrunk**
in the wash.*

shrivel
shrivels shrivelling shrivelled
verb

to become small and
wrinkled, or dry out.
*Water your plants or they
will **shrivel** and die.*

shrub
shrubs *noun*

a large plant that is smaller
than a tree, often with many
stems and little or no trunk.

shrug
shrugs shrugging shrugged *verb*
to raise your shoulders to
show that you do not care
or do not know.

shudder
shudders shuddering shuddered
verb

to shake or tremble violently
for a short time.
*The thought of spiders makes
me **shudder**.*

shuffle
shuffles shuffling shuffled *verb*
1 to mix things up to change
their order.

*He **shuffled** the cards.*
2 to move by dragging your
feet along the ground.

shut
shuts shutting shut *verb*
to close something.
*He **shut** the book carefully.*

■ opposite **open**
shut *adjective*

shutter
shutters *noun*

1 a hard cover for a window.

*The house has **shutters**
at every window.*
2 the part of a camera inside
the lens that opens and closes
to allow light to fall onto
the film.

shy
adjective

timid and lacking confidence
with people.

■ comparisons **shyer shyest**
shyly *adverb*

sick
adjective

ill, or not healthy.

■ comparisons **sicker sickest**

A B C D E F G H I J K L M N O P Q R S T U V W X Y Z

side
sides noun
1 the edge of something.
Triangles have three **sides**.
2 the outside surfaces of something, but not the front or back.

A car viewed from the **side**.
3 a team or group of people that is against another group.
Which **side** *are you on?*

sideways
adverb
towards the side or from the side.
Crabs walk **sideways**.

siege
sieges noun
the action of surrounding a place to try to force the people inside to surrender.
■ say **seej**

sieve
sieves noun
a container made of plastic or metal, that has mesh or small holes for sorting solids from liquids, or fine grains from larger pieces.

■ say **siv**
sieve verb

sift
sifts sifting sifted verb
to sort through something carefully in order to separate larger pieces from smaller pieces.

***Sifting** for gold.*

sigh
sighs sighing sighed verb
to let out a long, deep breath slowly.
■ say **sye**

sight
noun
1 the ability to see.
She lost her **sight** *in an accident.*
2 something that can be seen.
The ship was a fine **sight** *as it sailed up the river.*
■ say **site**

sign
signs signing signed verb
1 to write your signature.

The boy **signed** *his friend's plaster cast.*
2 to use sign language to communicate with people who have hearing difficulties.
■ say **sine**

sign
signs noun
1 a symbol that represents something.
The **sign** *for pound is £.*
2 a movement that expresses a meaning.
He nodded his head as a **sign** *that he wanted to leave.*
3 a public notice that gives information.

A road **sign**.
4 anything that indicates something is going to happen.
Is there any **sign** *of snow?*

signal
signals noun
1 an action or object that is used to send a message without words.

He put his right arm out as a **signal** *that he wanted to turn right.*
2 the electrical current by which sounds and pictures are transmitted to radios, televisions, and telephones.

signature
signatures noun
your special way of writing your own name.

■ say **sig**-na-chur

significant
adjective
very important, or having a special meaning.
A **significant** *event.*

Sikh
Sikhs noun
a person who follows Sikhism, an Indian religion. Sikhs believe in a single God.
■ say **seek**

silent
adjective
not making any sound.
silence noun
silently adverb

silhouette
silhouettes noun
a dark outline of something seen against a pale background.
■ say sil-oo-**et**

silk
silks noun
a thin, soft fabric made from threads spun by a silkworm.

silly
adjective
not sensible.
What a **silly** *idea!*
■ comparisons **sillier silliest**

silver
noun
1 a precious metal found in the ground, which is used in making coins and jewellery.

silver

silver ring

2 the colour of the metal silver.
silver adjective

similar
adjective
almost, but not exactly, the same.

These mugs are **similar**.

simmer
simmers simmering simmered *verb*
to cook something so that it bubbles very gently.
*Leave the soup to **simmer** for 20 minutes.*

simple
adjective
1 easy to understand or solve.
*A **simple** solution.*
■ opposite **complicated**
2 plain.

simple earrings   *ornate earrings*
■ comparisons **simpler simplest**

simplify
simplifies simplifying simplified *verb*
to make something easier.

sincere
adjective
honest, or not pretending.
*She was **sincere** when she said she was sorry.*
■ say sin-**seer**
sincerely *adverb*

sing
sings singing sang sung *verb*
1 to make a musical sound with your voice.

*She likes to **sing**.*
2 to perform by singing.
*She is **singing** in an opera.*

single
adjective
something that is only for one person, or only one of something.
single bed

sink
sinks sinking sank sunk *verb*
1 to go down below the surface of water.
*The boat was **sinking** fast.*
2 to go down slowly.
*The Sun **sank** below the horizon.*

sink
sinks *noun*
a basin with a water supply, taps, and a drain.

*kitchen **sink***

sip
sips sipping sipped *verb*
to drink in small amounts.

*He **sipped** his coffee slowly.*
sip *noun*

siren
sirens *noun*
a device that makes a loud noise, and is used as a warning signal.
*A fire-engine's **siren**.*
■ say **sye**-ren

sister
sisters *noun*
a female person who has the same mother and father as someone else.

sit
sits sitting sat *verb*
1 to rest your body by supporting your weight on your bottom, rather than on your feet.

2 to rest or be positioned.
*The bird **sat** on its perch.*
3 to take an exam.

site
sites *noun*
an area of ground used for a particular purpose.

*A building **site**.*

situation
situations *noun*
what is happening in a particular place at a particular time.

*He found himself in a desperate **situation**.*
■ say sit-yoo-**ay**-shun

size
sizes *noun*
a measurement of how large or small something is.

*These shoes are the wrong **size**.*

sizzle
sizzles sizzling sizzled *verb*
to make a hissing sound during cooking.
*The sausages **sizzled** under the grill.*

skate
skates skating skated *verb*
to slide along on a hard surface wearing special shoes with blades or wheels.

skating *noun*   *roller **skate***

skateboard
skateboards *noun*
a small board on wheels that people stand on to ride along.

skeleton
skeletons *noun*
a group of connected bones that support a person's or animal's body. There are 206 bones in a human skeleton.

seal **skeleton**

horny shield layer

ribs

bony layer

tortoise **skeleton**

bird **skeleton**

horn

frog **skeleton**

tusk

goat skull

elephant skull

skull (cranium)

collar bone (clavicle)

jawbone (mandible)

shoulder blade (scapula)

breast bone (sternum)

upper arm bone (humerus)

rib cage

spine

main forearm bone (ulna)

small forearm bone (radius)

hip bone (pelvis)

coccyx

hand bones (carpals)

metacarpal

phalanx

bony plates

radial

fish **skeleton**

thigh bone (femur)

kneecap (patella)

spine

main shin bone (tibia)

rib

skull

small shin bone (fibula)

foot bones (tarsals)

metatarsal

phalanx

monkey **skeleton**

snake **skeleton**

human **skeleton**

crocodile **skeleton**

sketch
sketches *noun*
1 a quick drawing.

*A **sketch** of a ship.*
2 a short play.

ski
skis skiing skied *verb*
to move over snow or ice on two long pieces of wood, metal, or plastic attached to special boots.

■ say **skee**
ski *noun*

skid
skids skidding skidded *verb*
to slide out of control.

*The car **skidded** on the icy road.*

skill
skills *noun*
an ability to do something.
*Juggling is a difficult **skill** to learn.*
skilful *adjective*

skin
skins *noun*
1 the thin, protective layer that animals and people have on the outside of their bodies (see **mammal** on page 124).
2 a thin layer that covers the flesh of vegetables and fruit (see **fruit** on page 85).

skip
skips skipping skipped *verb*
1 to move along, hopping lightly from one foot to another.
*She **skipped** down the road.*
2 to jump over a turning rope.

skipping rope

3 to miss something out deliberately.
*We'll **skip** the next question.*

skirt
skirts *noun*
a piece of clothing worn by a girl or woman, that hangs down from the waist.

skull
skulls *noun*
the bone frame of the head that protects the brain and supports the face (see **skeleton** on page 188).

*ram's **skull***

sky
skies *noun*
the air around the Earth as we see it. The sky usually looks blue.
*Not a cloud in the **sky**.*

skyscraper
skyscrapers *noun*
a very tall building with many storeys.

slam
slams slamming slammed *verb*
to shut something with a bang.
***Slam** the door.*

slang
noun
everyday words and phrases that are not normally used in writing or formal speaking.

slant
slants slanting slanted *verb*
to slope sideways.

*The wooden shelf **slanted** to the right.*

slap
slaps slapping slapped *verb*
to hit quickly with the palm of your hand.
slap *noun*

slave
slaves *noun*
someone who is forced to work without being paid and is not free to leave.

sledge
sledges *noun*
a low platform with curved strips of metal or wood underneath. Sledges are used to carry people and things over snow and ice.

sleek
adjective
smooth and shiny.
*Seals have **sleek** fur.*

sleep
sleeps sleeping slept *verb*
to rest your body and mind with your eyes closed.

sleep noun

sleeve
sleeves *noun*
the part of a piece of clothing that covers the arm.

sleeve

a b c d e f g h i j k l m n o p q r s t u v w x y z

A B C D E F G H I J K L M N O P Q R **S** T U V W X Y Z

sleigh
sleighs noun

a large sledge, usually pulled by an animal and used for travelling over snow or ice.

- say **slay**

slender
adjective

long and thin.
*A **slender** branch.*

slice
slices noun

a thin, flat piece cut from something.

*a **slice** of bread*

slice verb

slide
slides sliding slid verb

to move smoothly over a surface.
*She **slid** across the ice on her skates.*

slide
slides noun

1 a piece of children's play equipment for sliding down.

2 a transparent photo in a cardboard or plastic frame.

slight
adjective

very small in amount.
*There's a **slight** chance he'll come.*

- say **slite**
- comparisons **slighter slightest**

slightly adverb

slim
adjective

fairly thin.

- comparisons **slimmer slimmest**

slime
noun

an unpleasantly wet and slippery substance.
*Snails leave a trail of **slime** as they move along.*

slimy adjective

sling
slings noun

a piece of material used to support an injured arm.

sling

slip
slips slipping slipped verb

1 to move, or to move something easily or quietly.
*She **slipped** the note under the door.*
2 to slide or fall over by accident.
*He **slipped** in the mud.*

slipper
slippers noun

a soft, comfortable, loose shoe worn indoors.

slippery
adjective

smooth and difficult to grip.
*She couldn't keep hold of the **slippery** fish.*

slit
slits noun

a long, narrow, straight cut.
slit verb

slither
slithers slithering slithered verb

to slide along.
*Snakes **slither** over sand.*

slope
slopes noun

ground that slants.

*They practised on the artificial ski **slope**.*
slope verb

slot
slots noun

a small, narrow opening for putting something in.

*She put a coin in the **slot**.*
slot verb

slouch
slouches slouching slouched verb

to sit, stand, or walk so that your shoulders are bent over and your back is not straight.

- rhymes with **ouch**

slow
adjective

1 taking a long time, or not hurrying.

*Tortoises are very **slow**, while hares move fast.*
2 behind the time.
*This watch is 5 minutes **slow**.*

- comparisons **slower slowest**
- opposite **fast**

slowly adverb

sly
adjective

doing things in a sneaky or secretive way.
*She had a **sly** plan to trick her brother.*

- comparisons **slyer slyest**

slyly adverb

smack
smacks smacking smacked verb

to slap with the hand, usually as a punishment.

small
adjective

little in size, or not great or big.

small tin of paint   big tin of paint

- comparisons **smaller smallest**
- opposite **big**

smart

adjective

1 quick and intelligent.
*A **smart** remark.*
2 well-dressed.

*He looked very **smart** in his new suit.*

■ comparisons **smarter smartest**

smash

smashes smashing smashed *verb*

to break something into pieces.

*The plates **smashed** on the ground.*

smear

smears smearing smeared *verb*

to spread something sticky or messy.

*He **smeared** glue onto the back of the picture.*

■ say **smeer**
smear *noun*

smell

smells smelling smelled or **smelt** *verb*

1 to use your nose to notice odours.

***Smelling** a rose.*
2 to have an odour.
*The barn **smelled** of hay.*

smell

smells *noun*

1 the sense you use to notice odours through your nose.
***Smell** is one of the five senses.*
2 the odour of something, usually unpleasant.
*What a **smell**!*

smile

smiles smiling smiled *verb*

to show you are happy by widening your mouth and turning up the corners of your lips.

smile *noun*

smoke

noun

the cloud of gas and small ash particles that rises from a fire.
smoke *verb*

smooth

adjective

having an even surface, without sharp edges or lumps.
*As **smooth** as silk.*

■ opposite **rough**

smoulder

smoulders smouldering smouldered *verb*

to burn very slowly, without any flames.

■ say **smole**-der
smouldering *adjective*

smudge

smudges *noun*

a dirty mark made by rubbing or smearing something onto a surface.

*She had a **smudge** of chalk on her cheek.*
smudge *verb*

smuggle

smuggles smuggling smuggled *verb*

to take something into a place secretly and illegally.

smuggler

*They **smuggled** their cargo into the country under cover of darkness.*

snack

snacks *noun*

a small amount of food eaten between meals or instead of a meal.

snail

snails *noun*

a slow-moving animal with a spiral shell. Snails live on land or in water and eat mainly plants. When in danger, snails pull their soft bodies back into their shells.

snake

snakes *noun*

a long, thin reptile with no legs. Snakes eat insects, eggs, fish, or animals. Some snakes are poisonous, while others kill by squeezing their prey tightly.

*vine **snake***

snap

snaps snapping snapped *verb*

1 to make a sudden cracking noise.
***Snap** your fingers.*
2 to break suddenly.

*She **snapped** the stick in half.*
3 to talk in a quick, angry way.
*"Why haven't you done your homework?" he **snapped**.*

snarl

snarls snarling snarled *verb*

to growl fiercely, showing the teeth.
*The guard dog **snarled** at the burglar.*

a b c d e f g h i j k l m n o p q r **s** t u v w x y z

191

A B C D E F G H I J K L M N O P Q R S T U V W X Y Z

snatch
snatches snatching snatched
verb
to take hold of
something suddenly.
*I snatched my coat and ran
out of the house.*

sneak
sneaks sneaking sneaked *verb*
to move or act in a quiet
or secret way.

*He sneaked out of the room
when no one was looking.*
sneaky *adjective*

sneer
sneers sneering sneered *verb*
to show scorn about
something or someone.
*"My bike is better than yours,"
she sneered.*
sneer *noun*

sneeze
sneezes sneezing sneezed *verb*
to force air out of your nose in
a sudden, uncontrolled way.

sneeze *noun*

sniff
sniffs sniffing sniffed *verb*
1 to breathe in noisily
through your nose.
*Stop sniffing and blow
your nose!*
2 to breathe in through
your nose, trying to
smell something.
*Dogs find out about things
by sniffing them.*

snip
snips snipping snipped *verb*
to cut something
with scissors in one,
quick movement.

Snipping the top off the packet.

snore
snores snoring snored *verb*
to breathe noisily
as you sleep.

snorkel
snorkels *noun*
a short tube that a swimmer
holds in his or her mouth in
order to breathe underwater.

snorkel
snorkels snorkelling snorkelled
verb
to swim using a snorkel.

snout
snouts *noun*
an animal's long nose and
jaws (see **dinosaur** on page
61, **mammal** on page 124,
and **reptile** on page 168).

snow
noun
soft, white flakes of ice
that fall from the clouds
in cold weather.
snow *verb*
snowy *adjective*

snowball
snowballs *noun*
a ball shape made
by pressing
snow together.

snowdrift
snowdrifts *noun*
snow that has been blown
into a pile by the wind.

snowflake
snowflakes *noun*
a group of ice
crystals that
falls as a tiny
piece of snow.

snowman
snowmen *noun*
a figure that
you build
with snow.

snowplough
snowploughs *noun*
a machine used to clear
snow off the roads or off
railway tracks.

snowstorm
snowstorms *noun*
a storm during
which a lot of snow falls.

snug
adjective
comfortable
and warm.

*The cat looked very snug
curled up inside the basket.*

snuggle
snuggles snuggling snuggled *verb*
to lie close together in order to
keep warm.

soak
**soaks soaking
soaked** *verb*
to make
or become
thoroughly wet.

*The rain had
soaked her hair.*

soap
soaps *noun*
a substance used for washing.

soar
soars soaring soared *verb*
to fly high in the air.

*The eagle soared over
the valley.*

sob

sobs sobbing sobbed *verb*
to cry noisily, catching
your breath.

*The little boy was **sobbing** in
the corner.*

soccer

noun
another name for football.
Soccer is played by two teams
of 11 players. The winning
team is the one that scores
the most goals by kicking or
heading a large ball into a net.

social

adjective
to do with people living
together in communities.
Social history.
■ say **so**-shul

society

societies *noun*
1 all the people who live in
a group or in a country, and
their way of life.
*Laws protect **society**.*
2 a club or an organization.
*An animal welfare **society**.*
■ say sow-**sye**-eh-tee

sock

socks *noun*
a piece of
clothing that
covers your
foot and the
lower part of
your leg.

socket

sockets *noun*
a hole that something, such
as a plug or bulb, fits into.
*An electric **socket**.*

soft

adjective
1 easy to put out of shape by
touching, or not firm or hard.
*A **soft** pillow.*
■ opposite **hard**
2 gentle or smooth
to the touch.

*A **soft** ball of wool.*
■ opposite **rough**
3 not harsh or loud.
*A **soft** sound.*
■ comparisons **softer softest**

software

noun
programs that are put into
a computer to make it work.

soil

soils *noun*
the top layer of earth in
which plants can grow.

soil

*You can grow some vegetables
in pots of **soil**.*

solar

adjective
having to
do with the
power of the
Sun or any
other light.

solar panel

*A **solar**-powered calculator.*

sold

*from the verb **to sell***
*She **sold** her bike when
she grew too big for it.*

soldier

soldiers *noun*
a person who
is part of
an army.

*a Roman
soldier*

■ say **sole**-jer

sole

soles *noun*
1 the bottom part
of your foot.

sole

2 the bottom of a shoe.

3 an edible type of flat fish.

sole

adjective
one or only.
*He was the **sole** survivor
of the crash.*

solemn

adjective
serious.
*A **solemn** promise.*
■ say **sol**-em

solid

solids *noun*
a substance that keeps its
shape, and is not a liquid
or a gas.
*Ice, rock, and jelly are **solids**.*

solid

adjective
1 made of the same
thing all the
way through.

*This cat is carved from
a **solid** block of wood.*
2 firm or strongly made.
*They built a **solid** wall
around the castle.*

solo

adjective
on your own.
*She made a **solo** flight
around the world.*
■ say **so**-low

solo

solos *noun*
a piece of music that is played
or sung by one person.

*She played a violin **solo**.*

solution

solutions *noun*
1 the answer to a problem.
*The **solution** to the crossword.*
2 a liquid that has something
dissolved in it.
*A **solution** of salt and water.*
■ say so-**loo**-shun

A
B
C
D
E
F
G
H
I
J
K
L
M
N
O
P
Q
R
S
T
U
V
W
X
Y
Z

solve
solves solving solved *verb*
to find the answer to
a problem
or mystery.

*To **solve** the puzzle you must
end up with one marble in
the middle.*

some
adjective
1 several or a few, but not
a definite number or amount.
*Could you buy **some**
apples, please?*
2 part of, but not all.
*I ate **some** cake.*
♦ **Some**body has taken
my ruler.
♦ I must get there **some**how.
♦ Will **some**one lay the
table please.
♦ Let's get **some**thing to eat.
♦ **Some**times I go to the
swimming pool after school.
♦ You must have put
it **some**where.

somersault
**somersaults somersaulting
somersaulted** *verb*
to roll or leap forwards
or backwards so that your
whole body turns over.

■ say **summer**-salt
somersault *noun*

son
sons *noun*
a person's male child.
■ say **sun**

sonar
noun
a device that finds and
records the depth of water.
Sonar works by sending out
sound waves and measuring
how long it takes for the echo
to return. Submarines use
sonar to navigate at sea.

■ say **so**-nar

song
songs *noun*
a piece of music with words
that you sing.

soon
adverb
after a short time.
*It will **soon** be lunchtime.*

sore
adjective
aching or
hurting.

*His head was **sore** where
he had bumped it.*
■ comparisons **sorer sorest**

sorry
adjective
feeling sad or unhappy
about what has happened.
*I am **sorry** that I trod on
your toe.*
■ comparisons **sorrier sorriest**
■ opposite **pleased**

sort
sorts *noun*
a group of similar things,
or a type of something.
*What **sort** of holiday will
you have this year?*

sort
sorts sorting sorted *verb*
to arrange
things into
different types
or groups.

*He **sorted** the socks and put
them in pairs.*

sought
*from the verb **to seek**
The two countries
sought peace.*
■ say **sort**

soul
souls *noun*
the spiritual part of a person.
Some people believe that
the soul continues after
a person's body is dead.

sound
sounds *noun*
something that can be heard.

soup
soups *noun*
a liquid food made from fish,
meat, or vegetables, cooked
in water
or milk.

*vegetable **soup***
■ say **soop**

sour
adjective
with a sharp taste, like
vinegar or a lemon.
■ rhymes with **power**

source
sources *noun*
the place where something
comes from or is found.
*The **source** of a river.*

south
noun
one of the four main
directions on a compass.
South is to your right when
you are facing the rising Sun.

north

west *east*

south

southern *adjective*

souvenir
souvenirs *noun*
something that you keep
to remind you of a person,
place, or event.
*Holiday **souvenirs**.*
■ say soo-ven-**neer**

sow
sows sowing sowed sown *verb*
to put seeds in the soil
so that they will grow
into plants.

*She **sowed** some seeds
in the window box.*
■ say **so**

spider

spiders *noun*

a small animal with eight legs. Spiders spin nets of thin, sticky threads called webs, which they use to trap insects for food. They kill their prey with poison.

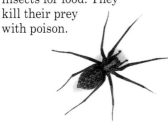

spike

spikes *noun*

a sharp point, often made of metal or wood, or a pointed part of an animal or plant.

spill

spills spilling spilled or **spilt** *verb*

to let something drop or overflow from a container.

*She **spilt** her drink.*

spin

spins spinning spun *verb*

1 to turn around quickly, or to make something turn quickly.

2 to produce threads. Spiders and silkworms spin threads by producing them from their bodies. People spin raw cotton and wool to make threads.

spine

spines *noun*

1 the column of bones that makes up the backbone of a skeleton (see **skeleton** on page 188).

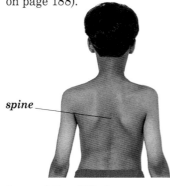

spine

2 one of the stiff, sharp points on an animal, like a porcupine, or on a plant, like a cactus (see **fish** on page 79, **plant** on page 151, and **sea life** on page 178).
3 the part of a book where the pages are joined and that holds the book together.

spiral

spirals *noun*

an object shaped in a curve that turns around a central point.

spire

spires *noun*

a tall, pointed structure at the top of a tower.

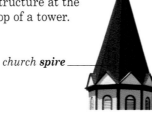

*church **spire***

spirit

spirits *noun*

1 a person's mind and feelings.
*In good **spirits**.*
spiritual *adjective*
2 a being, such as a ghost, that does not have a body.

spit

spits spitting spat *verb*

to force saliva or something else out of your mouth.
*She **spat** out the rotten apple.*

spite

noun

deliberate nastiness.
*He ignored him out of **spite**.*
spiteful *adjective*

splash

splashes splashing splashed *verb*

to scatter water or another liquid.

*The children **splashed** about in the pool.*
splash *noun*

splinter

splinters *noun*

a thin, sharp piece that has broken off something hard, such as wood or glass.

split

splits splitting split *verb*

1 to divide into parts.

*She **split** the logs with an axe.*
2 to tear or crack, perhaps by mistake.
*The bag **split** open.*

splutter

splutters spluttering spluttered *verb*

to make a series of short hissing or spitting noises.
*The sauce **spluttered** in the pan.*

spoil

spoils spoiling spoiled or **spoilt** *verb*

1 to destroy or damage something.
*Don't draw on that – you'll **spoil** it.*
2 to give a child so much that he or she becomes demanding and unpleasant.

spoke

from the verb **to speak**
*They **spoke** in a whisper in case anyone was listening.*

sponge

sponges *noun*

a soft, flexible material used for washing and cleaning. Some sponges are made of plastic, but real sponges are made from the skeletons of sea creatures.

■ say **spunj**

*bath **sponge***

sponsor

sponsors sponsoring sponsored *verb*

to give money to support a charity or event. Sometimes money is given in return for a person completing an activity.
*The sports shop **sponsored** the cross-country race.*
sponsor *noun*

spoon

spoons *noun*

a small utensil with a curved bowl at one end. Spoons are used for eating or stirring.

*plastic **spoon***

*metal **spoon***

sport

sports *noun*
an activity or game that needs physical effort or skill. People play sport for exercise or pleasure.

badminton

head

shaft

feathers

shuttlecocks

handle

racket

table tennis

blade

bat   ball

windsurfing

ball

tee

mast

sail

batten

boom

buoyancy aid

wetsuit

board

sailboard

golf

shaft

wood   iron   putter

head

golf clubs

American football

face guard

armpad   football helmet

shoulder and chest pads

athletics

spike

track shoes

basketball

basketball ring

basketball

net

singlet

shorts

trainers

squash

strings

frame

throat

shaft

ball

grip

racket

field hockey

goalkeeper's shoe cover

field hockey shoe

head

field hockey stick   ball

ice hockey

skates   *blade*

puck

shaft

blade

ice hockey stick

cricket

ball

bail

grip

blade

stump

wicket   bat

baseball

webbed pocket

ball

barrel

fielding glove   bat

a b c d e f g h i j k l m n o p q r **s** t u v w x y z

197

A B C D E F G H I J K L M N O P Q R **S** T U V W X Y Z

spot

spots *noun*

1 a small, round area that is a different colour from the area around it.
This cup and saucer are covered in white **spots**.
2 a place.
It was a perfect picnic **spot**.

spot

spots spotting spotted *verb*
to notice or see.
Can you **spot** *my car?*

spotlight

spotlights *noun*
a strong light pointed at a small area, usually on a stage.

spout

spouts *noun*
the part of a container that a liquid is poured from.

teapot **spout**

spray

sprays spraying sprayed *verb*
to scatter a fine shower of liquid onto something.

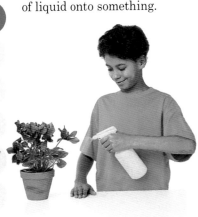

He **sprayed** *the plant with water.*
spray *noun*

spread

spreads spreading spread *verb*
to open something out or make it cover a bigger area.

He **spread** *the blanket out on the ground.*
■ say **spred**

spring

springs *noun*

1 the season between winter and summer when the weather becomes warmer and many plants start to grow.
2 a coil of thin metal that jumps back into shape after it has been pressed together or pulled apart.

3 a place where water flows out of the ground.

spring

springs springing sprang sprung *verb*

1 to jump upwards in a lively way.

She **sprang** *over the gymnastic apparatus.*
spring *noun*
2 to appear or grow quickly.
New houses **sprang** *up all over the hillside.*

sprint

sprints sprinting sprinted *verb*
to run very fast.

sprint *noun*

sprout

sprouts sprouting sprouted *verb*
to begin to grow.

Green shoots **sprouted** *from the bean.*
sprout *noun*

spy

spies *noun*
a person who gathers information in secret.
spy *verb*

square

squares *noun*
a shape with four equal sides and four right angles (see **shape** on page 182).
square *adjective*

squash

squashes squashing squashed *verb*

1 to crush something so that it becomes flat.
2 to squeeze together.

We all **squashed** *onto the sofa.*
■ say **skwosh**

squeak

squeaks squeaking squeaked *verb*
to make a short, shrill sound, like the sound a mouse makes.
squeak *noun*

squeal

squeals squealing squealed *verb*
to make a long, shrill sound like the sound a piglet makes.
squeal *noun*

squeeze

squeezes squeezing squeezed *verb*
to press hard, often in order to push something out.

She **squeezed** *the paint out of the tube.*

squirm

squirms squirming squirmed *verb*
to twist the body from side to side, or to wriggle.
The rabbit **squirmed** *under the fence.*
■ say **skwurm**

squirrel

squirrels noun

a small, furry rodent. Some types of squirrel live in trees, while others live on the ground. Squirrels eat nuts, berries, fruits, and insects.

squirt

squirts squirting squirted verb

to shoot out a thin jet of liquid.

He **squirted** the washing-up liquid into the bowl.
■ rhymes with **dirt**

stab

stabs stabbing stabbed verb

to pierce or wound with a knife or other pointed object. *She **stabbed** the potato with a fork to see if it was cooked.*

stable

stables noun

a building where horses or other animals are kept.

*a **stable** for horses*

stack

stacks noun

a pile of things, one on top of another.

*A **stack** of plates.*
stack verb

stadium

stadiums or **stadia** noun

a sports ground surrounded by seats for spectators.

staff

noun

a group of people who work together in a business, school, or other organization.

*The **staff** at the garage wear a uniform.*

stag

stags noun

a male deer, especially a red deer that is over four years old.

stage

stages noun

1 a platform used for plays and other performances.
2 a point reached in the progress of something. *They made the long journey in several **stages.***

stagger

staggers staggering staggered verb

to walk in an unsteady way. *They **staggered** home after the long walk.*

stain

stains noun

a dirty mark that is difficult to remove.

*coffee **stain***
stain verb

stair

stairs noun

one of a series of steps, set one after the other.

*A flight of **stairs**.*

stalactite

stalactites noun

a spike of rock that is formed from dripping water and hangs down from the roof of a cave.
■ say **stal**-ak-tite

stalagmite

stalagmites noun

a spike of rock that is formed by dripping water and builds up on the floor of a cave.

■ say **stal**-ag-mite

stale

adjective

no longer fresh. ***Stale** bread is hard and dry.*

stalk

stalks noun

1 the stem of a plant or a leaf (see **plant** on page 151).
2 a long, thin part of an animal (see **sea life** on page 178).

leaf stalk

stall

stalls noun

1 an area divided off in a stable or barn for one animal.

2 a table used to display and sell goods, usually at a market.

■ rhymes with **call**

stall

stalls stalling stalled verb

to come to a stop suddenly, without meaning to. *The old car **stalled** at the traffic lights.*

stammer

stammers stammering stammered verb

to stutter or speak with difficulty, often stopping in the middle of words and repeating sounds.
stammer noun

a
b
c
d
e
f
g
h
i
j
k
l
m
n
o
p
q
r
s
t
u
v
w
x
y
z

A
B
C
D
E
F
G
H
I
J
K
L
M
N
O
P
Q
R
S
T
U
V
W
X
Y
Z

stamp
stamps *noun*
a sticker you put on an envelope or parcel to show that you have paid for it to be delivered.

stamp
stamps stamping stamped *verb*
to bring your foot down very hard.

stamp noun

stand
stands standing stood *verb*
to be in an upright position.

*She **stood** on a box to look over the fence.*

standard
standards *noun*
a level of quality that is considered acceptable, or how good something is.
*The **standard** of spelling in this class is very high.*

standard
adjective
ordinary or usual.
*Headlights are **standard** equipment on all cars.*

stank
from the verb **to stink**
*The boat **stank** of fish.*

staple
staples *noun*
a small, thin strip of metal used to join sheets of paper together.
■ say **stay**-pul

star
stars *noun*
1 an object in the sky that appears as a ball of light. The Sun is the nearest star to Earth.

2 a shape with five or more points (see **shape** on page 182).
3 a famous actor, actress, or other performer.

stare
stares staring stared *verb*
to look for a long time at something with your eyes wide open.

*The cat **stared** at the mouse.*

starfish
starfish *noun*
a star-shaped sea animal, usually with five arms. Starfish eat plants and sea animals, such as crabs and other shellfish. They sense things through tentacles on their arms (see **sea life** on page 178).

start
starts starting started *verb*
to begin.

*The runners lined up, ready to **start** the race.*
start *noun*

startle
startles startling startled *verb*
to give someone a surprise or a shock.

*His son **startled** him.*

starve
starves starving starved *verb*
to suffer or die from lack of food.
starvation *noun*

state
states *noun*
1 the condition of something, or what it is like.
*In an untidy **state**.*
2 a group of people under one government. A state can be a whole country or part of a country.
*The United **States** of America.*

state
states stating stated *verb*
to say something clearly.
statement *noun*

station
stations *noun*
1 a place where buses and trains stop so that people can get on and off.
2 a building used by a public service, such as the police.
*A police **station**.*
■ say **stay**-shun

statue
statues *noun*
a figure of a person or animal made from stone, wood, or another hard material.

Statue of Liberty

■ say **stat**-tyoo

stay
stays staying stayed *verb*
1 to remain in one place.
*Dad **stayed** at home while we went to the show.*
2 to live somewhere for a short time.
*I went to **stay** with my cousin during the holidays.*
3 to continue to be in one state.
*It **stayed** sunny all week.*

steady
adjective
1 firm.
*He held the ladder **steady**.*
2 continuous or unchanging.
*A **steady** fall of snow.*
■ say **sted**-ee
■ comparisons **steadier**
steadiest
steadily *adverb*

steak
steaks *noun*
a thick slice of fish or meat, usually beef.
■ say **stake**

steal

steals stealing stole stolen *verb*
to take something that does not belong to you, without the owner's permission.

*Magpies **steal** shiny things.*

steam

noun
the gas that water turns into when it boils. Steam can be used as a source of power.

steel

noun
a hard, strong metal made from iron mixed with a small amount of carbon. Steel can also be combined with other metals. Stainless steel is a mixture of steel, chromium, and nickel.

grater   *hand whisk*

*Many kitchen utensils are made of **steel**.*

steep

adjective
slanting up or down sharply.
*A **steep** hill.*

■ comparisons **steeper steepest**

steer

steers steering steered *verb*
to control the direction something is going in.
*She **steered** her car into the driveway.*

stem

stems *noun*
the main stalk of a plant that grows up out of the soil (see **growth** on page 94 and **plant** on page 151).

step

steps *noun*
1 the movement made by lifting your foot and putting it down when you walk along or dance.
step *verb*
2 a level surface for putting your foot on to help you climb up or down, usually as part of a staircase or ladder.

3 a stage in a series of things to do.
*The first **step** in learning to swim is to enjoy being in the water.*

stepladder

stepladders *noun*
a portable ladder with flat steps that can stand up without leaning on anything.

stereo

stereos *noun*
equipment for playing recorded sound. The sound comes from two different directions, so that it sounds natural.

■ say **ster**-ree-oh
stereo *adjective*

stern

adjective
firm or strict.
*A **stern** warning.*

stern

noun
the back part of a ship or boat (see **boat** on page 31).

*The dinghy was kept at the **stern** of the yacht.*

stethoscope

stethoscopes *noun*
an instrument used by doctors for listening to the heart and lungs.

stick

sticks *noun*
1 a thin piece of wood.
2 something long and thin.
*A **stick** of celery.*

stick

sticks sticking stuck *verb*
1 to glue or fasten one thing to another.
*She **stuck** the model aeroplane together with glue.*
sticky *adjective*
2 to press a sharp point into something.
*He **stuck** a pin into the balloon.*

stiff

adjective
not easy to bend or move.

*This folder is made of **stiff** plastic card.*

■ comparisons **stiffer stiffest**

still

adverb
1 up until now.
*He is **still** there.*
2 even so, or nevertheless.
*I don't like rice pudding, but I **still** have to eat it.*
3 an even larger amount.
***Still** more snow fell.*

still

adjective
not moving or without sound.

stilt

stilts *noun*
one of a pair or set of long poles used to support a person or thing high off the ground.

*pair of **stilts***

3 to project out.

*The bread **stuck** out of the basket.*

a b c d e f g h i j k l m n o p q r **s** t u v w x y z

A B C D E F G H I J K L M N O P Q R S T U V W X Y Z

sting
stings stinging stung *verb*
to prick the skin, or to cause a sharp pain. Some insects sting when they are frightened or angry, injecting a poison into the skin.

stink
stinks stinking stank stunk *verb*
to have a strong, bad smell. *This bin **stinks**!*
stink *noun*

stir
stirs stirring stirred *verb*
to mix something by moving it around with a spoon or similar tool.

stitch
stitches *noun*
a loop of thread or wool made with a needle in sewing or knitting.

cross **stitch**

stitch *verb*

stock
stocks stocking stocked *verb*
to keep a supply of something.
*Do you **stock** writing paper in this shop?*
stock *noun*

stolen
*from the verb **to steal***
*A painting was **stolen** from the gallery.*

stomach
stomachs *noun*
1 the part of your body where food goes after you have eaten it, to be partly digested.

stomach

2 the outside part of your body at the front between your ribs and your hips.
■ say **stum**-uk

stone
stones *noun*
1 the hard material that rocks are made of.

*A bird table made of **stone**.*

2 a small, loose piece of rock.

*The field was full of **stones**.*

stood
*from the verb **to stand***
*They **stood** at the bus-stop for an hour.*

stool
stools *noun*
a seat without a back or arms.

*kitchen **stool***

stop
stops stopping stopped *verb*
1 to come, or bring, to an end. *The rain **stopped**.*
2 to prevent something from happening.

*The man **stopped** the boy from running into the road.*

stop-watch
stop-watches *noun*
a watch that can be started and stopped to measure how much time something takes (see **time** on page 216).

store
stores storing stored *verb*
to put something away for when you need it.

*They **stored** the sports equipment in the cupboard.*

storey
storeys *noun*
all the rooms on one floor of a building.

stork
storks *noun*
a large bird with a long beak and long legs that lives near shallow water. Storks eat fish, insects, rodents, and snakes. They live in large nests built in trees and on cliffs.

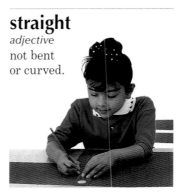

marabou **stork**

storm
storms *noun*
a period of bad weather, with strong winds and thunder and lightning, or snow.

story
stories *noun*
a tale, or a description of an event, either real or imaginary. *Tell me a **story**.*

stove
stoves *noun*
a piece of equipment used for cooking or heating.

straight
adjective
not bent or curved.

*She drew a **straight** line.*
■ say **strate**
■ comparisons **straighter straightest**

strain
strains straining strained *verb*
1 to try so hard that it hurts or tires you.
*Be careful not to **strain** yourself when you exercise.*
strain *noun*
2 to pass something through a sieve in order to filter out larger pieces.

strand
strands *noun*
1 any thread that is twisted together with others to make a stronger line.
2 anything that looks like a rope or string.
*A **strand** of hair.*

stranded
adjective
unable to leave somewhere.

*He was left **stranded** on the island.*

strange
adjective
unusual or unfamiliar.
■ comparisons **stranger** **strangest**

stranger
strangers *noun*
a person you have not seen before or who is new to a place.

strap
straps *noun*
a strip of leather or other material, used for fastening or holding things.

shoulder **strap**

straw
straws *noun*
1 stalks of dried wheat or other cereal plants. Straw is used for farm animals and pets to lie on.

2 a hollow tube used for drinking liquids through.

strawberry
strawberries *noun*
a small, red fruit that is soft and sweet and grows on a plant.

stray
strays straying strayed *verb*
to wander away from someone or somewhere.

*One duckling **strayed** from its mother.*

streak
streaks *noun*
a long, thin mark or smear.
*After the football game his clothes were covered with **streaks** of mud.*

stream
streams *noun*
1 a small river.

2 a steady flow of something.
*A **stream** of cars rushed along the street.*

streamlined
adjective
having a smooth shape that allows quick and easy movement through air or water.

*This cycling helmet has a **streamlined** shape.*
streamline *verb*

street
streets *noun*
a road in a city or town.
*What is the name of the **street** you live in?*

strength
strengths *noun*
the quality of being strong or powerful.

*The weight-lifter had incredible **strength** in his arms.*

strengthen
strengthens strengthening strengthened *verb*
to make something strong or stronger.
*You can **strengthen** your muscles by exercising.*

stress
stresses *noun*
1 a strain on a person or thing.
*He is under a lot of **stress**.*
2 an extra force laid on part of a word when speaking. In the word "stretcher", the stress is on the first syllable.

stretch
stretches stretching stretched *verb*
1 to pull something so that it becomes longer or bigger.
2 to straighten or reach out as much as you can with part of your body.

*She **stretched** out her arms.*

3 to reach one place from another.

*The road **stretches** all the way to the mountains.*

stretcher
stretchers *noun*
a light bed with handles that is used to carry someone who is hurt.

strict
adjective
keeping closely to the rules.
*The teacher was very **strict**.*
■ comparisons **stricter strictest**

a b c d e f g h i j k l m n o p q r s t u v w x y z

stride
strides striding strode *verb*
to walk with long steps.

stride *noun*

strike
strikes *noun*
the action of stopping work in order to get better pay and working conditions, or to protest about something.
On strike.

strike
strikes striking struck *verb*
1 to hit something hard.

The tree was **struck** by lightning.
2 to stop work in order to protest about something.

string
strings *noun*
a long, narrow cord used for fastening or as part of a musical instrument (see **musical instrument** on page 133).

strip
strips *noun*
a long, narrow piece of something.
*A **strip** of paper.*

stripe
stripes *noun*
a long, narrow band of colour.

This swimsuit has blue **stripes**.
striped *adjective*
stripy *adjective*

stroke
strokes stroking stroked *verb*
to rub gently with the hand.

He **stroked** the rabbit.

stroll
strolls strolling strolled *verb*
to walk slowly in a relaxed way.
*They **strolled** through the woods.*
stroll *noun*

strong
adjective
1 tough.
*A **strong** rope.*
2 powerful.
*Elephants are very **strong**.*
■ comparisons **stronger strongest**
■ opposite **weak**

structure
structures *noun*
1 something that has been built.

The Eiffel Tower is a tall, steel **structure**.

2 the way that something is put together or organized.
*A company's **structure**.*

struggle
struggles struggling struggled *verb*
to try hard, or to fight hard.
*He **struggled** with the maths problem for a long time.*

stubborn
adjective
determined to have your own way.

A **stubborn** mule.
■ say **stub**-ern

stuck
from the verb **to stick**
1 *I **stuck** the label on the jar.*
2 *The thorn **stuck** in her leg.*

student
students *noun*
a person who is studying at school, college, or university.
■ say **stew**-dent

studio
studios *noun*
1 a room where an artist or photographer works.
2 a room or building where television programmes or films are made.
■ say **stew**-dee-oh

television **studio**

study
studies studying studied *verb*
1 to look at something carefully.

She **studied** the flower through a magnifying glass.
2 to learn about a subject from books and lessons.
*She **studied** for her exams.*

stuffy
adjective
without fresh air.
*The room was **stuffy** so she opened the window to let some fresh air in.*

stumble
stumbles stumbling stumbled *verb*
to trip up and almost fall.

stump
stumps *noun*
a short part of something left behind after the rest has been cut or worn away.

tree **stump**

stunt
stunts *noun*
a dangerous action that is done as part of a film or performance.

*The **stunt** involved jumping over the cars on a motorbike.*

stupid
adjective
foolish, or not intelligent.
- say **stew**-pid
- comparisons **stupider stupidest**
- opposite **clever**

sturdy
adjective
strong and well made.
*A **sturdy** table.*
- comparisons **sturdier sturdiest**

stutter
stutters stuttering stuttered *verb*
to stammer or speak with difficulty, often stopping in the middle of words or repeating sounds.
stutter *noun*

style
styles *noun*
1 the way that something is done or made.
*Which **style** of tennis racket do you prefer, wooden or metal?*
2 a fashion or design.

*A 1950s **style** car.*
- say **stile**

subject
subjects *noun*
something you are talking, writing, or learning about.

submarine
submarines *noun*
a vessel that can travel underwater.

- say sub-ma-**reen**

substance
substances *noun*
a material or object that can be seen or felt.
*There was a sticky **substance** on the table.*

substitute
substitutes *noun*
someone or something that is used in place of another person or thing.

butter

margarine

*Margarine is used as a **substitute** for butter.*
- say **sub**-sti-tyoot

subtract
subtracts subtracting subtracted *verb*
to take one number away from another number.

$$8-5=3$$

*Five **subtracted** from eight equals three.*
subtraction *noun*

subway
subways *noun*
an underground tunnel for pedestrians beneath a road.

succeed
succeeds succeeding succeeded *verb*
to manage to do what you were trying to do.
*They **succeeded** in moving the heavy piano up the stairs.*
- say suk-**seed**

success
successes *noun*
a thing that works out well.
*His magic act was a complete **success**.*
- say suk-**sess**
successful *adjective*

such
adjective
1 of a particular kind.
*Pins, needles, and **such** things.*
2 so much.

*There was **such** a lot of work to do, he didn't know where to begin.*

suck
sucks sucking sucked *verb*
to pull liquid into your mouth, or to hold something in your mouth and lick it.

*He **sucked** his drink through a straw.*

suddenly
adverb
quickly and without warning.

***Suddenly** she had an idea.*
sudden *adjective*

suffer
suffers suffering suffered *verb*
to feel pain, or to be ill.
*She is **suffering** from measles.*

suffocate
suffocates suffocating suffocated *verb*
to die because you are unable to breathe.
- say **suf**-a-kate

sugar
noun
a sweet substance made from plants and used in food and drinks.

brown sugar

- say **shoog**-er

suggest
suggests suggesting suggested *verb*
to mention a new idea or plan to someone.
*I **suggested** going to the park to ride our bikes.*
- say su-**jest**
suggestion *noun*

a b c d e f g h i j k l m n o p q r **s** t u v w x y z

suicide
noun
killing yourself deliberately.
- say **soo**-i-side

suit
suits *noun*
a jacket and skirt or trousers, designed to be worn together.

- rhymes with **boot**

suit
suits suiting suited *verb*
to look good on someone.
*Does this **suit** me?*

suitable
adjective
right for a particular purpose or occasion.

*These boots are **suitable** for walking over rough ground.*
- say **soo**-ta-bul

suitcase
suitcases *noun*
a large bag with a handle that is used for carrying clothing and other things when you travel.

sulk
sulks sulking sulked *verb*
to be silent because you are in a bad temper.
sulky *adjective*

sum
sums *noun*
1 a total made by adding two or more numbers together.

$$3+49=52$$

*The **sum** of 3 and 49 is 52.*
2 an exercise in arithmetic.
*Have you done your **sums**?*

summary
summaries *noun*
a short form of a story or a piece of information that just gives the main points.
*They gave a **summary** of the news at the end of the programme.*

summer
summers *noun*
the warmest season of the year. Summer comes between spring and autumn.

summit
summits *noun*
the highest point of something.

*The two climbers finally reached the **summit** of the mountain.*

Sun
noun
the star that is the centre of our solar system (see **universe** on page 229).

sun
noun
the light and heat that we get from the Sun.
*The cat was sitting in the **sun**.*

sunflower
sunflowers *noun*
a tall plant with large, yellow flowers. The seeds can be eaten or used to make cooking oil.

sunglasses
noun
glasses with dark lenses that you wear to protect your eyes from sunlight.

sunlight
noun
the light from the Sun.

sunrise
sunrises *noun*
the time when the Sun is coming up over the horizon in the morning.

sunset
sunsets *noun*
the time when the Sun is going down below the horizon in the evening.

sunshine
noun
bright sunlight.

superb
adjective
extremely good.
*A **superb** performance.*
- say soo-**purb**

superior
adjective
higher in rank or position.
*Soldiers must salute their **superior** officers.*
- say soo-**peer**-ee-er
- opposite **inferior**

supermarket
supermarkets *noun*
a large shop that sells food and other items. People select the goods they want and pay for them at the exit.

supersonic
adjective
faster than the speed of sound.

*Concorde is a **supersonic** aircraft.*
- say soo-per-**son**-ic

superstition
superstitions *noun*
a false belief based on fear or lack of knowledge about something.
*A common **superstition** is that it is unlucky to walk under ladders.*
- say soo-per-**stish**-un
superstitious *adjective*

supper
suppers *noun*
a small meal eaten in the evening.

supply

supplies *noun*
a quantity of something that
may be needed.

*The farmer kept a **supply**
of grain in the barn.*
supply *verb*

support

supports supporting supported
verb
to hold something or someone
up to stop it, or them,
from falling.

*She **supported** her friend
who had hurt his leg.*
support *noun*

suppose

supposes supposing supposed
verb
to think that something is
true or likely.
*I **suppose** you are right.*

sure

adjective
certain, or with no doubt.
*I am **sure** you will enjoy your
stay here.*
■ say **shoor**

surf

surfs surfing surfed *verb*
1 to balance on a special
board while riding on waves
as they begin to break near
the seashore.
2 to explore the internet.

surfer

surfboard

surface

surfaces *noun*
the outside or top
of something.

*These buttons have
shiny **surfaces**.*
■ say **sur**-fis

surgeon

surgeons *noun*
a doctor
who treats
patients by
doing operations.

■ say **ser**-jun

surgery

surgeries *noun*
1 a medical operation that
involves cutting open part
of a patient's body.
2 a place where you go
to see a doctor or dentist
for treatment.
■ say **ser**-jer-ee

surname

surnames *noun*
the last part of someone's
name that shows which
family they belong to.

surprise

surprises *noun*
something that happens
when you do not expect it.
*She got a **surprise** when
she received the parcel!*
surprise *verb*
surprising *adjective*

surrender

**surrenders surrendering
surrendered** *verb*
to give yourself up.

*The kidnappers finally
surrendered to the police.*

surround

**surrounds surrounding
surrounded** *verb*
to be or to go on all sides
of something.

*The bench
surrounded
the tree trunk.*

survive

survives surviving survived *verb*
to continue to live after an
event in which you might
have died.
*They all **survived** the crash.*

survivor

survivors *noun*
a person who is still alive
after experiencing an event
that might have killed them.
*He was one of three **survivors**
of the shipwreck.*
■ say sur-**vye**-ver

suspect

suspects suspecting suspected
verb
1 to think that someone
is guilty of something.
*I **suspect** her of being a thief.*
suspect *noun*
2 to suppose that something
is likely.
*I **suspect** it will rain.*

suspend

**suspends suspending
suspended** *verb*
to attach something
by its top so that it
hangs down.

*The baskets are
suspended from
a hook.*

suspense

noun
the feeling of being anxious
or excited about what might
happen next.
*This film is full of **suspense**.*

suspicious

adjective
1 suspecting something bad.
*I became **suspicious** when
my friends didn't answer
the telephone for a week.*
2 behaving in a way that
makes people
suspect you.

*A **suspicious** character
was climbing into the house.*
■ say sus-**pish**-us

a b c d e f g h i j k l m n o p q r **s** t u v w x y z

swallow
swallows swallowing swallowed *verb*

to make your food go down your throat and into your stomach.

The snake **swallowed** *the egg whole.*

swallow
swallows *noun*

a small bird with long wings and a forked tail. Swallows eat mainly insects and are found in most parts of the world.

swam
from the verb **to swim**
I **swam** *across the pool.*

swamp
swamps *noun*

an area of wet or marshy land.

A mangrove **swamp**.

swan
swans *noun*

a large bird that lives in and around water. Swans feed on water plants, which they grasp with their sharp-edged bills. Swans are related to geese.

■ say **swon**

swap
swaps swapping swapped *verb*

to give one thing in return for something else.
He **swapped** *his toy for her tennis racket.*

swarm
swarms *noun*

a large number of insects moving together.
A **swarm** *of bees.*
■ say **sworm**

sway
sways swaying swayed *verb*

to swing or lean from side to side.

The trees **swayed** *in the wind.*

swear
swears swearing swore sworn *verb*

1 to make a solemn promise.
She **swears** *that she didn't do it.*
2 to speak rude or unpleasant words.

sweat
noun

the salty liquid that comes out of your skin when you are hot.
She was covered in **sweat** *after the race.*
sweat *verb*

sweatshirt
sweatshirts *noun*

a thick, cotton jumper with long sleeves.

sweep
sweeps sweeping swept *verb*

1 to clean up dust, dirt, or other mess using a brush.

2 to push away.
The flood **swept** *the car off the road.*

sweet
adjective

1 containing sugar or tasting like sugar.
Grapes are very **sweet**.
2 very pleasant or kind.
It was **sweet** *of you to bring me flowers.*
■ comparisons **sweeter sweetest**

sweet
sweets *noun*

a small piece of snack food, made mostly of sugar.

swell
swells swelling swelled swollen *verb*

to become larger.

The male frigate bird's throat **swells** *up to attract females.*

swelling
swellings *noun*

a swollen place on the body.
She had a **swelling** *where she had bumped her head.*

swerve
swerves swerving swerved *verb*

to turn quickly to one side when you are moving.

The cyclist **swerved** *to avoid the hole.*

swift
adjective

moving quickly.
■ comparisons **swifter swiftest**

swim
swims swimming swam swum *verb*

to move through water using arms, legs, or fins.

swim *noun*

swimming pool
swimming pools *noun*

a large, artificial area of water for swimming in.

swing

swings swinging swung *verb*
to move backwards and
forwards, usually while
hanging from a support.

swing

swing noun

swirl

swirls swirling swirled *verb*
to move with a twisting or
circular motion.

*The boat and leaves
swirled around as they
floated downstream.*

switch

switches *noun*
a lever or button used to turn
equipment or a machine on
and off.
switch *verb*

swivel

swivels swivelling swivelled *verb*
to turn around on
a central point.

Swivelling around on a chair.

swoop

swoops swooping swooped *verb*
to move downwards
through the air in a
curving movement.

*The stunt plane **swooped** down
out of the sky.*

sword

swords *noun*
a weapon
with a long
blade and
a handle.

*18th-century **sword***
■ say **sord**

swore

*from the verb **to swear**
She **swore** she was telling
the truth.*

syllable

syllables *noun*
a word or part of a word made
up of a single sound. The word
"once" has one syllable and
the word "single" has two.
■ say **sil**-a-bul

symbol

symbols *noun*
a sign or object that reminds
you of something else, or
represents something else.

*A dove is a **symbol** of peace.*
■ say **sim**-bul

symmetrical

adjective
having two halves that match
each other.

*This cut-out shape is
symmetrical through
its middle.*
■ say sim-**meh**-trik-kal
symmetry *noun*

sympathy

noun
a caring feeling shown by
someone for someone else.
*When you're hurt, it's nice
to get **sympathy**.*
■ say **sim**-pa-thee
sympathetic *adjective*

symptom

symptoms *noun*
a sign that shows you have a
particular illness or disease.
*One of the **symptoms** of
measles is red spots.*
■ say **simp**-tom

synagogue

synagogues *noun*
a building where Jews
go to worship.
■ say **sin**-a-gog

synthetic

adjective
made with artificial
materials rather than
natural ones.

*This frog is made from
synthetic fur.*
■ say sin-**thet**-ik

syringe

syringes *noun*
a tube with a nozzle or hollow
needle attached that is used
for sucking up and squirting
out liquid. Doctors
use syringes to
give injections.

■ say ser-**ringe**

syrup

syrups *noun*
a sweet, sticky
liquid food, often
made from sugar.

*maple **syrup***

■ say **si**-rup

system

systems *noun*
a group of things that work
together in an organized way.
■ say **sis**-tum

a
b
c
d
e
f
g
h
i
j
k
l
m
n
o
p
q
r
s
t
u
v
w
x
y
z

A B C D E F G H I J K L M N O P Q R S T U V W X Y Z

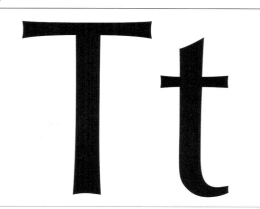

table
tables *noun*
1 a piece of furniture with a flat surface and legs underneath to support it.

2 a list of facts or figures written in columns.
A multiplication table.

tablet
tablets *noun*
a small, hard piece of medicine.

tackle
tackles tackling tackled *verb*
1 to try to solve something. *They had to tackle some difficult maths problems.*
2 to seize and try to throw someone to the ground, usually in a sport such as rugby or American football.

tactful
adjective
trying to avoid hurting someone's feelings.
She was very tactful when talking about his new haircut.
■ opposite **tactless**
tactfully *adverb*

tactics
noun
methods used to make something happen.
The team used clever tactics to win the match.
tactical *adjective*

tadpole
tadpoles *noun*
a young frog or toad. Tadpoles live in water. As they grow their tails get smaller and they grow legs.

tail
tails *noun*
the part that sticks out beyond the back end of an animal's body.

lizard's tail

tailor
tailors *noun*
a person who makes or mends clothes. Tailors usually make clothes to fit a particular person.

take
takes taking took taken *verb*
1 to get hold of or carry. *She took her coat off the peg.*
2 to bring or lead. *My parents took me to the cinema.*
3 to make use of something. *Take the first turning on the left.*
4 to require or need. *It takes three hours to cook.*
5 to travel by or on something. *Let's take the bus.*
6 to remove or steal.

The thief took a wallet from someone's coat pocket.

tale
tales *noun*
a story about things that may not be true.
A fairy tale.

talent
talents *noun*
a special natural skill or ability.

She showed a talent for dancing at an early age.

talk
talks talking talked *verb*
to say words, or to speak.
He talked to his sister on the telephone for an hour.
■ say **tork**
talk *noun*

talkative
adjective
talking a lot.
Our parrot is very talkative.

tall
adjective
1 very high.

The tall office block was surrounded by shorter ones.
■ opposite **short**
2 having a particular height.
He is 1.5 metres tall.
■ comparisons **taller tallest**

tambourine
tambourines *noun*
a musical instrument that is held in the hand and shaken or tapped to provide a rhythm.

■ say tam-bor-**een**

tame
adjective
used to living or working with human beings.
The bird they rescued from the cat became very tame.
■ comparisons **tamer tamest**
■ opposite **wild**

tan
tans *noun*
a brown skin colour caused by the Sun's rays.
tan *verb*

tangle
tangles tangling tangled *verb*
to twist into an untidy mass of knots.

The kittens tangled the wool.
tangle *noun*

tank
tanks noun
1 a large container for liquid or gas.
2 a heavy vehicle with guns that moves along on metal belts instead of wheels.

tanker
tankers noun
a vehicle or large ship that carries oil or other liquids.

tantrum
tantrums noun
a noisy display of bad temper.

*He had a **tantrum** when he was told to tidy his room.*

tap
taps tapping tapped verb
to hit gently with your fingers.

*She **tapped** on his shoulder.*
tap noun

tap
taps noun
a device that you turn to control the flow of liquid or gas from a pipe.

tape
tapes noun
1 a long, narrow strip of material such as paper, plastic, or metal.

*three types of sticky **tape***

2 a strip of plastic coated with magnetic powder that is used for recording sounds, video pictures, and computer information.

tape measure
tape measures noun
a tape marked in centimetres or inches that is used for measuring length.

tar
noun
a thick, dark, sticky liquid that is made from coal or wood. Tar is used in making road surfaces.

target
targets noun
an object that you try to hit when shooting or throwing something.

*archery **target***

tartan
adjective
decorated with a special pattern of lines and squares. Tartan patterns originally came from Scotland.

tartan scarf

task
tasks noun
a piece of work or a duty. *My **task** was cleaning the car.*

taste
noun
1 one of the body's five senses which we use to find out the flavour of something.
2 the flavour of something when you have licked it or put it in your mouth.

*She tried the soup to see if she liked the **taste**.*
taste verb
tasty adjective

tattoo
tattoos noun
a permanent picture or design printed on someone's skin, using needles filled with coloured ink.

tax
taxes noun
money that people have to pay to a government, which is used to provide public services.
tax verb

taxi
taxis noun
a car that you can hire to travel in by paying the driver money (see **car** on page 39).
■ say **tak**-see

tea
noun
a drink made by pouring boiling water onto the chopped, dried leaves of the tea plant.

tea plant leaves

*cup of **tea***

teach
teaches teaching taught verb
to help someone learn about a subject or learn a skill. *He has **taught** history for three years.*

teacup
teacups noun
a cup used for drinking tea.

team
teams noun
a group of people who work or play sports together.

*American football **team***

teapot
teapots noun
a container with a spout, lid, and handle that is used for making and serving tea.

a b c d e f g h i j k l m n o p q r s **t** u v w x y z

211

A B C D E F G H I J K L M N O P Q R S **T** U V W X Y Z

tear
tears tearing tore torn *verb*
to make a hole or split in something by pulling hard.

*The dog **tore** his trousers.*
■ rhymes with **care**
tear *noun*

tear
tears *noun*
a drop of salty water that comes from your eyes when you cry.

■ rhymes with **deer**

tease
teases teasing teased *verb*
to bother someone by saying or doing things in a playful, but annoying way.
*He **teased** his little sister about her dolls.*

technology
noun
science that is put to use in everyday life.
*Medical **technology**.*
■ say tek-**nol**-o-jee
technological *adjective*

teenager
teenagers *noun*
a person between the ages of 13 and 19 (see **growth** on page 94).

telephone
telephones *noun*
an instrument that allows you to talk to and hear people who are far away, by means of electrical signals. Telephone is often shortened to phone.

telescope
telescopes *noun*
an instrument with lenses inside it. When you look through it distant things appear closer and larger.

television
televisions *noun*
a piece of electrical equipment that receives pictures and sound that are broadcast by a television station. Television is often shortened to TV.

*flat screen **television***

tell
tells telling told *verb*
to put something into words, or let someone know something.
***Tell** me a story.*

temper
tempers *noun*
1 a mood.
*Are you in a good **temper** today?*
2 an angry mood.
*She threw the book across the room in a **temper**.*

temperature
temperatures *noun*
a measurement of how hot or cold something is.

*She took the child's **temperature**.*
■ say **temp**-ra-cher

temple
temples *noun*
a building where people go to worship.

*Buddhist **temple***
■ say **tem**-pul

temporary
adjective
lasting for only a short time.

*The box was a **temporary** bed for the cat.*
■ say tem-per-ra-ree
■ opposite **permanent**
temporarily *adverb*

tempt
tempts tempting tempted *verb*
to try to persuade someone to do something that they wouldn't usually do or shouldn't do.
*Can I **tempt** you to take another slice of cake?*
■ say **temt**
temptation *noun*

tendency
tendencies *noun*
the way that a person or thing usually or often behaves.
*She has a **tendency** to be late.*
tend *verb*

tender
adjective
1 easy to chew or cut.
*A **tender** piece of steak.*
2 feeling sore when touched.

*The lion had a **tender** paw after treading on a thorn.*
3 gentle and loving.
*He gave his baby a **tender** smile.*
tenderly *adverb*

tennis
noun
a game that is played with a racket and ball on a court divided by a net. The players try to hit the ball over the net in a way that makes it hard for their opponent to return it (see **sport** on page 197).

tennis court

tense

adjective

1 nervous.
2 stretched tight.
Tense muscles.

■ opposite **relaxed**

tense

noun

a form of a verb that shows whether the action is taking place in the past, present, or future.

tent

tents *noun*

a portable shelter made of waterproof material stretched over a frame of poles.

term

terms *noun*

one of the periods of time during a year when a school or university is open for teaching.

terminal

terminals *noun*

a building at the end of a travel route where passengers arrive and depart.

terrible

adjective

very bad or unpleasant.
*It was a **terrible** day.*

terrify

terrifies terrifying terrified *verb*
to frighten very badly.

*Heights **terrified** him.*

territory

territories *noun*

an area of land that is controlled by a country's laws or lived in by an animal.
*The pride of lions never left their own **territory**.*

■ say **ter**-ri-tree

terror

noun
great fear.

terrorist

terrorists *noun*

a person who uses, or threatens to use, violence to force people to do something, usually for a political cause.
terrorism *noun*
terrorize *verb*

test

tests testing tested *verb*
to try something out.

*She **tested** the liquid to see if it was an acid.*
test *noun*

text

noun
the words of something written or printed.

text message

noun
a written message sent between mobile phones.

textile

textiles *noun*
a cloth or fabric made by weaving or knitting.

texture

textures *noun*
the way something feels when you touch it.

*Sandpaper has a rough **texture**.*
■ say **tex**-cher

thank

thanks thanking thanked *verb*
to say that you are grateful for something.
*They **thanked** him for their presents.*
thank you *interjection*

thaw

thaws thawing thawed *verb*
to melt or to make something melt.
*The snow started to **thaw** in the sunshine.*
thaw *noun*

theft

thefts *noun*
the act of stealing.
*He reported the **theft** of the painting to the police.*

theme

themes *noun*
a main subject, idea, or topic.

*The **theme** of the fancy dress party was cartoon characters.*

theory

theories *noun*
an idea about how or why something happens.
*She tested her **theory** with scientific experiments.*
■ say **thee**-er-ee

thermometer

thermometers *noun*
a device that measures temperature.
■ say thur-**mom**-it-er

*wall **thermometer***

A
B
C
D
E
F
G
H
I
J
K
L
M
N
O
P
Q
R
S
T
U
V
W
X
Y
Z

thesaurus
thesauruses or **thesauri** *noun*
a book that groups
words that have similar
meanings together.
- say thi-**saw**-rus

thick
adjective
1 large in width
or depth.

thick candle

2 packed closely together.
A **thick** *forest.*
- opposite **thin**
3 having a certain
measurement in width
or depth.
*The plank was three
centimetres* **thick**.
- comparisons **thicker thickest**

thief
thieves *noun*
a person who steals things.
- rhymes with **beef**

thigh
thighs *noun*
the part of your leg between
your knee and your hip.

thigh

- rhymes with **sky**

thimble
thimbles *noun*
a small, hard covering worn
on the end of your finger
when you are sewing.
The thimble protects your
finger and helps you push
the needle through the fabric.

thin
adjective
1 small in width
or depth.

thin candle

2 hardly covered.
A **thin** *layer of snow covered
the ground.*
- opposite **thick**
3 not having much fat.
A **thin** *man.*
- opposite **fat**
- comparisons **thinner thinnest**

thing
things *noun*
1 an object that is not alive.
2 an idea or an action.
There are four **things** *I want
to do this evening.*

think
thinks thinking thought *verb*
to use your mind to create
ideas or opinions.

She **thought** *about what she
could eat for lunch.*

thirsty
adjective
needing something to drink.

He was very **thirsty** *after a day
without water.*
- comparisons **thirstier thirstiest**

thistle
thistles *noun*
a wild plant with prickly
leaves and purple, white,
or yellow flowers.

thorn
thorns *noun*
a sharp spike
on the stem
of a plant. — *thorn*

thorough
adjective
complete in every way.
He had a **thorough** *search
for his book.*
- say **thur**-er
thoroughly *adverb*

thought
thoughts *noun*
an idea or opinion that you
have been thinking about.
- say **thort**

thoughtful
adjective
caring about other people's
feelings and needs.

It was **thoughtful** *of her
to help him.*
- say **thort**-ful
- opposite **thoughtless**

thread
threads *noun*
a thin yarn such as cotton
or silk, that is
used for sewing.
- say **thred**

*sewing
thread*

*embroidery
thread*

thread
threads threading threaded *verb*
to pass a length of thread
or rope through a hole
in something.

Threading beads onto a string.

threat
threats *noun*
a warning that something
may happen.
There's a **threat** *of rain
in the air.*
- say **thret**
threaten *verb*

thrill
thrills *noun*
an excited feeling.
It was a real **thrill** *to ride
on the rollercoaster.*
thrilling *adjective*

throat
throats *noun*
the tube that leads from your
mouth, through your neck,
to your stomach and lungs.
- say **throwt**

throne
thrones *noun*
a special chair used by a
ruler of a country or a region.

through
preposition
from one side or end
to the other.
*She drove **through** the tunnel.*
■ say **throo**

throw
throws throwing threw thrown
verb
to send something out
of your hand and through
the air forcefully.

thud
thuds *noun*
a dull sound made
when a heavy object falls
on something.
*The book dropped to the floor
with a **thud**.*

thumb
thumbs *noun*
the short, thick finger set
apart from your other fingers
at the side
of your hand.

thumb

■ say **thum**

thunder
noun
a loud, rumbling sound that
comes after a flash of
lightning during a storm.

thunderstorm
thunderstorms *noun*
a storm that has thunder
and lightning.

tick
ticks *noun*
1 a written mark that
shows that something
is correct, or has been chosen.
2 a clicking sound made
by a clock.
tick *verb*

ticket
tickets *noun*
a piece of paper that shows
that you have paid to do
something, such as travel
by public transport
or go into
a cinema.

tickle
tickles tickling tickled *verb*
to touch someone's skin
lightly, making them laugh
or squirm.

tide
tides *noun*
the regular change in the
level of the sea that happens
twice a day.

*The **tide** is out.*

tidy
tidies tidying tidied *verb*
to put in order.

*He **tidied** his room.*

tie
ties tying tied *verb*
1 to fasten something with
a knot or bow.

*She **tied** a ribbon in her hair.*
2 to score the same number
of points as someone else
in a contest.
*They **tied** for first place.*
tie *noun*

tie
ties *noun*
a thin strip of fabric worn
around the neck and knotted
under the collar of a shirt.

tiger
tigers *noun*
a large, wild mammal that is
part of the cat family. Tigers
live in many regions of Asia,
from tropical forests to cold
plains. They hunt at
night for their food.

tight
adjective
fitting closely.
*A **tight** fit.*
■ say **tite**
■ comparisons **tighter tightest**
■ opposite **loose**
tighten *verb*
tightly *adverb*

tightrope
tightropes *noun*
a rope stretched high above
the ground that acrobats
balance on.

tile
tiles *noun*
a thin piece of decorated
baked clay or other
material that is used as
a wall or floor covering.

till
tills *noun*
a machine used in shops,
restaurants, and businesses
that adds up your bill and
stores the money that you
give in payment.

tilt
tilts tilting tilted *verb*
to move or be moved into
a sloping or leaning position.
*The huge pile of books
tilted dangerously.*

timber
noun
cut wood that is used for
building and making things.

a b c d e f g h i j k l m n o p q r s t u v w x y z

215

time

times *noun*

1 all of the past, present, and future. Time is measured in periods such as centuries, years, months, weeks, days, and hours.

2 a particular point in the day.
What's the time?

3 a period in the past, present, or future.
In Roman times, many roads were built throughout Europe.

4 an occasion or event.
I go swimming three times a week.

Telling the time

24-hour clock

o'clock

quarter past

half past

quarter to

Time-measuring devices

pocket watch

stopwatch

digital alarm clock

nurse's watch

back view

front view

wristwatch

front view

back view

carriage clock

Months of the year

January
February
March
April
May
June
July
August
September
October
November
December

calendar

Time periods

past

present

future

Days of the week

Monday
Tuesday
Wednesday
Thursday
Friday
Saturday
Sunday

diary

timetable
timetables *noun*
a chart that shows the times when events should happen, or when jobs should be done.

*He checked the **timetable** to find out when the coach left.*

timid
adjective
easily frightened or shy.
*The bird was very **timid** and flew away when I moved.*
timidly *adverb*

tin
tins *noun*
1 a light, soft, silvery metal.

tin ore   *tin* can

2 a metal container for putting things in or for preserving food.

tingle
tingles tingling tingled *verb*
to have a slight stinging feeling in a part of your body.
*Fizzy drinks make my mouth **tingle**.*

tinkle
tinkles tinkling tinkled *verb*
to make a light, ringing sound.
*The bells **tinkled** as the sleigh moved along.*

tiny
adjective
very small.
■ comparisons **tinier tiniest**

tip
tips tipping tipped *verb*
1 to move something so that it is not upright.
2 to turn something over so that the contents fall out.
*She **tipped** the dirty water out of the bucket.*

tip
tips *noun*
1 the narrow, pointed end of something.

*Touching the **tip** of his nose.*
2 a helpful hint or piece of useful information.
*Do you have any **tips** for getting rid of stains?*
3 a small, extra gift of money, given in return for a service.
*I left the waiter a **tip**.*
4 a place where rubbish is dumped.

tiptoe
tiptoes tiptoeing tiptoed *verb*
to walk slowly and quietly on your toes.

tired
adjective
feeling that you would like to sleep or rest.
*She felt **tired** after working in the garden all day.*

tissue
tissues *noun*
1 a thin, soft paper used for wiping or for wrapping things.

2 a material that makes up a part of a living thing.
*Brain **tissue**.*
■ say **tish**-yoo

title
titles *noun*
1 the name of a creative piece of work such as a book, film, or painting.
2 the part of someone's name that shows their rank or job. "Dr", "Mrs", and "Lord" are all titles.
■ say **tie**-tul

toad
toads *noun*
an insect-eating amphibian with rough, dry skin that usually lives on land. Toads move along with short hops. They hibernate in winter.

green toad

toadstool
toadstools *noun*
a poisonous fungus with an umbrella-shaped top.

toast
noun
1 bread that is grilled on both sides until it is crisp and brown.
2 the action of wishing someone well by raising your glass and drinking.
*Let's drink a **toast** to the bride and groom.*
toast *verb*

tobacco
noun
a plant whose leaves are dried and used in cigarettes and pipes.

toboggan
toboggans *noun*
a flat sledge that is used for sliding down slopes.

today
adverb
on this day.
*I'm going to the zoo **today**.*
today *noun*

toddler
toddlers *noun*
a young child who is learning or has just learnt to walk (see **growth** on page 94).

toe
toes *noun*
one of the five separate parts at the end of your foot.

toe

toffee
toffees *noun*
a chewy sweet made from sugar and butter.

together
adverb
with each other.
*Shall we go **together**?*

toilet
toilets *noun*
1 a bowl connected to a drain that can be flushed with water. People use toilets to get rid of body waste.
2 a room with a toilet.

a b c d e f g h i j k l m n o p q r s **t** u v w x y z

told

*from the verb **to tell***
*She **told** her friends what she had done at the weekend.*

tomato

tomatoes *noun*
a soft, juicy, red fruit that can be eaten raw in salads or cooked (see **fruit** on page 85).

*ripe beef **tomato***

tomorrow

adverb
on the day after today.
*I'm going on holiday **tomorrow**.*
tomorrow *noun*

tone

tones *noun*
the quality of a sound or a voice.
*He spoke in a low **tone**.*
■ rhymes with **own**

tongue

tongues *noun*
a flexible flap of muscle in your mouth that you use to eat, taste, and speak.

tongue

■ say **tung**

tonight

adverb
on the evening and night of the present day.
*Let's go to the concert **tonight**.*
tonight *noun*

tonsil

tonsils *noun*
one of two small lumps of tissue at the back of your throat.

took

*from the verb **to take***
*He **took** the packet out of the cupboard.*

tool

tools *noun*
a piece of equipment that helps you do a job.

tool box

saw
screwdriver
hammer

tooth

teeth *noun*
1 one of the hard, white, bone-like structures inside your mouth, which you use for biting and chewing.

tooth

2 one of the pointed parts on an object such as a saw or a comb.

comb

tooth

toothbrush

toothbrushes *noun*
a small brush with a long handle that you use for cleaning your teeth.

top

tops *noun*
1 the highest point of something.

*The bird sat on the very **top** of the cactus.*
■ opposite **bottom**
2 a lid.

top

3 a spinning toy.
4 a piece of clothing for the upper part of your body.

*pyjama **top***

topic

topics *noun*
a subject that is spoken or written about.
*The fire was the main **topic** of conversation for weeks.*

topple

topples toppling toppled *verb*
to fall over.
*The dominoes **toppled** over.*

toothbrush
toothbrushes *noun*

torch

torches *noun*
a portable lamp powered by a battery and small enough to be held in the hand.

tore

*from the verb **to tear***
*She **tore** her sleeve on a nail.*

tornado

tornadoes or **tornados** *noun*
a violent, whirling wind that causes great damage to the land and buildings.

■ say tor-**nay**-doh

tortoise

tortoises *noun*
a slow-moving reptile with a hard shell. Tortoises live in hot regions. They eat grass and other plants and can live a long time (see **reptile** on page 168).
■ say **tort**-tus

toss

tosses tossing tossed *verb*
1 to throw into the air lightly and carelessly.
*We **tossed** the ball around before the game.*
2 to throw a coin and guess which side will face upwards in order to decide something.
*We **tossed** a coin to see who should have the first turn.*
toss *noun*

A B C D E F G H I J K L M N O P Q R S T U V W X Y Z

total

totals *noun*
the entire amount of
everything added together.
*The **total** of 2, 3, and 4 is 9.*
■ say **toe**-tal

total

adjective
complete.
***Total** darkness.*

toucan

toucans *noun*
a colourful bird with a large
beak that lives in the
rainforests of South America.
Toucans nest in holes in trees
and feed on fruit, insects,
small lizards, and eggs.
■ say **too**-can

touch

touches touching touched *verb*
to put your hand or another
part of your body
on something.

*Can you **touch** the floor
with your hands, while
keeping your legs straight?*
■ say **tuch**
touch *noun*

tough

adjective
1 strong and not easy to
break or damage.

*Crash helmets are made of
tough plastic.*
■ opposite **weak**
2 very difficult.
*A **tough** problem.*
■ opposite **easy**
■ say **tuff**
■ comparisons **tougher toughest**

tour

tours *noun*
a journey that takes you to
see several places.
*We went on a sightseeing **tour**
of the city.*
■ rhymes with **poor**

tourist

tourists *noun*
a person who
travels and
visits places
for pleasure.

tournament

tournaments *noun*
a series of contests or
matches in a sport or game.
*A chess **tournament**.*

tow

tows towing towed *verb*
to pull something
along behind.
*The truck **towed** the
car to the garage.*
■ say **toe**

towards

preposition
in the direction of.

*The horse trotted
across the field **towards** her.*

towel

towels *noun*
a piece of soft, thick cloth
or paper that is used for
drying things.

tower

towers *noun*
a tall, narrow structure.
*The Eiffel **Tower**.*
■ rhymes with **our**

town

towns *noun*
a place with houses and other
buildings, where people live,
work, and shop. A town is
smaller than a city but larger
than a village.

toy

toys *noun*
an object to
play with.

jack-in-the-box

trace

traces tracing traced *verb*
1 to copy a picture by
placing a sheet of thin paper
over it and drawing around
the outline.

*She **traced** the picture
of a tiger from a book.*
2 to follow or discover
something by observing
marks or clues.
*She **traced** her family's history
back three centuries.*

trace

traces *noun*
a small mark or track left
behind by something.
*There were **traces** of a fire
in the cave.*

track

tracks *noun*
1 a mark or marks left
by someone or something
that is moving.

*The fox left **tracks**
in the fresh snow.*
2 a path or rough road.
*They drove the truck up
a bumpy **track**.*
3 a course used for races.
*They did four laps around
the running **track**.*
4 rails laid on the ground
for trains to run on.

a b c d e f g h i j k l m n o p q r s **t** u v w x y z

A
B
C
D
E
F
G
H
I
J
K
L
M
N
O
P
Q
R
S
T
U
V
W
X
Y
Z

tractor

tractors *noun*

a farm vehicle with large wheels that is used for pulling heavy loads or machinery over rough ground.

trade

trades *noun*

a business.
The tourist trade.

tradition

traditions *noun*

a special event, belief, or way of doing something that has continued in the same way for many years.
It is a tradition to celebrate the New Year with a party.
■ say tra-**dish**-un
traditional *adjective*

traffic

noun

vehicles, ships, or aircraft moving along a route.

There was a lot of traffic on the bridge.

tragedy

tragedies *noun*

1 a very sad and unfortunate event.
The train crash was a terrible tragedy.
2 a play with a sad ending.
Shakespeare's Romeo and Juliet *is a tragedy.*
■ say **traj**-e-dee

tragic

adjective

bringing great sadness.
A tragic accident.
■ say tra-jik
tragically *adverb*

trail

trails trailing trailed *verb*

1 to drag something along behind or let something hang loosely.

He trailed his toy train behind him.
2 to walk or move slowly behind someone.
The children trailed along behind their mother.

trail

trails *noun*

1 a path or track.
A nature trail.
2 a track, scent, or other sign left by something that has passed by.

He left a trail of rubbish behind him.

trailer

trailers *noun*

a small vehicle or container that can be towed behind a car, lorry, or tractor.

train

trains *noun*

a railway engine that pulls carriages or trucks behind it.

train

trains training trained *verb*

1 to practise sports skills or do exercises to get fit, often for an event.
She trains for three hours a day.
2 to teach or to learn a skill.
He trained his dog to sit.
training *noun*

traitor

traitors *noun*

a person who turns against his or her country or friends by helping an enemy.

trample

tramples trampling trampled *verb*

to crush something by stepping on it.

The dog trampled all over the flowers.

trampoline

trampolines *noun*

a piece of gymnastic equipment made of strong fabric and attached to a frame by springs.

■ say **tram**-po-leen

trance

trances *noun*

a kind of sleep, or a dazed state, when you are not completely conscious.
■ say trahns

transfer

transfers transferring transferred *verb*

to move something from one person or place to another.
He transferred his money to a savings account.

translate

translates translating translated *verb*

to turn words in one language into words of another language.
She translated the French poem into English.

transparent

adjective
able to be seen through.

This glass jug is transparent.
■ say trans-**pa**-rent

transplant

transplants *noun*

an operation to move an organ or tissue from one person or part of the body to another.
A heart transplant.

transport
noun

a way of carrying goods or people from one place to another. Different methods of transport are used to travel on land, on water, or in the air.

rudder

elevator flap

envelope   gondola   **airship**   nose cone

tank

cab

air deflector

dairy tanker

engine   propeller
cockpit
fuselage

landing   hull   float
wheel

sea plane

tail fin

rotor blade   engine housing   boom

instrument   G-HUMT
panel

stabilizer   tail rotor

hood

seat   saddle

pedal

rickshaw

landing
skid

helicopter

fairing   windscreen   cab   horn   engine   double-decker
carriage

motorbike

disc brake   exhaust pipe

passenger train   track

saddle   pommel
saddle
saddle   pump   handlebar
mud guard   reflector   bridle
frame

stirrup

pedal   **camel**

chain   **mountain bike**   **horse**

lifeboat   funnel   deck

rudder   hull   **paddle steamer**   paddle wheel

transport
transports transporting transported *verb*

to carry people or things from one place to another. *The goods were **transported** by train.*
transportation *noun*

trap
traps trapping trapped *verb*

to catch an animal or person and hold them in some way so that they cannot get away.
trap *noun*

trapdoor
trapdoors *noun*

a small door cut into a floor, on a stage, or in the ceiling.

trapeze
trapezes *noun*

a high swing used by acrobats for performing stunts.

trash
noun

rubbish, or something that is worthless or useless.

traumatic
adjective

upsetting enough to have a long-lasting effect on someone. *Giving evidence in the trial was very **traumatic**.*
■ say **traw**-ma-tik
trauma *noun*

travel
travels travelling travelled *verb*

to go from one place to another.

*We **travelled** around the lakes and mountains on holiday.*
travel *noun*

trawler
trawlers *noun*

a boat that is used to catch fish by dragging a large net behind it along the bottom of the sea.

tray
trays *noun*

a flat board, often with a rim, that is used for carrying food and drinks.

treacherous
adjective

very dangerous.

*The sea can be **treacherous** for a small boat.*
■ say **trech**-er-us

tread
treads *noun*

the raised part of a tyre.
■ say **tred**

tread

tread
treads treading trod trodden *verb*

to put your foot on something.

*The elephant **trod** on his foot.*

treason
noun

the act of being a traitor to your country by trying to destroy the government or the ruler, or by helping the enemy during a war.
■ say **tree**-zun

treasure
treasures *noun*

a large amount of gold, jewels, or other valuable things.

■ say **tre**-zhur

treasurer
treasurers *noun*

a person who looks after the money and accounts of a government, a club, or a company.

treat
treats *noun*

a special thing that gives someone pleasure.

*They were taken to the fair as a birthday **treat**.*
■ say **treet**

treat
treats treating treated *verb*

1 to behave in a certain way towards people, animals, or things. *She **treats** her pet hamster very well.*
2 to try to make someone well.

*She **treated** the cut on his head.*
treatment *noun*

treaty
treaties *noun*

an agreement made between countries.

*Signing a peace **treaty**.*

tree

trees *noun*
a tall plant with branches, leaves, and a main stem called a trunk. Trees are either deciduous or evergreen.

Leaves

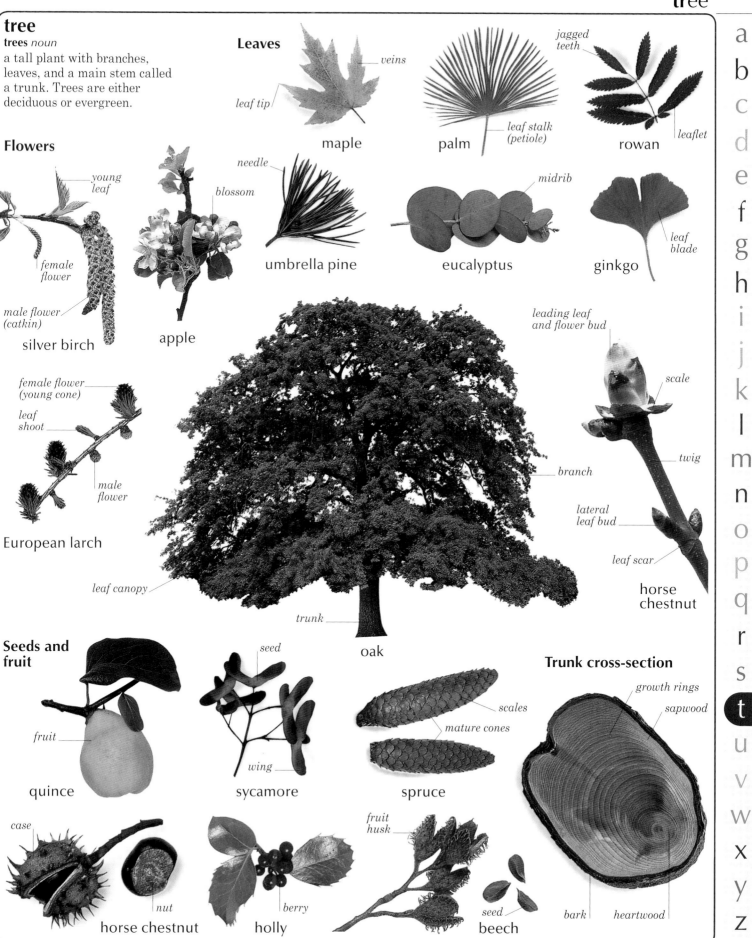

veins

leaf tip

maple

leaf stalk (petiole)

palm

jagged teeth

leaflet

rowan

Flowers

young leaf

blossom

needle

umbrella pine

midrib

eucalyptus

leaf blade

ginkgo

female flower

male flower (catkin)

silver birch

apple

female flower (young cone)

leaf shoot

male flower

European larch

leaf canopy

trunk

oak

branch

leading leaf and flower bud

scale

twig

lateral leaf bud

leaf scar

horse chestnut

Seeds and fruit

fruit

quince

seed

wing

sycamore

scales

mature cones

spruce

Trunk cross-section

growth rings

sapwood

case

nut

horse chestnut

berry

holly

fruit husk

seed

beech

bark

heartwood

tremble
trembles trembling trembled *verb*
to shake with fear or cold.

trial
trials *noun*
1 the legal process by which a judge and jury decide whether a person is guilty or innocent of a crime.
*She is on **trial** for theft.*
2 an experiment or test to see what something is like or to see if it works.
*The new sports car passed its **trials** successfully.*
■ say **try**-al

triangle
triangles *noun*
1 a shape with three sides (see **shape** on page 182).
triangular *adjective*
2 a musical instrument. A triangle is played by hitting one of the metal sides with a small metal rod.

trick
tricks *noun*
1 a skilful action that is done to entertain someone.

*A magic **trick**.*
2 something done to deceive someone.
trick *verb*

trickle
trickles trickling trickled *verb*
to flow very slowly.
*The raindrops **trickled** down the window.*

tricycle
tricycles *noun*
a vehicle with three wheels that is moved by turning the pedals around, like a bicycle.

*child's **tricycle***
■ say **try**-sik-ul

trim
trims trimming trimmed *verb*
to cut the edges or ends off something, such as hair, in order to make it neat.

*The hairdresser **trimmed** his hair.*

trip
trips tripping tripped *verb*
to stumble and fall.
*I **tripped** over the book that she'd left on the floor.*

trip
trips *noun*
a journey.
*We went on a school **trip** to the museum.*

tripod
tripods *noun*
a frame with three legs that is used as a support for a camera.

■ say **try**-pod

triumph
triumphs *noun*
a great success.
*Winning the race was a **triumph**.*
■ say **try**-umf
triumphant *adjective*

trod
*from the verb **to tread***
*She **trod** in a puddle and splashed her clothes.*

trolley
trolleys *noun*
a small cart on wheels that is used for carrying things.
*A supermarket **trolley**.*

trombone
trombones *noun*
a large, brass musical instrument, played by blowing through a mouthpiece. The notes are produced by sliding a long, bent tube backwards and forwards.

*tenor **trombone***

trophy
trophies *noun*
a cup, medal, or other prize that is given to the winner of a contest.

*tennis **trophy***
■ say **trow**-fee

tropical
adjective
from the hot, wet area of the world near the equator.
***Tropical** fruit.*

trot
trots trotting trotted *verb*
to move the way a horse does when it is walking fast. One of the horse's front hooves and the opposite back hoof are on the ground at the same time.

trot *noun*

trouble
troubles *noun*
a situation or problem that is worrying or difficult.
*If you smash that window, you'll be in **trouble**!*
■ say **trub**-ul

trough
troughs *noun*
a narrow, open container for animals to eat or drink from.
■ say **trof**

trousers
noun
a piece of clothing that you wear on your legs.

trout

trout *noun*
a type of edible fish that is part of the same family as the salmon. Most trout live in fresh water, but some species migrate to the sea after laying their eggs. They feed on insects, small fish, and shrimps.

rainbow **trout**

trowel

trowels *noun*
a hand tool like a small spade. Curved trowels are used for gardening. Flat ones are used for spreading plaster or cement.
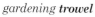
gardening **trowel**
■ rhymes with **owl**

truce

truces *noun*
an agreement to stop fighting for a short time.
The armies called a **truce**.
■ rhymes with **noose**

truck

trucks *noun*
a large vehicle used for carrying goods from one place to another.

trudge

trudges trudging trudged *verb*
to walk in a tired way.

They **trudged** *home through the snow.*

true

adjective
real and accurate.
A **true** *story.*
■ opposite **false**

trumpet

trumpets *noun*
a small, brass musical instrument, made of a long, curved, narrow tube with an end like a funnel. Notes are produced by pressing valves down and blowing through a mouthpiece.

valve

trunk

trunks *noun*
1 the main stem of a tree (see **tree** on page 223).
2 the main part of the body of a person or animal, not including the head, arms, and legs.

trunk

3 the long nose of an elephant (see **mammal** on page 124).
4 a large box with a hinged lid, used for storing things.

trust

trusts trusting trusted *verb*
to believe that someone or something is honest and reliable.
I **trusted** *my friend not to give away the secret.*
trust *noun*
trustworthy *adjective*

truth

noun
something that is true.
Do you always tell the **truth**?
■ say **trooth**

try

tries trying tried *verb*
1 to make an effort to do something.
He **tried** *to climb up the tree.*
2 to test something to see if it works, or to put something on to see if it fits.

She **tried** *on the gloves.*
3 to decide in a trial, within a court of law, whether someone is innocent or guilty of a crime.
The court **tried** *him for theft.*

T-shirt

T-shirts *noun*
a shirt made from knitted cotton with short sleeves and no collar.

tub

tubs *noun*
a rounded, open container that is used to store things or wash things.

tube

tubes *noun*
1 a long, hollow pipe.
A cardboard **tube**.
2 a long, narrow container made of plastic or thin metal. The contents are removed by squeezing.

tube of toothpaste

tuck

tucks tucking tucked *verb*
1 to fold or push into place.

Tuck *your shirt into your trousers.*
2 to cover up in a snug way.
I like being **tucked** *up in bed.*

tuft

tufts *noun*
a bunch of grass, threads, hair, or feathers that grows or is tied closely together.

tug

tugs tugging tugged *verb*
to give something a quick, hard pull.
My sister **tugged** *at my sleeve.*

tulip

tulips *noun*
a plant with a large, cup-shaped flower that grows from a bulb.

■ say **tyoo**-lip

tumble

tumbles tumbling tumbled *verb*
to fall and roll over.
She **tumbled** *down the hill.*

tuna

tuna or **tunas** *noun*
a large, edible sea fish. Tuna feed on squid and other fish. They are fast swimmers and migrate long distances every year.
■ say **tyoo**-na

a b c d e f g h i j k l m n o p q r s t u v w x y z

A B C D E F G H I J K L M N O P Q R S **T** U V W X Y Z

tune
tunes *noun*
a series of musical notes put together in a certain order to form a melody.
*He sang a song and I played the **tune** on the piano.*

tunnel
tunnels *noun*
an underground passage.

turban
turbans *noun*
a head covering consisting of a long strip of cloth wrapped around the head, worn especially by Muslim and Sikh men.

turkey
turkeys *noun*
a large bird that lives wild in the forests of North America. Turkeys feed on acorns, seeds, berries, and insects. Turkeys are reared on farms for their meat in many parts of the world.

turn
turns turning turned *verb*
1 to go around.
The watch hands **turn** *clockwise.*
2 to change direction.
*He **turned** to see what was happening behind him.*
3 to become.
*His fingers **turned** blue with the cold.*

turn
turns *noun*
a chance or duty that comes to each of a number of people in order.
*It's your **turn** to wash up.*

turnip
turnips *noun*
a type of plant with a round root which is eaten as a vegetable.

turquoise
noun
1 a green-blue stone that is often used in jewellery.

2 the colour of the stone turquoise.
■ say **ter**-kwoyz

turtle
turtles *noun*
a reptile that is part of the same family as the tortoise. Turtles live in water and feed on plants and small animals. Some turtles lay their eggs on land.

green
turtle

tusk
tusks *noun*
a long, pointed tooth that sticks out of the mouth of certain animals (see **mammal** on page 124).

twig
twigs *noun*
a small branch of a tree or shrub (see **tree** on page 223).

twin
twins *noun*
1 one of a pair of children or animals born to their mother at the same time.
*Identical **twins**.*
2 one of two things that are exactly the same.
twin *adjective*

twinkle
twinkles twinkling twinkled *verb*
to shine with small flashes of light.
*The stars **twinkled** in the sky.*

twirl
twirls twirling twirled *verb*
to spin in a quick, light way.

*She **twirled** around to show them her new skirt.*

twist
twists twisting twisted *verb*
to turn or wind something.

*She **twisted** her head around.*

type
types typing typed *verb*
to write using the letter and number keys on a typewriter or other keyboard.
■ say **tipe**

type
types *noun*
1 a group of people or things that are alike in some way.
*The shop sold two **types** of boots.*
2 printed letters.
*This book has small **type**.*

typewriter
typewriters *noun*
a machine with a keyboard, used for printing letters and numbers on paper.

typical
adjective
being a good example of something, or showing all its usual qualities.
*They lived in a **typical** city street.*
■ say **tip**-i-kul
typically *adverb*

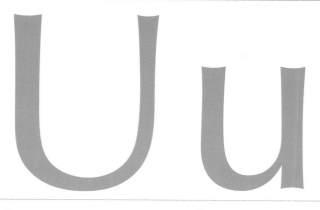

Uu

ugly
adjective
unpleasant to look at.
■ say **ug**-lee
ugliness *noun*

ulcer
ulcers *noun*
a sore patch on your skin
or in your stomach.
■ say **ul**-ser

umbrella
umbrellas *noun*
a covered frame, held up
by a stick that is used to
protect a person from the
rain, or as a shade from
the Sun. Umbrella frames
are covered with cloth or
plastic and can be folded
up when not in use.

umpire
umpires *noun*
someone who makes sure
that players follow the rules
of a game or sport.
umpire *verb*

unanimous
adjective
agreed by everyone.
*The leader was elected
by a **unanimous** vote.*
■ say yoo-**nan**-i-mus

uncle
uncles *noun*
the brother of someone's
parent, or their
aunt's husband.

uncomfortable
adjective
1 not able to relax.

*She was too **uncomfortable**
to go to sleep.*
2 causing an unpleasant
feeling or slight pain.
***Uncomfortable** shoes.*
■ opposite **comfortable**

unconscious
adjective
1 not able to think and feel,
possibly because of an illness
or accident.
*The falling brick knocked
him **unconscious**.*
2 done without thinking.
*He has an **unconscious** habit
of scratching his chin.*
■ say un-**kon**-shus
■ opposite **conscious**

uncover
**uncovers uncovering
uncovered** *verb*
to remove the cover, unwrap,
or reveal something.

*The archaeologists **uncovered**
a Roman mosaic.*

under
preposition
below or beneath
something, or to
a lower place.

*She is holding
the ball **under**
her arm.*

undercover
adjective
done in secret to obtain
information.
*The police were working on
an **undercover** investigation.*

underdone
adjective
not cooked for long enough.

underground
adjective
below the ground.

*An **underground** cave.*
underground *adverb*

underline
**underlines underlining
underlined** *verb*
to draw a line under
something, usually to
stress it or to show that
it is important.

You **must** reply.

underneath
preposition
below something, or in
a lower place.

*The children played
underneath the table.*
underneath *adverb*

understand
**understands understanding
understood** *verb*
to know what
something means.
*Did you **understand**
the question?*

understudy
understudies *noun*
a person who learns a part
in a play or performance so
that he or she can take over if
the usual actor cannot perform.
understudy *verb*

underwater
adjective
found under the surface
of the water, or used under
the surface of the water.

*The diver swam among
the **underwater** plants
and animals.*
underwater *adverb*

a b c d e f g h i j k l m n o p q r s t **u** v w x y z

underwear

noun

the clothes that you wear next to your skin and under your other clothes.

vest

pants

undo

undoes undoing undid undone
verb

to unfasten or untie.

Undoing a knot in a rope.

■ say un-**doo**

undress

undresses undressing undressed *verb*

to take clothes off.

■ opposite **dress**

uneasy

adjective

not feeling comfortable or happy.
She felt uneasy about leaving the door unlocked.
uneasily adverb

unemployed

adjective

without a job.
He's been unemployed for almost a year.
■ opposite **employed**
unemployment *noun*

uneven

adjective

not smooth or level.

The road had a very uneven surface.
■ opposite **even**
unevenly *adverb*

unexpected

adjective

surprising, or happening when you do not think it will.

The unexpected rain made everyone leave the beach.
■ opposite **expected**
unexpectedly *adverb*

unfair

adjective

not right or honest.
That's unfair – you've got more than me!
■ opposite **fair**

unfortunate

adjective

having or bringing bad luck.

It was unfortunate that he'd left a roller skate on the floor.
■ opposite **fortunate**
unfortunately *adverb*

unhappy

adjective

sad or miserable.
She felt unhappy when she failed the exam.
■ opposite **happy**

unhealthy

adjective

1 not well or not fit.
You look unhealthy.
2 bad for your health.
It's unhealthy to eat snacks all the time.
■ say un-**hel**-thee
■ opposite **healthy**

unicorn

unicorns *noun*

an imaginary animal in myths and fairy tales. A unicorn is like a horse, but has a long, spiralled horn on its forehead.
■ say **yoo**-ni-korn

unicycle

unicycles *noun*

a machine for riding on, with pedals, a saddle, and one wheel. Unicycles are sometimes used for performing acrobatic tricks.

■ say **yoo**-ni-sye-kul

uniform

uniforms *noun*

special clothes worn by members of a group to show that they belong to that group. Many school pupils and members of the armed forces wear uniforms.

19th-century army general's uniform

■ say **yoo**-ni-form

union

unions *noun*

1 two or more people, places, or things that are joined together to become one.
Russia was once a part of the Union of Soviet Socialist Republics.
2 a group of workers that join together to take care of the welfare of employees.
■ say **yoo**-nee-un

unique

adjective

being the only one of its kind.
Every snowflake is unique.
■ say yoo-**neek**

unit

units *noun*

1 a single part of something.
A kitchen unit.
2 a fixed amount used as a standard by which other things are measured.
A metre is a unit of length.

unite

unites uniting united *verb*

to join together or to do something together.
The towns united in their fight against the factory's pollution.
■ say **yoo**-nite

universe

noun

all of space, and everything that exists in it. The universe includes Earth, the other planets, and all the stars.

Satellites

solar panel

dish antenna

European Communications Satellite 1 (ECS 1)

command antenna

solar panel

Landsat

The Solar System

Mercury

Venus

Earth

Mars

Space exploration

antenna

magnetic sensor

television camera

solar panel

star detector

dish antenna

Mariner 10

flap door

main mirror casing

small mirror casing

solar panel

antenna

Hubble Space Telescope

Spacecraft

engine nozzle

antenna

heat shield

Apollo Service Module

Apollo Command Module

Apollo Lunar Module

docking window

manoeuvring engines

landing leg

foot pad

hatch

engine nozzle

upper part of the *Saturn V* rocket

ring

Jupiter

power supply

radio antenna

extendable boom

television camera

dish antenna

Voyager space probe

rudder and speed brake

flight deck windscreen

fin

fuselage

United States

heat-shield tiles

wing

Space Shuttle

main engine nozzle

ringlets

Saturn

rings

Uranus

solar panel

antenna

docking module

rings

unmanned cargo craft

main module

Soyuz TM spacecraft

solar panel

Neptune

Mir space station

a b c d e f g h i j k l m n o p q r s t **u** v w x y z

229

A B C D E F G H I J K L M N O P Q R S T U V W X Y Z

university
universities *noun*
a place where students go for the highest level of education.

*They received their degrees after studying at **university**.*
- say yoo-nee-**vur**-si-tee

unkind
adjective
cruel or not caring.

*She was very **unkind** to her little sister.*
- opposite **kind**

unknown
adjective
never seen or heard of.
*Motorways were **unknown** in the 19th century.*
- say un-**noen**

unlikely
adjective
not probable.
*An **unlikely** story.*
- opposite **likely**

unload
unloads unloading unloaded *verb*
to take things out of a vehicle or container.

*He **unloaded** the shopping from the trolley.*
- opposite **load**

unlock
unlocks unlocking unlocked *verb*
to open something by undoing a lock.

*He **unlocked** his bicycle.*
- opposite **lock**

unlucky
adjective
having bad luck, or bringing bad luck.
*It's thought to be **unlucky** to walk under ladders.*
- comparisons **unluckier unluckiest**
- opposite **lucky**

unnecessary
adjective
not needed.
*It's **unnecessary** to wear a coat in very hot weather.*
- say un-**nes**-i-sair-ee
- opposite **necessary**

unoccupied
adjective
vacant, or not being used.

*The house had been **unoccupied** for months.*
- opposite **occupied**

unorganized
adjective
with no order or plan.
*The trip was very **unorganized**.*
- opposite **organized**

unpack
unpacks unpacking unpacked *verb*
to take things out of a container.

***Unpacking** a suitcase.*
- opposite **pack**

unpleasant
adjective
not pleasing, or not nice.
*An **unpleasant** smell.*
- opposite **pleasant**

unscrew
unscrews unscrewing unscrewed *verb*
to loosen by turning, or to undo screws.

*She **unscrewed** the numbers from the door.*

untidy
adjective
in a mess.
*Her room was always **untidy**.*
- say un-**tie**-dee
- opposite **tidy**

untie
unties untying untied *verb*
to undo something that is knotted, such as rope or thread.

*She **untied** the rope and rowed away.*
- opposite **tie**

until
preposition
up to the time of.
*We were awake **until** midnight.*

untrue
adjective
false or not based on facts.
*The story about the two-tailed dog was **untrue**.*
- opposite **true**

unused
adjective
not in use or never used.
*An **unused** notebook.*
- say un-**yoozd**
- opposite **used**

unusual
adjective
rare or not ordinary.

*A very **unusual** guitar.*
- say un-**yoo**-zhoo-al

unwell
adjective
ill or sick.
*When I had flu, I felt **unwell** for days.*
- opposite **well**

unwrap
unwraps unwrapping unwrapped *verb*
to take the wrapping or covering off something.

*She **unwrapped** her present.*
- say un-**rap**
- opposite **wrap**

up
preposition
towards a higher position.
*I walked **up** the hill to the house at the top.*
- opposite **down**

up
adverb
to or in a higher position.
*Stand **up**!*
- opposite **down**

upright
adverb
sitting or standing up straight rather than bent over.

*The dog stood **upright** on its hind legs.*
- say up-**rite**
upright *adjective*

uproar
noun
a state of noisy activity.
*The crowd was in an **uproar**.*

upset
upsets upsetting upset *verb*
1 to make someone sad or anxious.
*The accident **upset** him.*
2 to knock something over.
*The cat **upset** the vase of flowers.*
upset *adjective*

upside-down
adverb
with the top part underneath, or turned the wrong way up.

*He hung **upside-down** from the bar.*
upside-down *adjective*

upstairs
adverb
to or on an upper storey.

*The lights are on **upstairs**.*
- opposite **downstairs**
upstairs *adjective*

upwards
adverb
towards a higher position.

*She let go and the balloons drifted **upwards**.*
- opposite **downwards**

uranium
noun
a silvery white, radioactive metal used for producing nuclear energy.

- say yoo-**ray**-nee-um

urge
urges urging urged *verb*
to try to persuade someone to do something.
*He **urged** them to be careful when playing by the river.*
- say urj

urge
urges *noun*
a powerful feeling that makes you want to do something.
*A sudden **urge** to sneeze.*

urgent
adjective
needing immediate action or attention.
*An **urgent** message.*
- say **ur**-jent
urgently *adverb*

urine
noun
liquid waste from the body.
- say **yoor**-rin

use
uses using used *verb*
to put something into action.

*The cat **uses** a cat flap to come in and go out of the house.*
- say **yooz**

use
uses *noun*
1 the value of something for a certain purpose.

*This penknife has many **uses**.*
2 the state of being used.
*Steam trains are still in **use** in some areas.*
- say **yoos**

useful
adjective
able to be used for all sorts of tasks, or good for a certain task.

*This gadget is **useful** for unscrewing lids.*
- say **yoose**-ful
- opposite **useless**
usefully *adverb*

usual
adjective
most often done or seen.
*I left work at the **usual** time.*
- say **yoo**-zhoo-al
usually *adverb*

utensil
utensils *noun*
a tool used for a particular job, especially one used in the kitchen.

*A whisk is a kitchen **utensil**.*
- say yoo-**ten**-sil

a b c d e f g h i j k l m n o p q r s t **u** v w x y z

231

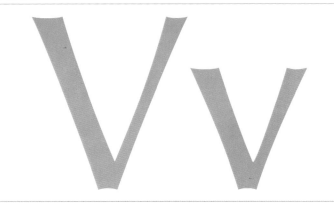

Vv

vacant
adjective
empty or not used.
*She parked in
the **vacant** space.*
■ say **vay**-kant

vaccination
vaccinations *noun*
an injection of a substance
called a vaccine that stops you
from getting
a particular
disease.

■ say vak-si-**nay**-shun

vacuum
vacuums *noun*
a space from which all,
or almost all, of the air
has been removed.
■ say **vak**-yoom

vacuum cleaner
vacuum cleaners *noun*
a machine that cleans
by sucking up dirt.

vacuum flask
vacuum flasks *noun*
a container used for keeping
liquids hot or cold. Flasks
have double walls
with a vacuum
between them.

vague
adjective
not clear or not definite.
*A **vague** idea.*
■ say **vayg**
vaguely *adverb*

vain
adjective
1 too proud of what you can
do, what you look like, or
what you own.
*Vain people look in the mirror
all the time.*
■ comparisons **vainer vainest**
2 unsuccessful.
*They made a **vain** attempt to
put out the fire.*
vainly *adverb*

valley
valleys *noun*
an area of low land between
hills, often with a river or
stream flowing through it.

valuable
adjective
1 precious,
or worth a
lot of money.

*This **valuable** Chinese
ornament once belonged
to an emperor.*
2 useful or worthwhile.
Valuable help.
■ say **val**-yoo-bul
■ opposite **worthless**
value *noun*

van
vans *noun*
a covered vehicle that is
smaller than a lorry and
is used for carrying goods.

vandal
vandals *noun*
a person who deliberately
damages things.
vandalize *verb*

vanilla
noun
a sweet food flavouring
made from the pods of
a tropical orchid, also
called vanilla.

vanilla pods

vanish
vanishes vanishing vanished *verb*
to disappear suddenly.
*The magician waved his wand
and the rabbit **vanished**.*

vapour
vapours *noun*
1 the gas that certain liquids
or solids give off when they
are heated.
2 steam, mist, or smoke in
the air.
■ say **vay**-pur

variety
varieties *noun*
1 change or difference.
*It is important to have
variety in your work,
or you will be bored.*
2 a selection of
different things.
*The shop had a **variety**
of mugs for sale.*
3 a particular type.
*What **variety** of fruit is that?*
■ say va-**rye**-e-tee

various
adjective
of several different kinds.
*I bought **various** things
when I went shopping.*
■ say **vair**-ee-us

varnish
varnishes *noun*
a type of clear paint that
makes a surface tough and
shiny when it is dry.

*wood **varnish***
varnish *verb*

vase
vases *noun*
a jar used as an ornament
for displaying flowers.

■ say **varz**

vegetable

vegetables *noun*

a plant, or part of a plant, that is grown for food. Vegetables contain vitamins and minerals that keep us healthy.

■ say **vej**-tab-bul

okra

pumpkin

flesh

seed

leaf

Brussels sprouts

stem

courgette

aubergine

leaf

leaf

stem

root

beetroot

kohlrabi

radish

corn-cob

husk

sweetcorn (maize)

seed

sweet potato

root tuber

spear

asparagus

leaf

radicchio

leaf

stem

celery

stalk

seed

peppers

skin

stalk

flower head

globe artichoke

chinese leaf

A
B
C
D
E
F
G
H
I
J
K
L
M
N
O
P
Q
R
S
T
U
V
W
X
Y
Z

vegetarian
vegetarians *noun*
someone who does not eat
meat or fish.
■ say vej-it-**tair**-ree-an

vehicle
vehicles *noun*
something that is used to
transport people or things on
land, in the air, or in space.

■ say **vee**-i-kul

veil
veils *noun*
a covering for the face
or head that is made
of thin fabric.

■ rhymes with **pale**

vein
veins *noun*
1 any one of the tubes that
carries blood from other parts
of the body to the heart.
The vena cava is
the major vein
in the body.

vena cava
heart

velvet
noun
a type of fabric
covered in short,
soft fibres.

velvet *adjective*

ventriloquist
ventriloquists *noun*
a person who can speak
without moving his or her
lips. Most ventriloquists use
dolls and make it seem as if
the doll is talking.

■ say ven-**tril**-o-kwist

verb
verbs *noun*
a word that describes what a
person or thing is doing. A
sentence usually needs a verb
in order to make sense.

verse
verses *noun*
1 a section of a poem or song.
2 a general name for poetry.
*He wrote a book of **verse**.*

2 one of the fine tubes in
a leaf or in an insect's wings.

vein

■ say **vane**

version
versions *noun*
A different kind or form of
the same thing.
*I like this **version** of the story.*

vertical
adjective
standing straight up,
at right angles to
the horizon.

*a **vertical** line*

very
adverb
extremely, or by
a great amount.
*This book is **very** long.*

vessel
vessels *noun*
1 a craft that is used for
transport by water, usually
anything larger than a boat.

2 a container in which liquid
can be kept.
*Bring the mixture to the boil
in a heat-proof **vessel**.*
■ say **ves**-ul

vest
vests *noun*
a piece of underwear worn
on the top half of the body.

vet
vets *noun*
a person who is trained to
treat sick animals. Vet is
short for veterinary surgeon.

vibrate
vibrates vibrating vibrated *verb*
to make tiny, rapid,
shaking movements.
*The drill **vibrated** noisily.*
■ say vye-**brate**
vibration *noun*

vicious
adjective
likely to hurt people
or things.
*A **vicious** dog attacked him.*
■ say **vish**-us

victim
victims *noun*
a person who has been
harmed or killed by
something or someone.
*The **victim** of an accident.*

victory
victories *noun*
success in
a contest
or battle.

*The racing driver was thrilled
with his **victory**.*
■ say vik-**tree**

view
views *noun*
1 everything that you can see
from a certain place.

*There was a good **view** of
the city from the window.*
2 an opinion.
*In my **view**, more people
ought to travel by train.*
■ say **vyoo**

a b c d e f g h i j k l m n o p q r s t u v w x y z

village
villages *noun*
a community in the country that is smaller than a town.

vinegar
noun
a sour liquid used to flavour or preserve food.

■ say **vin**-i-ger

vintage
adjective
old and of good quality (see **car** on page 39).

violent
adjective
using strong and damaging force.
*The **violent** storm threw cars across the street.*
violence *noun*
violently *adverb*

violin
violins *noun*
a wooden musical instrument with four strings. The violin body is held below the chin and played with a bow.

bow

violin

virus
viruses *noun*
a type of germ that causes a disease such as flu.
■ say **vye**-rus

visible
adjective
able to be seen.
*The mountain was **visible** for miles.*
■ opposite **invisible**

visit
visits visiting visited *verb*
to go to see a person or a place.

*I went to **visit** her in the hospital.*
visit *noun*

vitamin
vitamins *noun*
one of a group of natural substances found in foods that we need to eat to keep healthy.

parsley

pepper

*Foods containing **vitamin** C.*

vocabulary
vocabularies *noun*
1 all the words in a language.
2 all the words that are known and used by a person.
■ say vo-**kab**-yoo-la-ree

voice
voices *noun*
the sound that comes out of your mouth when you speak or sing.
*He's lost his **voice**.*
■ say **voys**

volcano
volcanoes *noun*
a mountain that is created by lava from inside Earth. Volcanoes sometimes erupt, sending lava and ash down onto the surrounding country.

volcanic *adjective*

volume
volumes *noun*
1 a book, usually one of a series.

*The fourth **volume** of an encyclopedia.*
2 the amount of space inside something, or the amount of space that something fills.

*This jug has a **volume** of one litre.*
3 an amount.
*This road has a huge **volume** of traffic travelling along it.*
4 the loudness of a sound.
*Can you turn up the **volume** on the television?*

volunteer
volunteers *noun*
a person who offers to do something without being told or paid to do it.
volunteer *verb*

vomit
vomits vomiting vomited *verb*
to be sick.
vomit *noun*

vote
votes voting voted *verb*
to show your choice or opinion by putting up your hand or by marking a name on a piece of paper with a cross.

*He **voted** for the candidate by putting a cross on the paper.*
vote *noun*

vow
vows *noun*
a solemn promise.
vow *verb*
■ rhymes with **how**

vowel
vowels *noun*
a sound represented by the letters a, e, i, o, or u (see **alphabet** on page 16).
■ rhymes with **owl**

vulture
vultures *noun*
a large bird of prey that feeds on dead animals. Vultures have a good sense of smell and good eyesight. Their feet are adapted for walking rather than holding onto branches.

Egyptian vulture

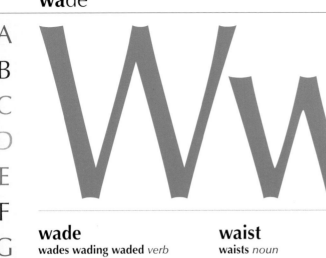

wade
wades wading waded *verb*
to walk through water.
*We **waded** across the stream.*

wafer
wafers *noun*
a thin, crisp biscuit that is
often eaten with ice-cream.
■ say **way**-fer

waffle
waffles *noun*
a crisp, thick pancake with
squares pressed into it.
Waffles are made from
eggs and flour.

■ say **wof**-ul

wage
wages *noun*
the money paid to some
in return for work.
*He collected his **wages**
every Friday.*
■ say **wayj**

wagon
wagons *noun*
a vehicle with
four wheels used
for transporting
heavy loads.
A wagon can be
pulled by a train
or a horse.

waist
waists *noun*
the narrower part of your
body between your chest and
your hips.

waist

wait
waits waiting waited *verb*
to stay in a place or delay
doing something until
a certain event happens.
Wait for me!
wait *noun*

waiter / waitress
waiters / waitresses *noun*
someone whose job it is to
serve you with a meal.
■ **waiter** is male and **waitress**
is female.

wake
wakes waking woke woken *verb*
to stop sleeping or to stop
someone else from sleeping.
*I **woke** up very early
this morning.*
awake *adjective*

walk
walks walking walked *verb*
to move along on foot.
■ say **wawk**
walk *noun*

walker
walkers *noun*
a person who takes long walks
for exercise and pleasure.

wall
walls *noun*
a vertical surface made
of stone, brick, or another
material. Walls are used
to enclose a space or to form
the outside structure and
inside divisions of a building.

*There was a high **wall** around
the garden.*

wallaby
wallabies *noun*
a plant-eating marsupial
from Australia that looks
like a small kangaroo.
■ say **wol**-a-bee

wallet
wallets *noun*
a small, soft case for
carrying money.

■ say **wol**-it

walrus
walruses *noun*
a very large sea mammal that
lives on the ice in the Arctic
and hunts for its food in
the icy waters. Walruses have
very tough skin and whiskers.
They have a thick layer of fat
called blubber to keep them
warm instead of fur.

wand
wands *noun*
a long, slender stick used
for performing magic tricks.
In fairy tales, wands
are used for casting
magic spells.

■ say **wond**

wander
wanders wandering wandered
verb
to go from place to place
without any real purpose
or destination.
*My friends love to **wander**
around the shops.*
■ say **won**-der

want
wants wanting wanted *verb*
1 to wish to have
or do something.
*I **want** a puppy for
my birthday.*
2 to need or
require something.
*Do you **want** any help?*

war
wars *noun*
a period of fighting between
countries or groups of people.
■ say **wore**

wardrobe

wardrobes *noun*

1 a cupboard for clothing.
2 a collection of clothes.
*A winter **wardrobe**.*

■ say **wore**-drobe

warehouse

warehouses *noun*

a large building used for storing goods.

warm

adjective

1 having a temperature that is between cool and hot.

*The hot water bottle felt nice and **warm**.*
2 friendly and kind.
*She gave us a **warm** welcome.*

■ comparisons **warmer warmest**
■ opposite **cool**
warmth *noun*

warn

warns warning warned *verb*

to tell or signal to someone that there may be a problem or danger ahead.

*The sign on the fence **warned** of radioactivity in the area.*

■ say **worn**
warning *noun*

warship

warships *noun*

a ship armed with weapons that is used during a war.

wash

washes washing washed *verb*

to clean yourself or something else with water and soap.

wash *noun*

wasp

wasps *noun*

a type of flying insect that can sting. A wasp uses its sting to defend itself and to catch other insects for food.

■ say **wosp**

waste

wastes wasting wasted *verb*

1 to use more of something than you really need or want.
*Don't **waste** electricity!*
2 to fail to use something.
*They **wasted** their chance to win the match.*
waste *noun*

watch

watches watching watched *verb*

to look at and pay attention to someone or something for a time.

***Watching** birds.*

watch

watches *noun*

a small instrument for telling the time, usually worn on the wrist (see **time** on page 216).

water

noun

a clear liquid that falls as rain and forms streams, rivers, lakes, and oceans.

■ say **wor**-ter

water

waters watering watered *verb*

to supply with water.
*Will you **water** my plants while I'm away?*

water cycle

noun

the process by which water travels around Earth and its atmosphere. Water from rivers and oceans evaporates into the air, where it gathers to form clouds. The water then falls as rain to fill the rivers and oceans.

waterfall

waterfalls *noun*

a place where a river falls over a steep cliff.

watermelon

watermelons *noun*

a large, juicy type of melon with green skin. The flesh is red and contains black seeds.

waterproof

adjective

not allowing water to pass through it.

*A **waterproof** coat.*

watt

watts *noun*

a unit for measuring electrical power.
*A 100-**watt** light bulb.*

■ say **wot**

wave

waves *noun*

1 a moving ridge on the surface of a liquid.

2 a vibration of sound or light that travels through the air and moves in a similar way to a wave in liquid.

wave

waves waving waved *verb*

1 to signal to someone by moving your hand or an object from side to side.

*She **waved** goodbye as the ship sailed away.*
wave *noun*
2 to move backwards and forwards.
*The branches **waved** in the strong wind.*

wax

waxes *noun*

a solid, oily substance that melts when it is heated. Wax is used to make many things, including furniture polish and candles.

a
b
c
d
e
f
g
h
i
j
k
l
m
n
o
p
q
r
s
t
u
v
w
x
y
z

A B C D E F G H I J K L M N O P Q R S T U V **W** X Y Z

way
ways *noun*
1 a direction or route.

*The sign showed the **way** to the village.*
2 a method.
*What is the right **way** to use a video camera?*
3 a manner of behaving.
*She stared at him in a very rude **way**.*

weak
adjective
having little strength or power.

*Baby birds are very **weak** when they are born.*
■ comparisons **weaker weakest**
■ opposite **strong**
weakness *noun*

wealthy
adjective
having a lot of money or possessions.
*The inventor sold his idea and became very **wealthy**.*
■ say **wel**-thee
■ comparisons **wealthier wealthiest**
wealth *noun*

weapon
weapons *noun*
a tool that can be used to hurt someone.

*In the past, spears and swords were used as **weapons**.*
■ say **wep**-on

wear
wears wearing wore worn *verb*
to have on, or covering your body.

*He is **wearing** a South American cowboy outfit.*
■ say **ware**

weary
adjective
very tired.

*She felt **weary** after her long walk.*
■ say **weer**-ree
■ comparisons **wearier weariest**
weariness *noun*

weather
noun
the condition of the atmosphere at a certain place and time, such as the air temperature and whether or not it is raining.

*a **weather** map*
■ say **weth**-ur

weathered
adjective
having changed shape or colour due to the effects of the Sun, wind, or rain.
***Weathered** rock.*

weave
weaves weaving wove woven *verb*
1 to pass threads over and under one another to make cloth.

*He is **weaving** a mat out of wool.*
woven *adjective*
2 to move in and out between objects.
*The river **weaves** its way around the hills and down to the sea.*

web
webs *noun*
1 a fine net of sticky threads made by a spider to trap flies.
2 a collection of pages linked electronically via the internet.

wedding
weddings *noun*
an occasion when two people get married.

weed
weeds *noun*
a wild plant that grows where it is not wanted.

*Burdock is a common **weed**.*

week
weeks *noun*
a period of seven days.

weekend
weekends *noun*
Saturday and Sunday, the days when many people do not go to school or work.

weep
weeps weeping wept *verb*
to show you are unhappy by crying.

weigh
weighs weighing weighed *verb*
1 to measure how heavy something is.

*He **weighed** some beans.*
2 to have a certain weight.
*The package **weighed** half a kilo.*
■ say **way**

weight
weights *noun*
1 the measurement of how heavy something is.
2 a piece of metal with a known heaviness, used with weighing scales to work out how much something weighs.
■ say **wayt**

weird
adjective
strange
and mysterious.

*The tree had
a **weird** shape.*
- say **weerd**
- comparisons
weirder weirdest

welcome
welcomes welcoming welcomed
verb

to show someone that you are
glad they have come.
*He went to the door to **welcome**
his guests.*
welcoming *adjective*

welfare
noun

a person's health, happiness,
and comfort.
*A headteacher has to consider
the **welfare** of the pupils.*

well
wells *noun*

a deep hole made in
the ground
to obtain
water, gas,
or oil.

well
adjective
in good health.
*Are you **well** today?*

well
adverb
1 in a good or suitable way.
*He behaved very **well**.*
2 thoroughly.
*Water the plants **well**.*

went
*from the verb **to go***
*I **went** to the shops to buy
some food.*

wept
*from the verb **to weep***
*He **wept** when his dog died.*

west
noun
one of the four main
compass directions. West
is the direction in which
the Sun sets.

north

west   *east*

south

western *adjective*

western
westerns *noun*

a film about cowboys
and other people living in
the western USA, usually
during the 19th century.

wet
adjective
1 covered or soaked
with water.

2 rainy.
Wet weather.
3 not yet dry.
Wet paint.
- comparisons **wetter wettest**
- opposite **dry**

whale
whales *noun*

a very large sea mammal with a breathing hole in the top of
its head. Whales eat fish or tiny water animals (see **mammal**
on page 124).

*sperm **whale***

what
adjective
which thing or which kind.
What is your favourite colour?
- say **wot**

wheat
noun
a type of cereal that is
grown on farms. The grains
from wheat are used for
making flour.

*durum **wheat***

- say **weet**

wheel
wheels *noun*
a circular object that turns
around a fixed, central point.
Most land vehicles move on
wheels (see **car** on page 39
and **transport** on page 221).

wheelbarrow
wheelbarrows *noun*
a small cart with one wheel
at the front, used for pushing
heavy loads by hand.

wheelchair
wheelchairs *noun*
a chair with wheels. People
use wheelchairs to move from
place to place if they have
difficulty in walking.

when
adverb
at what time.
When did you arrive?

where
adverb
at, in, or to what place.
Where are you going?

which
adjective
what particular thing or
things out of a selection.
Which car is yours?

whine
whines whining whined *verb*
1 to make a long, high cry.
*Dogs **whine**.*
2 to complain unnecessarily.
*The toddler **whined** about
going to bed.*

whip
whips *noun*
a rope or strip of leather that
is attached to a handle and is
used for urging animals
to do something.

*a cowboy's
whip*

a b c d e f g h i j k l m n o p q r s t u v w x y z

A B C D E F G H I J K L M N O P Q R S T U V **W** X Y Z

whirl
whirls whirling whirled *verb*
to turn yourself or an object
around quickly.

*He **whirled** the
lasso around
his head.*

whirlwind
whirlwinds *noun*
a very strong wind that
blows in spirals, causing
great damage.

whisk
whisks whisking whisked *verb*
1 to move quickly and lightly.
*She **whisked** the child out of
the way of the bike.*
2 to beat a mixture lightly
and quickly.

***Whisk** the egg whites until they
are stiff.*

whisker
whiskers *noun*
one of the stiff hairs that
grows near the mouth of
certain animals (see
mammal on page 124 and
pet on page 148).

whisper
whispers whispering whispered
verb
to speak in a very quiet voice.

*She **whispered** her secret into
his ear.*
whisper *noun*

whistle
whistles whistling whistled *verb*
to make a high,
shrill sound
by blowing
air through
your lips.

■ say **wis**-ul

whistle
whistles *noun*
a device that you blow into to
make high, shrill sounds.

white
noun
a colour.

whizz
whizzes whizzing whizzed *verb*
to move along very fast.

whole
adjective
complete, or with
nothing missing.

*They bought a **whole** quiche
for the party.*
■ say **hole**
whole *noun*

why
adverb
for what reason.
Why did you go?

wicked
adjective
behaving in a bad way
on purpose.
*A **wicked** person.*
wickedness *noun*

wide
adjective
1 being a large size, or long
distance, from one side to
the other.

*A **wide** river.*
■ comparisons **wider widest**
■ opposite **narrow**
2 having a certain
measurement from one side
to the other.
*The carpet is one metre **wide**.*
wide *adverb*
width *noun*

widow / widower
widows / widowers *noun*
a person whose husband or
wife has died.
■ **widow** is female and **widower**
is male.

wife
wives *noun*
a married woman.

wig
wigs *noun*
a false covering of
hair for the head
(see **costume** on
page 51).

wild
adjective
1 in a natural environment,
or not controlled
by people.

*Meadowsweet
is a **wild** flower.*
2 uncontrolled, violent,
or crazy.
*The children went **wild**
in the theme park.*
■ rhymes with **child**
■ comparisons **wilder wildest**

wilderness
wildernesses *noun*
a wild area of land where
no one lives.
■ say **wil**-der-ness

will
verb
a word used to show that
the action of a verb is
happening in the future.
*I **will** go out this afternoon.*
■ opposite **will not** or **won't**
■ always used with another verb

will
wills *noun*
1 the power to choose and control your own actions.
She forced me to do it against my will.
2 a document containing instructions about what should happen to a person's possessions after his or her death.

3 determination.
She had the will to win.

willing
adjective
in agreement with something that you are asked to do.
Are you willing to help in the garden?

win
wins winning won *verb*
to come first in a game or competition.

She was very pleased when she won the game.
■ opposite **lose**

wind
winds *noun*
a current of air.

The wind blew his umbrella inside-out.
■ rhymes with **sinned**
windy *adjective*

wind
winds winding wound *verb*
1 to twist or coil something up.

He wound the clock.
2 to turn in a curving way.
They could see the car winding its way up the hill.
■ rhymes with **find**

windmill
windmills *noun*
a building with large sails, which uses wind power to turn a machine that grinds grain, pumps water, or makes electricity.

window
windows *noun*
an opening in a building or vehicle that lets in light and air, often covered with glass.

wine
noun
an alcoholic drink made from the juice of grapes.

wing
wings *noun*
1 one of the parts of a bird, insect, or bat that is used for flying (see **bird** on page 28, **insect** on page 108, and **mammal** on page 124).
2 one of the large, flat parts on each side of an aeroplane that acts in a similar way to a bird's wings (see **transport** on page 221).

wink
winks winking winked *verb*
to open and close one eye briefly as a signal to another person.

winter
noun
the coldest season of the year. Winter comes between autumn and spring.

wipe
wipes wiping wiped *verb*
to clean or dry something by rubbing.

He wiped the mirror's surface with a duster.

wire
wires *noun*
a long, thin, metal thread that can be bent. Wires can be used to carry electrical power.

copper wire

wise
adjective
having a lot of knowledge and experience.
The wise old lady gave me good advice.
■ say **wize**
■ comparisons **wiser wisest**
■ opposite **foolish**

wish
wishes wishing wished *verb*
to feel or say that you want something.
I wish I owned a car.
wish *noun*

witch
witches *noun*
a woman who practises magic.

wither
withers withering withered *verb*
to become dry.

Their plant withered while they were away on holiday.

without
preposition
not having or not using.

He went outside without his shoes.

witness
witnesses *noun*
a person who sees an event happen.
Three witnesses saw him stealing the car.
witness *verb*

wizard
wizards *noun*
a man who practises magic.

a b c d e f g h i j k l m n o p q r s t u v **w** x y z

A
B
C
D
E
F
G
H
I
J
K
L
M
N
O
P
Q
R
S
T
U
V
W
X
Y
Z

wobble
wobbles wobbling wobbled *verb*
to move
unsteadily.

*He wobbled
on his ice-skates.*

woke
from the verb **to wake**
He woke her very early.

wolf
wolves *noun*
a wild mammal that is part
of the dog family and lives
in cold regions. Wolves live in
packs and hunt other animals
for food.

woman
women *noun*
an adult human female.
■ say **wum**-an

wombat
wombats *noun*
a marsupial that lives in
Australia. A wombat looks
like a small bear and lives
underground, eating leaves,
roots, and bark.

won
from the verb **to win**
We won the match.
■ say **wun**

wonder
noun
a feeling caused by
an extraordinary
or amazing thing.
*They looked in wonder
at the bright lights in the sky.*
■ say **wun**-der

wonder
wonders wondering wondered
verb
to question or think about
something in a curious or
doubtful way.
*I wonder how she managed
to arrive first?*

wonderful
adjective
amazing or extraordinary.
A wonderful idea.
■ say **wun**-der-ful

wood
noun
1 the hard material from
a tree's trunk or branches
used to make furniture and
objects or to burn for fuel.

The train is made of wood.
wooden *adjective*

2 a group of trees
growing together.

woodwind instrument
woodwind instruments *noun*
one of a group of musical
instruments that is
played by blowing.
Some, such as
the clarinet, are
made from wood
while others, such
as the flute, are
made from metal.

alto clarinet

wool
noun
the soft hair of sheep and
some other animals, which
can be used to make cloth,
clothes, carpets,
and blankets.

sheep's wool

ball of wool

woollen
adjective
made from wool.

woollen hat

word
words *noun*
1 a sound or group of sounds
that stands for an idea,
an object, or an action.
2 the group of letters you use
to write down these sounds.

word processing
verb
writing, correcting, and
storing documents
electronically.

wore
from the verb **to wear**
He wore a yellow T-shirt.

work
works working worked *verb*
1 to use effort to
do something.
*I worked hard when I painted
the house.*
2 to do a job or task.
My father works in a factory.
work *noun*
3 to operate efficiently.

*This washing machine is not
working properly.*

world
noun
the planet Earth and all the
people and things on it.

worm
worms *noun*
a small animal with a soft
body and no legs or backbone.

earthworm

worry
worries worrying worried *verb*
to feel anxious.
I am worried about my exams.
■ say **wur**-ee
worry *noun*

worse
from the adjective **bad**
very bad.
*Last week's weather was bad,
but today, it is worse.*

worship
worships worshipping worshipped *verb*
to respect and love, usually in a religious way.

The ancient Egyptians **worshipped** *many gods.*

worst
from the adjective **bad**
extremely bad.
This is the **worst** *storm I've ever seen.*

worth
adjective
having a value.

The crown was **worth** *a lot of money.*

worthless
adjective
having little or no value.
He found an old vase, but it turned out to be **worthless***.*

would
verb
1 a word used to talk about an action that depends on something else.
I **would** *go to the park, but I have to wait here.*
2 a word used to ask for something.
Would *you like some tea?*
■ rhymes with **good**
■ opposite **would not** or **wouldn't**
■ always used with another verb

wound
wounds *noun*
an injury to the body where the skin is torn or cut in some way.

She put a dressing on the **wound***.*
■ say **woond**
wound *verb*

wound
from the verb **to wind**
He **wound** *the string round the parcel.*
■ rhymes with **sound**

wove
from the verb **to weave**
She **wove** *the wool into cloth.*
■ rhymes with **stove**

wrap
wraps wrapping wrapped *verb*
to fold paper or fabric around something.

He **wrapped** *the present in coloured paper.*
■ say **rap**

wrapper
wrappers *noun*
a piece of paper, plastic, or foil that is used to cover something you buy.

sweets in their **wrappers**

■ say **rap**-er

wreath
wreaths *noun*
a decoration made from flowers, leaves, or branches tied together in a circle.

■ say **reeth**

wreck
wrecks wrecking wrecked *verb*
to destroy or ruin.

He crashed into the stone post, **wrecking** *the car.*
■ say **rek**

wrestle
wrestles wrestling wrestled *verb*
to struggle with someone and try to force him or her to the ground.
■ say **res**-ul

wriggle
wriggles wriggling wriggled *verb*
to twist and turn from side to side.
■ say **rig**-ul

wring
wrings wringing wrung *verb*
to twist something hard using both hands.
■ say **ring**

He **wrung** *the water out of the cloth.*

wrinkle
wrinkles *noun*
a small crease or fold in skin or fabric.
■ say **ring**-kul

wrist
wrists *noun*
the joint between your hand and your arm.

wrist

■ say **rist**

write
writes writing wrote written *verb*
1 to form letters and words on a surface.
2 to create something, such as a letter, by using words.
I **wrote** *to my sister last week.*
■ say **rite**

wrong
adjective
1 not correct.
The **wrong** *answer.*
2 bad.
It's **wrong** *to steal.*
■ say **rong**
■ opposite **right**

a b c d e f g h i j k l m n o p q r s t u v w x y z

243

A B C D E F G H I J K L M N O P Q R S T U V W **X** **Y** Z

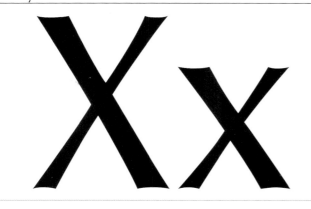

X-ray
X-rays *noun*
a special photograph that shows your bones and other parts that are inside your body.

chest **X-ray**

X-ray *verb*

xylophone
xylophones *noun*
a musical instrument with wooden bars on a frame. Each bar produces a different note when it is struck.

■ say **zye**-le-fown

yacht
yachts *noun*
a small ship with a sail that is usually used for racing or pleasure, rather than for transporting goods or passengers.

■ say **yot**

yak
yaks *noun*
a wild ox with long hair and horns that lives in the mountains of central Asia. Yaks eat grass and are often used by people as a source of food or for carrying loads.

yap
yaps yapping yapped *verb*
to bark in a shrill way.

yard
yards *noun*
an outdoor area near a building, enclosed by a fence or a wall.

yarn
yarns *noun*
wool, cotton, or another material spun into a thread for knitting or weaving.

yawn
yawns yawning yawned *verb*
to open your mouth and breathe in deeply, usually because you are tired or bored.

■ rhymes with **corn**
yawn *noun*

year
years *noun*
a period of 12 months. A year is the time that it takes Earth to travel once around the Sun.
yearly *adverb*

yeast
noun
a yellow-brown substance made up of tiny fungi. Yeast is used in bread and cakes to help them rise with air.

fresh **yeast**   *dried* **yeast**

yell
yells yelling yelled *verb*
to shout or scream loudly.

He **yelled** *at the neighbour's cats that were fighting outside the window.*
yell *noun*

yellow
noun
a colour.

yesterday
adverb
on the day before today.
I went to the zoo **yesterday**.
yesterday *noun*

yet

adverb

up to the present time.
*The letter hasn't arrived **yet**.*

yoga

noun

a system of exercises and
deep breathing, aimed at
making a person healthy
and relaxed in
mind and body.
- say **yo**-ga

yoghurt

yoghurts *noun*

a sour food made by adding
bacteria to milk.
- say **yog**-urt
- also spelt **yogurt**

yoke

yokes *noun*

a wooden frame that fits
over the shoulders of two
oxen or other work animals
so that they can pull a load.
The yoke keeps the
animals together.

yolk

yolks *noun*

the yellow part of an egg.

yolk

- say **yoke**

young

adjective

in the early part of life.

*The grandmother held the
young child in her arms.*
- say **yung**
- comparisons **younger
youngest**
- opposite **old**

youth

noun

1 the state of being young.
*In my **youth**, I had dark hair.*
2 young people in general.
*A place for the **youth** of
the town to meet.*
3 a young man or boy.
- say **yooth**

yo-yo

yo-yos *noun*

a toy that spins up and down
on a string.

Zz

zebra

zebras *noun*

a striped African mammal
that is part of the horse
family. Zebras live in herds
on open plains and eat grass
and shrubs.

zero

zeros *noun*

nothing or none.

zigzag

zigzags *noun*

a line with a series of sharp
turns and angles in it.
zigzag *adjective*

zigzag *verb*

zinc

noun

a blue-white, brittle metal.

zip

zips *noun*

a device with two
rows of teeth that
can be opened and
closed. Zips are used
to fasten clothing
or bags.

zip *verb*

zodiac

noun

the 12 sections into which
astrologers divide the sky.
Each part is represented
by a sign.
- say **zoe**-dee-ak

zone

zones *noun*

an area that is divided off for
a particular purpose.
*A no-parking **zone**.*

zoo

zoos *noun*

a place where people
can observe and learn
about animals.

zoom

zooms zooming zoomed *verb*

to move very fast.

*The four motorbikes **zoomed**
past me.*

Abbreviations

An abbreviation is a short form of a word or phrase. Some abbreviations are made by just shortening a word. For example, **ad** is short for **advertisement**, and **max** is short for **maximum**. Other abbreviations, such as **CD** for **compact disc**, are made from the first letters of the words that they stand for. On this double page you will find a useful alphabetical list of common abbreviations.

ac alternating current
(An electrical current that travels first in one direction, then in another.)

ad advertisement

AD in the year of our Lord
(From the Latin *anno Domini*. Used in dates to count the year after the birth of Jesus Christ, eg, AD 400.)

AIDS Acquired Immune Deficiency Syndrome
(A disease that makes a person unable to fight illnesses.)

am before noon
(From the Latin *ante meridiem*. Used with times, eg, 9 am.)

anon anonymous

approx approximately

asap as soon as possible

Ave avenue

b born

BA Bachelor of Arts
(A title given to someone who has an arts degree.)

BC Before Christ
(Used in dates to count the years before the birth of Jesus Christ, eg, 30 BC.)

BSc Bachelor of Science
(A title given to someone who has a science degree.)

BST British Summer Time
(The time used in Britain during the summer.)

C Celsius or Centigrade

c about
(From the Latin *circa*. Used with uncertain dates.)

CD compact disc

CIA Central Intelligence Agency
(A US government agency that deals with spies and secrets that are important to the country.)

CID Criminal Investigation Department
(A part of the police force that deals with serious crimes.)

cm centimetre

Co Company
(Used after the names of some companies.)

c/o care of

cont continued

d died

dc direct current
(An electrical current that travels in only one direction.)

dept department

DIY do-it-yourself
(Used to describe repairs and decorating that people do to their own homes.)

DJ disc jockey

Dr doctor

DVD digital versatile/video disc

E east

EAL English as an additional language.

EFL English as a foreign language

eg for example
(From the Latin *exempli gratia*.)

Email electronic mail

ESP extra-sensory perception
(An ability some people are said to have, which makes them aware of things without using their senses.)

etc and all the rest
(From the Latin *et cetera*.)

F Fahrenheit

FBI Federal Bureau of Investigation
(An agency of the American Department of Justice.)

ft foot

flu influenza

g gram

GB Great Britain

GMT Greenwich Mean Time
(The time used in Britain during the winter, and from which time all around the world is measured.)

GP general practitioner
(The title given to a doctor who works in a surgery, rather than in a hospital.)

HGV heavy goods vehicle

HIV Human Immunodeficiency Virus
(The virus that causes AIDS.)

HM His or Her Majesty

HMS His or Her Majesty's Ship

hp horse power

HP hire-purchase
(A way of buying goods by paying in instalments.)

HQ headquarters

HRH His or Her Royal Highness

ICT Information and Communication Technology

ID identification

ie that is
(From the Latin *id est*.)

in inch

Inc Incorporated
(Used in the names of some US companies.)

Inst Institute

IOU I owe you

IQ intelligence quotient
(A test score that claims to measure a person's intelligence.)

IVF in vitro fertilization
(a medical technique where a woman's eggs are fertilized outside the womb.)

Jr junior

kg kilogram

km kilometre

kph kilometres per hour

l litre

lab laboratory

lb pound (in weight) (From the Latin *libra*.)

LCD liquid crystal display

LED light-emitting diode

LP long-playing record

Ltd Limited (Used after the names of some British companies.)

m metre or mile

MA Master of Arts (A title given to someone with a BA, who completes a higher arts degree.)

max maximum

MD Doctor of Medicine (From the Latin *Medicinae Doctor*.)

memo memorandum (A message to remind someone about something.)

MI5 Military Intelligence 5 (The British government organization that deals with spies and secrets that are important to the country.)

min minimum

misc miscellaneous

Miss Mistress (A title that goes before an unmarried woman's name.)

mm millimetre

MP Member of Parliament

mpg miles per gallon

mph miles per hour

mp3 MPEG (Moving Pictures Expert Group) 1 audio layer 3 (A type of digital computer file used to store music.)

Mr Mister (A title that goes before a man's name.)

Mrs Mistress (A title that goes before a married woman's name.)

Ms (A title for a married or an unmarried woman.)

MSc Master of Sciences (A title given to someone with a BSc, who completes a higher science degree.)

Mt mount or mountain

N north

NASA National Aeronautics and Space Administration

NATO North Atlantic Treaty Organization (A military group of countries including the USA and much of western Europe.)

NB take notice (From the Latin *nota bene*.)

NE north east

NHS National Health Service

no number (From the Italian *numero*.)

NW north west

OK all correct

oz ounce

p page

PC police constable or personal computer

PE physical education

PhD Doctor of Philosophy (A title given to someone who has studied a subject to an advanced level at university.)

PLC Public Limited Company

pm after noon (From the Latin *post meridiem*. Used with times, eg 3 pm.)

PO Post Office

POW prisoner of war

pp on behalf of (From the Latin *per procurationem*.)

PR public relations

pro professional

Prof professor

PS postscript (From the Latin *post scriptem*. An extra note written at the end of something, such as a letter.)

PTA Parent Teacher Association

PTO please turn over

RAM random-access memory (The part of the memory in a computer that you use to work on.)

Rd road

ref referee

Revd Reverend

RIP rest in peace (From the Latin *requiescat in pace*. Often written on a grave.)

ROM read-only memory (The part of the memory in a computer that stores permanent information which cannot be altered.)

rpm revolutions per minute (The measurement of how fast records and other things turn.)

RSVP please reply (From the French *répondez s'il vous plaît*. Used on an invitation to a party, wedding, or other event.)

S south

sci-fi science fiction

SE south east

Soc Society

sq square

Sr senior

St Saint or street.

SW south west

tel telephone

temp temporary

3-D three-dimensional (Having height, width, and depth.)

TV television

UFO unidentified flying object

UK United Kingdom

UN United Nations

Unesco United Nations Educational, Scientific, and Cultural Organization

Unicef United Nations Children's Fund (Formerly UN International Children's Emergency Fund.)

US or **USA** United States of America

UV ultraviolet

v against (From the Latin *versus*.)

VAT value-added tax

VDU visual display unit

VIP very important person

W west

WHO World Health Organization

www world wide web

yd yard

Spelling guide

If you are having trouble finding a word in the dictionary, it may be because you are looking under the wrong spelling. There can be many different ways of spelling the same sound. Letters sometimes make a different sound to the usual. They may even be completely silent, like the **k** in **kneel**, or the **g** in **gnat**. The spelling guide below will help you to work out the correct spelling of difficult words.

Sound	As in	Other ways to spell this sound
a (say **air**)	hair	care, wear, there, their, prayer
a (say **ay**)	cake	rain, straight, break, veil, bouquet, obey, hay
a (say **ar**)	father	heart, calm, clerk
ch	chin	catch, question
e	ten	any, said, friend, bury, head, leopard
e (say **ee**)	me	meet, seat, key, quay, machine, field, city
f	fall	laugh, telephone
g	get	ghost, guess
h	help	whole
i	fit	damage, pretty, women, busy, build, myth
i (say **eye**)	ice	height, eye, sigh, buy, fly, dye
j	jump	trudge, soldier, adjective, magic
k	kiss	come, anchor, sack, biscuit, walk, unique
l	leg	island
m	miss	comb
n	nose	gnat, kneel, pneumonia
o	not	swan, cauliflower, knowledge
o (say **oh**)	go	sew, though, boat, brooch, slow
o (say **or**)	sort	autumn, awful, broad, ought
o (say **ow**)	now	out, bough
o (say **oy**)	boy	boil
oo	zoom	threw, move, shoe, soup, through, blue, fruit, queue
qu (say **kw**)	quite	choir
r	red	rhyme, wrong
s	saw	cell, psychology, science
s (say **zh**)	pleasure	mirage, confusion
sh	she	ocean, machine, special, sure, conscience, expansion, nation
t	top	debt, bought
u	up	son, does, flood, double
u	pull	woman, wool, would
u (say **ur**)	fur	germ, heard, bird, worm, journey
v	very	of
w	wish	what
y	yard	use, onion
z	zebra	busy, scissors, xylophone

Word building

The charts on this page show how you can take one word and build a new one from it by adding a group of letters called a prefix or a suffix. Prefixes, such as **dis-**, **un-**, or **mis-**, are joined to the front of a word. They are often used to change a word to its opposite. For example, adding the prefix **in-** turns **visible** into **invisible**. Suffixes, such as **-ful**, **-ism**, or **-ment**, are joined to the end of a word. They are often used to change a word from one part of speech to another. For example, adding the suffix **-er** turns the verb **teach** into the noun **teacher**. These charts show some common prefixes and suffixes.

Prefixes

Prefix	Meaning	Example	Prefix	Meaning	Example
anti-	against	antiseptic	non-	makes the opposite	non-fiction
dis-	makes the opposite	disagree	post-	after	postwar
ex-	out of, or from	export	pre-	before	prehistoric
ex-	former	ex-president	re-	again	replace
in-	makes the opposite	independent	sub-	under	submarine
inter-	between	international	super-	above, or more than	superhuman
mis-	makes the opposite	misfortune	trans-	across	transplant
multi-	many	multicoloured	un-	makes the opposite	unpleasant

Suffixes

Suffixes that make nouns

Suffix	Meaning	Example
-age	a result	wreckage
-ance	an action or state	importance
-ant	a person	assistant
-ee	a person	referee
-ence	an action or state	difference
-er/-or	a person	teacher
-ery	a type or place of work	bakery
-ess	makes a feminine form	waitress
-ful	as much as will fill	spoonful
-ing	an action or result	painting
-ion	a process, state, or result	decoration
-ism	a belief or condition	Judaism
-ist	a person	florist
-ment	an action or state	measurement
-ness	a quality or state	happiness

Suffixes that make adjectives

Suffix	Meaning	Example
-able	able to be	inflatable
-en	made of	woollen
-ful	full of	beautiful
-ible	ability	flexible
-ish	a little	greenish
-less	without	careless
-like	similar to, like	lifelike
-ous	full of	joyous
-some	a tendency to	quarrelsome

Suffixes that make adverbs

Suffix	Meaning	Example
-ly	in a manner	quickly
-ward(s)	shows direction	forwards
-ways	shows direction	sideways

a b c d e f g h i j k l m n o p q r s t u v w x y z

Facts and figures

Metric measures

Length
10 millimetres = 1 centimetre
100 centimetres = 1 metre
1,000 metres = 1 kilometre

Area
10,000 square centimetres =
1 square metre
1,000,000 square metres =
1 square kilometre

Weight
1,000 grams = 1 kilogram
1,000 kilograms = 1 tonne

Volume
10 millilitres = 1 centilitre
10 centilitres = 1 decilitre
10 decilitres = 1 litre

Imperial measures

Length
12 inches = 1 foot
3 feet = 1 yard
1,760 yards = 1 mile

Area
144 square inches = 1 square foot
9 square feet = 1 square yard
4,840 square yards = 1 acre
640 acres = 1 square mile

Weight
16 ounces = 1 pound
14 pounds = 1 stone
112 pounds = 1 hundredweight
20 hundredweight = 1 ton

Volume
20 fluid ounces = 1 pint
8 pints = 1 gallon

Temperatures

Degrees Centigrade / Celsius
Boiling point of water   100°C
Freezing point of water   0°C
Normal body temperature   37°C

Degrees Fahrenheit
Boiling point of water   212°F
Freezing point of water   32°F
Normal body temperature   98.6°F

To convert Centigrade to Fahrenheit:
multiply by 9, divide by 5, and add 32.
(eg: **20°C** x 9 = 180;
180 ÷ 5 = 36; 36 + 32 = **68°F**)

To convert Fahrenheit to Centigrade:
subtract 32, multiply by 5, and
divide by 9.

Counties in the United Kingdom

England
Avon
Bedfordshire
Berkshire
Buckinghamshire
Cambridgeshire
Cheshire
Cleveland
Cornwall
Cumbria
Derbyshire
Devon
Dorset
Durham
East Sussex
Essex
Gloucestershire
Greater London
Greater Manchester
Hampshire

Hereford and Worcester
Hertfordshire
Humberside
Isle of Wight
Kent
Lancashire
Leicestershire
Lincolnshire
Merseyside
Norfolk
Northamptonshire
Northumberland
North Yorkshire
Nottinghamshire
Oxfordshire
Shropshire
Somerset
South Yorkshire
Staffordshire
Suffolk

Surrey
Tyne and Wear
Warwickshire
West Midlands
West Sussex
West Yorkshire
Wiltshire

Northern Ireland
Antrim
Armagh
Down
Fermanagh
Londonderry
Tyrone

Scotland
Borders
Central
Dumfries and Galloway

Fife
Grampian
Highland
Lothian
Orkney
Shetland
Strathclyde
Tayside
Western Isles

Wales
Clwyd
Dyfed
Gwent
Gwynedd
Mid-Glamorgan
Powys
South Glamorgan
West Glamorgan

Cardinal numbers

1	one				
2	two				
3	three				
4	four				
5	five				
6	six				
7	seven				
8	eight				
9	nine				
10	ten				
11	eleven				
12	twelve				
13	thirteen				
14	fourteen				
15	fifteen				
16	sixteen				
17	seventeen				
18	eighteen				
19	nineteen				
20	twenty				
21	twenty-one				
30	thirty				
40	forty				
50	fifty				
60	sixty				
70	seventy				
80	eighty				
90	ninety				
100	one hundred				
500	five hundred				
1,000	one thousand				

Ordinal numbers

1st	first
2nd	second
3rd	third
4th	fourth
5th	fifth
6th	sixth
7th	seventh
8th	eighth
9th	ninth
10th	tenth
11th	eleventh
12th	twelfth
13th	thirteenth
14th	fourteenth
15th	fifteenth
16th	sixteenth
17th	seventeenth
18th	eighteenth
19th	nineteenth
20th	twentieth
21st	twenty-first
30th	thirtieth
40th	fortieth
50th	fiftieth
60th	sixtieth
70th	seventieth
80th	eightieth
90th	ninetieth
100th	one hundredth
500th	five hundredth
1,000th	one thousandth

Roman numerals

1	I
2	II
3	III
4	IV
5	V
6	VI
7	VII
8	VIII
9	IX
10	X
11	XI
12	XII
13	XIII
14	XIV
15	XV
16	XVI
17	XVII
18	XVIII
19	XIX
20	XX
21	XXI
30	XXX
40	XL
50	L
60	LX
70	LXX
80	LXXX
90	XC
100	C
500	D
1,000	M

Symbols and punctuation marks

+	plus	%	per cent	&	and	?	question mark
−	minus	°	degree	@	at	!	exclamation mark
×	multiply	√	square root	©	copyright	–	dash
÷	divide	π	pi	.	full stop	*	asterisk
=	equals	£	pound	,	comma	( )	brackets
>	greater than	$	dollar	;	semi-colon	" "	speech marks
<	less than	€	euro	:	colon	'	apostrophe

a
b
c
d
e
f
g
h
i
j
k
l
m
n
o
p
q
r
s
t
u
v
w
x
y
z

Countries of the world

On the next four pages is a list of the world's countries, arranged in alphabetical order. Under each country's name are its capital city, the name of the people who live there, and its currency. When a country has two capital cities, they are both listed. If there is a common abbreviation or symbol for the currency, such as $ for **dollar**, this is shown in brackets after the name of the currency.

Afghanistan
Capital city: Kabul
People: Afghans
Currency: Afghani (AF)

Albania
Capital city: Tirana
People: Albanians
Currency: Lek

Algeria
Capital city: Algiers
People: Algerians
Currency: Algerian Dinar (DA)

Andorra
Capital city: Andorra la Vella
People: Andorrans
Currency: Euro (€)

Angola
Capital city: Luanda
People: Angolans
Currency: Readjusted Kwanza (Kz)

Antigua & Barbuda
Capital city: St John's
People: Antiguans
Currency: Eastern Caribbean Dollar

Argentina
Capital city: Buenos Aires
People: Argentinians
Currency: New Argentine Peso

Armenia
Capital city: Yerevan
People: Armenians
Currency: Dram

Australia
Capital city: Canberra
People: Australians
Currency: Australian Dollar (AU$)

Austria
Capital city: Vienna
People: Austrians
Currency: Euro (€)

Azerbaijan
Capital city: Baku
People: Azerbaijanis
Currency: New Manat

Bahamas
Capital city: Nassau
People: Bahamians
Currency: Bahamian Dollar

Bahrain
Capital city: Manama
People: Bahrainis
Currency: Bahraini Dinar

Bangladesh
Capital city: Dhaka
People: Bangladeshis
Currency: Taka (Tk)

Barbados
Capital city: Bridgetown
People: Barbadians
Currency: Barbados Dollar

Belarus
Capital city: Minsk
People: Belarusians
Currency: Belarussian Rouble

Belgium
Capital city: Brussels
People: Belgians
Currency: Euro (€)

Belize
Capital city: Belmopan
People: Belizeans
Currency: Belizean Dollar

Benin
Capital city: Porto-Novo
People: Beninese
Currency: CFA Franc*

Bhutan
Capital city: Thimphu
People: Bhutanese
Currency: Ngultrum (Nu)

Bolivia
Capital city: La Paz, Sucre
People: Bolivians
Currency: Boliviano (B)

Bosnia & Herzegovina
Capital city: Sarajevo
People: Bosnians
Currency: Marka

Botswana
Capital city: Gaborone
People: Batswana (singular Motswana)
Currency: Pula (P)

Brazil
Capital city: Brasília
People: Brazilians
Currency: Real

Brunei
Capital city: Bandar Seri Begawan
People: Bruneians
Currency: Brunei Dollar

Bulgaria
Capital city: Sofia
People: Bulgarians
Currency: Lev

Burkina
Capital city: Ouagadougou
People: Burkinabé
Currency: CFA Franc*

Burma (Myanmar)
Capital city: Nay Pyi Taw
People: Burmese
Currency: Kyat (K)

Burundi
Capital city: Bujumbura
People: Burundians
Currency: Burundi Franc

Cambodia
Capital city: Phnom Penh
People: Cambodians
Currency: Riel

Cameroon
Capital city: Yaoundé
People: Cameroonians
Currency: CFA Franc*

Canada
Capital city: Ottawa
People: Canadians
Currency: Canadian Dollar (C$)

Cape Verde
Capital city: Praia
People: Cape Verdeans
Currency: Cape Verde Escudo

Central African Republic
Capital city: Bangui
People: Central Africans
Currency: CFA Franc*

Chad
Capital city: N'Djamena
People: Chadians
Currency: CFA Franc*

Chile
Capital city: Santiago
People: Chileans
Currency: Chilean Peso

China
Capital city: Beijing
People: Chinese
Currency: Renminbi (known as Yuan)

Colombia
Capital city: Bogotá
People: Colombians
Currency: Colombian Peso

Comoros
Capital city: Moroni
People: Comorans
Currency: Comoros Franc

Congo
Capital city: Brazzaville
People: Congolese
Currency: CFA Franc*

Congo, Democratic Republic
Capital city: Kinshasa
People: Congolese
Currency: Congolese Franc

Costa Rica
Capital city: San José
People: Costa Ricans
Currency: Costa Rican Colón (¢)

Croatia
Capital city: Zagreb
People: Croatians
Currency: Kuna

Cuba
Capital city: Havana
People: Cubans
Currency: Cuban Peso

Cyprus
Capital city: Nicosia
People: Cypriots
Currency: Euro (€)
(Turkish Lira in
Northen Cyprus)

Czech Republic
Capital city: Prague
People: Czechs
Currency: Czech
Koruna

Denmark
Capital city: Copenhagen
People: Danes
Currency: Danish
Krone

Djibouti
Capital city: Djibouti
People: Djiboutians
Currency: Djibouti Franc

Dominica
Capital city: Roseau
People: Dominicans
Currency: Eastern
Caribbean Dollar

Dominican Republic
Capital city: Santo Domingo
People: Dominicans
Currency: Dominican
Republic Peso

East Timor
Capital city: Dili
People: East Timorese
Currency: US Dollar ($)

Ecuador
Capital city: Quito
People: Ecuadoreans
Currency: US Dollar ($)

Egypt
Capital city: Cairo
People: Egyptians
Currency: Egyptian
Pound

El Salvador
Capital city: San Salvador
People: Salvadorans
Currency: Salvadorean
Colón (¢), US dollar ($)

Equatorial Guinea
Capital city: Malabo
People: Equatorial Guineans
or Equatoguineans
Currency: CFA Franc*

Eritrea
Capital city: Asmara
People: Eritreans
Currency: Nakfa

Estonia
Capital city: Tallinn
People: Estonians
Currency: Kroon

Ethiopia
Capital city: Addis Ababa
People: Ethiopians
Currency: Ethiopian
Birr (Br)

Fiji
Capital city: Suva
People: Fijians
Currency: Fiji Dollar

Finland
Capital city: Helsinki
People: Finns
Currency: Euro (€)

France
Capital city: Paris
People: French
Currency: Euro (€)

Gabon
Capital city: Libreville
People: Gabonese
Currency: CFA Franc*

Gambia
Capital city: Banjul
People: Gambians
Currency: Dalasi (D)

Georgia
Capital city: Tbilisi
People: Georgians
Currency: Lari

Germany
Capital city: Berlin
People: Germans
Currency: Euro (€)

Ghana
Capital city: Accra
People: Ghanaians
Currency: Cedi

Greece
Capital city: Athens
People: Greeks
Currency: Euro (€)

Grenada
Capital city: St George's
People: Grenadians
Currency: Eastern Caribbean
Dollar

Guatemala
Capital city: Guatemala City
People: Guatemalans
Currency: Quetzal (Q)

Guinea
Capital city: Conakry
People: Guineans
Currency: Guinea Franc

Guinea-Bissau
Capital city: Bissau
People: Guinea-Bissauans
Currency: CFA Franc*

Guyana
Capital city: Georgetown
People: Guyanese
Currency: Guyanese Dollar

Haiti
Capital city: Port-au-Prince
People: Haitians
Currency: Gourde (G)

Honduras
Capital city: Tegucigalpa
People: Hondurans
Currency: Lempira (L)

Hungary
Capital city: Budapest
People: Hungarians
Currency: Forint (Ft)

Iceland
Capital city: Reykjavik
People: Icelanders
Currency: Icelandic Krona

India
Capital city: New Delhi
People: Indians
Currency: Indian Rupee

Indonesia
Capital city: Jakarta
People: Indonesians
Currency: Rupiah (Rp)

Iran
Capital city: Tehran
People: Iranians
Currency: Iranian Rial

Iraq
Capital city: Baghdad
People: Iraqis
Currency: New Iraqi
Dinar (ID)

Ireland
Capital city: Dublin
People: Irish
Currency: Euro (€)

Israel
Capital city: Jerusalem
People: Israelis
Currency: Shekel

Italy
Capital city: Rome
People: Italians
Currency: Euro (€)

Ivory Coast
Capital city: Yamoussoukro
People: Ivoirians
Currency: CFA Franc*

Jamaica
Capital city: Kingston
People: Jamaicans
Currency: Jamaican Dollar

Japan
Capital city: Tokyo
People: Japanese
Currency: Yen (Y)

Jordan
Capital city: Amman
People: Jordanians
Currency: Jordanian Dinar

Kazakhstan
Capital city: Astana
People: Kazakhstanis
Currency: Tenge

Kenya
Capital city: Nairobi
People: Kenyans
Currency: Kenya Shilling

Kiribati
Capital city: Tarawa Atoll
People: I-Kiribatis
Currency: Australian Dollar
(AU$)

Kosovo (disputed)
Capital city: Pristina
People: Kosovars or
Kosovacs
Currency: Euro (€)

Kuwait
Capital city: Kuwait City
People: Kuwaitis
Currency: Kuwaiti Dinar

Kyrgyzstan
Capital city: Bishkek
People: Kyrgyz
Currency: Som

a
b
c
d
e
f
g
h
i
j
k
l
m
n
o
p
q
r
s
t
u
v
w
x
y
z

A
B
C
D
E
F
G
H
I
J
K
L
M
N
O
P
Q
R
S
T
U
V
W
X
Y
Z

Laos
Capital city: Vientiane
People: Laotians or Laos
Currency: New Kip (KN)

Latvia
Capital city: Riga
People: Latvians
Currency: Lats

Lebanon
Capital city: Beirut
People: Lebanese
Currency: Lebanese
Pound (£L)

Lesotho
Capital city: Maseru
People: Basotho (singular
Mosotho)
Currency: Loti (M)

Liberia
Capital city: Monrovia
People: Liberians
Currency: Liberian Dollar

Libya
Capital city: Tripoli
People: Libyans
Currency: Libyan Dinar

Liechtenstein
Capital city: Vaduz
People: Liechtensteiners
Currency: Swiss Franc

Lithuania
Capital city: Vilnius
People: Lithuanians
Currency: Litas

Luxembourg
Capital city: Luxembourg-Ville
People: Luxembourgers
Currency: Euro (€)

Macedonia
Capital city: Skopje
People: Macedonians
Currency: Macedonian Denar

Madagascar
Capital city: Antananarivo
People: Malagasy
Currency: Ariary

Malawi
Capital city: Lilongwe
People: Malawians
Currency: Malawi Kwacha

Malaysia
Capital city: Kuala Lumpur,
Putrajaya
People: Malaysians
Currency: Ringgit

Maldives
Capital city: Male
People: Maldivians
Currency: Rufiyaa

Mali
Capital city: Bamako
People: Malians
Currency: CFA Franc*

Malta
Capital city: Valletta
People: Maltese
Currency: Euro (€)

Marshall Islands
Capital city: Majuro
People: Marshallese
Currency: US Dollar ($)

Mauritania
Capital city: Nouakchott
People: Mauritanians
Currency: Ouguiya (UM)

Mauritius
Capital city: Port Louis
People: Mauritians
Currency: Mauritian Rupee
(Mau Rs)

Mexico
Capital city: Mexico City
People: Mexicans
Currency: Mexican Peso

Micronesia
Capital city: Palikir
(Pohnpei Island)
People: Micronesians
Currency: US Dollar ($)

Moldova
Capital city: Chisinau
People: Moldovans
Currency: Moldovan Leu

Monaco
Capital city: Monaco-Ville
People: Monégasques or
Monacans
Currency: Euro (€)

Mongolia
Capital city: Ulan Bator
People: Mongolians
Currency: Tugrik

Montenegro
Capital city: Podgorica
People: Montenegrins
Currency: Euro (€)

Morocco
Capital city: Rabat
People: Moroccans
Currency: Moroccan Dirham (DH)

Mozambique
Capital city: Maputo
People: Mozambicans
Currency: New Metical (Mt)

Namibia
Capital city: Windhoek
People: Namibians
Currency: Namibian Dollar

Nauru
Capital city: None
People: Nauruans
Currency: Australian Dollar
(AU$)

Nepal
Capital city: Kathmandu
People: Nepalese
Currency: Nepalese Rupee

Netherlands
Capital city: Amsterdam
Seat of government: The Hague
People: Dutch
Currency: Euro (€)

New Zealand
Capital city: Wellington
People: New Zealanders
Currency: New Zealand Dollar
(NZ$)

Nicaragua
Capital city: Managua
People: Nicaraguans
Currency: New Córdoba

Niger
Capital city: Niamey
People: Nigeriens
Currency: CFA Franc*

Nigeria
Capital city: Abuja
People: Nigerians
Currency: Naira (N)

North Korea
Capital city: Pyongyang
People: North Koreans
Currency: North Korean Won

Norway
Capital city: Oslo
People: Norwegians
Currency: Norwegian Krone

Oman
Capital city: Muscat
People: Omanis
Currency: Omani Rial

Pakistan
Capital city: Islamabad
People: Pakistanis
Currency: Pakistani Rupee

Palau
Capital city: Melekeok
People: Palauans
Currency: US Dollar ($)

Panama
Capital city: Panama City
People: Panamanians
Currency: Balboa (B)

Papua New Guinea
Capital city: Port Moresby
People: Papua New Guineans
Currency: Kina (K)

Paraguay
Capital city: Asunción
People: Paraguayans
Currency: Guaraní (G)

Peru
Capital city: Lima
People: Peruvians
Currency: New Sol (NS)

Philippines
Capital city: Manila
People: Filipinos
Currency: Philippine Peso

Poland
Capital city: Warsaw
People: Poles
Currency: Zloty (Zl)

Portugal
Capital city: Lisbon
People: Portuguese
Currency: Euro (€)

Qatar
Capital city: Doha
People: Qataris
Currency: Qatar Riyal

Romania
Capital city: Bucharest
People: Romanians
Currency: New Romanian
Leu (lei)

Russian Federation
Capital city: Moscow
People: Russians
Currency: Russian Rouble

Rwanda
Capital city: Kigali
People: Rwandans
Currency: Rwanda Franc

Saint Kitts & Nevis
Capital city: Basseterre
People: Kittitians, Nevisians
Currency: Eastern Caribbean
Dollar

Saint Lucia
Capital city: Castries
People: St Lucians
Currency: Eastern Caribbean Dollar

Saint Vincent & the Grenadines
Capital city: Kingstown
People: St Vincentians
Currency: Eastern Caribbean Dollar

Samoa
Capital city: Apia
People: Samoans
Currency: Tala

San Marino
Capital city: San Marino
People: Sammarinese
Currency: Euro (€)

São Tomé & Príncipe
Capital city: São Tomé
People: São Tomeans
Currency: Dobra

Saudi Arabia
Capital city: Riyadh, Jiddah
People: Saudi Arabians
Currency: Saudi Riyal

Senegal
Capital city: Dakar
People: Senegalese
Currency: CFA Franc*

Serbia
Capital city: Belgrade
People: Serbs
Currency: Dinar

Seychelles
Capital city: Victoria
People: Seychellois
Currency: Seychelles Rupee

Sierra Leone
Capital city: Freetown
People: Sierra Leoneans
Currency: Leone (Le)

Singapore
Capital city: Singapore
People: Singaporeans
Currency: Singapore Dollar (S$)

Slovakia
Capital city: Bratislava
People: Slovakians
Currency: Slovak Koruna

Slovenia
Capital city: Ljubljana
People: Slovenians
Currency: Euro (€)

Solomon Island
Capital city: Honiara
People: Solomon Islanders
Currency: Solomon Islands Dollar

Somalia
Capital city: Mogadishu
People: Somalis
Currency: Somali Shilin

South Africa
Capital city: Pretoria, Cape Town, Bloemfontein
People: South Africans
Currency: Rand (R)

South Korea
Capital city: Seoul
People: South Koreans
Currency: South Korean Won

Spain
Capital city: Madrid
People: Spaniards
Currency: Euro (€)

Sri Lanka
Capital city: Colombo
People: Sri Lankans
Currency: Sri Lanka Rupee (SL Rs)

Sudan
Capital city: Khartoum
People: Sudanese
Currency: New Sudanese Pound or Dinar

Surinam
Capital city: Paramaribo
People: Surinamers
Currency: Surinamese Dollar

Swaziland
Capital city: Mbabane
People: Swazis
Currency: Lilangeni (E)

Sweden
Capital city: Stockholm
People: Swedes
Currency: Swedish Krona

Switzerland
Capital city: Bern
People: Swiss
Currency: Swiss Franc

Syria
Capital city: Damascus
People: Syrians
Currency: Syrian Pound

Tajikistan
Capital city: Dushanbe
People: Tajiks
Currency: Somoni

Tanzania
Capital city: Dodoma
People: Tanzanians
Currency: Tanzanian Shilling (T Sh)

Thailand
Capital city: Bangkok
People: Thais
Currency: Baht (B)

Togo
Capital city: Lomé
People: Togolese
Currency: CFA Franc*

Tonga
Capital city: Nuku'alofa
People: Tongans
Currency: Pa'anga (Tongan Dollar)

Trinidad & Tobago
Capital city: Port-of-Spain
People: Trinidadians, Tobagonians
Currency: Trinidad and Tobago Dollar

Tunisia
Capital city: Tunis
People: Tunisians
Currency: Tunisian Dinar

Turkey
Capital city: Ankara
People: Turks
Currency: New Turkish Lira

Turkmenistan
Capital city: Ashgabat
People: Turkmens
Currency: Manat

Tuvalu
Capital city: Fongafale (Funafuti Atoll)
People: Tuvaluans
Currency: Australian Dollar and Tuvaluan Dollar

Uganda
Capital city: Kampala
People: Ugandans
Currency: New Uganda Shilling

Ukraine
Capital city: Kiev
People: Ukrainians
Currency: Hryvna

United Arab Emirates
Capital city: Abu Dhabi
People: Emiratis
Currency: UAE Dirham

United Kingdom
Capital city: London
People: British
Currency: Pound Sterling (£)

United States of America
Capital city: Washington DC
People: Americans
Currency: US Dollar ($)

Uruguay
Capital city: Montevideo
People: Uruguayans
Currency: Uruguayan Peso

Uzbekistan
Capital city: Tashkent
People: Uzbekistanis
Currency: Som

Vanuatu
Capital city: Port Vila
People: Ni-Vanuatu
Currency: Vatu

Vatican City
Capital city: Vatican City
People: Citizens of the Vatican
Currency: Euro (€)

Venezuela
Capital city: Caracas
People: Venezuelans
Currency: Bolívar (Bs)

Vietnam
Capital city: Hanoi
People: Vietnamese
Currency: Dông (D)

Yemen
Capital city: Sana
People: Yemenis
Currency: Yemeni Rial

Zambia
Capital city: Lusaka
People: Zambians
Currency: Zambian Kwacha (K)

Zimbabwe
Capital city: Harare
People: Zimbabweans
Currency: Zimbabwe Dollar (Z$)

* The CFA Franc is used in a number of French-speaking African countries. CFA stands for "Communauté Financiere Africaine".

a b c d e f g h i j k l m n o p q r s t u v w x y z

Acknowledgements

Dorling Kindersley would like to thank the following people for their help in the production of this book:

Additional design assistance
Bronwen Davies, Susan Downing, Karen Fielding, David Gillingwater, Tim Lewis, Sharon Peters, Peter Radcliffe, Sarah Scrutton, Hans Verkroost, Martin Wilson

Additional editorial assistance
Monica Byles, Helen Drew, Stella Love

Picture research
Kathleen Collier, Catherine O'Rourke, Lucy Pringle, Jenny Rayner, Joanna Thomas

Additional illustrations
Janos Marffy, Liz Roberts

Additional photography
Simon Battensby, Paul Bricknell, Geoff Brightling, Jane Burton, Peter Chadwick, Matthew Chattle, Gordon Clayton, M. Crockett, Geoff Dann, Tom Dobbie, Philip Dowell, Michael Dunning, Andreas von Einsiedel, Jo Foord, Philip Gatward, Mike Good, Christi Graham, Frank Greenaway, Peter Hayman, Stephen Hayward, Alan Hills, Jacqui Hurst, Colin Keates, Gary Kevin, Dave King, Bob Langrish, Cyril Laubscher, Bill Ling, Liz McAulay, Andrew McRobb, Diana Miller, Graham Miller, Ray Moller, David Murray, Jack Nicholls, Martin Norris, Ian O'Leary, Stephen Oliver, Daniel Pangbourne, Roger Phillips, Martin Plomer, Laurence Pordes, Susanna Price, Dave Rudkin, Karl Shone, Steve Shott, James Stevenson, Clive Streeter, Harry Taylor, Kim Taylor, David Ward, Matthew Ward. Philip Dowell © 1990 and 1991 page 90 goat and kid; page 111 jaguar; page 118 leopard; page 183 sheep. Jerry Young © 1990 and 1991 page 168 rattlesnake, flying gecko, milkshake, today lizard, starred tortoise, and leopard gecko; page 217 green toad; page 242 wolf.

Models
Shiran Abay, Di Anguige, Sarah Ashun, Oliver Barber, Lindsey Bender, Marvin Campbell, Louis Chan, Puishan Chan, Danny Cole, Andy Crawford, Ebu Djemal, Helen Drew, Andrea East, Josey Edwards, David Gillingwater, Emily Gorton, Julia Gorton, Kashi Gorton, Steve Gorton, Sheena Haria, Laura Hobbs, Paul Holden, Marcus James, Stella Love, Naomi McLean, Rachael Malicki, Jamie May, Ryan Munroe, Emily Parsons, Jade Reading, Jonathon Reed, Tim Ridley, Matthew Saunders, Sarah Scrutton, Silpa Shah, Lee Simmons, Cheryl Telfer, Nicola Tuxworth, Aubrey Weiner, Martin Wilson, David York.

Additional acknowledgements
Anatomical models on pages 20, 98, 114, 120, 122, 202 and 232 supplied by Somso Modelle, Coburg, Germany.

Chest page 43, chest of drawers page 65, and fan page 75 loaned by Gore Booker, Covent Garden, London; drum page 67 loaned by Foote's Musical Instruments, London; leotard page 118 loaned by Porselli, Covent Garden, London; cup page 55 loaned by Whittard, Covent Garden, London; chess set page 43 loaned by the British Museum Shop, London.

Thanks to Clark Denmark at the Centre for Deaf Studies, Bristol University for advice.

Thanks also to the BCP contributors: Gemma Casajuana (Conversion manager), Miguel Cunha (Conversion coordinator), Colleen Dixon (Conversion DTP), Marc Staples (Conversion DTP)

Picture agency credits
KEY: a-above; b-below/bottom; c-centre; f-far; l-left; r-right; t-top.

The publisher would like to thank the following for their kind permission to reproduce their photographs:

Action Plus/Tony Henshaw 198cr. Ayrton Metals Ltd and The Platinum Advisory Centre 112car, 112cbfr. Beaulieu Motor Museum 39cl, 222tr. The Bridgeman Art Library/Bonhams, London 112cb. Kremlin Museums, Moscow 54tl. British Museum 17cfr, 35tfl, 99fl, 112ca. British Museum/Museum of Mankind 221cafl. John Bulmer 224tr. Christies's Images 9cbl, 131cbr. The Coleman Company 38tfr.Bruce Coleman Limited/Erwin and Peggy Bauer 226bfl; John Cancalosi 179tfl; Peter Davey 42cafr, 211tfr; P. Evans 18cr; Christer Fredriksson 22car; Frans Lanting 70tl; Luiz Claudio Marigo 124tc; William S. Paton 104bfl; Eckart Pott 166br; Andy Purcell 8bfl, 142car; Hans Reinhard 6c, 7tl, 25bfr, 58cfl, 70tfl, 163cbl; Dr Frjeder Sauer 147bfr; Konrad Wothe 97tr. Compix/A and J Somaya 56tr. Corbis Theo Allofs 66ftr; Andrea Rugg Photography/Beateworks 115cl; Atlantide Phototravel 25cl, 103tl, 169crb; Bilderbuch/Design Pics 169bl; B. Bird/Zefa 211fcrb; Christophe Boisvieux 22ftl; Ron Chapple 171crb; Mike Chew 20cra; Philip Coblentz/Brand X 176clb; Chris Collins 242br; CS Productions/Brand X 200tr; Wolfgang Deuter/Zefa 153br;

Dex Image 199fcr; ER Productions 174clb; Fancy/Veer 208fcrb; First/Zefa 45fcra; Bertrand Gardel/Hemis 130br; Uden Graham/Redlink 162fcrb; Mike Grandmaison 176cr; John Harper 46fbl; Ian Hodgson/Reuters 203fbr; Jose Luis Pelaez, Inc. 186cra; Sean Justice 63bl; Jutta Klee 57fbr; Kulka/zefa 192crb; Frans Lanting 163fbl; Klaus Leidorf/Zefa 15fbl; Robert Llewellyn 141cla; John Lund 222bl; Mango Productions 120fcrb; Lawrence Manning 232fbl; Robert Marien 226fcla; Kevin Mason/Loop Images 91ftr; MM Productions 150cr; Moodboard 132fclb, 169fcla, 185cla, 212fcl; David Muench 91tr; Ron Nickel/Design Pics 24tl; Richard T. Nowitz 220fclb; Owaki - Kulla 130tr; Carl Purcell 171fcla; Radius Images 227fbl; Jose Fuste Raga 162br; Eddy Risch/EPA 73ftl; Bill Ross/Corbis Outline 139tr; Charles E. Rotkin 165fbr; Galen Rowell 119fcrb; Kevin Schafer 235tr; Ted Spiegel 77fbl; Thinkstock 190ftl, 196crb; Stefano Torrione/Hemis 139fclb; Visuals Unlimited 228fcrb; R. Wallace/Stock Photos/zefa 71ftr; Weatherstock 215tl; P. Wilson/Zefa 237fcra; Jim Zuckerman 241cr. DK Images Jerry Young 15ftr, 171br; NASA 68fcra, 172ftl; Philips Domestic Applicances and Personal Care 69tr; Rough Guides 192bl, 208fclb; The Science Museum, London 43br. Massey Ferguson 152bfr. Ermine Street Guard 195cbl. Getty Images 192cr; Altrendo Travel 235ftl; Image Bank/Tim Graham 160fcrb; Daryl Benson 215bl; Alistair Berg 181fclb; Philippe Bourseiller 232bl; C Squared Studios 219clb; Rosemary Calvert 218fcla; Gabriel M. Covian 227crb; Andy Crawford 113cra; Creative Crop 162tr; CSA Plastock 171fcr; Dex Image/Luxe Party 125fbl; Digital Vision/Erik Von Weber 114cra; Digital Vision/Robert Glusic 116cra; Digital Vision/Steve Wisbauer 118cr; Digital Vision/VisionsofAmerica/Joe Sohm 45tl; Sergio Dionisio 34bl; Dorling Kindersley 105fclb; EschCollection 234fbr; David Evans 240crb; Don Farrall 218fcra; Stephen Ferry/Liaison 62tr; James Forte 198bl; Jill Fromer 200cla; fStop/Stephan Zirwes 116br; Yasuhide Fumoto 212clb; Gallo Images/Travel Ink 125fbr; Glowimages 20ftl; Gorilla Creative Images/Harri Tahvanainen 136clb; Gavin Gough 200ftr; Frank Greenaway 171tr; Iconica/2008 ML Harris Photography 41cla; Iconica/Caroline von Tuempling 95fcr; Image Bank/PM Images 49fbl; Image Bank/Sasha Weleber 101cfb; Mathew Imaging/WireImage 21fbr; Seth Joel 195crb; Johner 222tl; Taylor S. Kennedy 206fcra; Pornchai Kittiwongsakul/AFP 14br; Darryl Leniuk 165fcra; Lonely Planet Images/Lee Foster 23br; Lonely Planet Images/Peter Hendrie 110fcra; David Madison 174cla; Simon McComb 237crb; Ethan Miller 38fcra; Mr. Sunshine 202clb; National Geographic/David Evans 59fclb; National Geographic/Paul Nicklen 107fcr; Mark Nolan 42ftl; Thomas Northcut 224tr; Per-Anders Pettersson 113fcr; PhotoAlto/Matthieu Spohn 127bl; Photodisc 88bc, 111bl, 193fcrb; Photodisc/Don Farrall 154ftr; Photodisc/Jack Hollingsworth 50cla; Photodisc/Jeff Maloney 114fbl; Photodisc/Kim Carson 25fcrb; Photodisc/Paul Burns 103fcla; Photographer's Choice/Michael Rosenfeld 37clb; Photographer's Choice/Simeone Huber/Slow Images 40ftl; Photographer's Choice/Tom Walker 144bl; Photographer's Choice/Travelpix Ltd 60br; Photographer's Choice RF/George Diebold 12tr; Photographer's Choice RR/Fry Design Ltd 146tr; Photographer's Choice RR/Geoff Du Feu 50fcr; Photonica/Sabine Scheckel 84tl; Photonica/Silvia Otte 62fclb; Andrea Pistolesi 212crb; Plush Studios 165bl; Poncho 167cra; Pool Photo 59ftl; Mike Powell 203crb; Rich Reid 206br; Robert Harding World Imagery/Christian Kober 169cla; Lew Robertson 150cra; Rubberball Productions 88bl; Rubberball Productions/Mike Kemp 111cla; Pete Ryan 163cr; David Sanger 242clb; Science Faction/Jim Reed 96fbl; Zack Seckler 203fcrb; Erik Simonsen 175br; Check Six 211ftl; John Slater 196cra; Luke Stettner 63bc; Stockbyte 12ftr; Stone/Jeff Hunter 117bl; Stone/Kevin Cooley 34tr; Stone/Oliver Benn/Royal Philharmonic Orchestra 142tl; Stone/Rex Butcher 157br; Stone/Roger Tully 64fcla; Stone/Walter Hodges 109fbr; Taxi/Francesco Bittichesu 154fclb; Taxi/Jasper White/jasper@jasperwhite.co.uk 88fbl; Taxi/Kevin Cooley 47fcra; Alan Thornton 166fcrb; Travel Ink 166cl; UpperCut Images/John Churchman 129fbl; Slaven Vlasic 130fcrb; Gary Wade 201cla; Gordon Wiltsie 196clb, 206clb; Yashoda 43fcra. Greenwich Maritime Museum 31tr, 31tl, 31cr, 31car, 109cl. Robert Harding Picture Library/G and P Corrigan 131tl. Michael Holford 112cal. The Image Bank/Charles S. Allen 5cl, 6bfr, 39b; Gary Crallé 24cbr; Gary Gay 103tr; Alvis Upitis 23tfr. NASA 21fcla, 68tr, 68 cafr, 172 tfl. National Museum of Denmark, Copenhagen 112tl. Natural History Photographic Agency/Peter Johnson 100cl; David Woodfall 17bfr; Norbert Wu 111tfr. Nature Photographers Ltd/David Hutton 115bfr. Oxford Scientific Films 76bfr, 99cafr, 131cfl. The Pitt Rivers Museum 183cbfr. Planet Earth Pictures/Robert Canis 131cafr. Quadrant 220br. Rough Guides 192 bl. Rough Guides/ Alex Robinson 208 bfl. Science Photo Library 224cal/John Burbridge 80cbfr; CNRI 83cbfr; Peter Menzel 162cbr; Astrid and Hanns-Frieder Michler 245br; Claude Nuridsany and Marie Perennou 192cbr; Jim Selby 232cfl; US Department of Energy 231tr. Tony Stone Images 120cbfl, 244bfl/Tim Beddow 226cfl; Dave Bjorn 207tr. Thistle Quilters/The Quilter's Guild 161cafr. Warwick Castle 95br. The Worshipful Company of Goldsmiths/Andrew Grima 112bfl.

Jacket images: Front: Corbis: Corbis: Matthias Kulka/Zefa cb; © 2008 The LEGO Group: MINDSTORMS is a trademark of the LEGO Group clb; Science Photo Library: Mehau Kulyk cr. Back: Alamy Images: Trip tr; Corbis: Tim Davis/Davis Lynn Wildlife clb; Kulka/zefa tc.

Every effort has been made to trace the copyright holders. Dorling Kindersley apologizes for any unintentional omissions and would be pleased, in such cases, to add an acknowledgement in future editions.

All other images © Dorling Kindersley
For further information see: www.dkimages.com

A B C D E F G H I J K L M N O P Q R S T U V W X Y Z